MERGER

MERGER

Peter F. Hartz

William Morrow and Company, Inc.
New York

For Matthew and his farfar and farmor . . .

With love to Kathy and special thanks to Eric and Maureen,
Suzanne Katz, Joey, Ivy, Maggie in NYC, Bill and Harriet in
Baltimore, Jimmy, Paul and Rich in D.C., Jo-Ann, and Lynn,
Danny, Jay, Phyllis, Nana.

Copyright © 1985 by Peter F. Hartz

Library of Congress Cataloging in Publication Data

Hartz, Peter F.
Merger.

Includes index.
1. Consolidation and merger of corporations—United
States—Case studies. 2. Bendix Corporation.
3. Martin Marietta Corporation. I. Title.
HD2746.5.H37   1985   338.8'362904'0973   84-22679
ISBN 0-688-03983-9

Printed in the United States of America

3 4 5 6 7 8 9 10

BOOK DESIGN BY JAMES UDELL

In 1982, there were 2,346 mergers between companies in the United States—more than $54 billion changed hands. In 1983, there were 2,533 mergers worth $73 billion and during 1984, there were 2,543 mergers worth an astounding $122 billion. Most were stories quietly told on the pages of daily business newspapers. *Merger* is the true story of a business strategy that evolved into the most interesting war in American corporate history.

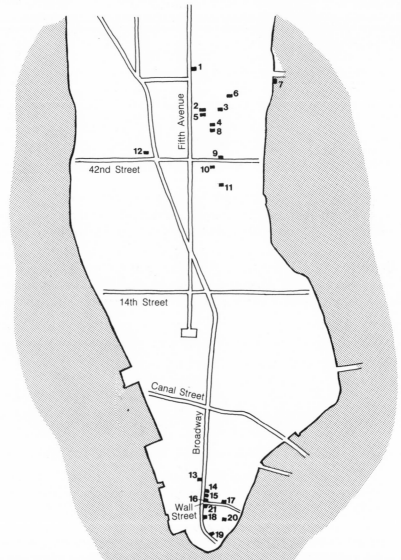

Jaye Zimet © 1985

1. Bendix N.Y. headquarters on twenty-first floor of the GM Building
2. First Boston Corporation—Bendix bankers **3.** Citibank corporate headquarters **4.** Martin Marietta "headquarters" at Waldorf-Astoria **5.** Suite 4509
at the Helmsley Palace **6.** Skadden, Arps—Allied lawyers **7.** Marine Heliport
#3 **8.** Wachtell, Lipton—Martin Marietta and UTC lawyers **9.** Hill & Knowl-
ton—Bendix PR firm **10.** Dewey Ballantine "uptown"—101 Park Avenue—
Martin Marietta lawyers **11.** St. Regis Corporation—N.Y. site of Allied
board meetings **12.** New York Times **13.** Wall Street Journal **14.** Dewey
Ballantine "downtown"—140 Broadway **15.** Lazard Frères—United Technologies banker **16.** Hughes, Hubbard & Reed—Bendix lawyers **17.** Kidder,
Peabody—Martin Marietta bankers **18.** Barrett, Smith & Shapiro—Martin
Marietta attorneys **19.** Fried, Frank, Harris, Shriver & Jacobson—Bendix
lawyers/Salomon Brothers—Bendix bankers **20.** Citibank corporate office—
site of Martin Marietta purchase of Bendix stock **21.** NYSE

ONE

I t's hard to keep a secret on Wall Street.

Money has a way of creating its own loyalties.

On August 19, 1982, Marty Weinstein was sitting at his small desk, smoking a Golden Lights cigarette and talking on the telephone. A short, round man with wavy gray hair and bright blue eyes, Marty was in the midst of a troubling conversation.

The closing bell of the New York Stock Exchange was about to ring.

As the point man for the investment banking house of Salomon Brothers, Weinstein's job was to play the stock market. Five days a week, from his cubicle on the fortieth floor of One New York Plaza, Weinstein worked "the street."

It had been a little more than thirty days since the Salomon trading desk completed a secret acquisition of common stock of the Martin Marietta Corporation for the Bendix Corporation. Buying the stock in small lots to avoid raising suspicions, the Salomon trading desk picked up 1,632,500 shares—exactly 4.9 percent of the outstanding shares of Martin Marietta—the limit the law allowed without publication.

In July, a banker from another investment banking firm— Kidder, Peabody—called on behalf of Martin Marietta to ask about the purchases.

"Our client wants to know who's buying their stock."

"Just institutional holders," a Salomon trader said. "Nothing to worry about."

They seemed to accept the bluff.

But now the rumors were flying down Wall Street.

It was obvious that someone had received a tip.

There on the stock sale sheets was the evidence. At 3:58 P.M., just two minutes before the close of the Big Board, someone spent a little more than $2.5 million to buy ninety thousand shares of Martin Marietta stock. That kind of volume was way out of line with the normal trading pattern.

"This is going to bust wide open if we don't do something," Marty Weinstein said to the managing director of the mergers and acquisitions department of Salomon Brothers. Jay Higgins was the man who dealt with the client—the Bendix Corporation. The two men were in Higgins' office.

"Calm down," Higgins replied. A tough, sometimes abrasive man with deep acne scars on his face, Higgins was already overworked without adding a new panic.

"Jay, the store is flying, we should shut it down," Weinstein said.

"What exactly are you hearing, Marty?" Higgins asked.

"We got a leak that is starting to look like Niagara Falls. For God's sake, a retail broker called me up to say that a guy came in and wanted to buy every share of Martin Marietta he could come up with. Our sales guys are hearing rumors that a move is being made against Martin. I'm getting calls. People are asking. I think we should shut down trading."

"Let me talk to the Bendix guys," Higgins said.

In the Southfield, Michigan, headquarters of the Bendix Corporation, a small group of executives had been monitoring the situation for several days. Their complex financial package assembled over the past weeks with the help of Jay Higgins was being shot to hell. The tipster was driving up the price of Martin Marietta stock, and every half point was adding millions of dollars to the Bendix plan.

Between Tuesday and Thursday, the stock price seesawed from 25¼ to 28⅞ per share. By Friday's close of the New York Stock Exchange, Martin Marietta common stock leaped to 30⅝.

Something had to be done. And done quickly, before the speculators took the deal away.

* * *

"The Bendix board meeting is now Tuesday," the caller from Michigan said.

Arthur Fleischer, Jr., a tall, senior securities lawyer with the law firm of Fried, Frank, Harris, Shriver & Jacobson, received the message calmly, showing no trace of disappointment that his planned vacation at East Hampton on the seashore of Long Island was no more.

"Has Bill decided to go ahead?" Art asked, looking out his twenty-seventh-floor window at Battery Park and the southern tip of Manhattan. His office was in the same high-rise as Salomon Brothers. Out Fleischer's window in the distance—the Statue of Liberty.

"This looks like it," the caller from Michigan said, adding, "we're watching the market closely out here, and we don't like what's happening."

As the firm's chief lawyer in the mergers and acquisitions area, Fleischer was familiar with the issue at hand. A list of ten names of huge companies had been given to him months before by William M. Agee, the forty-four-year-old chairman and chief executive officer of the Bendix Corporation.

Ten days ago, when Bill Agee stopped off at Fleischer's office for a chat, he repeated a name on the list, Martin Marietta—a large aerospace company—but added that he had not yet made up his mind. With the stock market still on a general downward swing, Agee explained that a move probably would not come before Labor Day—provided there were no leaks.

But here it was two weeks before the September holiday.

After asking his secretary to see if several Fried, Frank partners were available for a discussion in his office, Fleischer got on the phone. First he called a lawyer at Hughes, Hubbard & Reed, a prestigious law firm with a unique address—One Wall Street—which placed its offices at the corner of Wall and Broadway, opposite Trinity Church.

Hughes, Hubbard & Reed had also been retained by Bendix Corporation.

"I assume you've heard from our friends in Detroit," Fleischer said. "I expect that I will call you over the weekend. How are the corporate papers coming?"

"It's in the works. I guess we're losing about two weeks because of the leaks," the lawyer said.

"Yeah. I'm getting my people started this weekend on drafting the litigation papers to get declaratory judgments against the applicable state laws. I'm assuming your guys will be in the office this weekend?"

"Sure."

"Right. Okay, my people will be in touch."

With over 160 attorneys in the New York office, Fleischer's firm was one of the leading law firms in the country specializing in the sophisticated financial transactions of Wall Street. Teams of lawyers were organized into corporate, litigation, tax, and antitrust groups. During the 1960s, when corporate America was rushing to consolidate and expand its gains through merger of companies into massive conglomerates, the partners of Fried, Frank, Harris, Shriver & Jacobson developed a major practice in the field, known as M&A in street shorthand.

Arthur Fleischer—along with several other lawyers from competitive firms—was considered the best in the business. During the formative early 1960s, Fleischer worked for the Securities and Exchange Commission. As a lawyer in private practice, his time went for $350 an hour. His treatise *Tender Offers: Defenses, Responses, and Planning* was on every M&A lawyer's bookshelf. Among Fleischer's recent clients were Mobil Oil Corporation and Connecticut General. From years of experience, Arthur had trained his considerable analytical abilities to follow logical lines of thinking, to see clearly, to look ahead, to make strategy.

With his two teenage daughters and wife, Susan, Fleischer drove east Friday night on Southern State Parkway to Route 27 —Montauk Highway—to East Hampton.

Saturday and Sunday were cool and blustery. A storm front was on the way, holding temperatures down in the sixties. But after several weeks of hot, muggy weather in the city, the change was a relief.

Fleischer spent most of the weekend on the phone—to the office, checking on the progress of drafting the litigation papers; to Hughes, Hubbard, to touch bases. He called Michigan to talk with Hal Barron, the general counsel of Bendix, who served as the "contact man" between the teams of lawyers.

Coordination was paramount—even in a straightforward transaction.

* * *

A handsome man, in good shape, with a ready smile, stylish eyeglasses, and brown hair parted neatly at the corner of his forehead, Bill Agee commanded one of the largest corporations in the world. His salary topped $850,000 a year with all the perks of power at his disposal.

Since being named chairman of the board and chief executive officer of the Bendix Corporation in 1977 at the age of thirty-nine, Bill Agee had led the company to ever-increasing profits. Revenues had grown each year at an average of 10 percent. Employment swelled to almost seventy-two thousand people working in the automotive, aerospace, and industrial sectors.

Agee was the youngest man to run any of the top hundred American corporations. *The New York Times* in January 1980 said "Bill Agee appears to be winning a place among elite American executives."

Agee was the all-American boy from Idaho by way of Harvard.

It seemed he could do no wrong.

Nine months later, his reputation was in shambles.

The cause—his own public admission that he was "very close friends" with a twenty-nine-year-old blond Bendix employee hired as his executive assistant and then rapidly promoted to vice president for strategic planning. Her name—Mary Cunningham.

The admission made the national news. It was widely assumed that Bill and Mary were having an affair. Both Agee and Cunningham protested that their friendship was strictly platonic. Mary was married—albeit separated. Bill had only a month before finalized the divorce sought by his wife, Diane (née Walker), the mother of his three children. Despite their protests, Bill and Mary found themselves in the middle of a maelstrom of public opinion.

Mary Cunningham resigned. *Time* magazine would write "[the] story has gathered enough momentum in the past five weeks to eclipse national interest in who shot J.R."

A year and a half later, on June 6, 1982, Agee married Mary Cunningham.

With his name out of the news, Bill Agee went back to work.

For several years, while analysts were praising Bendix as a significant contributor to the economy, perhaps even a standout in a tough recession, Bill Agee was looking down the road to the mid-1980s and beyond. He knew the profile of his company had to change if the glowing financial results were to continue.

In his early years as chairman, he had a saying "No one customer, no one project." That line summed up what was the central problem for Bendix. In 1977, the sales of Bendix automotive parts such as brakes and Fram air, oil, and fuel filters for cars and trucks accounted for 61 percent of the company's earnings. Bendix was relying on one customer—the American automobile market—for its profits.

In 1980, Agee was quoted in *Fortune* magazine, "Automobile brakes are in the winter of their life, and so is the entire automobile industry." That was a tough attitude to take when your corporate headquarters were located in a Detroit suburb and the Bendix blue logo was bonded in the perceptions of the public with the car. Several Detroit leaders took offense, including Lee Iacocca, chairman of Chrysler Corporation.

Seeking to diversify his earnings and lessen his risk, Bill Agee decided to maintain his market positions in the automotive field but not to expand. He was going to look elsewhere for future profits.

By the time the American automobile manufacturers were drowning in a sea of red ink, Bill Agee had already redirected some of his assets and altered his balance sheet. Nonetheless, several areas of his business were slumping, threatening to produce Bendix's first year of lower earnings since 1970.

Agee needed a bold move.

To amass cash for a major acquisition, Agee sold the Bendix forest products business, an interest in ASARCO, Incorporated, and the stock of a Bendix subsidiary, United Geographical Corporation.

The result: $700 million in the bank earning peak interest rates. The money managers of America saw Bill Agee as brilliant —although suspect because of his celebrity status. The joke on Wall Street was that Bill Agee was making more money on his money than he could on his operations.

By 1982, the stock market was a disaster.

Scores of corporations were undervalued.

It was a buyers' market.

The Bendix cash was burning a hole in Bill Agee's pocket.

On Sunday, August 22, Bill and Mary and Bendix's president, Alonzo McDonald, sat together in the bright and cheery

living room of the Agees' condominium in the fashionable Detroit suburb of Orchard Lake. A tall, lanky Georgian who had
served as White House staff director for President Carter, Mc-
Donald had come to brief the chairman on the latest developments. The sudden rise in the price of Martin Marietta stock was
forcing a decision.

A Bible was displayed on a side table near the entryway of
the condo. A devout Catholic, Mary had a passion to remember
the events of her life. Among her files—all the press coverage
of her tumultuous career and her celebrated relationship with
Bill Agee.

It had been almost two years since Mary quit Bendix. In her
former position as VP for strategic planning at Bendix, Mary had
put the name of Martin Marietta at the top of the list of acquisition targets.

But in 1980, the price was too high. The company was doing
well.

Then the Martin Marietta management poured hundreds of
millions of dollars into losing operations in aluminum. The
money was spent just in time for a recession that would decimate
their aluminum markets and send their cement business into a
deep slump.

The one gem that shone through all that bauxite and cement
was the Martin Marietta aerospace operations. The defense
business was booming. While Bendix was a subcontractor on
defense projects, Martin Marietta was one of a handful of prime
systems contractors.

They had the Pershing missile and a host of tactical missiles.
They had the MX missile. They worked on the Space Shuttle.
Martin Marietta was the kind of acquisition that would fulfill Bill
Agee's vision of the future of Bendix.

Badly beaten by the recession in its aluminum and cement
businesses, the stock price of the aerospace giant fell from a high
of $50 in the first quarter of 1981 to a high of $35.25 a year later.
And it was heading lower.

At bargain prices, Martin Marietta was irresistible.

"I'm glad we got our summer vacations out of the way early,"
Al McDonald said.

Mary poured each man a glass of white wine.

"To the new Bendix Corporation," Agee said to the touch-
ing of glasses.

TWO

Tuesday, August 24, was a sunny, warm day in New York City. The day's high would hit eighty-four degrees. At the tip of Manhattan, in the maze of narrow streets collectively known as Wall Street, the day began early, long before the opening of the New York Stock Exchange at 10:00 A.M. Because of the towering office buildings of lower Manhattan, there were places that seem trapped forever in shadows despite the bright sunlight.

Tuesday morning, in preparation for the Bendix board of directors' meeting at 4:00 P.M., a meeting of the Bendix acquisition team was scheduled at Hughes, Hubbard & Reed, the Bendix law firm at One Wall Street.

Bill Agee and Mary Cunningham had flown in the night before from Michigan on one of the Bendix jets. They checked into the Helmsley Palace, an ornate—even gaudy—luxury hotel at the corner of Fifty-first Street and Madison Avenue.

The Palace had memories for Bill Agee. He and Mary celebrated their betrothal with a reception in late June in the conspicuously elegant Versailles Room. More than two hundred guests were invited from the elite of the New York social, business, and media worlds—Katharine Graham of the Washington Post, economist Milton Friedman, television personalities Jane Pauley and Barbara Walters, and the mayor of New York.

Later, at a second celebration, in Michigan, Bill Agee, to the bewilderment of many of his employees, crowned Mary the "First Lady of Bendix." It was obvious that despite her resignation almost two years before, Mary Cunningham was by virtue of her marriage still very much involved with Bendix.

The Helmsley Palace was also convenient.

Within walking distance, the Bendix New York offices on the twenty-first floor of the General Motors Building on Fifth Avenue; and the fifth-floor office in the Park Avenue headquarters of Joseph E. Seagram & Sons, where Mary worked. She joined the company in 1981 and was promoted within a year to executive vice president for strategic planning of the newly formed Seagram Wine Company.

The Hughes, Hubbard offices were the picture of the New York legal and financial establishment. The law library, housing thousands of leather-bound volumes, was walled by glass doors allowing a view of a quaint circular staircase. Antique furniture and oriental throw rugs complemented the black-and-white tile hallways and dark-paneled walls.

The feeling was old money.

Although the law firm had handled Bendix legal business since 1940, senior partner Jack Fontaine, fifty-one, had a more personal connection. His dad, A. P. Fontaine, had been chairman of Bendix for almost a decade from the early 1960s. After A. P. Fontaine came Mike Blumenthal, who recruited and promoted Bill Agee. Jack found Bill Agee to be a man skilled in the use of power. Friendly and open, Agee could also withhold his opinions in a way that kept his advisers off balance.

Gathered in the conference room at Hughes, Hubbard were some of the very best M&A advisers money could buy. Cigars were more common than cigarettes. These men were the statesmen of the business—experienced dealmakers who charged their clients by the hour. A lot of very expensive meters were ticking.

There is an unwritten rule on Wall Street that corporate executives not schooled in the fine art of merging companies should leave the deal-making to the professional dealmakers— the bankers and lawyers. There was a sense of familiarity in the room. Many of the advisers knew each other from other deals. It seemed the only things that really changed were the corporate players—the advisers just moved over one chair.

But this time it would be different.

Bill Agee was running the show.

Two weeks before, Jay Higgins from Salomon Brothers—Bendix's banker—learned the lesson firsthand. Al McDonald and Agee had come to Salomon's offices to meet with Salomon M&A guru Ira Harris.

Harris had no intention of getting involved with the day-to-day workings of the deal. He invited Jay Higgins into the meeting.

"What about the legal front?" Higgins asked.

"You don't need to worry about that," Agee said.

"We should get together with the lawyers," Higgins interjected.

"Everything is under control. We'll get you together at the appropriate time."

Bill Agee was pulling the strings of his power.

Among the high-priced, old-hand talent at Tuesday's meeting was Dick Cheney, an exuberant and rotund PR man with a penchant for bow ties, from the firm of Hill & Knowlton. He planned to discuss the communication plan and general strategy for dealing with the press. Bendix PR director Bob Meyers, a hawk-eyed man balding at the crown, was coordinating with Cheney.

Jack Fontaine, Art Fleischer, and Hal Barron, chief counsel of Bendix, took turns focusing on the legal plan, the actions to be taken by Bendix and the anticipated legal responses of "Georgia." While all three men respected the sheer cloth of secrecy, they knew the real name behind the code: the Martin Marietta Corporation—a company with gross sales of over $3 billion a year, with the majority of its sales to the United States government.

Mindful of that constituency, Michael Rowny, a young but seasoned strategic planner at Bendix, presented the Washington plan—an elaborate, finely tuned course of action to be initiated upon announcement of a move by Bendix. Rowny was familiar with the power politics of Washington, having worked for McDonald in the Carter White House. If the Bendix board approved the proposed deal today, Rowny would go to Washington tonight to be prepared for the public announcement on Wednesday at 9:00 A.M.

Listening to a piece of the discussion, Dick Cheney piped up,

"You know, here I am talking about the plan, but I don't even know who the target is. But that's fine."

Cheney knew PR types were always the last to know.

"But I will say this," Cheney continued. "From a PR point of view, a hostile takeover bid could make Bill Agee vulnerable to personal attacks."

Everyone in the room knew what Cheney meant.

In March 1982, Bill Agee had made a pass at the RCA Corporation.

Hard pressed by disastrous financial results, RCA's 1981 profits were down 81 percent from the year before. The stock price had fallen and would have fallen even farther except for the healthy dividend voted by the RCA board of directors.

When RCA did cut its dividend, Agee pounced—buying almost 7 percent of RCA common stock. The management of RCA panicked. Everyone on Wall Street knew that Bill Agee was looking to buy some big company.

Was this Bill Agee's big move?

RCA's chairman immediately turned to his advisers. Among them was an internationally known lawyer, Martin Lipton, fifty-one, a sensitive and cagey man.

Lipton gave RCA a brilliant defense. He wrote a simple line —cleared by RCA's chairman, Thornton Bradshaw—that sent shock waves reverberating through Wall Street and Washington. The attack was skillfully aimed at Bill Agee's soft underbelly —Mary Cunningham.

"Mr. Agee has not demonstrated the ability to manage his own affairs, let alone someone else's."

Subjected to ridicule, Bill Agee again found the glare of national publicity shining in his eyes. Promptly, he called a cease-fire with RCA. Few people believed Bill Agee's reason for backing down—the soaring price of RCA stock—as the professional speculators attempted to cash in on the fight.

To anyone who would listen, Agee was adamant that he never intended to take over RCA—just buy low and sell high. But the sting of the personal attack had left its mark.

Dick Cheney did not need to remind anyone. It could be tried again.

"I think the chairman by now is well aware of that possibility," said Bob Meyers, the Bendix PR head brought to the company by McDonald. He too had worked as an assistant to

McDonald at the White House for one year after having spent nineteen years in the Foreign Service. Despite such experience, Meyers had never been in a corporate takeover before. As was his way after years of political training, he was first and foremost loyal, and second, cautious.

"It's important to remember," Cheney said, "if the price is right and no one outbids you, personal attacks tend to boomerang. But if this new move turns into a fight, the personal attacks will mount. It could get rough."

"Those calls we'll give to you," Al McDonald said.

"Yeah," Cheney said, leaning back in his chair. "Another way to look at it is if Bill is successful, everybody will forget whatever nastiness has been said about him."

The General Motors Building in New York City is a fifty-story tower faced with white Cherokee marble occupying a full block of Fifth Avenue between Fifty-eighth and Fifty-ninth streets on the edge of Central Park. Across Grand Army Plaza is the Plaza Hotel; next door, the windows of the toy store F. A. O. Schwarz.

With barely twenty employees, the Bendix New York offices on the twenty-first floor were modest by corporate standards. In keeping with the United Nations flag flying in the building's courtyard, the office handled licensing Bendix products to LDCs —corporate shorthand for less-developed countries.

The offices gave visiting Bendix executives an official base for discussions with the New York financial community, politicians, and national media leaders. Bendix scuttlebutt had it that the offices also gave Bill Agee a desk just several blocks from Mary.

The board of directors' meeting was set for 4:00 P.M. sharp, but Bill knew the directors would assemble early, as was their custom, to chitchat before getting down to the business at hand.

Agee was ready.

He regarded the board meeting as the beginning of the culmination of his three-year plan of action.

Limousines began arriving at 3:35 P.M.

Prior to the board meeting, Bill Agee sat in his corner office, which looked out onto the green of Central Park. Through his secretary, he placed an overseas telephone call to Interlaken, Switzerland. Hugo Uyterhoeven, a Harvard professor and Bendix board member, picked up the phone in his hotel room. It was almost 11:00 P.M. in Switzerland.

"Hugo," Agee began, "I'm sorry to disturb you at this hour, but there have been some developments I wanted to discuss with you. A board meeting is scheduled within a matter of minutes."

"Fine, Bill."

"Since we talked last week, the market has begun to move. If we are going to keep the acquisition of Martin Marietta a viable option, it's becoming a now-or-never situation. We are in a dangerous position regarding leaks. The value of Martin Marietta stock is up almost a hundred million dollars today."

At minutes before the close of the market, Bill Agee had been handed a summary sheet by Mike Rowny, who had closely monitored the situation with his trading floor contacts all during the day. Rumors were hitting the market hard. Martin Marietta stock was up $2.50, against the general direction of the market.

"Are you recommending making an offer?" Uyterhoeven asked.

"I am."

"What kind of price?"

"Forty-three a share," Agee said. "I wanted to be able to inform the board of your opinion. I have already spoken with Tav, who also is unavailable, and he is for it."

"My feeling is unchanged from our last meeting," Uyterhoeven said.

"Good. I'll speak with you soon."

With Uyterhoeven and Tav—William Tavoulareas, the olive-skinned president of Mobil Oil Corporation—both absent, eleven directors filed into the central, windowless conference room of the Bendix offices.

As the directors found seats at the oval table, the mood was upbeat and relaxed. No agenda for the meeting had been provided in advance. There was some questioning among the directors as to what Agee was up to, but the questions were not pointed.

Despite considerable turmoil over the past several years, the Bendix board continued to be committed to their CEO—Bill Agee. His old mentor, Mike Blumenthal, after an unexpectedly short stint in Washington as Jimmy Carter's Secretary of the

Treasury, had wanted to rejoin the Bendix board. Agee refused. There was another rub, involving compensation for Blumenthal. The two men disagreed. Blumenthal became the head of the Burroughs Corporation and an adamant Agee critic.

Several Bendix directors also served as directors of Burroughs. Agee forced them to choose. Two resigned from the Bendix board. Another, Bob Purcell, quit five months later, citing a "loss of confidence in management."

Among the ten men and one woman seated in the conference room were four "inside" directors—men who worked for Bendix: Al McDonald, president; William Purple, the silver-haired president of the Bendix aerospace group; Fred Searby, the new industrial group president; and Paul Hartz, chairman of Fram Corporation, a Bendix company, and a director since 1967. Hartz had been a Bendix director longer than anyone else on the board.

The "outside" directors present were a distinguished group —Jack Fontaine, lawyer; Jonathan Scott, former chairman of Great Atlantic & Pacific Tea Company (A&P stores); Lt. Gen. (Ret.) Thomas P. Stafford, the astronaut who commanded *Apollo 10*, and who also commanded the American crew for the joint U.S./Soviet space linkup; Coy Eklund, at sixty-seven the oldest member of the board, chairman of Equitable Life; Wilbur Cohen, a professor who served in President Kennedy's cabinet; Donald Rumsfeld, the former Secretary of Defense who was hired by G. D. Searle & Company as its president; and Jewel Lafontant, a striking black woman lawyer from Chicago who was also on the Mobil, Equitable and TWA boards of directors.

Bill Agee walked briskly into the paneled room and moved to the head of the table. As usual, he was in shirt sleeves and tie, his suit coat left on a hanger in his office. After acknowledging the final seating of the directors, Bill Agee nodded to Hal Barron, who then proceeded to distribute an eleven-page memorandum entitled "Acquisition of Georgia."

"Gentlemen and Jewel," Agee began, nodding to Lafontant, seated to his left, "I'd like you to take a minute for review of this position paper. It concerns my request for board authorization to pursue the acquisition of the Martin Marietta Corporation, which is here code-named Georgia."

The memorandum addressed to the board was broken down into topics labeled Proposal; Background on Georgia; Aerospace; Aluminum; Chemicals; Concrete and Aggregates; Other; Financials; Shareholders; The Combination; The Approach; Request for Authority; Earnings and Debt Ratio Summary; Pro Forma Balance Sheet of Bendix, Georgia, and Combined Company.

The directors intently read the memorandum, some reading more closely than others, some seemingly waiting for Bill Agee's explanation. The only sound in the room was made by Rumsfeld, an imposing man with black, slicked hair, pouring himself a glass of water from a pitcher on the table. In keeping with his connection to the Pentagon, Rumsfeld wore military high-gloss black shoes.

"We propose that Bendix make a cash offer to buy up to forty-five percent of Martin Marietta's common shares for forty-three dollars per share," Agee said, methodically going through the memorandum, detailing for the directors the products and assets of Martin Marietta, a huge conglomerate with 1981 sales of $3.3 billion.

"Many of their Defense Department contracts are in the early stages of their life," Bill Agee said, "with excellent prospects for growth and profitability. The aerospace segment produced an operating profit in 1981 of one hundred thirty-six point five million dollars and has continued to improve in the first half of 1982 at a record pace.

"Martin Marietta is a financially strong company," Agee said. "However, the continuing depressed economic climate and recent heavy capital expenditures have caused Martin Marietta to increase its debt ratio from thirteen percent at the end of 1980 to thirty percent this July one.

"Together, Bendix and Martin Marietta would have sales of almost eight billion dollars and about double Bendix's current profits and assets.

"We would intend to propose to Martin Marietta management that they accept the Bendix offer on a friendly basis. Nevertheless, the Martin Marietta board and management may well resist our offer. However, our investment banking adviser, Salomon Brothers, believes there is a good chance our offer will succeed on purely economic grounds.

"I have spoken with Tav and Hugo regarding this move," a confident Bill Agee said. "Both of them have stated that they are in favor of the proposal."

To demonstrate his thoroughness of preparation and to allow full deliberation by the board, Agee presented a series of experts to discuss specific issues related to the offer for Martin Marietta.

First up was Jerry Shapiro, an almost shy fifty-eight-year-old antitrust lawyer from Hughes, Hubbard & Reed. At the behest of Jack Fontaine, his partner at Hughes, Hubbard, Shapiro had begun in July to consider the antitrust issues in a potential Bendix bid for Martin Marietta. A methodical man who joined his firm in 1949, Shapiro was a lawyer at heart. An avid Beethoven fan whose wife was an opera singer, Shapiro heard music in the precision of a legal argument.

"My primary mission," Shapiro said, "is to ensure that in the event of board approval of the offer, Bendix does not receive a second request for information from the Justice Department, which would disrupt the delicate timing mechanism of our offer.

"In that regard, we must anticipate the possibility of a lawsuit with antitrust counts being considered by Martin Marietta if they chose to resist our offer. The area most likely to be scrutinized will be tactical missiles. However, it is the thinking of my firm that such a case cannot succeed on the merits. We have developed a solid line of reasoning to show that the success of our offer would not materially damage competition in the business of making missiles."

"Where is the market overlap?" Donald Rumsfeld asked.

"They are the prime contractor on certain missile programs —Titan III, Pershing II, the MX. Bendix supplies components for several missiles, such as Pershing, out of the Bendix Eatontown and Teterboro, New Jersey, plants."

"I understand they're having trouble with the Pershing," Bill Agee said to Rumsfeld. "I think we can help straighten them out."

After handling a range of questions from the directors, Shapiro retired from the boardroom, and Arthur Fleischer, from Fried, Frank, Harris, Shriver & Jacobson—Agee's acquisition counsel—was invited in.

Initially moving to a position at the oval conference table, Fleischer looked confident. This was his first appearance before the Bendix board. Fleischer had the markings of a classic adviser. Tall and commanding, Fleischer never showed arrogance of opinion; low-key but tough, he would defer to others but often had the last word.

As Agee's key outside legal adviser, Fleischer described to the board the timetable of events from the publication of the offer through consummation.

"There are no substantive barriers that would preclude Bendix from acquiring the Martin Marietta Corporation," Fleischer concluded. "Our broad litigation strategy is first and foremost to get our offer through to a successful conclusion."

"Are there immediate legal actions to be taken by us?" Agee asked to flesh out an understanding for the directors.

"Yes. Many states have on their books so-called takeover laws that purport to be applicable to offers in their states. A Supreme Court decision has rendered one of these statutes unconstitutional. Using that precedent, we will sue in six states to seek declaratory judgments and injunctions against enforcement. I do not anticipate a problem. We will commence litigation at the same time as the offer."

Next up were financial advisers from Salomon Brothers, one of the largest and most successful investment banking firms in the world. Agee had insisted that John Gutfreund, the cochairman of the firm, address the board.

"The offer is fair," Gutfreund said.

The memorandum included the financial implications of a $5 raise in price if that was necessary during the course of negotiations with Martin Marietta management.

"What do you think their response is going to be?" Rumsfeld asked.

"The consensus opinion," Bill Agee answered, "is that Martin Marietta—due to its recent heavy debt load to finance capital expenditures and poor showing in the stock market—will not be in a position to vigorously resist our offer."

"What is your plan for approaching Martin Marietta?" Bill Purple asked. A tough, almost crude man, Purple had been known when traveling to carry a small-caliber gun strapped under his pant leg. As the head of the Bendix aerospace group, he was an executive who knew the industry. He could already hear the howls.

"I plan to phone Tom Pownall, the president of Martin Marietta, in the morning. At the same time, a letter will be delivered notifying him of our offer. I would like the authorization of the board to negotiate directly with him."

"I've known Tom Pownall since he was an advance man in

Nixon's 1960 campaign," Rumsfeld said across the table, adding, "he's one helluva good guy."

With the discussion near a conclusion, Coy Eklund, the gray-haired, blue-eyed chief executive officer of the Equitable Life Assurance Society, neatly deposited the proposal onto the table and pushed back his chair. He excused himself for another engagement.

In reality, Eklund was bothered. Although his function as CEO was clearly and purposely separated from the insurance giant's $40 billion investment funds, Eklund suspected that Equitable had a substantial position in Martin Marietta stock. To avoid the appearance of conflict of interest (the deal Agee was proposing was worth tens of millions of dollars in profits to Equitable), Eklund decided to remove himself temporarily from the Bendix board of directors.

Finally, a motion in favor of the proposal was made and seconded, and the directors voted with a show of hands. The "Acquisition of Georgia" passed unanimously.

THREE

The Martin Marietta corporate headquarters is a graceful, three-story building set on rolling green lawns and flanked by a man-made pond. Some corporate architects have reached for grandiose statements in their designs. The PepsiCo building in Purchase, New York, as an example, also has a pond—in the shape of a giant letter P.

Not so with the Martin Marietta building, sitting low and streamlined among the pine trees of Bethesda, in Montgomery County, Maryland. Close by, across the banks of the Potomac, was the firm's main client—the Pentagon.

In October 1981, a young banker from New York came to make a sales presentation. At thirty-three, Martin A. Siegel was as smooth as they come. "Handsome" was a word used to describe Siegel. So were "cunning," "politic," and "brilliant." With dark hair and eyebrows, brown eyes, flashing white teeth, a perfect tan, and finely manicured hands, Siegel could easily have passed as a New York actor. In fact, he was the head of the M&A department of the investment banking firm of Kidder, Peabody. In his twelve years in the business, Siegel had built a reputation as a doer, handling as many as fifteen important deals in a year.

His specialty was defense against hostile takeovers.

Business Week magazine called Siegel "a canny virtuoso of defensive tactics with an enviable string of triumphs. . . . If the takeover game has become corporate America's version of professional football, Siegel ranks as a kind of all-star middle linebacker."

At the 1981 presentation before Martin Marietta management, Siegel attempted to put the fear of Wall Street into these men of industry.

"Never forget that there are people out there who may want to take your company away from you," Siegel said. "You've got to be prepared."

Charlie Leithauser, Martin Marietta's chief financial officer, was impressed with Siegel. Normally, Charlie refused to be impressed by anything. But Siegel had a straight-ahead attitude that Leithauser liked.

Siegel outlined the vulnerability of Martin Marietta to a hostile takeover attempt: The stock was depressed by poor earnings (and substantial losses) of certain divisions of the corporation; in addition, the company had minimal cash reserves and weak borrowing power.

Martin Marietta's chairman, J. Donald Rauth, liked the pitch and gave Siegel the account. It seemed only the prudent thing to do.

Over the intervening months, Marty Siegel had several associates laboriously compile a financial analysis of the company. They went to Martin Marietta facilities and spoke with the presidents of the operating companies. "We'll kick all the tires," Siegel said.

A whole list of recommendations was submitted.

Not much was done. Until something happened in March 1982.

Newsweek magazine, in its March 22 issue, did a summary of the events in Bendix's investment in the RCA Corporation. The headline was "The Voice of a New Master?" Bill Agee was pictured in a shirt and tie but no jacket, his hand outstretched in a gesture of command. Thornton Bradshaw was also pictured, looking very old by comparison, his eyes heavy and sad. Toward the end of the one-page article, Arthur Davis, an analyst with Prescott, Ball & Turben in Cleveland, was quoted as predicting that RCA was just one example of upcoming investments by Bendix in growth areas.

"I see him in the future maybe buying into Martin Marietta," Davis said.

That raised a few eyebrows in Bethesda.

By late August, the hallways of Martin Marietta were rife with rumors.

Robert W. Powell, Jr., the treasurer of the Martin Marietta Corporation, was a tall, friendly man, fast with numbers, a sure touch with people. As a matter of usual corporate overview, the investor relations department monitored purchases of Martin Marietta stock. They were the ones who noticed the sudden surge in buying in July.

The latest rumors were making Powell nervous.

"Golly," Powell said to Charlie Leithauser, "maybe we ought to stop kicking the tires and start the engine."

Some assignments were made—just in case.

Powell got on the phone with Siegel.

"Marty, looks like we've got something developing. Is Bendix gonna make a move on us?"

"I don't think they're gonna do it," said Siegel.

In the past several days there had been a flurry of activity regarding Bendix and another of Siegel's clients: Gould, Inc. Bendix had accumulated a substantial position in Gould stock, and then Bendix chairman Bill Agee had called up Gould chairman Bill Ylvisaker and said "Let's talk."

When Ylvisaker gave a firm "No" to a proposed joint project, Agee appeared to back off. Siegel was waiting for the next move.

Bob Powell was worried that Martin Marietta could be Agee's next move.

He tracked down Tom Pownall, the president of the company. Pownall, a hands-on kind of man, was down at the Marietta aerospace plant in Orlando, Florida, where the company manufactures the Pershing missile, the politically sensitive armament destined for deployment by President Reagan in Europe.

"Well, look," Pownall said after hearing Powell out, "we've got this system for these kinds of things. We've spent some money to get it in place and we've never exercised it. I don't know if the rumors are real or not, but let's be ready."

Before he left the office that night, Bob Powell took his secretary, Marcia Ortega, aside.

"We've got a very sensitive situation going on," Bob said to

Mrs. Ortega, a native of Panama. "I don't want you to discuss it with our people, but you may have to get in touch with me. Here is a list of phone numbers where you can get me."

On Saturday, Bob Powell and his son Steven packed up their car for the long drive of New England they had planned for months. Steven was a senior in high school. He wanted to go to college in New England.

On Sunday they drove north on Interstate 95, headed for Maine. On Monday they visited Bates, Colby, and Bowden. Then Middlebury and Vermont on Tuesday. They did a whirlwind tour of St. Lawrence, and by late morning on Wednesday, Bob Powell was in the admissions office of Hobart College.

"Is your name Powell?" an admissions officer asked. "Call your office."

"What's up, Marcia?" Bob asked.

"The thing that you thought might happen has happened. Come home."

Shortly after 8:30 A.M., Wednesday, August 25.

"This is Bill Agee from the Bendix Corporation. I would like to speak with Tom Pownall."

"Mr. Pownall, a Mr. Agee is on the phone to speak with you," the secretary said.

Down the hall in his general counsel's office, Pownall rubbed his jaw hard. He had an "oh, shit" feeling about this one.

A sturdy man with a firm handshake and a keen sense of duty, Pownall has been described by his associates as a quiet but decisive man—the kind of person who listened to a variety of opinions before announcing his own decision.

His face was a study in masculinity. His eyes were commanding, his forehead a lattice of deep wrinkles. Military in his bearing, Tom Pownall could really stick out his chin.

Since 1963, when he joined Martin Marietta after serving over twenty years in the Navy and Air Force, Pownall had gone about his job at an even pace, advancing slowly but steadily up the ranks of the corporation. In April 1982 the chairman of Martin Marietta, J. Donald Rauth, made Pownall the president and chief executive officer of the company. After a forty-two-year career with Martin Marietta (and a recent bout with cancer), Rauth planned to retire in January 1983. At that point Pownall would become chairman.

"Tell Agee I'm unavailable," Pownall said into the speaker box.

Minutes later, a receipted letter was delivered to Pownall.

The contents were a note from Bill Agee and a press release.

Pownall skimmed the six-paragraph letter quickly and then the three-page press release.

"Oh, hell, look at this," Pownall said to his general counsel, Frank Menaker, Jr., forty, a dark-haired lawyer with round, dark-framed glasses. "You better get the guys together so we can talk about this."

Charlie Leithauser, as senior vice president and chief financial officer, was the principal executive to whom Tom Pownall had entrusted the job of dealing with the New York financial community. A thin man, close to retirement, who combed his gray-white hair into a wave, Leithauser was old school. He did everything by the book. He had a reputation for being a tough son-of-a-bitch. The first assignment for Leithauser following the letter from Agee was to contact the investment bankers—Kidder, Peabody.

Shortly after 9:00 A.M., Leithauser called New York. Marty Siegel was out of town. Leithauser was given a telephone number to reach him. He was in Memphis attending the board meeting of another client.

"Bendix has come at us," Leithauser said when he reached Siegel in his hotel room. Momentarily, Siegel said nothing. He had been wrong about Agee.

"What about the Stock Exchange?" Leithauser asked.

"They should be notified and trading in Martin Marietta stock suspended," Siegel said.

"Okay, we haven't opened yet," Leithauser said, checking his watch. "We'll tell them what's happening. There is a meeting at 4:00 P.M. here. Menaker is getting the lawyers from Dewey, Ballantine to come down. You should be here."

"Charlie, I'll get my team together, but I've got a problem. You know, Memphis isn't the easiest place to connect out of."

"Don't worry about it. We'll send the G-2," Leithauser said, referring to a company jet.

With a prepared defensive book—thanks to Martin Marietta's foresight and the legwork provided by Kidder, Peabody—the team was able to hit the pavement running, after the briefing by Pownall. Everyone had assignments, although once preliminary calls were made, the reality and confusion of the situation began to sink in.

Charlie Leithauser arranged a meeting of his finance staff and—knowing Bob Powell was out of town—several of the treasury's staff. Perhaps twenty people, representing the accounting and audit departments, crowded into the room. Among them was Tom Mendenhall, the young assistant treasurer for cash and banking. The meeting was more a briefing than a call to action.

"I just want to tell you the news personally," Leithauser began. "I know it comes as a shock to many of you, but you should know we are somewhat prepared. We're going to develop a defensive strategy. Everyone is going to be called on to do something, we don't know what yet. At the moment we're trying to get people from all over the country to meet here this afternoon."

As the meeting ended, Mendenhall asked Leithauser:

"What should we do about money?" That was Mendenhall's area of responsibility, and with his boss—Bob Powell—not present, he was on the edge of his seat to be sure he was thinking of all possibilities. This was the most exciting thing that had happened in his career.

Mendenhall, with his dark hair and youthful expression, looked almost boyish next to Leithauser. Mendenhall had a hard-earned respect for Charlie's toughness.

"That's a good question. We gotta talk to the banks," Leithauser responded.

"What are we talking about? How much money?"

"What are we good for now? Three hundred?" Leithauser asked.

"Yeah, three hundred million dollars, plus a little more from our seasonal lines of credit."

Leithauser thought about it for several seconds.

"See if you can line up four hundred more," he said, quickly adding as Mendenhall began to look excited, "but don't pay anything for it. Start the process, talk to the people, but don't sign it up."

"Can I ask why you want seven hundred million dollars?"

"Cause that's how much Bendix has!" Leithauser said, guessing.

* * *

Dow Jones & Company, which publishes *The Wall Street Journal,* also serves the business community with a ticker tape news service known as the "broad tape," which electronically distributes news over telephone lines almost as it happens. The news is printed out—line by line—in banking and brokerage offices around the country.

The Dow Jones editors have an electronic means of prioritizing the news. When something is hot, a buzzer sounds on the teletype machine.

Buzzers were blaring all over the country on August 25.

The story of Bendix's announcement hit the wire at 10:15 A.M.:

BENDIX ANNOUNCES $43-A-SHARE
OFFER FOR MARTIN MARIETTA

A polished brass telescope stood in the corner of Ivan Boesky's office on the twenty-ninth floor of an office tower at One State Street Plaza in the heart of the New York financial district. Ivan Boesky was a man respected on Wall Street. He was an arbitrageur—a professional stock market speculator.

Beginning in 1975 with $700,000, Boesky shimmied the capital of his firm to more than $90 million in five years. A lawyer, accountant, and securities analyst, Boesky had an instinct for deals that had made him one of the richest men in America.

His office was a clutter of activity. The latest stock prices ran on a computerized ticker tape across one wall. Teletype machines from Reuters and Dow Jones printed out the latest news on continuous paper behind his desk between flags of the United States and Israel. Bronze statues of bulls in various stages of arousal were scattered throughout the room. Boesky used the horns of one sleepy bull's head as a hat rack.

At forty-five, Boesky was gray-haired with a long, thin face and darting eyes.

Standing at his desk, an office loudspeaker microphone bent to his mouth, a telephone in another hand, gold cuff links offsetting his starched white shirt and suit vest, Boesky was poised for action—connected to the world of business by computer, by telephone, by sense of smell.

When the announcement hit the tape at 10:15 A.M., it was as

if a fire alarm had sounded. Boesky dropped the telephone and grabbed his microphone.

"Bendix is making a bid for Martin Marietta! Let's get on this one! I want some answers. Perry Cohen? Can you hear me, Cohen? Bring in your research!"

Within minutes, Boesky and his research director analyzed the situation, looking closely at terms of the Bendix offer and the "spread"—the difference between where the stock was on the market and what Bendix was offering.

Hostile merger attempts have great risks. Many times the deal does not go through as planned. Boesky and his research director assessed the risk in the proposed Bendix and Martin Marietta deal.

The investing public also had to make decisions.

A stockholder could hold on to his Martin Marietta stock in hopes that Bendix would succeed and deliver the promised $43 a share. If a stockholder did not want to take the risk, he could sell his stock—discounted down from the $43 offer—to an arbitrageur.

Ivan Boesky was willing to take the risk.

"Buy Martin Marietta," Boesky instructed his staff.

When the market opened on Martin Marietta stock at 2:19 P.M. after the delay requested by the company "pending news," 323,000 shares changed hands. The price was $40 a share—up almost $7 from yesterday's close.

When the story first broke, a staffer at the Park Avenue law firm of Wachtell, Lipton, Rosen & Katz clipped the story—along with others—and began his usual rounds of distributing the news to interested partners.

Dick Katcher, a forty-one-year-old athletic lawyer with a bad back and a good sense of humor, had his name on the list for stories about Bendix. He had been involved with his partner Martin Lipton in representing RCA Corporation early in the year and wanted to keep an eye on Bill Agee.

When the release crossed his desk, already loaded down with papers, Katcher read it, paused briefly, and then went back to work.

Behind his desk was a wall of collected and bound papers from the many deals he had worked on. Clear plastic trophies on a shelf commemorated still more deals—RCA's acquisition of CIT, Norton Simon's securing of Avis; the list went on, a tangible history of his career. In one corner, a small Japanese dwarf pine. In a drawer, a photograph of his wife, Susan, from whom he was recently separated.

Joanne Martinuzzi, Martin Lipton's secretary, tapped on Katcher's door.

"Mr. Siegel from Kidder, Peabody just called looking for Mr. Lipton. He said it was urgent. I told him Mr. Lipton was not in the office. Perhaps you would take the call. Here's his number."

"Where's 901?" Katcher asked, looking at the area code.

"He said he was in Memphis."

After several tries, Katcher got Siegel.

"You've seen the story about Bendix going after Martin Marietta?" Siegel asked after hearing that Lipton was unavailable. "We're representing Martin Marietta, and Kidder, Peabody would like you guys to represent us. How's it look?"

A cardinal rule of Wall Street is to get someone to do for you what he has already done for someone else. Siegel wanted to get Bill Agee to go away. Martin Lipton's firm had done it before. Maybe they could do it again.

Dick called back Siegel after some checking for conflicts.

"We'd be delighted to represent you."

"Great. There's a four-o'clock meeting this afternoon in Bethesda at Martin Marietta. Call Doug Brown in my office and he'll handle all the details."

"What do you have on Martin Marietta?" Dick asked. He knew the name, and that they had bought Harvey Aluminum, they had cement plants, big in aerospace, and that Martin Marietta had been in a famous 16b case.

"Doug will bring books on both companies," Siegel said. "And most of the Martin directors are going to be there tomorrow, so maybe you'll stay over. See you soon."

Dick called his secretary, Eleanor, and asked her to get him a messenger. While he waited, Dick smoked a Merit cigarette and doodled with a colored pen on a yellow legal pad.

"Go to bookkeeping and get money," Dick said to the messenger, "and then go down and buy me toothpaste, shaving cream, a hair brush, underwear, socks, and a shirt."

Once packed and ready to leave, Dick took one last phone call. It was from Jay Higgins, the head of the M&A department of Salomon Brothers. Jay was a close friend of Katcher. During the summer, when Dick was first separated from his wife, Susan, he had no place to go. Susan and the kids were at the house in Mamaroneck. Jay let Dick stay at his apartment for several weeks while he was on Long Island.

"I guess you heard we're representing Bendix," Higgins began.

"I guess everybody has heard by now."

"Are you guys going to be involved?" Higgins asked.

"Yeah. Siegel at Kidder wants us to represent him."

"I'd just like you to know that we're prepared to meet and talk about it. We would like to get together," Higgins said.

"I'll pass it on."

"How are you and Susan?"

"Better."

"I'll send you our tender offer papers."

"Thanks."

At the airport, Dick looked for Doug Brown. With Doug were two more soldiers from Kidder, Peabody—Ed Midgley and Peter Wood. Katcher had never met them before but recognized them because they were the men in suits carrying the bulging briefcases.

On the 1:00 P.M. shuttle flight to Washington's National Airport, Katcher read up on Martin Marietta and Bendix and the terms of the proposed deal as carried by the wire service. Brown had two fat notebooks—one analyzing Martin Marietta, one Bendix.

Midgley rented a car and drove them through suburban Maryland to Bethesda—less than ten miles in a straight line from the Pentagon.

FOUR

The Edward A. Garmatz Federal Court House, at the corner of Lombard and Hanover, stands facing the new Baltimore, with its back to the Chesapeake. Named after a local politician who was later indicted and acquitted of bribery, the courthouse is a collection of courtrooms and judicial chambers beginning at the lowest levels of judicial review on the first several floors and rising to the Appeals Court on the ninth floor. As is the case with most federal courthouses, when a lawyer says he will appeal to a higher court, he means it literally.

John Henry Lewin, Jr., from Maryland's biggest law firm—Venable, Beatjer & Howard—represented Bendix in Maryland. He was hired forty-eight hours before and had worked feverishly to prepare a preemptive lawsuit challenging the constitutionality of a Maryland statute that attempted to prevent hostile corporate takeovers.

Lewin had beaten the statute before, in the Sunshine Mining case.

On Wednesday morning he was waiting in his office for a telephone call from New York. On his desk, a coffee mug labeled "J L 2." A picture of George Washington was on the wall. Lewin was wearing a blue shirt with a striped tie. His round glasses offset his reddish face.

The phone rang. "Go file," the man said.

Those simple instructions, timed to the delivery of Bill Agee's letter to Tom Pownall, set in motion the first blow of the Bendix legal plan.

At the courthouse during the afternoon, the Bendix lawyers —Lewin and his New York counterpart—were joined by the lawyer representing the State of Maryland and an attorney from the law firm of Miles & Stockbridge representing Martin Marietta. The group met in the conference room of Federal District Judge Joseph H. Young. There were several other people milling around the room.

Judge Young went about introducing himself, shaking hands with everyone. When he got to a man and a woman standing apart from the lawyers, he asked who they were. They identified themselves as reporters from the *Baltimore Sun.*

"Out," Young said, pointing to the door. He was not wearing his black court robes, but the authority in his voice left little doubt who was in charge.

"But Your Honor, this involves a Maryland corporation. The public has a right to know of your deliberations!"

"Out," the judge repeated.

After about an hour of discussion with the Bendix team pointing to the precedent of the U.S. Supreme Court decision of *Edgar* v. *Mite,* Judge Young granted John Henry Lewin's request. Martin Marietta and the State of Maryland were temporarily restrained from enforcing the Maryland takeover statute. Young set a hearing date of September 2 on Bendix's motion that Martin Marietta be permanently restrained.

For now, Bendix had frozen the Maryland law.

Martin Marietta would find no relief here.

FIVE

Roy Calvin, the vice president in charge of public relations and anything-else-Tom Pownall-wants-to-gimme was standing in the broad hall of the second floor of Martin Marietta's headquarters.

As usual, he had a cigarette in his hand, threatening to drop a long, white ash. Adjusting his black-rimmed glasses, Calvin watched secretaries and executives go in and out of offices. The pace was up. But Calvin had his doubts that anybody knew what the hell they were doing.

Four hours before, the Bendix Corporation announced its intention to buy the Martin Marietta Corporation. Calvin noticed a variety of people from other departments wandering around the third floor. Some of the secretaries whose desks lined the hall were being visited by friends from other floors.

Everybody wanted to know: "What's going on?"

The scope of the challenge was beginning to unfold.

Frank Menaker, the general counsel, was being flooded by calls from attorneys across the country. Martin Marietta had been sued by Bendix in Maryland, Louisiana, Nebraska, Oklahoma, South Carolina, and Utah.

Menaker called a short meeting with his staff of five assistant general counsels.

"Clear your desks," he said.

"What can we do?" Doris Rush, an assistant general counsel, asked.

"Find out more about these state takeover statutes," Menaker said.

Rush went into the law library—a small, narrow room just wide enough for one table—and started looking up state statutes. Another lawyer, a younger woman, joined in. Their thinking was that if Bendix had started these moves in a series of states, maybe there were states with takeover laws that they missed. Perhaps a counterattack could be launched.

After hours of pouring through heavy legal volumes, they realized nothing had been missed. The Bendix team had been very thorough and pulled off their first move with military precision.

Wednesday was the hottest day of August. The Washington, D.C., area usually is hot and humid in the summer. Wednesday was no exception. The temperature peaked at ninety-two degrees. By the time the New York advisers began streaming into Marietta headquarters, it was a relief to get indoors.

Dick Katcher arrived with Doug Brown and two more soldiers from Kidder, Peabody. Marty Siegel had not yet arrived on the G-2 from Memphis.

Leonard Larrabee, an experienced New York corporate lawyer, arrived with three of his partners. Larrabee's law firm— Dewey, Ballantine, Bushby, Palmer & Wood—had been retained months before in anticipation of a hostile move against the corporation. A ruddy man bursting with energy, Larrabee looked much older than his fifty-two years. His nasal accent revealed him to be a true New Yorker—born, raised, and still living in New Rochelle.

As if to get the lay of the land, various members of the invited teams of lawyers and bankers wandered in the broad hall of Martin Marietta's executive wing, which was sparsely decorated with the exception of a large bronze eagle, enraged with talons extended. Dick Katcher peeked into an open office. Doris Rush looked up from her work and asked him to come in.

A tall, stately lawyer, neatly dressed, with platinum hair set in a flip at her shoulders, Rush offered a quick smile and pointed to a chair for Dick to sit. She lit a cigarette.

"This is all a bit new to me," Doris said. "We've never been in this situation before. Could I ask you a question?"

"Certainly." Katcher was the friendly type. With his curly hair, thick sideburns, and quick wit, he had been mistaken for the comedian Gene Wilder. Once, during the past summer, separated from his wife, Dick was at the yacht club. A passerby refused to leave Dick alone until he admitted that at least he was Gene Wilder's brother.

"How does the timing of this thing work?" Rush asked, turning her cigarette lighter in her hands. "I know there are a series of deadlines."

Katcher went on to explain the intricate mechanism of regulation that allows one corporation to attempt to buy the stock —and control—of another corporation. Several key filings were required by the Securities and Exchange Commission. The first —a 14D-9—required Martin Marietta to answer the Bendix offer, yes, no, or maybe.

Beyond that, a series of deadlines was established regarding the process of Bendix buying the Martin Marietta stock. First, all the Martin Marietta stockholders must be notified and allowed sufficient time to deliver or "tender" their stock to Bendix. At a later date, established by law, Bendix would be allowed to buy the stock.

Bendix could buy Martin Marietta stock at 12:01 A.M. on September 17.

"In twenty-three days," Doris Rush said.

"Right."

"Okay," Rush said, jotting a note to herself.

"But even if someone tenders their shares to Bendix, they can still change their mind and withdraw them anytime before Bendix buys on the seventeenth," Katcher said.

"Got it."

"Good. Then when I get confused, I'll ask you," Dick said with a smile.

When Marty Siegel arrived, he was greeted by Charlie Leithauser. After shaking hands with several Marietta executives, Siegel was led to a room on the third floor. Moving decisively, Siegel quickly assumed command. While Leithauser and the Martin Marietta executives were frazzled wondering where to begin, Siegel was calm, smiling, full of confidence.

"Which phones can we use?" Siegel asked.

"Any phone you want," Leithauser responded.

Siegel checked with his office in New York.

"Kathy," he said to his secretary, "I haven't had a chance yet. Will you call Jane [his wife] and tell her we better cancel our vacation plans."

Next, Siegel got the bad news from the stock market. Almost nine hundred thousand shares of Martin Marietta had changed hands in the less than two hours of open trading. It was obvious that the arbitrageurs (or "arbs," as they are called) were jumping in with both feet.

That meant trouble.

Siegel knew that the Bendix stock market strategy was to try to panic the Martin Marietta stockholders into selling their shares at a modest profit to the arbs, who were short-term speculators. Once the arbs had boxes of the stock, they would be natural allies of Bendix. Men like Ivan Boesky bore no allegiance to any company. His goal was to buy low, sell high.

An immediate job for Siegel's team would be to communicate with Boesky and the other arbitrageurs. Martin Marietta— if they decided to resist the Bendix offer—had to convince the arbs that the Bendix takeover plan would not work.

With yellow legal pads scattered on a table, the lawyers were making notes of priorities. Things that must be immediately done. Issues to be researched. The bankers needed to complete a financial analysis of the adequacy of the Bendix offer. The lawyers had to prepare the filings with the SEC. Both groups had to lay out the options for Martin Marietta management in the event they chose to resist the offer.

Marty Siegel had a bold idea.

"What about hitting them hard?" Siegel said to Dick Katcher and Leonard Larrabee. "Martin Marietta is not in that bad shape. Maybe we can make an offer to buy Bendix as a defense?"

Leonard Larrabee mulled it over. In 1981, in the Conoco and Dome Petroleum transaction, Larrabee had wanted to try the same strategy, but Canada's Foreign Investment Review Act had blocked the move.

Having seen the idea of a countertender offer tried several times before within the past year, Dick Katcher was quick to say, "That will work only if we can take control first. Where is Martin Marietta incorporated?"

"Maryland."

"We'll have to check the statute. Where is Bendix incorporated?"

"Delaware."

"I remember from the Cities Service-Mesa deal that Delaware has no waiting period," Katcher said. "A majority stockholder can take control immediately, unless their charter negates that. We'll need to take a look at the Bendix charter."

"I'll get Doug to call the office to get ahold of the Bendix charter and bylaws," Siegel said.

"It could be an opening," Larrabee said.

Charlie Leithauser came back into the room.

"I'd like to talk with Mr. Rauth and Mr. Pownall," Siegel said to Leithauser.

Leithauser led Siegel followed by Larrabee and Katcher down the hall to Chairman Rauth's office, where Tom Pownall and Frank Menaker were huddled. Leithauser introduced the three outsiders. Menaker recognized Katcher's name.

"I've read some of your articles."

The first objective from the advisers' point of view was to assess the reaction of Pownall and Rauth to the bid for Martin Marietta. Siegel knew from the advance work done on the financials that the $43 a share bid by Bendix was not the kind of price that would excite a sale. After all, less than a year before, the value of the Martin Marietta stock was over $50 a share, and everyone had been hurt by the recession—albeit Martin Marietta more than many other companies.

Pownall was noncommittal. He wanted to study the situation.

"If the bid is fair, we ought not to oppose it. If this is the time to sell, we'll sell. I want the opinions of you guys. But if we wanted to resist, what the hell would we do?"

Siegel ticked off the list of standard defensive responses of a company that comes under attack from another company: Martin Marietta could fight in court. Or put a block of stock in friendly hands who would refuse to sell out. Or buy back its own stock. Or look for a friendly company to buy Martin Marietta. Or make an acquisition that would present an antitrust problem for Bendix. There were scores of weapons in Siegel's arsenal.

"Can we stop this in court?" Pownall asked.

Katcher and Larrabee and Frank Menaker explained the role of litigation in most tender offers. At best, the other side may have made a mistake in their Securities and Exchange Commission filings. Perhaps they could be fought on an improper disclosure basis. Perhaps on an antitrust basis.

"The bottom line," Siegel said, "is don't count on the courts to save the company."

Pownall grimaced. This was all so new to him.

"You should also know that the market does not look very good. Volume on Martin stock was very heavy today—some nine hundred thousand shares—and price is up to thirty-nine and an eighth. People are selling their stock to the arbs."

"The arbs," Pownall asked, rubbing his jaw. "So what have we got?"

"We could try another tactic," Siegel said.

"Shoot."

"We could make an offer to buy Bendix."

Pownall looked dumbfounded. He had never been in a hostile merger fight before. Marty Siegel was practically the first investment banker he had met. He looked to Frank Menaker, whose expression was similarly confused.

"Look," Siegel said, "we haven't explored it. It would be an aggressive strategy that might force Agee to think twice. But if nobody's interested, we won't waste time on it."

"Well, if we decide to oppose, we'll consider it. If it seems viable after our preliminary discussions, it'll be something that gets presented to the directors."

"When are you calling a meeting?"

"I've talked to some of them already. Tomorrow—as you know—we're gonna get together informally just to get up to speed. I guess we'll schedule a formal board meeting for Monday."

"I'll take care of that," Don Rauth said in a gentle voice.

At 6:00 P.M., the Martin Marietta executives excused themselves from the deliberations for a prior commitment—the retirement dinner of Bernie Gamson, the president of the aluminum company. It was held in Bethesda at the Congressional Country Club.

"We'll have some sandwiches sent in for you guys," PR head Roy Calvin said to Marty Siegel.

Siegel and Larrabee and their teams gathered in the meeting room that quickly became known as the "War Room." It had a conference table, a chair and desk, a credenza, and another chair, in the corner.

As the men filed into the room, Dick Katcher turned to Robert Myers, a lawyer from Dewey, Ballantine and asked, "How do we find a Maryland corporation statute?"

Myers was a small man—immaculately dressed, starched shirt, cuff links, a pipe in his jacket pocket.

Together they left the War Room and headed for the small law library. They pulled several volumes off the shelf and began thumbing through the pages.

"Here it is," Myers said, pointing to the regulations governing the actions of stockholders of a Maryland corporation. For Bendix to take control of Martin Marietta, Agee would first have to call a Martin Marietta stockholders' meeting and use his planned stock purchases to elect a new loyal board of directors.

Katcher and Myers found something interesting that could stop Agee. A stockholders' meeting of a Maryland corporation required a minimum ten-day notice. But control of a Delaware incorporated company could be achieved immediately by the written consent of 51 percent of the company stockholders.

Both men looked at each other. Katcher reached into his jacket and brought out his pocket calendar.

"First of all, they can buy our stock on September seventeenth, correct?" Katcher said.

"At one minute after midnight, correct."

"That means they can call a special meeting and take control of Martin Marietta at the earliest by Sunday, September twenty-sixth. Now, if we announce a bid to buy Bendix this Monday, which is August thirtieth, then we can buy on the twenty-first and act by written consent immediately. That gives Martin Marietta a five-day advantage!"

"We can take control before they can!" Myers said excitedly.

"That's nice," Katcher said, playing with Myers.

Both men knew it could never be that easy. Both states had statutes regarding who is eligible to vote their shares at a stockholders' meeting. If Bendix bought Martin Marietta, then Martin Marietta would be a subsidiary of Bendix and prohibited under Delaware law from voting any Bendix shares against its corporate parent.

"That's bad," Katcher said.

The two men also found a similar statute in Maryland law.

"So then if both companies buy, neither one can vote the shares?" Katcher reasoned aloud.

"Let's hope we can find a judge who thinks so," Myers said, knowing that a stalemate appeared to be the best Martin Marietta could achieve if Bendix decided to push ahead.

"Remember the Pabst case?" Katcher said. "Pabst provided Olympia the money to buy Pabst. The court looked at this subsidiary issue and decided that the key issue was control. The key thing was who had control. If Martin Marietta fights back and buys Bendix, maybe they could take control first?"

"Let's let New York go over this one," Myers said.

Katcher and Myers left the library and returned to the boardroom, where Leonard Larrabee was making notes. They thrashed out a rough division of labor. There were so many things to look at. There were the antitrust issues, the margin regulations, the 14D-9 filing with the Securities and Exchange Commission, and the complex preparation—just in case—of the countertender offer materials to buy Bendix.

Larrabee looked at Katcher and said, "We need more troops."

At 5:00 A.M. on Thursday, the Martin Marietta white Gulfstream jet picked up Bob Powell, the Marietta treasurer, at an upstate New York county airport. After taking off, the plane made a great swing to pick up several members of the Martin Marietta board of directors. In New Hampshire, near Lake Winnipesaukee, they picked up Charlie Hugel, the executive vice president of AT&T; in Portland, Maine, Gene Zuckert (a lawyer) and his wife.

To pass the time on the trip back to Bethesda, Powell, Hugel, and Zuckert took turns reading the newspaper.

On the front page of *The New York Times* was a story about eighty U.S. Marines landing at Beirut Harbor at dawn to help monitor the withdrawal of Yassir Arafat and the PLO guerrillas.

There in black and white deeper in the *Times* was the tombstone announcement "Notice of Offer to Purchase for Cash Up to 15,800,000 Shares of Common Stock of Martin Marietta Corporation at $43 Net Per Share by The Bendix Corporation."

In the business section, the headline in the *Times* read: "$1.6 Billion Martin Bid by Bendix—$43 Share Offer Is Called Low."

"Several analysts doubted that Martin Marietta would view the offer with favor," the *Times* article said. "Francis Carey, an analyst at Fahnestock, said he believes the $43-a-share price is too low, adding that: 'I don't think the Martin management will roll over and play dead.' "

Bob Powell smiled at Hugel and Zuckert.

Tom Pownall did not know how to roll over and play dead.

By the time Hugel, Zuckert, and Powell got back to Bethesda, the other directors were already gathered in the boardroom. As the stragglers entered the room and said their hellos and expressed understandable shock at the happenings, Chairman Don Rauth introduced the various outsiders to the directors.

With bright blue eyes and thin, reddish-gray hair, Rauth showed his age, sixty-four, but no ill effects from his bout with colon cancer. His treatments at the Mayo Clinic had arrested the disease.

The long bank of drapes running down the far wall of the room were pulled open, giving the room diffused natural lighting. Before getting down to business, the men spoke informally with each other.

Tom Pownall had chatted with director Jack Byrne.

At fifty, Byrne was the youngest man on the board. In 1976 he had taken charge of Geico Corporation, a huge Washington, D.C., auto insurer that was close to bankruptcy. He spent a horrible summer trying to salvage the company. Before it was clear he had succeeded, Marietta chairman Don Rauth asked Byrne to join the board.

"Tom, don't be too quick here about Agee," Byrne advised Pownall. "All I know about the man, really, is that he said something awfully sensible in *The New York Times* a while ago."

Agee had written an editorial in the March 25 edition under the headline "How Companies Should Use Their Cash: Lessons from Bendix."

Byrne was so impressed at the time, he made a Xerox copy of the editorial and distributed it to his portfolio managers.

"Agee seems like a smart guy. If that article represents the man, he may not be too bad a guy to work for."

Tom Pownall smiled and said very little.

Although today's meeting was not officially called to order and no minutes would be kept, the gathering represented almost the complete board of fourteen accomplished businessmen. Among the well-known names—Griffin Bell, President Carter's first Attorney General, now a senior partner of the

Atlanta law firm of King & Spalding; and Melvin Laird, former Secretary of Defense.

Rauth turned the floor over to Tom Pownall.

It was obvious from Rauth's deferential attitude that Pownall was now in charge. Erect in his bearing, Pownall seemed fit for the challenge.

"Let me give you just a bit of background before we start," he said. "I got a call this morning from Bill Agee from Bendix. I didn't take it. A couple of minutes later, I got this letter."

With that Pownall read Agee's letter to the board.

The directors sat—mostly quiet, many grim-faced.

"Let me introduce a couple of fellows," Pownall said. "First, this is Marty Siegel from Kidder, Peabody. He will be in charge of the financial analysis of the Bendix offer."

"That won't take long," a director quipped.

In preliminary chats, Pownall had spoken with the directors, sounding them out about the Bendix price. It seemed everybody thought it was low. Some of the directors—particularly the financial types such as Frank Ewing, a self-made millionaire— thought Agee's price was far too low.

Tom Pownall did not have a magic number in his own head.

He had never sat down and figured out what the company was worth on a per-share basis. One thing for certain, he thought, if he was pressed to give a dollar value of the company, it would be higher than he could explain.

Martin Marietta was a living thing to Tom Pownall. Not just a business. The value of the company was somehow a long list of names and faces who had worked on projects such as Viking, the exploration of Mars, the Titan rocket, and the Pershing missile since 1958, and a host of other projects for the nation's defense. The value of all that in Pownall's mind was not a number, trailing a long line of zeroes.

Pownall was not certain what to think of Bill Agee.

He had met the man once socially in 1980 at a party in Agee's Detroit home. Not much was said. From what he knew, Pownall thought Agee had done a hell of a good job running Bendix. But the automobile business was not the prime systems aerospace business.

"There are a great many options the board must consider. We're going to get our guys to look at this from all the angles, and I hope to have some answers by the formal board meeting on Monday."

"Where will that be?" asked a director.

Pownall, looking around, said, "I assume here."

"If I may," Dick Katcher said, "we're gonna have a lot of paper and people on this in New York. That's where the support staff is. All of our offices are there, all our facilities."

"We'll get you as many secretaries and typewriters as you need," interjected a Martin Marietta staffer.

The meeting was set—Monday, August 30. Time to be announced. In Bethesda.

Jack Byrne, sitting at the long conference table, did an odd thing. He loosened his red tie and removed it from around his neck. The tie bore a pattern of naval pennants that signaled "Don't Give Up The Ship." Byrne scribbled a note on a piece of paper, wrapped the tie in it, and asked Gene Zuckert to pass it down to Pownall.

Pownall read the note and smiled.

"This tie was given to me when all hell was breaking loose at Geico. I wore it until we turned the company around. It might be useful to you in this crisis. I tender it to you. P.S. I need a tie. Will you pass yours down?"

As Pownall removed his own tie, the directors were filled in and everyone had a good laugh. Before the day was over, almost everyone on the executive floor knew about Pownall's new tie. Everybody wanted to see it.

Tom Pownall held an open meeting for employees in the headquarters building. Hundreds of office workers attended. Pownall, a strong, steady man, tried to calm nerves. Although he had little to offer by way of information, his direct approach and we're-in-this-together attitude was appreciated.

"I can't tell you what we're gonna do," he said, standing to address the large group, "but we're studying every angle. You can be sure that we are going to do what's best for the company and its shareholders. Our customers will be taken care of. I can tell you that we are in control."

Pownall wanted to believe that himself.

SIX

Martin Marietta assistant treasurer Tom Mendenhall had a lot on his mind. On Thursday morning, at home in Manassas, Virginia, on the other side of the Potomac, Mendenhall stood quietly before the bathroom mirror. He was thinking.

At thirty-three, his dark brown hair was turning wispy at the top of forehead. He kept his hair closely cropped, just sitting over the ridge of his ears. There was a devilishness in his small, curled smile that kept him looking young.

His wife, Linda, wanted to know what was going on.

"I've got to raise seven hundred million dollars," Tom said matter-of-factly.

That was the figure Charlie Leithauser had mentioned the day before. "But don't pay for anything yet, just line it up," he had said.

That was just like Charlie—the tough old bird.

Mendenhall drove faster than normal, barreling up Interstate 66 to the Beltway and then down to Martin Marietta headquarters in Bethesda.

A steady stream of calls were returned to Mendenhall during the morning as he battled to reach the loan officers of the ten banks involved in the company's existing credit line. He talked with Chase Manhattan Bank, Citibank, Morgan, Bankers Trust,

Chemical, Manufacturers Hanover, Mellon, Toronto Dominion, and Continental Illinois.

Over his term as assistant treasurer, Mendenhall had tried to develop relationships, not just handle transactions with the banks. Having worked for a bank himself (First Pennsylvania Bank), Mendenhall wanted the bank loan officers to like the people as well as the numbers of Martin Marietta.

He was up front with his contacts.

"Look, at this stage I can't pay for anything," Mendenhall said to the loan officer from Bankers Trust. "I'm not even sure what we're gonna do with the money. All I know is the big guys here want me to line up commitments. How much are you good for?"

"We're prepared to stand with you," the officer from Mellon Bank said. "You'll just have to tell us how much you need. By the way, how much is Bank of America putting out?"

Good question, Mendenhall thought.

Bank of America was the key.

If B of A was not involved in a big way, Mendenhall had his doubts that the package Charlie wanted could be put together. The other banks needed a leader.

At just after noon, Mendenhall finally reached Tom Tegart, the loan officer at the Bank of America in Los Angeles.

"Tom, we've got some fireworks going on here," Mendenhall said.

"That's what I gather from the newspapers."

"Look, I'm trying to put together a whole new loan package. I want Bank of America as our lead bank. Make some airline reservations. I'll talk with you later in the day. But I think you better get in here by tomorrow."

Friday, August 27:

Some people at Martin Marietta in the treasury and legal departments thought Tom Mendenhall was a bit off the beam. His desk was a shambles. He ran around the office with a determined look on his face, talking to no one.

He was always on the phone, tapping a pencil and bouncing a knee.

Suddenly he appeared at Doris Rush's door.

Grabbing slips of paper from his pockets, he merrily shouted: "We got fifteen million dollars from Chemical. And another fifteen here. And somewhere," he said, madly going through the papers in his hands, "I know there's another twenty-five in here."

Mendenhall knew nothing of the strategy. He heard different possibilities bantered about. Mendenhall was comfortable leaving those important decisions to the likes of Charlie Leithauser, Frank Menaker, and Tom Pownall.

"No matter what is decided," Mendenhall's boss, Bob Powell, said, "it's going to take lots of money, so keep it up."

Tom had not seen Charlie Leithauser in twenty-four hours. Finally he bumped into him in the hall. Charlie was on his way to a meeting. Both men were brief.

"How are things going?" Leithauser asked.

"We've got a lot of banks with us, Charlie."

"Who's not with us?"

"I don't know yet," Mendenhall said, not sharing his concerns about several banks.

"We heard from Maryland National Bank," Leithauser said, lightening. "They've committed twenty-five million dollars. Be sure to put them on your list."

"Great."

"Did Bob tell you?"

"Tell me what?"

"The bankers and lawyers in New York say we may need eight hundred million."

Mendenhall was given a batch of telephone numbers of the advisers in New York. He dialed the number of Leonard Larrabee, the lawyer from Dewey, Ballantine. Larrabee had earlier expressed an interest in the status of arranging the money.

"Tom, I'm glad you called. I'm sitting here with Ed Midgley from Kidder, Peabody, and we've been going over the company's existing credit agreement."

The credit line was a $300 million revolver, with a five-year term-out allowing the company to borrow and pay back for three years with the outstanding balance due in five years.

"There's a lot of stuff in the old agreement that would be trouble," Larrabee said. "We've got to file our financing arrangements with the SEC. The new agreement has got to be watertight."

"At this stage I'm still trying to line up commitments," Mendenhall said. "We haven't drafted anything."

"Just remember," Larrabee said in his nasal accent, "If the agreement is just a document that says 'if the banks agree, we can borrow the money,' the Bendix lawyers will rip us to shreds in court."

"The banks are bound to want some conditions," Mendenhall said.

"The less conditions the better," Larrabee said.

Mendenhall had sixty hours to get ten different banks to commit $800 million. Normally it would take weeks of loan committee meetings and review. Mendenhall had sixty hours, spread over a weekend—definitely not regular banking hours.

"At this point, all I can say is we need you," Mendenhall told a bank loan officer. "Our time fuse is very short. I need a phone number where I can reach you on Saturday, and you better make sure you can reach your decision-makers."

By midday on Friday, Tom Tegart from B of A in Los Angeles arrived at Martin Marietta with Tim Deason, a Bank of America lawyer from New York. The driver dropped them off at the side entrance, a set of double glass doors on a circular drive. The rolling lawns were perfectly manicured, the plantings still holding the last of the summer's bloom.

The two men were issued security badges and hustled to the elevator.

Mendenhall greeted Tegart as a friend and smiled at the introduction of Tim Deason. Mendenhall introduced several other treasury staffers, including Bill Armistead, who had come to Martin Marietta after working with the commercial side of Maryland National Bank. He knew the details of the existing loan agreement.

"And this is Doris Rush, an assistant general counsel here," Mendenhall said. "Don't let her scare you."

"Will you stop," Doris said, a smile rising. She was wearing a blue suit with a white lace blouse. She held behind her back a burning cigarette.

Rush had a reputation as a bulldog—she would not let go of a problem until it was solved. Mendenhall was glad to have her involved.

"Read 'em their rights, Doris," Mendenhall joked.

Treasurer Bob Powell wanted Mendenhall to be careful with the B of A team.

"These guys should not hear every conversation going on in

here," Powell said. There was a lot of discussion swirling through the executive offices. The New York bankers were in and out from one office to the next. The lawyers and Martin Marietta executives were debating Marty Siegel's strategy of launching a counterattack against Bendix.

Mendenhall was a little concerned about letting Tegart talk with Siegel's right-hand man, Doug Brown from Kidder, Peabody. Doug, a quick thinker and good investment banker, also had a tendency to think aloud. Mendenhall worried that too much information could swamp the bank team and lessen the chances of getting the agreement Martin Marietta wanted.

But Tegart wanted to talk with the investment bankers.

He was asking questions Mendenhall could not answer.

"When we loan money, we like to know what it is going to be used for," Tegart said softly. He knew that went to the point of strategy.

"All we want to do is increase our three-hundred-million-dollar credit line," Mendenhall said. "Until the board meeting on Monday, we don't know what we are gonna do—if anything —with the money."

"What are some of the things you're thinking about?" Tegart asked.

"There are many possibilities," Doug Brown said. An impetuous man, tough and shrewd, Brown was not afraid of talking with Tegart. He knew the banker needed more information than he was getting.

"Such as?" Tegart asked.

"Martin Marietta could try to buy Bendix," Brown said.

Tom Mendenhall felt his temperature rising.

"What if they own you? Would you still go through with buying their stock?" a taken aback Tom Tegart asked.

"It's a possible tactic," Brown said.

The conversation continued to touch a subject that the bank —considering loaning a great deal of money—had every right to know but that the Martin Marietta team could not answer: What did Martin Marietta plan to do with the money?

As it became obvious that there were many unanswered questions, Mendenhall found his mood careening like a roller coaster. While the atmosphere was cordial and it was obvious from the time and interest that the B of A team was investing that they wanted to come to an agreement, that did not lessen the obstacles; it perhaps even increased the frustration as they struggled for a formula.

Hearing Doug Brown talk in separate meetings, Mendenhall became even more depressed. Here it was Friday afternoon and the powers that be had again hiked their requests. They now wanted firm commitments for almost $900 million—with no strings attached. They wanted, in the words of Bob Powell, a "trust me, baby" loan.

"Well, I think we're going to have to get Krapf on the phone," Tegart said. He was kicking the decision upstairs to a higher level at the bank.

Tegart got Lyle Krapf, the head of North American operations for B of A, on the phone. After getting him up to speed, the rub quickly became apparent. Mendenhall turned to his boss, Bob Powell.

"Look, Bob," Krapf said during the conference call, "we are going to want some convenants in this agreement—just in case you decide to do something crazy. Maybe we'll have to put something in there dealing with the debt-to-equity ratio of the company to make sure the decisions made are fiscally responsible."

Bob Powell was getting irritated. He knew that this insistence on covenants was totally unacceptable. It would look terrible in the necessary filings with the SEC. Bendix would be able to ridicule the loan agreement. Besides, if the debt-to-equity-ratio covenant was included, that would eliminate the possible strategy of buying Bendix.

"You know if you guys want to jump ship," Mendenhall interjected, "I've got two or three other banks that want to be lead bank on this."

On an hour-by-hour basis, the Bendix team kept a close watch on the fluctuations of the New York Stock Exchange. As is always the case in financial deals involving publicly held companies, ultimately it is "the street"—the buyers and sellers of stock—who decide the outcome of an attempted takeover.

From his lower Manhattan office at One New York Plaza, high above the grounds of Battery Park, where strollers were out on a warm but cloudy afternoon, Jay Higgins, the investment banker from Salomon Brothers, sat at his desk beside his computer with his back to the window.

Higgins was not in a good mood.

Marty Weinstein had delivered a fresh intelligence report.

"So tell me again what the guy said," Higgins said.

"A lot of talk on the street is that Martin Marietta is going to come back at Bendix with something big. The phrase that this guy used was that Marietta was going to have 'a transaction-oriented response.' "

"A transaction-oriented response," Higgins repeated.

"That's what he said."

"What do you make of that?"

"The arbs I'm talking to think Marietta is gonna make some kind of offer of its own."

"For Bendix?"

"Maybe."

Both men went over the latest results on the stock market. Volume in Martin Marietta stock had been up—another 1,075,900 shares had traded hands. That was great news. But the price had slipped $1.25, down to $41. The Bendix offer was for $43 a share of Martin Marietta stock. Perhaps there was some erosion of confidence in Bendix on the street.

But the slippage in Marietta's price was not the real concern.

Higgins and Weinstein were worried about the price of Bendix stock.

It had shot up almost $4 a share. The market was moving up with the rumors of a Martin Marietta move against Bendix. The higher the price went, the greater the concern that the professional speculators were starting to play both sides of the street —maybe hedging their bets—just in case Martin Marietta could pull off a miracle.

"I'm gonna call Siegel," Higgins said, picking up the phone. When he got the Martin Marietta banker on the telephone, Higgins sounded calm and self-assured, a man certain of victory. The two bankers had been through many deals and were quick to come to the point.

"Hey, what do you think, let's sit down and talk," Higgins said. "The Bendix people want to talk."

"I've got two hundred retired generals down in Bethesda who are mad as hell and they say they're not going to talk about anything unless the offer is withdrawn," Siegel said emphatically.

"I know what Agee's going to say about that."

"Well, see you around," Siegel said.

Friday night, Dick Katcher had a date with his wife, Susan, an attractive woman with long, dark hair, a pretty smile, and a complexion younger than her age. They had things to talk over.

Earlier, at the office, Dick Katcher met with Len Larrabee to talk over a sticky legal problem. Not much could be accomplished. They both recognized that they were entering a new gray area where the courts would have little to go on. The two men were tired.

"Dick, you won," Larrabee said.

"Great. What did I win?"

"They've changed the plan. The Martin directors are going to meet in New York on Monday instead of Bethesda."

"Thank God."

"Pownall will be down here tomorrow," Larrabee said.

Third Avenue was a blaze of lights and activity as Katcher walked to his apartment. Friday night in New York.

Dick and Susan were having troubles in their relationship.

In May 1982, they had decided to separate. Dick moved out and stayed at Jay Higgins' apartment a couple of weeks. Then Dick got an apartment at 200 East 57th Street on the corner of Third Avenue, within walking distance to work. He visited on weekends with his kids.

Dick had married Susan in 1964 at the end of his first year at NYU Law School. She was teaching on the Lower East Side of Manhattan. He graduated in May 1966, and their first son, Daniel, was born in September. Susan retired from her job to be a full-time mother.

Dick's career progressed. Eventually he became a partner of a well-known Park Avenue law firm. Dick and Susan bought a house in Mamaroneck, New York, a well-to-do suburb northeast of the city. They became members of the Metropolis Country Club, a private golf and tennis club in Westchester.

Dick's job was demanding, requiring a rare tolerance for long hours, work on weekends, work away from home, being on call to clients. But the pay was good. And the sense of accomplishment was important. And Dick had a sense of humor about the whole thing. Or at least he tried to.

In 1979, Dick and Susan had a scare when their thirteen-year-old son Daniel reported a bump in his knee that turned out to be a tumor. Fortunately, the biopsy proved negative—it was nonmalignant. But the initial shock made Dick take a second look at his world. Maybe he did work too hard. Maybe he didn't spend enough time with his kids. Along the line, Dick became Daniel's basketball coach to share more of himself.

Susan—looking beautiful—knocked on the door.

"Hi," Dick said with a crooked smile. Talking was hard. Having a date with his wife seemed even harder.

"Have you thought about it?" Susan asked.

"How are the kids?" Dick asked.

"They miss their dad."

Dick and Susan went to P. J. Clarke's for a hamburger, and afterward, for a walk.

"Bill, let's get out of town for the weekend," Mary Cunningham said on Friday night. "Let's go up to the Cape tomorrow and stay with my mother."

Sitting in the living room of their suite on the forty-fifth floor of the Helmsley Palace, Bill Agee had his shoes off, his stocking feet up on the coffee table. Mary was in the small kitchen.

"It will be nice," Mary said, tired from her long day at Seagram.

Bill was reading a news summary telecopied from Berl Falbaum in the Bendix public-relations office.

Falbaum reported calls from *The Wall Street Journal, The New York Times,* the *Rocky Mountain News,* Reuters . . . "most news stories center on the expected Monday announcement by Martin Marietta. . . . All accounts fairly straightforward. Some stories quoted analysts as predicting a fight. . . . No editorial slant noted. . . . The *New York Post* had a little spicer language—'sizzling takeover bid . . . escape Agee's clutches.' . . . Expect a couple of slow news days until Marietta announcement. . . . Late in the afternoon, Standard & Poor's issued its credit watch on Bendix and Martin Marietta. . . . Only *The Wall Street Journal* called for reaction. . . . Issued release on Hart-Scott-Rodino Act shortly before 4:00 P.M. . . . We will have a news summary at 8:00 A.M. Monday, August 30, on weekend stories."

Next Wednesday was Mary's thirty-first birthday. Knowing the time demands of his schedule, Agee decided to leave New York and go to the Cape to celebrate early.

They flew to Cape Cod the following morning.

Mary's mother was happy to see them.

For her birthday, Bill gave Mary an idyllic painting of a child sitting on the seashore. He was in the backyard minding the barbecue when he heard the telephone ring. Mary came out of the house.

"It's Al."

"What are you hearing from our friends?" Agee asked McDonald, referring to the Bendix team of lawyers and bankers.

"I'm having a difficult job getting the guys to focus on working out the scenarios. The kind of 'what happens if' . . . I don't think there is much real belief that Marietta will come back at us."

McDonald still did not believe the rumors himself. He had a mathematical mind. The statistical chance seemed remote. At best it was a possibility. But the latest report from Jay Higgins was that it now looked like a probability. It was more than the bad news McDonald did not like. He was having trouble with Higgins. Sometimes pushy and opinionated, Higgins seemed to dislike his subordinate role in the scheme of things.

"What's the noise I'm hearing?"

"Bill, I'm in a phone booth."

McDonald was in Tennessee with his daughter. They were looking at Vanderbilt University.

"Al, you're my contact man. Lookit, you just turn the legal guys and everybody else upside down. Tell them that come hell or high water, I want to know that we're covered. Let's turn over every rock again."

Agee trusted McDonald to get the job done. But still, he wondered if the preparations had been handled properly.

"What's your feeling if Martin does decide to fight?" Bill asked.

"It's a negotiating tactic. At the end of the day," McDonald said, using a favorite phrase that meant when all is done, "the Bendix Corporation will own Martin Marietta."

SEVEN

Wh en Tom Mendenhall woke up early Saturday morning, he opened his eyes wide enough to see the familiar face of the alarm clock and beyond—the furnishings of the bedroom in his Manassas, Virginia, home.

His wife, Linda, was still asleep.

The conversations with the Bank of America had dragged into the late hours last night. The scene came back to Mendenhall.

Stretched out on the floor of a small office in Martin Marietta headquarters, draped in available chairs, surrounded by cans of flat Coke and scraps of food, consensus on the scope of a one-year straight loan had been reached. The Bank of America would be the leader of a consortium of banks.

"If you're dumb," Mendenhall remembered saying to Tom Tegart, the loan officer from the Bank of America, "you're only dumb for one year."

Getting out of bed, Mendenhall realized for the first time that if Martin Marietta fought Bendix and lost, he would be out of a job.

Mendenhall found himself stammering to his wife.

"If anybody calls the house, you don't know anything, okay, honey?"

Going to the closet and pulling out a suitcase, Tom was suddenly charged with energy.

"Where are you going?" Linda asked.

"I'm going to the office. I may stay tonight at a hotel and then probably straight to New York."

"How long are you going to be gone?"

"I don't know. I'm packing for at least five days. I don't know when I will see you again. But I will call."

"You haven't done anything wrong, have you?" Linda asked with a worried look on her face.

On Saturday morning, Tom Pownall, the chief executive officer of the Martin Marietta Corporation, was sitting in his office. Still wearing the red "Don't Give Up the Ship" necktie that board member Jack Byrne had given him, Pownall was thinking about job security too.

Tom Pownall thought of himself as a simple man.

The things he cherished were family, company, and country.

At sixty, his blue eyes were as bright as those of a much younger man. Born in Cumberland, Maryland, brought up in West Virginia, Pownall had a spunk that belittled his gray hair. He had mettle. A graduate of the U.S. Naval Academy, Pownall served aboard a cruiser following World War II and on destroyers during the Korean War.

After Korea, Pownall and his wife, Marilyn, and their two daughters, Susie and Fuzzie, lived in the lower-rent district of sunny La Jolla, California.

Later, Pownall worked in Dayton, Ohio, with the Convair Company, the forerunner of General Dynamics, before moving to Washington. In 1963 he joined Martin Marietta. For nineteen years he rose through the ranks before he became president and CEO.

Sitting at his desk, a bronze eagle statue on a credenza behind him, Pownall was thinking about all his years at Martin Marietta. He wondered how many of his employees were worried that the end of Martin Marietta was in sight. Pownall knew that for the company to be run effectively, he had to take care of his key people.

"Do we have the compensation committee on the phone yet?" Pownall asked Frank Menaker, the corporation's general counsel. Menaker had just walked into Pownall's office with Jim Simpson, the president of the chemicals operation.

The compensation committee of the board of directors was made up of four members: David Scott, chairman of Allis Chalmers Company; Bill Hagerty, president of Drexel University; John Hanigan, chairman of Genesco; and Charles Hugel, executive VP of AT&T.

To set up a conversation was no easy matter—Scott was in Milwaukee, Hagerty was in Philadelphia, Hanigan was in Nashville, and Hugel was in New York. After some confusion, the conference call was arranged. Only Hanigan could not be located.

"I've called this committee meeting at the request of management," David Scott said, abiding by formalities. He was chairman of the committee. A director since 1978, Scott knew the issue at hand, but he was quick to turn to Pownall. "Tom, why don't you tell us what you have in mind."

Pownall began discussing what is known on Wall Street as "golden parachute" employment contracts for key Marietta executives. Pownall wanted to guarantee certain employees that no matter what happened with Bendix, they would be taken care of.

"I don't want these guys looking over their shoulders during this mess with Bendix," Pownall said. "I'm going to let Jim Simpson talk about the specific proposals. I intend to bring this up at the board meeting on Monday, but I think it is appropriate that the compensation committee discuss the matter first. Jim, why don't you explain the proposal."

A silver-haired man with black Clark Kent glasses, Simpson had been the general counsel for Martin Marietta for ten years. In 1981 he accomplished something rather unusual for Martin Marietta—he successfully made the transition from corporate staff to operations.

"I was asked," Simpson said toward the speaker box, "to draw up contracts that in the event of management change at Martin Marietta, certain employees would be guaranteed their salaries, benefits, and stock options through August thirtieth, 1985. The considered employees include upper management—Pownall, Leithauser, Adams, Menaker, Powell, and myself as well as Caleb Hurtt, head of aerospace, and other line personnel.

"Why do you want to have these contracts?" director Hugel asked. "We've never had them before."

"The headhunters and raiders are out there," Pownall interjected. "They're looking for good Martin Marietta people who may be nervous. One of our friendly competitors would love to hire away our MX program manager or the Pershing program manager, and I've seen whole departments bail out after some key guy goes. And you don't have a program without people."

"How many people are we talking about—fifteen or five hundred?" a director asked.

"We are looking at twenty-nine people," Simpson said, "certainly division managers and key program personnel. We want to protect the people who have program responsibility."

"How much money are we talking about?" Scott asked from Milwaukee.

"Close to twenty million dollars."

A vote was taken, and subject to certain changes, the proposal was approved by the present members of the compensation committee. After the meeting, Simpson reached Hanigan and informed him of the proceedings and the vote. Hanigan joined the others to make it unanimous. The matter would be presented on Monday to the full board of directors, and assuming board approval, twenty-nine Martin Marietta executives would receive their paychecks for the next three years—no matter what happened.

"Okay, let's go to New York," Pownall told Charlie Leithauser, Frank Menaker, and the other members of his inner circle. A long day of meetings was planned. The Waldorf-Astoria had been chosen as Pownall's command center. With the board meeting set for tomorrow, Pownall wanted to hear the final arguments of his New York advisers before deciding.

And there was the question of the money.

Two days before, L. Robert Fullem, fifty-three, a senior law partner at Dewey, Ballantine, was on vacation in Martha's Vineyard when he got a call from his office passing along a message from Leonard Larrabee:

"Come home."

Once Fullem returned to New York, he quickly assumed a key position in the Martin Marietta defense team. After being briefed by Larrabee, Fullem took charge. Veterans of many corporate battles, both men knew that for the next thirty days they would eat, sleep, and breathe Martin Marietta and Bendix.

Bob Fullem's office was on the forty-sixth floor of 140 Broadway. Suiting his position as a senior partner in the law firm, Fullem had a corner office with expansive views of Manhattan.

To the left, across a vast forest of high-rises and the Hudson River, was New Jersey. To the right, the grace of the Brooklyn Bridge leading across the East River.

In the distance, two helicopters, headed in different directions, appeared to collide in midair above the needle of the Empire State Building. And then they were past each other.

Fullem was smoking a cigar when a Dewey, Ballantine partner knocked on his door.

"What have you got?" Fullem asked. The man was Robert Myers, an impeccably dressed lawyer with finely manicured hair and nails. Next to the tall and jowled Fullem, Myers looked short in stature.

Fullem had assigned Myers to head the team of litigating lawyers. Myers was searching for the rationale of a lawsuit against Bendix.

"Bendix may have given us an opening," Myers said. "This ran on the Dow Jones wire yesterday." He handed Fullem a piece of narrow paper ripped off of the teletype machine:

> 8:26 AM EDT AUG 27—82
> BENDIX WOULD CONSIDER SELLING SOME MARTIN MARIETTA UNITS
> Southfield Mich—DJ—Bendix Corp. said it is considering dismembering Martin Marietta Corp. if its $1.5 billion bid to acquire the Maryland aerospace and defense company is successful.

After Fullem read the story and looked up with a quizzical look on his deeply lined face, Myers handed over another story:

> 9:54 AM EDT AUG 27—82
> BENDIX HASN'T ANY PLANS TO BREAK UP MARTIN MARIETTA
> Southfield Mich—DJ—Bendix Corp. said it hasn't any plans to break up Martin Marietta Corp. should it be successful in its offer to acquire the company for $1.5 billion in cash and stock.

"What do you make of that?" Myers asked. "Here they come out and say they may break up Martin Marietta and then an hour later, they're back saying they have no intention of breaking it up."

"Sounds to me like they're trying to shut down a problem," Fullem said, his voice rising.

The Bendix "problem" was that federal regulations mandate that a company must properly disclose its full intentions when seeking to acquire another company. The apparently contradictory statements by Bendix could have been an inadvertent distortion of the facts by the wire service or perhaps a quickly suppressed hint of a hidden agenda. Maybe Bendix did intend to buy Martin Marietta and keep the cherries and spit out the pits. If that intention was not properly disclosed and could be proved in court, Martin Marietta could force Bendix to lose valuable time and momentum by having to reissue its disclosure documents.

"Sure," Fullem said, getting excited, "I mean, everybody knows that Martin Marietta is losing a bundle of money in aluminum, right?"

"And it's no secret that Agee wants the aerospace operation," Myers added.

"I'll bet Agee has plans to unload the losers!"

"And if he didn't disclose his intentions, we've got him!" Myers said.

Fullem suddenly turned quiet. He reexamined the news stories.

Bendix may have slipped.

"It's not great," Fullem said, "but it's the best we got. Draft a complaint and let's hit Bendix hard in court in Baltimore on Monday."

Early Saturday evening, at the end of a long day of meetings, the Martin Marietta legal teams from Dewey, Ballantine and Wachtell, Lipton were breaking up for dinner. Two lawyers from Wachtell, Lipton were going out with their wives and asked Dick Katcher if he wanted to join them. Dick begged off. He had something else in mind. Susan came over to the apartment that night. They went out to the Barclay Hotel and sat in the bar. They were both excited and toasted their decision to reconcile.

"Let's go home and tell the kids!" Susan said.

"I can't go tonight. This Bendix and Martin thing is going crazy. There are meetings early tomorrow. Some guys are going back to Dewey tonight. I promise I'll be home tomorrow night."

"Sunday night," Susan said in a dampened tone.

"Tomorrow night, I promise. We'll tell the kids and have a bottle of champagne."

Sunday morning, after a poor sleep in a Bethesda hotel, Tom Mendenhall called Doris Rush at her apartment.

"My God, what time is it?"

"Doris, this is your seven A.M. wake-up call. I need you in here. You can get mad at me later. Just get in here, would ya? I have the Citation scheduled to fly us to New York at wheels-up one P.M., which means we have to leave the office at noon, whether we have the finalized agreement or not. Do we have a finalized draft agreement, Doris?"

"Not yet."

"See you in the office."

The big powwow among all the banks was set for 5:00 P.M. —in a forty-second-floor conference room at the Dewey, Ballantine law offices in New York.

With Tom Tegart and Tim Deason from the B of A, and Doris Rush and Bill Armistead working feverishly at Martin Marietta headquarters to draft the agreement, Mendenhall was two doors down, going over and over his chit sheets of banks pledging money. He had verbal commitments for $800 million, but he didn't really know exactly how much he needed; $900 million had been mentioned.

When he got off the phone with one bank, Mendenhall ran down the empty hallway toward the office where the agreement team was assembling copy and marshaling secretarial help.

"We got another twenty-five million!" Mendenhall screamed, like he was the master of ceremonies at a telethon. Checking his watch, he said in a suddenly clear and firm tone, "Okay, ninety minutes to go."

"No . . ." Rush countered, "we're not ready."

"Ninety minutes and counting."

Mendenhall—through Bob Powell's secretary, Marcia—had spoken with Jim Fink, the chief Martin Marietta pilot. The small Citation jet was on a tight schedule. After picking up and dropping off Mendenhall and his party, the jet was heading north to pick up some directors for the board meeting tomorrow. "I can't wait for you," Fink had said. "It's one P.M. or never."

Mendenhall ducked into the hallway every fifteen minutes to call out the time. Finally, in a booming voice, he said, "That's it! We're outta here!"

66

Gathering together papers and the word-processing diskettes, the team headed out, getting to the airport just in time. On the five-seater plane with Doris, Tim Deason, Tom Tegart, and Bill Armistead, Mendenhall tried to catch up on some sleep. He was so excited it was impossible. Instead he drank two beers and ate three sandwiches.

In a conference room on the forty-second floor of 140 Broadway, Tom Mendenhall was pacing and checking his watch. Doris Rush was with him.

"Now, Doris, be nice to these people, we want them to give us a lot of money."

Rush smiled at Mendenhall's tease.

At about 5:00 P.M., the bankers and their respective legal counsels began arriving on the forty-second floor. They were ushered into the conference room.

Tegart and Deason from the Bank of America were seated when George Moyer and Mary Docherty from Citibank arrived with their lawyer from Sherman & Sterling; the loan officer from Bankers Trust and his counsel; Frank Tellier from Morgan with his counsel, Bruce Nichols from Davis, Polk.

Within ten minutes there were almost thirty-five people in the room.

Mendenhall was silently taking an attendance check. Only the representative from Seattle First National Bank was missing.

Copies of the banking agreement were distributed to the twelve bank teams. The bankers huddled with their lawyers, reviewing the terms and provisions of the agreement.

Although some banks had come to the meeting prepared to sign the agreement, it quickly became apparent that there would have to be negotiations before several of the larger banks would feel comfortable enough to commit hundreds of millions of dollars.

"Shouldn't we have some protections in here? What about covenants saying what you can and can't do with the money?"

"This has to be wide open. We can't accept substantial covenants," Mendenhall said.

"But Tom, shouldn't there be some kind of trigger that says we could get out of the commitment if something crazy happened?" Frank Tellier from Morgan asked.

"What's crazy?" Mendenhall asked.

"Well, borrowing the money if Bendix already owns you."

Mendenhall had a problem. He was not asking the banks to

give him the money on the spot. He was seeking their written pledges to loan Martin Marietta the money when he wanted it. The interest on loans totaling close to $1 billion was a pretty penny. Charlie Leithauser had been adamant about one thing: The company would not borrow the money a minute sooner than it had to.

"If there are outs in the agreement," a Martin Marietta lawyer offered, "then it would offer litigation opportunities for Bendix. If the use of the money is burdened with conditions, we would be hard-pressed to convince anybody that the banks are serious."

Most of the bankers seemed to understand the dilemma facing Martin Marietta. If the money was to be used to finesse a way around Bill Agee, the banking agreement had to be seen on Wall Street as airtight.

Then an even thornier issue surfaced.

"What about the margin regulations?" a bank lawyer asked.

The bankers sat back and listened to the discussion among the lawyers regarding one particularly difficult regulation, which they called Regulation U. The regulation stipulated that if a loan was going to be secured with stock, the borrower could borrow only 50 percent of the value of the stock. That could limit the amount Martin Marietta could borrow.

Listening to the lawyers argue back and forth for almost an hour about "Reg U" and "negative pledge," Mendenhall felt way out of his league. With a Dewey, Ballantine partner, Phil Coviello, Mendenhall ducked out of the meeting and found Bob Powell in Bob Fullem's office two floors up.

Coviello, a towering forty-nine-year-old lawyer, explained the Regulation U dilemma.

"Oh, my God, this could be a major problem," Fullem said, leaning back in his chair. "We've got to look at the asset sheet of the company."

The team—with Fullem and Larrabee leading—pursued various options to handle the situation. Bob Powell provided them with a breakdown of the assets of the corporation. Fullem and Larrabee were counting out loud. If the assets were deployed in a certain way among the subsidiaries of the corporation, perhaps a protection from the Reg U provisions could be found.

"We can't go on this kind of information," Fullem said adamantly. "We don't have enough time."

Mendenhall knew he had to come up with something to reassure the bankers that they could lend the money and that Martin Marietta would not be subject to legal challenge based upon violations of the margin regulations.

Unable to answer the question immediately, the participants were dragged into other pressing discussions. Confused and concerned, Mendenhall and Powell left Fullem's office.

In the hall, Powell turned to Mendenhall.

"Remember what it says in the old agreement about restrictions on the borrowing power of subsidiaries?"

"That everything is a restricted sub unless it's specifically unrestricted or it's created after 1979," Mendenhall said.

"Yeah, so why can't we create a new subsidiary?" Powell asked.

"Exactly what I was thinking."

"Let's talk to Fullem again."

They went back to Fullem's office and picked up the discussion. Fullem methodically lead them through the obstacles in regulation and the situation. They explained the old loan agreement and repeated their question.

"Yes, wait a minute," Fullem said, excitedly, "we could organize a new subsidiary to buy the Bendix stock. And we could set it up so the margin regulations would not even apply to the stock at all."

"Geez," Larrabee said, swinging his arms with nervous excitement.

"That's it!" Fullem said, slapping Mendenhall on the back.

Armed with an explanation, Mendenhall and the Dewey, Ballantine lawyers assured the bankers that the margin regulations would not be an obstacle. Obviously tired after hours of discussion, the men in the cigar-smoke-filled conference room were prepared to accept Mendenhall's representation of the issue.

Checking his chit sheet, Mendenhall knew he was $30 million short of the new target of $900 million in available credit. While the discussion was continuing among the bankers and their counsels, Mendenhall pulled the representatives of Citibank and the Bank of America out of the meeting.

"How much would you guys be willing to go up?" Mendenhall asked Tom Tegart from the Bank of America and George Moyer and Mary Docherty from Citibank.

"What do you need?"

"I need thirty million dollars more."

"Why do you need thirty million dollars more?" Docherty asked.

"'Cause my lawyers and investment bankers are telling me I need another thirty. Would you be willing to split it fifteen apiece? That'll give me the nine hundred million dollars I need."

"Yeah, no problem," the Citibank team said.

"Do you need more?" Tegart asked.

"No, Tom, really," Mendenhall said. "Just keep it in your pocket."

Excited to hit the mark finally, Mendenhall bounded up the staircase to the office where Bob Powell was meeting with lawyers from Miles & Stockbridge to review the resolutions governing the company's borrowing authorities. After seventy-two hours, Mendenhall was nearly in tears when he entered the room.

"We did it. We got the nine hundred million dollars!"

Bob Powell looked up at him, smiled, and said, "Fine. But what we really need is nine hundred thirty million dollars."

Stunned, Mendenhall stood waiting for reconfirmation.

"Don't ask again," he said, storming out of the room.

On his way back down the staircase, Mendenhall ran into Charlie Leithauser.

"How are things going?" Charlie asked.

"I need thirty more," Mendenhall said dejectedly.

"Well, I think I have an idea—"

"Don't bug me, Charlie, just don't bug me," Mendenhall said, dashing down the staircase.

He pulled Duncan Gibson from the Toronto Dominion Bank out of the meeting on the forty-third floor. Mendenhall had always considered the Canadian bank to be an ace in the hole. First of all, there were no legal lending limits in Canada. That meant they were almost a bottomless pocket. Or they were, at least, until the Dome Petroleum transaction in which several Canadian banks got hurt. Toronto Dominion was already in for $50 million to Martin Marietta.

"Duncan, I've got a problem. I need thirty million dollars more."

"I'll have to call the top people in Toronto. But I don't think I can reach them now."

"I've got to get the commitment for the money tonight."

"I can give you the highest assurance that you can get another thirty from us, but I can't confirm it tonight," Gibson said.

"Cross your heart and hope to die," Mendenhall said. "I'm going to go upstairs and stop bargaining."

"Go upstairs and stop bargaining."

Mendenhall went back up the staircase and into an office gathering with Bob Powell and the lawyers.

"You got your nine hundred thirty million dollars," he said, more reserved this time as general euphoria broke out around him.

EIGHT

In the street-level courtyard of the office building there was a modernist work of art—a giant red metal cube percariously perched on one corner. That pretty much characterized the way Tom Pownall felt standing before the window in Bob Fullem's office on the forty-sixth floor.

Mendenhall had returned to the bank meeting downstairs.

Tom Pownall was meeting with his senior advisers.

Gloriously, the Manhattan skyline lay before him, a million lights shining against the black night. Headlights raced up Broadway, Fifth, and Avenue of the Americas. The helicopters were still flying, signaling with small red warning lights.

Pownall was not talking much. It was obvious to the lawyers that he was thinking. Only four months ago, he was named chief executive officer. And now this mess with Bendix was taking over his life. This was not the way any man would choose his time at the handles of power.

"You know," one of the lawyers whispered to another, "there is a huge difference between those who don't have the responsibility and those who do."

Tom Pownall turned his back to the window.

He was ready for more discussion.

"Tom, I really think it will work," Marty Siegel said. Pownall thought the young, good-looking investment banker was sharp

72

as a razor. The tactic he was proposing was bold and daring.
And after days of bad news from the stock market, Pownall knew
he needed something dramatic to get Bill Agee's attention.

"If Martin Marietta makes an offer to buy the Bendix Corporation, it will send a clear signal to Agee," Siegel said. "I think
the financial package we're talking about will get the attention
of the street. Agee will know that his shareholders will sell to us.
I think he'll back down. He'll take his profit and run."

"How do you see it, Bob?" Pownall asked Fullem.

"I'm not certain Agee will walk away. Maybe. But if he does
buy our stock, and we follow through and buy Bendix stock, I
think there is a good chance that we will be able to take control
first. At worst it would be a Mexican standoff."

Fullem reviewed how the discrepancy between the state laws
of Maryland and Delaware gave them that edge. To take over
Martin Marietta, Bendix had to give ten days' written notice;
whereas Martin Marietta could take control of Bendix immediately upon becoming the majority shareholder.

If the threat was clear to Agee, maybe he would back off.

"My recommendation, Tom, is that you should call Agee
tomorrow after the board meeting and say, 'The board has
rejected your offer, we're going to make a bid, we have a time
advantage because of the Maryland/Delaware difference, and
we're gonna take you over unless you drop your bid against
us.' "

Fullem looked around the table for reaction.

"It could work," Frank Menaker said.

"There is a down side," Dick Katcher added. "You could be
telling Agee that you're scared and that you're not really serious
about your offer."

"If our objective is to get him to go away," Menaker asked,
"why not give him a chance to do that before we go public?"

"Just remember," Marty Siegel said, "Agee is very press-
oriented. It's gonna come out in the papers. And who knows
how he's gonna tell the story? It's not going to look good on the
street. The arbs will not be convinced that we are serious. It
could hurt the offer."

"Besides," Katcher emphasized, "sure, we got this difference
between Maryland and Delaware but this double-subsidiary
problem on who can vote the shares is unresolved. We don't
know how that will come out, do we?"

"If Bendix can get Delaware to say we can't vote our shares, we can more than likely get Maryland to do the same. The prospect of a stalemate is the kind of thing Agee will not over-look," Fullem said.

"I agree, but to call Agee and to try to scare him by relying on something that may turn out to be a quirk in the law is risky."

As is his manner, Pownall listened carefully to the lawyers. He weighed the benefits against the risks. He rubbed his jaw hard.

Tomorrow he would ask his directors for authorization to buy the Bendix Corporation.

"But I don't think I'll make the call. If I'm going to deal with Bill Agee, it's going to be from strength, not weakness."

While Pownall reluctantly accepted handshakes from Bob Fullem and Marty Siegel, Dick Katcher was huddled in the cor-ner, talking softly into the telephone with his wife, Susan, home in bed in Mamaroneck. Dick had promised he would be there to toast their decision to reconcile.

"I'm still at this meeting," he said. "I just can't make it tonight."

At about 11:00 P.M., while waiting for the Dewey, Ballantine secretaries to finalize the banking agreement for signatures, Mendenhall asked Tom Pownall to address the gathering of bankers.

The room was warm and loaded with the smell of cigars.

"We want to thank you," Pownall said, obviously tired but rising to the occasion. "In particular, I want to thank the repre-sentatives from the Bank of America who worked with us in Bethesda starting late last week. I know all of you have made considerable sacrifice to be here on Sunday. I also understand that there are personal risks. And you have been forced to work under a terrible time pressure.

"Thank you for your confidence in Martin Marietta."

At shortly after one in the morning on Monday, the bankers signed the finalized agreement. Bob Powell, the treasurer, signed the document for Martin Marietta. Exhausted, the bank-ers were quick to file out and hail cabs. Powell and Mendenhall, along with Doris Rush and Bill Armistead, joined Len Larrabee and his team in Fullem's office to review the drafting of the document that had to be filed with the SEC in regard to Martin Marietta's tender offer for Bendix Corporation.

There were certain portions that involved description of the financing component of the offer. Larrabee made it clear that everything had to be absolutely perfect.

"If we make one false statement, we could be accused of a manipulative device, and Bendix could have a field day," Larrabee said.

Reviewing the loan agreement, the question was raised about the missing signatures: one from Seattle First National Bank; and another from Ameritrust; another from Toronto Dominion.

"The Ameritrust and Toronto guys are coming in tomorrow, no problem," Mendenhall said. "They couldn't sign on their own authority but it's settled and they'll be in tomorrow. As soon as business opens in Cleveland and Toronto, they'll meet with me to sign."

"What about Seattle First?"

"The guy—Tim Crow—is sick. He just couldn't make it. I have a telegram from them authorizing the commitment."

"It doesn't look good with a blank signature."

"Yeah, this thing should be all signed before the board meeting tomorrow," Bob Powell said. "We'll get the signature."

Between them it was decided that Bill Armistead—a junior man in Martin Marietta's treasury department—would fly to Seattle as soon as possible to get the signature. Powell got on the phone and found Jim Fink, the Martin Marietta pilot, informing him of the situation. They decided that takeoff would be at 4:00 A.M.

At nearly two in the morning, Powell, Mendenhall, Rush, and Armistead piled into a cab and headed toward their hotel—the Waldorf-Astoria. The tension of the evening finally found a release. They started acting crazy.

"Do you realize you just borrowed one billion dollars?" Mendenhall said to Powell. "Holy cow!"

Laughing with excitement and exhaustion, they did impersonations of several bankers and lawyers on their way uptown to the hotel. They broke down remembering Coviello, a Princeton undergraduate, calling a troublesome lawyer in a Brooks Brothers suit a "preppie bastard."

By the time they reached the Waldorf, they were still in a party mood. On the way up to his room, Mendenhall stopped at the desk to check his messages, and there were two letters: one from Chemical Bank and one from Chase Manhattan Bank. Both had a problem joining the agreement. However, the letters pledged a total of $175 million worth of credit to back up Martin Marietta's commercial paper.

Up in Mendenhall's room, the team was too wired to sleep. They decided to order room service. At that hour, the only available food were shrimp cocktails and beer. They ordered several of each. After waiting an hour, they called down to room service and were told, "Oh, we don't have any Miller beer."

"Just send anything," Mendenhall said, thinking how incredible it was that here in New York you could borrow $1 billion but not get room service.

Shortly thereafter, two shrimp cocktails and three beers were delivered. Bill Armistead drank a beer, washed his face, put on his jacket, and left with encouraging words from Powell, Mendenhall, and Rush. Armistead caught a cab to Newark Airport.

"Do you work for Martin Marietta?" Jim Fink, the pilot, asked Bill Armistead, obviously looking for someone. Armistead boarded the company Gulfstream jet. He felt a bit foolish all alone with a steward in the twelve-seat jet on a forty-two-hundred-mile errand to collect a signature.

His instructions did not make him feel any easier. It was suggested to him that he take two copies of the agreement. Get them both signed and before returning, mail one. Just in case the plane crashed.

NINE

After less than a full hour of sleep, Bob Powell was up, getting dressed in his room at the Waldorf-Astoria. With an 8:00 A.M. board meeting scheduled at the Dewey, Ballantine uptown offices on Park Avenue, Tom Pownall wanted his troops to assemble at 7:00 A.M. for a dress rehearsal.

Powell and Charlie Leithauser had to explain to the board the financial implications of borrowing the money and making the countertender offer. Powell's assistant treasurer for financial planning, Tom Quinn, had spent the past three days working on a five-year plan.

"I never knew five years could go so fast," Quinn said sarcastically.

"Ah, you love it," Powell said. Both men were exhausted.

They met each other in the towering marble foyer of the Waldorf. Quinn was leaning against a gilded railing.

"Is that the stuff?"

"Yeah," Quinn said. "The projector is in that box, and the overhead graphs are in here."

"Good golly, this is heavy," Powell said.

Loaded down with briefcases and equipment for the board meeting, the two men went through the revolving door and found themselves on Park Avenue at Fiftieth Street. It was warm

—even this early in the morning. The sidewalks were already filled with people, mostly businesspeople on their way to work.

"I was told Dewey, Ballantine is just a couple of blocks away," Powell said. "Let's walk."

They soon realized that it is not "just" down the the street. The Dewey, Ballantine uptown law offices were at 101 Park, near Forty-first Street—nine long blocks away, past the Pan Am Building and Grand Central Station. The men were sweating by the time they arrived.

"What took you?" Tom Mendenhall asked. He left the hotel at the same time but had the uniformed top-hatted attendant wave up a cab.

"Don't ask," Powell said, feeling ridiculous. "Did you get the signature from Toronto Dominion?"

"He'll be here in about an hour."

Powell and Mendenhall were chatting when Charlie Leithauser came into the double-doored waiting area outside the conference room. Charlie, looking fresh and vigorous, his gray hair neatly oiled back from his forehead, stopped just long enough to catch Mendenhall's attention.

"I'd like to have those two letters of credit before the meeting," Charlie said.

"Oh, God," Mendenhall said. He suddenly realized that the letters of commitment from Chemical Bank and Chase Manhattan—worth $175 million—were in his other suit jacket, which was hanging in his hotel room closet.

Bob Powell was smiling at Mendenhall's panic.

From a nearby office, Mendenhall got on the phone, hoping to catch Doris in her room at the Waldorf.

"Thank God, I caught you. You've got to help me out."

"What's the problem?"

"You've got to get into my room somehow. I left the commitment letters for a hundred seventy-five million dollars in my jacket pocket."

"How could you lose a hundred seventy-five million dollars?" Rush asked, laughing.

"Doris, c'mon, I don't have time to come back, and I need them."

"Okay. What's the room number."

Doris Rush stood in the hallway near Mendenhall's room until a cleaning woman wheeled her supply dolly into the hallway. The maid was several doors down when Doris began her act by fumbling in her purse. Then loud enough, she said, "Oh, no!"

The cleaning woman looked up from her dolly.

"Would you believe it," Doris said, "my husband walked off with the key and he has stuff in his pocket that I need. Not only did he forget to bring it down with him, but now he's gone with the key."

"Menfolks is all alike," the cleaning woman said.

"Could you just let me in?" Doris said as gratefully as possible.

"Well, I'm not supposed to," the woman said, taking out her passkey. She stood at the door as Doris entered the room, opened the closet, and found the commitment letters.

When she told Mendenhall the story, he was taken aback.

"Why did you have to say you were my wife?" he asked half seriously. "You could have said it was your room."

"Oh, sure. What was I going to tell her after she let me in and there were all these men's clothes in the closet? What, that I'm a transvestite?"

In the conference room, Bob Powell had set up the projector. When Charlie Leithauser came in, the two men began their rehearsal—flashing overheads against the screen and reviewing their presentations to the directors.

Both men knew they carried a heavy load.

Their financial projections were anything but rosy. If the board decided to fight the Bendix offer with some fireworks of its own, it was going to cost dearly.

"Don't forget to mention that the company had planned three hundred seventy-five million dollars in capital spending and that that could be reduced to increase cash flow," a serious Charlie Leithauser said.

Charlie by nature was a conservative man. He felt almost physical pains discussing the trauma about to be experienced because of the Martin Marietta balance sheet. For the loans, the company would have to pay almost $100 million in interest.

A key indicator of economic health—the debt-to-equity ratio —would be turned upside down. Instead of having roughly 30 percent debt, Martin Marietta—if it fought Bendix.with Marty Siegel's counterattack strategy—would have an 80 percent debt.

"We are going to be hammered pretty good by the rating agencies," Powell said.

"Jesus, do you blame them?"

Both men were businesslike going about their preparations. Tom Pownall came into the room. Listening to the men review, Pownall had one question for his senior vice president and chief financial officer. He had asked it many times over the past several days.

"Charlie, can we do it? Can we take this on and come out of it?"

"I'd never wish it on anybody," Leithauser said, "but I think so."

"Are you guys ready?" Pownall asked, grim-faced, one hand in a fist.

Before the Martin Marietta board of directors' meeting, two men, wearing coats and ties, inspected the designated conference room. One had a scanning instrument in his hands, and he slowly walked the room, electronically looking for listening devices.

"What about the rooms above and below?" he asked.

"Yeah, they want us to be sure they're clean, too," the other man said.

With millions to be made or lost on the outcome of the fight between Bendix and Martin Marietta, all precautions were ordered. After nodding to one of the Dewey, Ballantine lawyers standing in the doorway, the surveillance men headed out.

Before 10:00 A.M., the directors began arriving.

Former Attorney General Griffin Bell, slightly hunched over, walked through the hallway past Tom Mendenhall, who was trying hard to look inconspicuous while at the same time staying close to the action. Public-relations VP Roy Calvin was sweeping the area, making certain the junior people were minding their own business.

Jack Byrne from Geico came into sight, wearing a smart blue three-piece suit and talking and joking with James L. Everett III, the chairman of Philadelphia Electric Company. Everyone called the fifty-six-year-old Everett "Lee." David Scott, the compensation committee chairman, was intent on his notes held in one hand, his thin briefcase in another.

Frank Ewing, a man who made millions in real estate; Bill Hagerty, president of Drexel University; John Hanigan, at seventy-one, the oldest man on the board—all crossed the threshold and disappeared into the meeting room.

And then Frank Bradley, Jim Clark, Charlie Hugel, and former Secretary of Defense Melvin R. Laird—a man who divided his time among eight boards of directors and his senior counselor position with Reader's Digest.

Looking clean-shaven and vigorous, Tom Pownall did not seem to notice anyone as he made his way to the meeting room. Jack Byrne's red tie was brilliant against his white dress shirt and dark business suit. Even in a business suit, there was something about the man that seemed martial—perhaps his upright posture or his leathery neck and purposeful chin.

Charlie Leithauser and Frank Menaker were with him. Behind them was Larry Adams, the sour-faced senior VP and chief operating officer. Adams, a white-haired man wearing metal glasses, was intently examining a passage of his notes.

And then there were the advisers: Bob Fullem, the senior Dewey, Ballantine partner, and Len Larrabee, his chief coordinator; and Marty Siegel, immaculately tailored, wearing a big smile, brimming with confidence.

The last men filed in.

Then the dark wooden door was shut.

After what seemed like only a matter of minutes later, the door opened and Charlie Leithauser lead a stream of lawyers, bankers, and other Martin Marietta executives out of the boardroom. And then the door shut again, leaving them to walk in the hall or duck into an adjacent office, where refreshments and morning coffee were waiting.

"Executive session," a staffer said to an inquisitive Tom Mendenhall.

And then one by one, the advisers—Marty Siegel, Bob Fullem, Charlie Leithauser, Bob Powell, and others—were summoned into the boardroom like witnesses to a trial.

Almost two hours later, the door opened and loud but friendly conversation followed the men out and over to the refreshment room.

"So now that we've rejected their offer, what's next?" a director asked. The man had a cup of coffee in one hand, a danish in the other.

"Management recommendations are next on the agenda," Pownall said with a smile, adding for the benefit of the larger group of directors in hearing range, "so don't anybody leave!" That got a laugh.

Director Jack Byrne asked Tom Pownall for a moment.

"Tom, I want you to know, I met with Johnny Gutfreund from Salomon Brothers on Friday on Geico business. We had a drink together at the Waldorf."

"What did he have to say?" Pownall asked, his blue eyes narrowing.

"Well, first I told him that I had no idea where this situation between Martin Marietta and Bendix was heading, but I told him that he may have underestimated his quarry."

Tom Pownall smiled at that. He was the big-game hunter—and now he was the hunted.

"He asked if he could call me now and again, and I said sure. He also asked me to pass along a message from Bill Agee."

Tom Pownall's expression brightened into a question.

"For whatever it's worth," Byrne said, "I think you oughta meet with Agee. And I don't think it matters a damn whether it's here or Cleveland. He'll meet you anywhere you want."

"That's the message?"

"Yup."

"Thanks."

"What do you think?"

"Jack, you know how it is, I'm not doing a damn thing until it's been looked at by everybody. I'll talk about it."

The men filed back into the boardroom, and again the door was shut.

Since the crisis began, an interesting change occurred in the personal dynamics between Martin Marietta chairman J. Donald Rauth and the president and chief executive officer, Tom Pownall.

Pownall was usually deferential to his chairman. But now the tables were turned. Rauth—a man who normally carried himself softly—became deferential to Tom Pownall the decisive activist.

Several directors were surprised. Don Rauth had barely said a word during the first session. It was as if the mantle of power had been passed.

At about 2:00 P.M., the directors emerged from the meeting room.

Tom Mendenhall was waiting in the lobby. He watched Mel Laird walking casually, with a wide smile. He soon realized that everyone was smiling, Pownall included. Even the sober Charlie

Leithauser had a thin, wrinkled grin. PR chief Roy Calvin requested the attention of the audience of milling lawyers, advisers, and Martin Marietta staffers.

"I would like to ask that everyone just stay on this floor for now. We don't want people going in and out. I don't want anybody talking to anybody outside until we're ready. We'll release you shortly."

Pownall, Calvin, some lawyers, and a representative from Kekst & Company, the outside PR firm hired at the suggestion of Wachtell, Lipton, went into a side room to draft the press release. Pownall also tape-recorded an audio message that would be played later at Martin Marietta locations.

When they emerged, Pownall nodded to Calvin, who read a statement to the group.

"We're gonna go at them at seventy-five dollars a share," Calvin said, an unlit cigarette in his hand. A cheer went up.

It seemed that everyone on Wall Street had a side bet about what the Martin Marietta board of directors was going to decide. An announcement was promised in the afternoon.

During morning trading, like a thermometer teased by a flame, the price of Bendix stock rose $4.50 and then fell back $2.00 on weak volume of 142,500 shares. The speculators were blowing hot, then cold.

The Martin Marietta team was exasperated. They wanted the price to remain low until the announcement. The bigger the spread between the trading price of Bendix stock and the price offered by Martin Marietta, the better the deal would look to Wall Street. But the rumors were damaging the strategy. At 2:38 P.M., Martin Marietta requested that trading in Bendix shares on the New York Stock Exchange be halted.

When the announcement finally crossed the wire, bells rang all over the country.

> 4:18 PM EDT AUG 30—82
> MARTIN MARIETTA SETS $75 A SHARE OFFER FOR BENDIX
> NY—DJ—Martin Marietta Corp. said its board authorized a cash tender offer for 11,900,000 shares of the Bendix Corp.'s common stock at $75 per share.
>
> Following the offer, Martin Marietta said it expects to seek a merger or similar business combination in which

remaining Bendix common shares would be converted into a combination of Martin Marietta preferred and-or common stock.

Thomas G. Pownall, president and chief executive of Martin Marietta said "Our board concluded that if these two corporations are going to be combined the interests of shareholders will be best served by combining the two corporations on the terms contemplated by the Martin Marietta offer rather than the Bendix offer.

"We believe it would be harmful for Martin Marietta's aerospace business to pass into the hands of a management lacking deep experience and continuity in the major systems business. . . . Given Martin Marietta's past performance and future potential, the timing of the Bendix takeover proposal is an attempt to buy Martin Marietta stock at bargain prices."

After the board meeting, Bob Powell, Jim Simpson, Tom Mendenhall, and Doris Rush went to the downtown Dewey, Ballantine offices to review language of the tender offer materials to be filed with the Securities and Exchange Commission.

"It's hard to keep the tassels going in both directions," Bob Powell said to Tom Mendenhall, imitating a stripper's gyration.

"Are you as tired as I am?" Mendenhall asked.

"Do I look tired?" Powell said facetiously.

The SEC requires the filing of several documents, including reports labeled 13D, 13G, 14D-1, 14D-9, 13E-3, and 13E-4. Dick Katcher from Wachtell, Lipton; Phil Coviello and Larrabee and Fullem from Dewey, Ballantine; and Doug Brown from Kidder, Peabody were gathered around a small conference table.

The scene was too familiar. Less than twelve hours ago, the banks had signed the loan agreement. And just a couple of hours ago, the Martin Marietta board agreed to borrow the money.

The team was examining a draft of the document word by word and line by line to ensure that all facts were included and accurate.

"This has got to be perfect," Larrabee said, his thin, nasal voice cracking. "Otherwise, Bendix will rip it to pieces."

For hours, the group reviewed the document. Alternately, Powell or Mendenhall or Rush would push back their chairs to stand up for a stretch or another cup of coffee.

"What are you going to say about white-knight activity?"

Doug Brown asked. In the parlance of Wall Street, a "white knight" was a company that agreed to buy another company to "rescue" it from the grasp of an attacking company. Whenever a takeover attempt is in the news, scores of companies line up to talk with the target to see if they want to be rescued. As the investment banker, Brown was in charge of handling the barrage of calls from interested third parties.

If Tom Pownall could not escape Agee, maybe he'd make another deal.

The bankers and lawyers were paid to keep every avenue open until the client was prepared to decide. Fight like hell (but always be ready to run) was the credo.

"Every investment banker in the world has called," Bob Powell said, adding, "and everybody's playing both sides against the middle."

"Have there been substantative discussions?" Larrabee asked.

"I've been pitching a few people," Doug Brown said at the end of the table. "Just to keep the door open. I'm getting calls and I'm taking calls and people are talking to me. It's something that is always out there. Siegel asked me to put together a list, and I'm contacting people just in case we need them."

"We gotta say something about that," Larrabee said.

"Don't say we are talking to white knights—that's too strong. The conversations are only exploratory at this stage."

"Yeah, but we gotta say something like we have not talked yet," Larrabee said, "but we intend to."

"Well, how about Martin Marietta expects to hold discussions with third parties?" Dick Katcher offered as a compromise.

"Okay."

Everybody was tired.

That phrase—"Martin Marietta expects to hold discussions with third parties"—would come back to haunt everyone in the room.

Dick Katcher finally jumped into a cab for the twenty-five-mile ride to his home on Fairway Drive in Mamaroneck. Susan was barely awake when he came in. It was Dick's first night home in months. In his own bed, next to his wife of eighteen years, with his two boys asleep down the hall, Dick prepared for a good night's sleep.

"We already drank the champagne," Susan said.

"Did you tell them what's happening?"

"Yeah, yesterday," Susan said, sleepily.

"What did they say?"

"I talked with Andrew," Susan said, referring to their youngest son, who was in seventh grade, "and I said, 'What's the best news you can imagine?' and he said, 'Daddy's coming home!' And then I called Daniel and I said, 'What's the best news you can imagine?' and he said, 'You got me tickets to see The Clash' and I said, 'Noooo. Guess again' and he said, 'Andrew's moving out' and I said, 'Noooo!' "

Within a five-minute walk of the Dewey, Ballantine offices on Broadway, a team of Bendix lawyers was meeting late into the night at the Hughes, Hubbard & Reed offices at One Wall Street, across the street from the soot-stained Trinity Church and its ancient graveyard of tipped and worn stones.

Hughes, Hubbard partner and Bendix director Jack Fontaine was uptown at the Helmsley Palace meeting with Bill Agee. Fontaine was checking in periodically with the lawyers assembled downtown.

The men were debating an issue.

Fontaine was giving instructions to the team, which was hosted by Hughes partner Bob Enright, thirty-seven, a man with curly brown fluffy hair, glasses with steel rims, freckles, a favorite brass belt buckle, and a predilection for tweed suits.

"Are we safe? And do we have to do anything to be in accordance with the law? Those are the questions," Fontaine said to Enright.

Enright could hear other voices in the room with Fontaine at the Palace. Everyone was talking at once.

"Examine the employee stock plan," Fontaine said, "and make sure that what we think is correct, is indeed correct."

Enright had worked intensively with the Bendix Salaried Employees Savings and Stock Option Plan in 1981 when Bendix bought back some of its own shares for strategic purposes.

Under the terms of the Bendix Plan (referred to by its initials as SESSOP), eligible employees could contribute by payroll deduction from 2 to 12 percent of their monthly base salaries, and these contributions were invested in U.S. government securities or in Bendix common stock. The corporation matched in Bendix stock the employee contributions up to 8 percent of their salaries.

SESSOP was administrated by a trustee—Citibank.

The white-collar employees of Bendix owned almost one quarter of the shares of the corporation. With Martin Marietta having announced an offer to buy Bendix common stock, the Bendix team was worried.

"Bill Agee wants confirmation that Citibank can't do anything with the four point five million Bendix shares they hold for the employees," Fontaine said.

"Well, one thing is certain," Enright said. "The rules of the plan do not allow Citibank to tender the shares to the Martin Marietta offer. Nowhere in the plan is the word 'tender' mentioned. The plan says that the trustee has 'no power to sell or otherwise dispose of shares held in trust' except as routinely required by participants."

"Just stay on top of this thing. We don't want any surprises. And Bob," Fontaine said, "Hal Barron wants to know if Andy Samet is there."

"Yes, he's here," Enright said, looking at Samet, a small man with thinning hair, from the in-house Bendix legal department.

"Talk with Samet. I'll be in touch."

Enright's office at Hughes, Hubbard, off the black-and-white-tiled foyer, was crowded with lawyers from Hughes, Hubbard and from Fried, Frank, Arthur Fleischer's firm. A janitor was in the hallway, polishing the tile floor with a giant buffer.

Enright closed the door.

"Okay, Andy, let's hear it," Enright said.

"I've got a lawyer in my department, Dick Sanderson," Samet said, "and he went to a seminar last year—one of those Practising Law Institute seminars. It was called 'Employee Benefit Plans: Mergers and Acquisitions.' The message was that in certain extraordinary circumstances the trustee of a plan might have to ignore the rules of the plan so as not to violate its fiduciary duties."

"That's seminar goobledygook," a lawyer said.

"Let's grab an associate and have him hit the books," one of the Fried, Frank partners said.

"Claude, would you handle this," Enright said to a young lawyer taking notes. The man departed for the glass-walled library. He returned with a large legal volume in his hands.

"There aren't many precedents," Claude Johnston said, "only the Grumman case, which is instructive but not directly related."

The lawyers talked it over.

This was a gray area in the law.

"How could a trustee deliberately violate the terms of the plan and the trust agreement?" a Fried, Frank attorney asked Samet.

"Yeah, I don't follow that," one of the attorneys said.

"Citibank could be sued to kingdom come," another lawyer said.

"It's good to turn over every stone," Enright said.

"This one seems more like a pebble," a man said.

Enright reported the conclusions to Fontaine, uptown. Hal Barron talked with Andy Samet for a while.

"Just to be on the safe side," Samet said, "if you remember the *Grumman* v. *LTV* case, Grumman got sued by the Labor Department for improper handling of their pension fund. What the Grumman board of directors did wrong was not getting independent counsel to render an opinion. Barron wants us to hire somebody experienced in these things to give independent advice to the board of directors."

"That would be the safest route," Enright said.

"Who the hell are we going to get?"

Andy Samet remembered Dick Pogue from Jones, Day, Reavis & Pogue in Cleveland. The firm was well respected. Dick was a smart guy, lots of common sense, with resources at his command. Jones, Day had represented Warner & Swasey when Bendix had acquired the company in a $290 million deal in 1980.

On Monday night, just hours after Martin Marietta had announced its offer for Bendix, Hal Barron, the general counsel for Bendix, hired Dick Pogue to review the company's obligations toward its stockholding employees.

On Tuesday morning, Tom Pownall was given a standing ovation by the office staff on the third floor of Martin Marietta headquarters when he emerged into the broad hall from the private elevator. People gathered like it was a parade. A modest man, Pownall seemed embarrassed. He walked briskly, acknowledging only the eyes that met his. It was a happy moment, full of smiles, loud cheers, and a few tears of pride.

Pownall had declared war.

Doris Rush, the assistant general counsel, stood in her doorway.

And then it was time to get back to work.

Rush sat down at her desk and fumbled with her cigarette case. She lit her cigarette. Feminine but not delicate, Rush was tall, trim, with distinctive platinum hair. She was a private person, a bit of a loner, not afraid of joining a group but never assuming membership. Her entire career, she had been the different kid on the block.

Doris Rush was a pioneer of sorts.

She had traveled a path not followed by many women of her generation. Her first job out of college (mathematics major) was with Sperry Corporation, a major defense contractor. Rush was hired along with three other women—it was the first time the corporation had women in nonsecretarial positions. Doris worked in the engineering department for several years while attending law school at night—courtesy of Sperry.

Rush was one of the few women graduates of St. John's University Law School, Class of 1958.

The aerospace industry is a male-dominated business and run by men who pride themselves on their patriotism and operational experience. These are usually hands-on men who have models of airplanes and spacecraft in their offices. They feel close affiliation with the military. It's more than a job.

When Rush was hired in 1974 by then general counsel Jim Simpson, they joked about her visibility.

"It's all right," Doris said. "If Martin Marietta is a company that is future-oriented enough to put Viking on Mars, I think I can expect that they're the kind of people who accept the future when it happens."

Now, before Doris finished her second cigarette, her boss—Frank Menaker—was standing in front of her desk. Menaker adjusted his round eyeglasses.

"I've got a project for you," Menaker said.

"Great."

"Doris, I want you to look at anything you can get your hands on in terms of the Bendix employee stock plan, trust agreements, the works. Bendix has twenty-three percent of their stock in the employee plan and if we can't get any of that pried loose, it's going to be hard for us to get fifty percent of their stock tendered to our offer. And I don't need to tell you what happens if we can't make a go of it."

"Good-bye, Martin Marietta. Hello, Bendix."

"Right."

"Can the Bendix employees tender their shares to us?"

"I'm asking you, Doris," Frank said.

"Who's in charge of those shares?"

"A trustee—Citibank."

"Okay, Frank, I'll get right on it."

As the in-house lawyer responsible for the Martin Marietta pension and stock plans, Doris had some familiarity with the issues. Plans such as those of Bendix and Martin Marietta were governed by rules enforced by the Department of Labor. The acronym for the rules was ERISA.

It just so happened that Doris had immersed herself in the ERISA regulation issues in March as part of her preparation for Frank for a planned June board meeting. She had spent at least seventy hours at the American University library in Washington reading everything she could find on fiduciary duty and ERISA.

Only a small fraction of Martin Marietta's stock was in the employee plan, unlike the Bendix situation, where SESSOP held over four million shares.

By late morning, Doris had an ashtray full of cigarette butts.

Don Taylor from the pension area wandered into her office.

"Oh, by the way," Taylor said, "I talked with Audra Misiunas of Bankers Trust."

"What were you talking to her about?" Rush asked, not looking up from her yellow legal pad. Bankers Trust was the trustee of Martin Marietta's stock plan.

"Audra said that a Bankers Trust committee had met to review the Bendix offer and had decided not to tender Martin Marietta shares to Bendix because the offer was too low."

"What?" Doris said, looking up.

"Audra said they will not tender our shares to Bendix."

"Where did they think they had the right to tender the shares in the first place?" Doris asked incredulously. "I mean, it's purely a profit-sharing plan. I've got my money in there. Why would the trustee think they had the right to tender shares from my account?"

"I told you what she told me."

Rush was intrigued. She called Misiunas at Bankers Trust.

"Our position in this kind of thing," Misiunas said, "is that we—as the trustee of the plan—have a fiduciary responsibility to the people in the plan to examine any offer. We are supposed to be representing the best financial interests of the people in the plan. We had to look at it."

"Thanks a lot," Rush said, realizing that she may have stumbled onto something. Maybe the Bendix trustee—Citibank—had some responsibility to look carefully at the Martin Marietta offer?

She would make some calls.

TEN

Tuesday morning, Bill Agee breakfasted with Mary in the Trianon Room, a formal dining room on the second floor at the Helmsley Palace. It was 7:00 A.M. sharp. Bill and Mary sat at a corner table, guarded by a towering potted plant.

Mary did not remember Bill coming to bed last night. She excused herself at close to 1:00 A.M., with Bill still talking in the living room with Arthur Fleischer and Al McDonald. It had been a busy evening. Lawyers were in and out. The phone rang constantly. Every minute of Bill's time was dedicated to a review of strategy—and planning the next move.

He had a smile for her when she retired.

The morning's *Wall Street Journal* carried a long story by Tim Metz and Virginia Inman:

> MARTIN MARIETTA SPURNS BENDIX OFFER AS "INADE-QUATE," COUNTERING WITH $75-A-SHARE BID FOR CONTROL OF SUITOR
>
> Martin Marietta's strong countermove is in line with a budding takeover defense plan that Wall Street arbitrageurs and investment bankers alike are calling "the Pac-Man strategy." "That's where my client eats yours before your client eats mine," a merger specialist at one major investment banking firm said. . . .

A Wall Street source close to Martin Marietta rejected any contention that the Martin Marietta offer is simply a defensive ploy devised to drive Bendix away. "You'll note there won't be any condition in the offer to let Martin Marietta drop it if Bendix acquires Martin Marietta shares. We mean business," the source said.

"William Agee, Bendix's chairman, is going to be very sorry he started this," a source close to the situation said.

Bill Agee folded the newspaper onto his lap. He wore a crisp white shirt, striped tie, dark business suit, calf-high stockings, and expensive brown shoes.

Mary had already seen *The New York Times* and the *Journal.* In yesterday's edition, the writers were biding their time, waiting for the Martin Marietta announcement. But that did not keep them from filling up their columns. Mary saw her name, and saw the "Bill and Mary Story" summarized for the hundredth time. And, of course, there was the recitation of the RCA encounter and Thornton Bradshaw's quote. Bob Cole of the *Times* concluded, "Mr. Agee could face such an attack again."

"The U.S. Open starts today at Flushing Meadow," Bill said, sipping on his juice. "Maybe we'll go this weekend."

"What time is the board meeting?" Mary asked. She adjusted her shoulder-length strawberry-blond hair.

"Ten," Bill said, checking his watch. "I've got to run."

"Call me."

Bill squeezed Mary's hand and headed out of the Trianon Room, down the ornate staircase that looked onto a walled courtyard bounded by Madison Avenue. Walking briskly, Bill went one crosstown block before turning north on Fifth Avenue.

Arthur Fleischer's book *Tender Offers: Defenses, Responses, and Planning* is a thorough analysis of the options available to a company attacked by another company. The familiar strategies of Wall Street are all there, footnoted. Every move, every responsibility, every legal recourse is detailed in this working paper of more than eight hundred pages. Every move but one.

In Fleischer's repertoire, there was only one line about the countertender strategy conceived by Marty Siegel for Martin Marietta:

"It has been suggested that a target might even announce a

tender offer for a bidder's shares, though this has not been attempted."

At the time of Fleischer's writing (1978), no one had tried it.

Early in 1982, several companies tried the strategy, with mixed results. NLT Corporation tried unsuccessfully to beat back American General Corporation. In May, Cities Service Company launched a tender offer to try to fight off Mesa Petroleum; this succeeded only in forcing a marriage with a third company.

To Arthur Fleischer, a contemplative, graying lawyer with a dry sense of humor, the countertender plan was a surprise. The Bendix strategists and investment bankers had discussed the possibility in earlier meetings. But they concluded such a step by Martin Marietta would be financially unlikely. In Fleischer's mind, the strategy also unwisely swerved from the more familiar defensive paths available to Martin Marietta.

This morning, waiting at the Bendix offices on the twenty-first floor of the GM Building on Fifth Avenue, Arthur Fleischer had a determined look set into his face. The curved lenses of his eyeglasses magnified the size of his blue-gray eyes.

In his methodical, calculated manner, Fleischer reworked the scenario in his mind, looking beyond the day's headlines to the end game. He was waiting in a mirrored alcove. Occasionally he used the telephone on a table next to him. A mature oriental woman sat behind the reception desk, a small Bendix gold logo above her work station.

"Are you sure you don't want to go in?" the woman asked.

"I'll just make one more call," Arthur said, appreciating the tranquillity of the waiting area. He was checking in with his litigation partner—Marc Cherno—who was coordinating Bendix courtroom strategy. Cherno's secretary had Arthur on hold.

"What's that construction?" he asked the Bendix receptionist, pointing toward a window, the telephone cradled in his neck.

"Condos of some sort," she said, adding wistfully, "before they started building, you could see the Fifty-ninth Street Bridge."

"Are you ready to file in Michigan?" Fleischer asked Cherno.

A fast-talking, fast-thinking lawyer, Cherno was in his office at the southern tip of Manhattan coordinating litigation plans in Maryland, Louisiana, Nebraska, Oklahoma, South Carolina, and Utah. He had a picture on his wall of a Daumier-like caricature of a court scene with a sleepy judge; downtrodden defendant; and shyster, loudmouthed lawyer.

Cherno was planning to attack the Martin Marietta directors and their decision in Michigan following the Bendix board meeting today.

"The complaint is almost ready," Cherno said. "We're charging violations of sections 10(b) and 14(e) of the Exchange Act."

"Fine. I'll call you when the meeting is over," Arthur said.

When Bill Agee arrived, he was bright and full of vigor. He threw out "hellos" to the staff as he moved directly to his office, picking up his messages from his secretary, Marie. In preparation for the board meeting, Agee chaired a behind-closed-doors briefing with his key advisers.

Among those present were Al McDonald; Hal Barron; Jay Higgins from Salomon Brothers; Jack Fontaine from Hughes Hubbard; and Art Fleischer from Fried, Frank.

"It's a bluff," Al McDonald said, trying to sit in an uncomfortable chair in the corner of the room. Unable to settle, he stood up. "It is obviously a negotiating tactic to drive up our price."

"I don't think the stock market is going to believe them," Jay Higgins said forcefully. But from the stony look on Bill Agee's face, Higgins knew he was in trouble with his client. Bill Agee clearly had not expected Martin Marietta to come back at him aggressively.

"I mean seventy-five dollars a share is not a credible offer," Higgins continued. "Book value on the company is almost that. The market in the next couple of days will tell them that it's not going to fly.

"Martin Marietta is offering to buy eleven point nine million shares or fifty percent of Bendix common stock on a fully diluted basis. Bendix stock closed yesterday at fifty-seven dollars. They're offering seventy-five dollars. If the Bendix stock does not move up dramatically today or tomorrow or the next day, they'll know their ass is bare."

"As you know, Bill," Hal Barron, the forty-five-year-old general counsel of Bendix interjected, "almost twenty-three percent of our stock is in the hands of Citibank, which serves as trustee for the SESSOP plan. And that block is untouchable. We've had that confirmed this morning."

"What have you heard?" Agee asked.

"Bernie called Citibank and talked with Joe McDermott, a VP over there. He's a guy we've worked with for years."

Bernie was Bernard Winograd, the Bendix treasurer.

"McDermott was very clear that he read the SESSOP trustee agreement the same way we do. Citibank won't touch the SES-SOP shares."

"Excellent," Agee said, smiling.

"And with that block secure," Higgins said, examining some notes, "Martin Marietta has to get seventy-two percent of the remaining shares—just to end up with fifty percent. It's going to be almost impossible. I don't think they will fill their proration pool."

Martin Marietta was seeking 50 percent of the outstanding Bendix shares by promising $75 a share—on a first-come, first-served basis. This body of stock waiting to be purchased was the proration pool.

If they couldn't fill the pool, Bendix stockholders were not selling in sufficient amounts.

And if that was the case, Martin Marietta was doomed to fail in its attempt to take over Bendix.

"What's the legal situation?" Bill asked, turning to Fleischer.

"They have sued against the state takeover laws in Delaware, Michigan, Missouri, and New Jersey. It presents us with an interesting opportunity. They filed in Michigan for a TRO, and Her Honor—Judge Taylor—denied their request. It looks like Michigan is a good court for us."

The tall, commanding lawyer thought Michigan was a good jurisdiction for more reasons than home-court advantage. In 1981, the Sixth Circuit of Appeals—seated in that area—issued a decision in the *Mobil* v. *Marathon* case restricting the flexibility of the target company's board and management to artificially thwart the tender offer process. Fleischer won that ruling for his client—Mobil.

"Our plan is to file a securities lawsuit in Detroit—charging the Martin Marietta directors with breach of duty and that their counteroffer is a manipulative device aimed at frustrating the tender offer process."

"Excellent," Agee said.

"What about this timing advantage for Marietta that I read in this morning's *New York Times?*" Agee demanded of Fleischer.

"It's a technicality," Fleischer said.

"Did you know about this before?"

"It was discussed in several meetings, but the consensus was that Martin Marietta would not come back at us as they have. A countertender was considered a remote possibility. As such, the related issues were 'what ifs' that had to be weighted accordingly. Bill, I distinctly remember you saying that you did not want to be paralyzed by possibilities."

"Correct."

Despite the apparent breakdown in planning, Agee liked Fleischer and respected the older man's experience and insight.

The consummate lawyer who knew that nothing could be predicted with 100 percent certainty, Fleischer had looked this one over very closely.

"I'm not worried about this alleged timing advantage. If we buy first, we will win," Arthur said, looking Bill in the eye.

"If these guys want to play hard ball, we've got to show them we intend to win," Agee said emphatically.

It was time to turn the screw tighter.

"What's your best thinking to shut them down?" Agee asked. "The amendment thing we discussed last night?"

"Yes. It is a move that would negate any alleged timing advantages," Fleischer said. "By amending our certificate of incorporation, we could thwart any hostile bid against Bendix."

In Arthur Fleischer's manual on defenses against hostile takeover bids, there was a broad section entitled "Advance Planning." The tactic he was recommending to Agee was straight out of the book—page six. In the jargon of Wall Street, these types of amendments were called "shark repellents." The attacking company was pictured as the shark. The amendments were legal devices to repel the attack.

The plan would require a vote by the Bendix stockholders.

That meant contacting the 29,043 Bendix stockholders.

"We have examined the timing," Fleischer said. "Martin Marietta—if they pursue their offer—will be able to buy Bendix stock on September twenty-first at midnight. We are planning to solicit votes for a meeting in the morning on the same day. Just the possibility of passage of the amendments will create a lack of confidence toward the Martin Marietta offer in the financial markets."

"A proxy fight in the middle of two tender offers," Fontaine said, shaking his head and smiling, "that will keep them off balance." None of the experts had ever seen a situation like this before.

"The New York Stock Exchange has a thirty-day rule on special stockholder meetings," Hal Barron said. "We're going to talk with them today—I think we can get them to waive the rule."

"Our people in Washington," Fleischer said, "will handle the necessary filings with the Securities and Exchange Commission."

Bill Agee removed his suit jacket and crossed the room among the seated advisers. He hung his jacket on a hanger at the back of the door.

"Thank you, gentlemen," he said without turning.

"Tav, how are you?" Bill Agee asked, extending his hand.

William Tavoulareas, the president of Mobil Oil Corporation, responded with a powerful handshake. The two men were standing in the hallway of the Bendix offices. The board meeting was scheduled to begin in a matter of minutes, at 10:00 A.M.

"We missed you at the last board meeting," Agee said.

Both Tavoulareas and Professor Hugo Uyterhoeven from Harvard Business School had missed the first board meeting when Agee presented the "Acquisition of Georgia."

"I understand you've been busy," Tavoulareas said with a smile.

Knowing the forceful personalities of Uyterhoeven and Tavoulareas, Bill Agee was certain that their presence today would have an impact on the board. Although "Tav" (as he was commonly addressed by his colleagues) had been a member of the Bendix board for only a year, he had become the senior statesman of the board (although, at sixty-two, he was not the oldest—Wilbur Cohen and Coy Eklund were both his senior in age). Tav's tough-minded approach and considerable corporate experience made him a logical leader.

The takeover game was familiar territory to him.

Brooklyn-born and a self-made man, Tav had an opinion of himself no less firm than his handshake. He had seen some battles. Less than a year before, he was a key figure in the proposed $5 billion takeover of Marathon Oil by Mobil. Marathon fought back with lawsuits while it searched for a "white knight" to come to the rescue. Twenty-three days later, Marathon announced an agreement to merge with U.S. Steel for a substantially higher price.

"Okay," Tavoulareas said after a private word with Agee.

Bill smiled as if to say he had it under control.

The two men walked into the windowless, paneled meeting room.

"First off, I would like to inform the board that director Coy Eklund has removed himself from our deliberations. Equitable has a substantial holding of Martin Marietta stock. Coy would prefer—for propriety sake—to withdraw. He sends his best wishes."

A quick glance around the table confirmed for Agee that two other members were absent—Professor Wilbur Cohen from Texas and Jewel LaFontant from Chicago. That made eleven directors present—five inside directors and six outside directors.

"Gentlemen, I am sure you have seen the latest developments in the papers," Bill said, addressing the board from the head of the conference table. "On Wednesday, August twenty-fifth, we commenced our offer to purchase the Martin Marietta Corporation. Yesterday they announced an offer to purchase the Bendix Corporation.

"As I see it," Agee said, calm and in command, "Tom Pownall is making an offer for Bendix in an effort either to coerce us into dropping our offer, or more likely, in an attempt to get a higher price from us.

"But be that as it may, these seem to be our options: one, remain the aggressor; two, adopt a wait-and-see approach; three, soften our stance without withdrawing the offer; and four, we could capitulate."

While Bill Agee spoke, Hal Barron, the board's secretary, jotted down notes on a yellow legal pad. William Tavoulareas, peeking over his black bifocal glasses, noticed that other directors had pads on the table and they too were making notes.

"Excuse me, Bill," Tavoulareas said, "if I could, I would like to make an observation. I see people are taking notes. I don't think that is a very good idea."

Several directors put down their pens.

"Everything in the world is discoverable in a court," Tavoulareas said, "and if people are taking notes—some Martin

Marietta lawyer is going to find a way to get those notes into a court. So if you are doodling, make it pretty."

Bill Agee respected Tav. In some ways, the men were alike.

Like Agee, Tavoulareas had also had his share of activities deemed suspect by the press. The *Washington Post* in 1979 had published two articles charging that Tavoulareas had "set up" his son in the oil tanker business with lucrative Mobil contracts.

Tavoulareas hired John Walsh from the Wall Street firm of Cadwalader, Wickersham & Taft. He sued the *Post* for libel. The *Post* hired the legendary lawyer Irving Younger, from the firm of Williams & Connolly in Washington.

By the time Tavoulareas sat in the Bendix board of directors' meeting, he was fresh from a $2.05 million verdict against the *Post*. Bill Agee, still pained by the slander he thought had been heaped on him and Mary since 1980, could not help but admire Tavoulareas's victory.*

Jay Higgins and his associate Harold Tanner from Salomon Brothers were invited into the meeting.

"Jay, what is your analysis of the Martin Marietta offer?" Agee asked.

"The bid is a two-tiered offer," Higgins said. His voice was determined—almost pugnacious—as though there were something he had to prove.

"The nature of the proposed transaction calls for a payment of seventy-five dollars in cash for fifty percent of the company —followed by a converting of the remaining Bendix shares into a package of Martin Marietta securities. Salomon Brothers considers this setup to be discriminatory to the Bendix shareholders, as the back end of the deal is only worth fifty-five dollars."

"How is it discriminatory?" Donald Rumsfeld asked. His black hair was shining under the white light of the boardroom. Rumsfeld did something that seemed untoward to several directors—he placed his shoe against the table and tilted back his chair.

"The Bendix shareholders who tender promptly will receive the cash. The other stockholders who aren't among the first fifty percent to tender will get the back-end stock deal worth twenty dollars less," Higgins said.

"It is important to remember," Agee said, "that twenty-three

---

*In May 1983, a federal judge overturned Tavoulareas's victory on the grounds that the *Post* had not been proven guilty of "actual malice."

percent of our outstanding shares are held by Citibank in the name of the Bendix Salaried Employees Savings and Stock Option Plan, and the terms of that agreement do not allow the trustee to tender the shares to any offer.

"If you look at the Marietta offer," Agee said, "it is plain that this is a retaliatory move. In effect, they are trying to stampede our shareholders into their pool by offering cash up front and then to hell with the loyal Bendix employees who don't tender. They get screwed on the back end of the deal.

"We have determined that in light of the Marietta offer," Agee said, "the board of directors will have independent legal counsel from the firm of Jones, Day in Cleveland—Dick Pogue is the lawyer—for the purpose of reviewing the employee stock plan. Hal—do you want to address this point?"

Hal Barron pushed back his chair and stood up.

"Our next scheduled board meeting is set for a week from today. In the event that changes in our plan are necessitated by law, we are recommending that a committee from the board be available to meet with special counsel Dick Pogue and the lawyers to review the situation."

"I have asked Jack Fontaine, Tav, and Jonathan Scott to form that committee," Bill Agee announced. "Before we continue the discussion, I would like to call a vote on the Martin Marietta offer."

A motion to reject the Martin Marietta offer was passed unanimously.

"All right," Agee said, "in light of the discriminatory nature of the Marietta offer—as explained by counsel—management is proposing to attack the offer head-on. Arthur will discuss the specifics, but we propose to offer to our shareholders for their approval, amendments to the company's charter."

Arthur Fleischer outlined the intention of the two proposed amendments. One amendment would establish a procedure for setting a minimum price in the second stage of any two-step transaction such as the Marietta offer.

That would protect the employees against discriminatory offers.

The second amendment would permit stockholders in the company to take action without calling a meeting only upon near-unanimous consent. That amendment would specifically block Martin Marietta from taking control of Bendix before Bendix could take control of Martin Marietta.

If the amendment passed, Marietta's claim of a tactical timing advantage—perceived or real—would disappear.

"As you know, the arbitrageurs and institutional investors would be expected to vote 'no' on such amendments, looking for a short-term profit," Agee said. "Typically in situations such as this, individuals tend to support the positions of management. With twenty-three percent of our stock held by employees in our SESSOP plan and a substantial amount in individual hands, we are in a strong position."

"Can we win?" Rumsfeld asked Fleischer.

"It's probably fifty-fifty," Fleischer said.

"Jesus, too bad we did not do this before," a director said.

"At that stage it seemed unnecessary," Agee said. "Besides, what kind of management would we be if unassailed we covered the company five ways to Sunday? I am not so worried about somebody offering to buy Bendix as I am about somebody—like Martin Marietta—offering a ridiculously low bid. That is not in the interests of our shareholders."

Hal Barron reviewed the timetable of the special stockholders' meeting. The record date—in order to be eligible to vote —would be September 10. In order to pass inspection with the SEC and the NYSE, the earliest possible date for the meeting would be September 21 in the morning. At midnight, Martin Marietta would be able to buy Bendix shares according to the SEC timetable of their offer.

"One more thing before we go," Agee said, "about the decision of the board to reject the Martin Marietta offer."

"In circumstances such as these," Art Fleischer said to the attentive group, "it is required when the board recommends to the shareholders to reject an offer for them to also indicate what the members of the board are doing personally as shareholders.

"Does anyone around the table intend to tender their shares to Martin Marietta?" Fleischer asked.

As if passing an invisible ball, the directors looked to each other. While the stock holdings of the outside directors were typically small, the insiders had substantial portfolios; Agee, 47,055 shares; McDonald, 14,752; Bill Purple, 29,472; Paul Hartz, 22,506. Without smiles or hesitation, the directors shook their heads, forswearing hundreds of thousands of dollars in profits.

ELEVEN

The headline "BENDIX DIRECTORS REJECT MARTIN MARIETTA TAKEOVER BID" hit the Dow Jones wire at 1:30 P.M., followed minutes later by the body of the story:

> "Our board believes," Agee was quoted, "that our tender offer for 45 percent of Martin Marietta's shares and our proposal to acquire the remaining shares in exchange for Bendix common stock is the proper means for achieving what now appears to be our common aim of combining the two companies.
>
> "We are determined to push our transaction through to completion. If Martin Marietta persists in its diversionary scheme, we will acquire more than 50 percent of Martin Marietta's shares in our initial cash offer.
>
> "We will not be coerced into dropping our offer. We do however repeat our willingness to negotiate any and all of the terms of our offer for Martin Marietta.
>
> "I again invite the principals of Martin Marietta to meet with our top management for discussions on how best to achieve the common objectives within the framework of our tender offer for Martin Marietta."

While the press release had tough talk, Bill Agee was concerned.

He needed to talk to somebody. To get some satisfaction, Agee decided to go over the head of Jay Higgins to the guru of the Salomon M&A department.

"Get me Ira Harris," Agee told his secretary.

In 1981, Salomon Brothers announced its intention to combine its investment banking business with Philipp Brothers. A stock issue was planned. Harris personally had 367,524 shares of the new stock worth $10,209,000.

Word came back that Harris was not in his Chicago office. He was on vacation in Hawaii. Agee had his secretary call back and get the name and number of his hotel.

Harris was staying at the Hyatt on Maui.

"Ira, are you aware of what's going on here?" Agee asked.

"I talk with Jay Higgins every day, Bill. These things take on a life of their own. You've got to give it time to unfold."

Agee had heard Jay Higgins say that line. It confirmed his feeling that Harris was the man he wanted.

"I really need your advice. I want to get you more involved. I mean, Jay's a good guy, but Ira, you're the pro of the outfit."

Bill Agee considered Higgins a competent nuts-and-bolts guy, but Higgins did not command his full respect. Since Martin Marietta came back with nine hundred million borrowed dollars to launch their counteroffer, Agee suspected Higgins' judgment.

"Higgins can do the job," Harris said.

"Pownall is refusing to talk to me."

"It'll work out. Just don't do anything that makes it look like you're worried, Bill."

"I may talk with a few friends."

"Don't put out negative vibes on the street," Harris cautioned.

"It's under control," Agee said. "When are you coming back?"

"This coming weekend."

"Why don't you come back earlier and meet with me?"

"Bill, I'll be back this weekend. Higgins can handle it."

"Sure," Agee said, hanging up.

"Mr. Rohatyn's office," Cathy Kelly answered.

"Is Felix in? This is Bill Agee."

"I'm sorry, Mr. Agee. Mr. Rohatyn is out of the office."

"Tell Felix that I want to see him today."

"Will he know what this is regarding?"

"Just tell him I want to meet today."

Bill Agee did not know he was about to open Pandora's box.

John Crudele was a reporter at the RFR (Reuters Financial Report), a news wire similar to the service offered by Dow Jones. He had handled the corporate takeover beat for four years, filing stories read each day by the brokers and lawyers and bankers.

Tuesday afternoon he sat in his office at 1700 Broadway trying to find something in the Martin Marietta 14D filing delivered this morning by messenger.

He read the dry, legalistic prose. Having read scores of filings before, he had a sense of what to look for—something in small print that perhaps told a bigger story.

Stories on the Reuters wire were given priority by a system of bells. When something was hot and needed to go out right away, a writer would signal his editor by assigning bells on his computer keyboard. It rang in the editor's office, and if the editor agreed, it rang in banking and brokerage offices throughout the country.

The most a story could be assigned was six bells.

At 3:03 P.M. on Tuesday, less than twenty-four hours after the official announcement from Martin Marietta, a twelve-word story from Crudele ran on the wire with six bells:

> Martin Marietta said it expects to hold discussions with interested third parties.

That simple statement sent shock waves through Wall Street.

The professionals monitoring the deal all knew what that simple statement meant. Martin Marietta was holding talks with another corporation. They were, in the parlance of Wall Street, looking for a "white knight," some friendly corporation to come to their rescue—inevitably at a higher price than Bendix was offering.

There is nothing sweeter on Wall Street than a bidding war.

Millions of dollars could be swooped up by Marietta stockholders.

On the floor of the New York Stock Exchange, it was madness. Brokers were huddled around a trading desk, screaming, waving slips of paper in the air, all trying to increase the number of Martin Marietta shares in their portfolios. Arb reps—such as Leigh Sircus from the Ivan F. Boesky Corporation—were yelling buy instructions.

More traders wanted to buy than to sell.

At 3:05 P.M., trading in Martin Marietta stock was halted on the New York Stock Exchange because of the sudden influx and imbalance of orders.

At the close, at 4:00 P.M., trading was resumed to execute the orders. A total of 509,000 shares traded hands at $40 per share, bringing the day's total to 849,800 shares.

The little twelve-word story convinced the Wall Street traders that Martin Marietta secretly realized the impossibility of its position. Most people on the street thought Bill Agee—or some new player—was going to succeed in buying the Martin Marietta Corporation.

The credibility of the Martin Marietta offer to buy the Bendix Corporation was devastated.

"For Christ's sake, that's not what we meant!" Bill Harwood from the Martin Marietta press office yelled into the phone at John Crudele.

More than once in the conversation, Crudele had to take the receiver from his ear.

"Every reporter and his brother is calling here wanting to know if we have made a deal to sell the company! I want you to correct that statement!"

"I'm not gonna change it," Crudele said.

"It's goddamn not true!"

"Hey, look, you guys are the ones who put it in there," Crudele said, getting tired of being leaned on.

"That's just legalities."

"I write what I see," Crudele said, hanging up.

At 4:36 P.M., a Martin Marietta press release crossed the wire, datelined Bethesda. It called the Reuters story "erroneous" and added that "Martin Marietta is not now actively engaged in discussions of such a nature with anybody." Few people took note of the story. The damage had been done.

Felix Rohatyn was a distinguished man with swarthy appearance, his dark eyes framed by glasses. He had a wide smile and a stellar reputation. His picture was seen in the social press, snapped at late-night parties at Elaine's or any number of fashionable New York spots where the rich, powerful, and famous rub shoulders with everybody else.

As chairman of the Municipal Assistance Corporation in the 1970s, Rohatyn huddled with the politicians and bankers to extricate New York City from bankruptcy. While the garbage piled up and social services threatened to break down, Rohatyn pulled off an extraordinary feat—his bailout plan worked.

Rohatyn also had made an enormous impact on Wall Street.

The rich and powerful sought his advice on a wide range of deals.

One important, long-standing client was United Technologies.

When Felix got Agee's urgent message, Rohatyn was downtown at a meeting. The first thing he did was to call Ed Large, one of five executive vice presidents at the huge conglomerate, headquartered in Hartford, Connecticut.

"Bill Agee wants to meet with me today," Rohatyn said.

"Is he aware of what we've been up to?" Large asked.

"I don't have a clue. Do you have any objections?"

"Hell, no," Large said. "I'd be interested in hearing what he says."

United Technologies was hearing from everyone in this deal. Doug Brown from Kidder, Peabody had called up days ago, wanting to speak with Harry Gray, the chairman of UT. You don't get to Harry that easily. Stillman Brown, another exec VP, in charge of finance and administration, took the call.

"Would you like to receive a package on Martin Marietta?" Doug Brown asked Stillman Brown.

"Sure. Why not?"

"I understand Harry Gray and Tom Pownall are old friends," Doug said.

"Yeah, I understand that, too."

"Do you think Harry may be interested in Martin Marietta?"

"Let me get back to you," Stillman said.

On the previous Friday (August 27), Rohaytn; Harry Gray; Stillman Brown; Jim Lyons, VP for strategic planning; and Ed Large met in the UTC headquarters, the biggest building in the state of Connecticut.

The building is gold-colored and reflective.

A helicopter pad is on the roof.

UTC makes helicopters and a thousand different things.

Harry Gray, sixty-three, a warm, dog-eared man, trained as a journalist and considered one of the shrewdest businessmen in America, sat listening to his advisers.

"Look, Agee's price of forty-three dollars a share is not that bad. If we wanted Martin Marietta, we would have to come in at some higher number—and I don't think I want some of Tom's businesses that much," Gray said, spreading his big hands.

Harry Gray carried in his wallet a 1973 clipping from *The New York Times*—ennobled in plastic. It was a report on a session Gray had with financial analysts.

Gray had been named CEO only several months before in late 1972, but with typical panache, he unveiled before the analysts an ambitious plan to increase the success of the then $2-billion-a-year United Aircraft.

"I'm interested in acquiring companies in energy, communications, electronics, automotive, transportation, and environmental systems."

During the next decade, Gray bought Otis Elevator, Carrier Air Conditioning, and many other companies.

Through its Pratt & Whitney company, UTC became the world's largest supplier of gas turbine engines. The Pentagon bought the F-100 engine to power the U.S. Air Force's premier fighters, the F-15 and F-16.

Another UTC company, Norden, developed the computers for the Peacekeeper (MX) missile command, control, and communications systems. Virtually all U.S. and overseas commercial and military aircraft are equipped with one or more products from another UTC company, Hamilton Standard.

Its automotive companies were major suppliers to Ford, Chrysler, and General Motors. Mostek, an integrated-circuit producer acquired by UTC in 1979, was a leading producer of computer memories.

And UTC owned Sikorsky Aircraft, the largest manufacturer of helicopters in the free world. Another UTC company, Inmont, was the largest U.S. manufacturer of printing inks.

Harry Gray surprised even himself. His goal was to double sales by the end of the decade. Instead sales soared, to $14 billion. Employment almost tripled, to 184,000. In 1982, UTC was the nation's seventh largest manufacturer and its third largest defense contractor. The company had a presence in thirty-seven countries.

On Wall Street, Harry Gray was revered.

But Harry wanted more.

A company his acquisition team had looked at for years was the Bendix Corporation. The UTC automotive operation got 90 percent of its business from original-equipment manufacturers such as Ford, Chrysler, and GM. Although Bendix was strong with OEMs, it also had a profitable after-market operation that made replacement parts. The product lines of UTC and Bendix would work well together.

But always the same problem occurred. For UTC to be successful in acquiring Bendix, it had to overcome a substantial antitrust dilemma. Bendix and a UTC company—Hamilton Standard—were among a small group of firms involved in the fuel controls business. A fuel control system in a military fighter allowed the pilot of an F-15, for example, to climb to an altitude of twelve miles in 120 seconds, burning as much as four gallons of fuel a second. With both companies making these devices, it would create a substantial problem with the Justice Department's antitrust division.

Sitting in Hartford with Rohatyn and his acquisition team, Harry was in no particular hurry. He knew opportunity comes to those who wait.

"Harry, do you still want to buy Bendix?" Rohatyn asked.

"Yeah," Harry said, smiling.

"Felix, it's the same problem as before," Stillman Brown said. "How can we get around the objections of Justice?"

The men kicked it around.

A suggestion from Rohatyn made them sit up.

"We could structure a deal where we buy Bendix with the guarantee that Martin Marietta buy the Bendix fuel controls problem from us."

The idea seemed simple enough. UTC could eliminate their antitrust dilemma, and in light of their present situation, Martin Marietta would be willing to pay a good price. The men agreed that from a financial point of view, an acquisition of Bendix looked pretty good.

"I don't know if it will stand up in court," Ed Large said.

"See if you can get comfortable," Harry said.

On Monday, August 30, Large went to New York to talk with

several lawyers, among them a friend, Marty Lipton from Wachtell, Lipton, Rosen & Katz. Large knew that he would be able to feel out Martin Marietta management by briefing Lipton.

"What do you think?" Large asked.

"I think it can work," Marty Lipton said.

"If we wanted to do this, do you think you could represent us?"

"I'm representing Kidder, Peabody," Lipton said. "Maybe we could work something out where I get one of the guys here to stay with Marty Siegel and Kidder, Peabody, and I come over to you guys."

"Think about it," Large said.

When Large returned to Hartford in the afternoon, he caught Harry in the hall.

"Harry, I want you to know that I'm comfortable with the concept now about our friends in Detroit. If we want to become a player, we should not let the antitrust problem stop us."

Harry got on the phone with Tom Pownall.

The two men had been friends for many years and traveled in similar social circles. The aerospace industry, despite its billions of dollars of contracts from military and civilian aviation and high public profile, was in many respects a small, private men's club.

And Bill Agee was not a member of the club.

"You've got yourself in one hell of a mess," Gray said, teasingly. Pownall had called him.

"Jesus, Harry, you wouldn't believe it."

"What can I do for you?"

"I thought you might be interested in looking at us."

"Gee, Tom, sure we are, but not at that price," Gray said. He knew Pownall would never want to work for Bill Agee.

"Tom, we've been looking at it and I think we have a slightly different idea. We haven't worked it all out yet, but maybe we could do something to help."

"What's your thinking?" Pownall asked.

"I'm looking at buying Bendix myself."

"Come on over for a drink, Felix," Bill Agee said. "Suite four-five-oh-nine."

Rohatyn arrived at the Helmsley Palace by limo. Tuesday

night was warm, almost balmy. The gilded entrance of the Palace was ablaze with light. A uniformed black man opened the door.

Acquaintances for several years, Agee and Rohatyn engaged in friendly discussion. Bill casually invited Mary Cunningham into the living room. Felix enjoyed a drink of champagne; Mary offered Bill an iced tea. When Bill decided to turn the conversation to the business at hand, Mary wandered from the couch to leave the two men alone.

"How did the market treat you today?" Rohatyn asked, knowing the answer.

"We're down two, to fifty-five. Marietta is up to forty."

"Are you pleased?" Felix asked.

"I'm thinking of adding to my team of advisers," Bill said.

"What's wrong with Salomon?"

"Nothing is wrong. I would just like to see a little more depth, and I was wondering if you were free if I decide to go in that direction."

"I may have a conflict," Rohatyn said, without naming names. "There's a possibility that a good client of mine could be interested in you or in the situation."

"I see."

"Would you be prepared to sell the company?"

"It's the old story, Felix. If the price is right and that's the best alternative for the company, that's my job," Agee said intently.

"Is price your concern with the Martin offer?"

"Well, lookit, the kind of lowball bid that they've come in with is ridiculous. I mean, the average price between the front and back ends for the whole company is something like sixty dollars at most. I wanted to get your thinking on that."

"I could have some of my people look at it. Maybe Bendix is worth sixty-five dollars."

"My thinking is closer to a hundred dollars," Agee said, adding, "lookit, I haven't really given it serious thought, but I can sure as hell tell you that when the board today said the Marietta offer was inadequate, they didn't mean by a couple of dollars."

TWELVE

In the morning, Bob Powell was sitting quietly in his office at Martin Marietta headquarters. *The New York Times* was spread open on his desk. Powell rubbed his hands over his weathered face.

Tom Mendenhall peeked into the office.

"Did you see this?" Powell asked. He jabbed a finger at the *Times*. He went back to rubbing his eyes with the heels of his hands. Mendenhall began to read.

The story just would not go away.

MARIETTA IS SEEKING "3D PARTIES"
By Robert J. Cole
   Wall Street professionals, who had voiced scepticism over the seriousness of Martin Marietta's bid for Bendix, said yesterday that the company's stated intent to search for a friendly suitor confirmed their assessment.
   In any event, many said, Bendix appeared to have a strong timing advantage—because it acted first—and that it stood either a good chance of winning Martin Marietta or, if it loses to another suitor, of emerging with a huge profit.
   "There's a serious credibility problem for Martin Ma-

rietta," said Guy P. Wyser-Pratte, a professional arbitrager for Bache Halsey Stuart Shields. "On the one hand they say they're serious in going for Bendix and that Agee will be sorry he started this, and then they announce they're looking for a white knight."

"Yeah, it's in *The Wall Street Journal,* too," Mendenhall said somberly.

"It's a fatal flaw," Powell said, almost to himself. He was a ranking company man at that meeting with Doug Brown, Dick Katcher, Len Larrabee, and the others at Dewey, Ballantine when the language was written. He felt personally responsible.

"Hey, what are you going to do?" Mendenhall said, trying to cheer him up.

"Tom," Powell said, suddenly looking up.

"Yeah?"

"I don't want you signing anything. I don't want your name on anything, okay?"

"What do you mean?"

"Look, I've got one of the golden-parachute contracts; you don't. If Bendix takes us over, I want you to be able to continue to work here. If you don't sign anything, they may never know that you've been in the middle of this."

Now Mendenhall was getting depressed.

Marty Siegel sat in his Kidder, Peabody office at 10 Hanover Square, near the waterfront of Manhattan's Battery Park. His thick, dark brown hair was parted neatly. He was tanned and close-shaven. Behind him, out his window, were the high-rise canyons of Wall Street.

Things were not going well for his client.

He told the Martin Marietta board of directors that the announcement of a countertender offer would send the price of Bendix stock way up—throwing a scare into Bill Agee.

It didn't happen.

On his desk, Siegel had a paperweight—of a reddish-brown tarantula frozen in clear plastic. It was a gift from a grateful client. Siegel tried to figure out the next move he would recommend to Tom Pownall and the Martin Marietta board of directors.

From years of experience, Siegel knew that on average only

one company in five was successful at repelling a takeover bid. Siegel had built his reputation at Kidder, Peabody by boosting those odds to one in three for his clients. But no matter what the percentages, Martin Marietta was in trouble.

At his left elbow was his desktop computer.

He punched in commands to see how the stock market was doing.

When the market opened in the morning, someone bought 251,000 shares of Martin Marietta stock at $40 a share. That was a $10 million investment. In a little more than two weeks, Bendix was promising to pay $43 a share. If all went according to the Bendix plan, that someone would make $753,000 in profit for his trouble.

Throughout the day, while fielding phones calls and directing his staff, Siegel kept an eye on the market. By the close, 1.6 million Martin Marietta shares traded hands—the heaviest volume the stock had ever experienced. To make matters worse, trading volume for Bendix shares was light—and the price actually fell $3.50.

It was a disaster. By the heavy volume in trading of Martin Marietta stock and the falling price of Bendix stock, the market had spoken. The pros thought Bendix would win.

Siegel knew he needed help badly.

"Harry Gray is a finisher," he told Tom Pownall. "We need him to come into this. It's the only way to get some credibility back. Maybe Agee will believe us and back off if he knows Harry is out there."

"Where does it stand?" Pownall asked.

"I talked to Felix Rohatyn—Harry's banker—last night. He called me at home. We're trying to work out the antitrust problem involving the fuel-controls-business overlap between Bendix and United Tech. To put it together, I think we need to get you and Harry together."

"I'm ready," Pownall said.

Siegel talked to Felix again.

"Let's get Tom and Harry together," Siegel said.

Publicity-conscious, the two men debated where the meeting should take place. Both men were worried about secrecy. Siegel suspected his office was being watched.

"We'll have the meet at Marty Lipton's office," Rohatyn said.

* * *

With Martin Marietta clearly on the defensive on Wall Street, Bill Agee wanted to shut the back door on Martin Marietta to force Tom Pownall to the negotiating table.

"How are we doing in Washington?" Bill asked Al McDonald.

To coordinate the Bendix strategy in Washington, Al McDonald had turned to Nancy Clark Reynolds, the Bendix lobbyist on Capitol Hill. She ran the Bendix National Affairs office from quarters on Maryland Avenue, a long, spacious road that passes the New Senate Office Building, the U.S. Supreme Court, and the back steps of the U.S. Capitol.

"I talked with Nancy this afternoon. I think we will see some results from her work over at the Pentagon," McDonald said. The two men were in Bill Agee's corner office at the GM Building.

"Will Carlucci sign?" Agee asked.

"Looks like it," McDonald said.

"Pownall will have to talk with me now," Agee said.

An attractive fifty-three-year-old political veteran with fine blondish hair wrapped in a bun, Reynolds was a seasoned veteran and a close personal friend of the President and Mrs. Reagan, as well as an old friend of Bill Agee's from Idaho.

In preparation for takeover activity, Reynolds transformed the National Affairs office—adding almost twenty telephones to a conference room, installing a telex machine for instant communications with Bendix, and an enormous Xerox machine that could collate hundreds of pages of documents.

In the basement of the office on Maryland Avenue, shelves were stocked with gray envelopes labeled with every representative and senator's name, cross-referenced by building, by floor, by office number, by committee. Lists were organized, checked, and rechecked. Material was constantly updated, waiting for instructions.

At McDonald's suggestion, Reynolds hired Anne Wexler, a Washington political consultant.

Wexler had worked with McDonald and Bendix strategic planner Michael Rowny in the Carter White House. McDonald was staff director there; Rowny was his deputy staff director. Wexler, a short-haired, wiry operative, was an assistant to the President for public liaison. The three had developed a solid working relationship over months of hard work.

With a cover letter from McDonald, they sent questionnaires to managers at all of Bendix's field operations, seeking intelligence about who was politically active and could be called upon when needed. They developed detailed index cards on each important senator or representative—including a breakdown of how much money was given to each by the Bendix Political Action Committee.

Wexler and Reynolds nicknamed the strike team "McDonald's Marauders."

Timed to the announcement of the Bendix bid to acquire the Martin Marietta Corporation, the Marauders made hundreds of calls to the powerful in Washington. Nancy called the White House and spoke with Ed Meese. He was pleased to know before the newspapers.

The overriding goal was to ensure that Washington would remain neutral—no one in power would publicly condemn Bendix, no senator or representative would call a committee meeting to review the situation. Nothing was to interfere with Agee's plan to buy the Martin Marietta Corporation on September 17, at 12:01 A.M.

"What we've got to worry about," Wexler said to Reynolds in the Bendix National Affairs office, "is the reputation of Tom Pownall. That guy is known and liked by almost everybody over at the Department of Defense."

"What are our people saying?" Reynolds asked.

"Pownall is hitting hard trying to get some committee to look into this takeover fight. And he is talking to people at DOD saying that Bendix does not have the management experience to handle security-clearance-type programs."

"We've got to get a leg up at DOD," Reynolds said.

"Let's use John Rhinelander," Wexler said.

Rhinelander's name was suggested to Mike Rowny, who flew to Washington the night before the announcement of the Bendix bid to buy Martin Marietta eight days ago.

During his service in the Nixon Administration as general counsel for the Health, Education, and Welfare Department, John Rhinelander had established close relationships with Cap Weinberger, Frank Carlucci, and William Taft.

Cap Weinberger became Reagan's Secretary of Defense. He in turn tapped Carlucci as his deputy, while William Taft became the general counsel of the Department of Defense.

As the advertising slogan says, the best business calls are personal calls. Rhinelander was retained by Bendix to call his friends at DOD.

An exchange of letters between Bendix and the DOD was suggested.

Rhinelander drafted a letter and sent it over to Bill Taft, who used it to draft a statement that Carlucci signed.

On Thursday, September 2, the Bendix PR department issued copies of an exchange of letters between Bill Agee and Frank Carlucci. Bendix had succeeded in getting the Deputy Secretary of the Department of Defense to go on record that the DOD did not "support or oppose Bendix' proposed acquisition of Martin Marietta."

The Marauders had done their job. Pownall was beaten in his own backyard.

"Pownall will have to talk with me now," Agee said confidently.

Thursday afternoon was a muggy eighty-five degrees in downtown Hartford.

Thunderstorms were predicted.

With a surge of power, a Sikorsky S-76 helicopter lifted off the pad atop the "Gold Building"—world headquarters for United Technologies Corporation. The sleek white helicopter swept over the downtown high-rises before turning southwest for the flight to New York City.

"I never get tired of this view," Ed Large said to no one in particular. The United Technologies executive vice president for legal and corporate affairs was looking at the graceful rolling green below bisected by the Connecticut River, which runs from Canada, dividing Vermont from New Hampshire before twisting into Long Island Sound.

It was a short hop to New York City.

Large was joined by Stillman Brown, the unflappable, low-key executive VP for finance and administration. Both men were on board because UTC chairman Harry Gray wanted them along.

The men were headed to New York for a 4:30 P.M. meeting with Tom Pownall and his team at the offices of Wachtell, Lipton.

"This deal makes sense," Harry said. Gray was upbeat, a

smile riding high on his weathered face. "It makes sense for Pownall—he can borrow less, keep his freedom, and pick up some good businesses," Brown said.

"What about Agee?" Large asked.

"Agee is a finance guy," Harry said. "Logic will prevail. If he sees us come in for Bendix, he'll deal. Felix said Agee talked price already. Everything I know about the man, he will come over if the ticket is right." With a tug on his earlobe, Gray added, "I could use a guy like him around here. How would you like Bill Agee working in finance, Stillman?"

"For me or with me?"

Harry only smiled.

The helicopter skimmed over the river on the East Side of Manhattan in the shadow of the Queensboro Bridge and landed at the Marine 3 aviation pad at Fifty-ninth Street. From there the men took a limo to the Wachtell, Lipton offices at 299 Park Avenue, between Forty-eighth and Forty-ninth streets.

Marty Lipton, fifty-one, was a courtly man, finely tailored in a dark blue suit and white shirt with cuff links. He had curly gray hair, thick glasses, and a round face. Waiting for Harry Gray to arrive, Lipton was sitting at his desk, having his shoes shined by an old smocked black man.

"Where are we going to put these guys?"

Lipton looked up. At the door was his partner Dick Katcher.

"Let's put the UTC team in conference room one and the Marietta people in two and we'll let Tom Pownall and Harry Gray talk here in my office."

"Fine," Katcher said, tapping the door with his knuckles. "Is Pownall ready?"

"Yeah, he's ready," Katcher said, "but I think his guys are worried about him being alone with Gray. I think they're scared Gray may get the better of their man."

A lot of people were in the halls at Wachtell, Lipton.

There were glimpses of Pownall talking with his main lieutenants—Frank Menaker, general counsel; and Charlie Leithauser, senior VP and chief financial officer. Marty Siegel had several people with him from Kidder, Peabody. And a small army of lawyers—including Bob Fullem and Leonard Larrabee from Dewey, Ballantine—were emptying from the hall into a conference room.

Felix Rohatyn was there.

Harry Gray swept in with his entourage. A vigorous man, Gray wore a dark business suit. A small emblem was on his lapel —he had been an Army captain in World War II, and the emblem commemorated the Silver star he received for gallantry in action. Rumors had circulated for several years that Gray was going to retire. First the pundits said when Harry reached sixty. Now the target was sixty-five. Few believed Gray would ever step down voluntarily.

The man enjoyed being chairman, chief executive officer, and president of one of the most powerful enterprises in the world.

"Tom, it's good to see you. Been a while," Gray said, seeing Pownall. The two men—old friends—walked smartly toward each other for a firm handshake. Pownall seemed almost as if he were at attention, his prominent chin jutting out.

The two men introduced some of their supporting casts.

"Well, what do you say, Tom, let's get the bankers talking to the bankers, and the lawyers talking to the lawyers. And you and I can sit down somewhere and talk this deal over."

"Harry, please feel free to use my office," Lipton volunteered.

By 10:00 P.M. it was raining hard in New York.

The promised thunderstorm was tracked by the Central Park Observatory, which registered almost one-quarter inch of rainfall in less than an hour. The rain beat against the windows of Marty Lipton's office.

At almost 11:30 P.M., Lipton's office was crowded with lawyers and executives from both companies. The meetings had lasted on and off for almost six hours—with the two men in charge spending several hours alone. Harry Gray sat in a chair, his arms spread over the arms of the chair, his hands looking for something to do. Gray looked well worn, his hair silver and thin, his face lined with wrinkles like his suit trousers after a long day's work.

"We'll have your understanding on paper tomorrow," Marty Lipton said to Gray and Tom Pownall. Harry nodded his head. This was between friends—but this was business. Every "i" would be dotted.

"Well, Tom, let's call it a night," Gray said to Pownall. "I've got to fly home in the rain."

"I'll present our agreement to my board tomorrow," Pownall said.

"Me, too," Gray said, adding to Marty Lipton and Felix Rohatyn, "see you in Hartford."

Gray stood up. Tom Pownall extended his hand.

The two men shook on their agreement. There was still a lot of detail work for their staffs to accomplish. Tom and Harry handled the broad framework. UTC would launch a deal of more than $1 billion to buy the Bendix Corporation, and if UTC was successful, Tom would pay Harry $600 million to take away the sticky areas that would attract the government bloodhounds.

"What are you doing for Labor Day?" Harry asked Pownall offhandedly.

"I can't plan that far ahead these days," Tom said with a grin.

"I'll be playing tennis in Nantucket. My game is really coming together. All right, then, Tuesday, UTC will announce to the world its offer for Bendix."

THIRTEEN

The trees lining Fifth Avenue were whipping against the black sky, the street lights making their leaves shimmer. The rain was easing off but still steady.

The fifty-story GM Building was awash in spotlights. On the twenty-first floor, Al McDonald was trying to wrap up his work before a planned late dinner at the River Club of New York at 477 East 52nd Street, six crosstown blocks from the office, near the East River.

Several secretaries remained, too—waiting for the Bendix president to call it a night.

"Go ahead," McDonald said, handling one last detail.

McDonald's secretary Martha grabbed her bag from the top of her desk; one of Agee's secretaries, Barbara, emerged from another office; they headed for the elevator.

"Hold the door!" another secretary called. Angie—who worked for Bob Meyers and Mike Rowny—emerged from the ladies' room.

The elevator doors opened into the lobby of the GM Building—all bright and shiny, potted plants giving a human scale to the towering lobby. Chandeliers hung on long chains like battleship anchors. The women followed the runner rug to the revolving door. Angie had to lean hard to get it to move. The wind was a squall in the building's courtyard.

They managed to cross the street.

It was raining too hard to go farther.

The three women huddled by the eave of F. A. O. Schwarz, waiting for a taxi to appear.

Martha noticed a dark shape coming from the GM Building. The man had no umbrella. He was running.

"Oh, no," Martha said under her breath to Barbara and Angie.

"Just look at me!" McDonald said, barely controlling his anger. "Where's my cab?"

"I forgot to call a cab," Martha offered weakly.

"See you in the morning," McDonald said in a harsh voice.

After more than a week, the pressure was hard to ignore.

Friday morning, September 3.

"Where is everybody?" Doris Rush asked Tom Mendenhall.

The executive wing of the Martin Marietta headquarters building seemed deserted. Pownall was gone, so was Leithauser, Adams, Simpson, Menaker, Powell. It was a ghost town on the third floor.

"I think there's a board meeting in New York," Mendenhall said. He was looking tired. The work load was unreal. "I talked with Leithauser this morning before he left."

"What did he say?"

"Not much."

"Are they up to something?" Rush asked.

"I don't think we're supposed to know, so I'm not asking. Charlie said that he didn't know what was going to happen next week. He said we should leave a phone number and try to get some rest over the weekend."

"Oh, that's right, it's Labor Day weekend," Rush said.

"Earth to Doris, Earth to Doris," Mendenhall said. He liked teasing Rush. She was older. The way she crinkled her face made it worthwhile.

"What are you going to do?" Mendenhall asked.

"Sleep. What about you?"

"I think I'll take Linda and the kids to St. Michael's. Her parents—the Bells—have a place there. Not bad, huh? The Bells of St. Michael's. Maybe I'll go sailing."

* * *

"I'll take sleep any day," Rush said.

"What are you working on?" Mendenhall asked.

"This Bendix SESSOP thing."

"Huh? Oh, the employees' shares, right. How's it going?"

"I want to talk with Frank."

"Charlie wants me to line up another three hundred million dollars in loans," Mendenhall said, talking as much to himself as Rush. "I can't pay anything, of course. Just line it up." Mendenhall snapped out of his trance. "What am I blabbing about? I'll see you, Doris. Next week we'll get them."

Mendenhall disappeared out of Doris's office. After a few minutes, Doris threw down her pencil and went out into the hall, headed for Menaker's office. She had some pressing questions for Menaker.

"I need to talk with Frank," Doris told Mary Lou, Menaker's secretary.

"Doris, I don't even know where he is. But I do know he doesn't want to be found."

"He's in New York," Doris said.

"I did not say that," Mary Lou responded.

Doris knew she would be unable to sleep over the weekend if she did not get some answers. She decided to call a lawyer at Dewey, Ballantine to see what they were doing to "get at" the Bendix SESSOP shares.

Maybe she would try out her theory on someone.

She called a Dewey, Ballantine lawyer—Carol Trencher. Carol was not available. Doris left urgent messages, which were not returned. Doris tried unsuccessfully to reach Bob Fullem. Finally, she spoke to an associate, Steve Matthews.

"Have you considered any way to get the Bendix employee shares to tender to our offer?" Rush asked.

"Citibank is the trustee," Matthews said.

"I understand that," Doris said. "I've been thinking that maybe there is a way to get Citibank to tender those shares to us."

"We're looking at that," the man said.

"How can I help?"

"Well, actually, Doris, Bob Fullem and several of us have looked at it and our opinion is that those shares are bound in a way that will prevent Citibank from doing much of anything. But keep up the good work."

Doris felt a letdown. Maybe this wasn't such a great idea, anyway. Discouraged, she took a call from Doug Brown at Kidder, Peabody.

"Menaker tells me you are the ERISA expert," Brown said, teasing.

"I wish I could talk with him."

"He'll get back to you," Brown said.

"I'm having a problem getting anybody to listen to an idea."

"Shoot."

"Well, it seems that a case could be made that the trustee of a plan has a fiduciary duty to examine an offer on the merits. They are supposed to be representing the interests of the people. Bankers Trust told me they were examining the Bendix offer to decide whether or not they should tender our damn shares to them! I've checked around and I think their approach is right. So why shouldn't Citibank be responsible for examining our offer? Maybe they should tender to us."

"You've checked into this?"

"Well, as far as I've gone, yeah."

"So what do you want to do?" Brown asked.

"I want to put the pressure on Citibank to tender the shares to us," Doris shouted.

"There's a problem," Brown said. "If you—the assistant general counsel of Martin Marietta—tell Citibank their responsibilities, nobody is going to listen."

"I know," Rush said. "Maybe I need an outside opinion. A written legal opinion from somebody they respect."

"Good idea. Go get them, Doris."

In New York, the Martin Marietta team of lawyers was expecting to see a draft of the agreement between Martin Marietta and United Technologies first thing Saturday morning. A meeting was scheduled for 11:00 A.M. at Dewey, Ballantine for the Marietta lawyers to review the document, which was prepared by Marty Lipton's team at Wachtell, Lipton.

Len Larrabee of Dewey, Ballantine was anxious to see how the agreement had been fleshed out. An experienced lawyer, Larrabee expected some surprises. After all, United Technologies was squarely in the driver's seat. Marietta needed them more than UTC needed Marietta.

"How's it going?" Larrabee said during a call uptown.

"Ed Large is looking the draft over," the Wachtell, Lipton lawyer said.

"Should we get it soon?"

"We'll call you," the man said.

Ed Large had come down from Hartford by helicopter.

He read the drafted agreement and went in to talk with Marty Lipton.

"Marty, did you write this?" Large asked.

"An associate utilized my notes," Lipton said.

"Well, c'mon, was that guy present at the meeting? This thing is not quite right."

It turned out that in addition to the "flavor" of the agreement, Large wanted included several points that had not even been mentioned on Thursday night. One dealt with Martin Marietta paying UTC's expenses in the event Pownall decided to back out of the agreement.

A tough, cool operator, Large spent several hours making the document acceptable to United Technologies.

As time dragged on into the afternoon, the Martin Marietta lawyers downtown at the Dewey, Ballantine offices were getting increasingly skeptical.

When the document finally arrived, Len Larrabee and Bob Fullem sat down with Frank Menaker, Charlie Leithauser, and Jim Simpson from Martin Marietta to review the document.

"At this stage, don't look for the fine points," Charlie Leithauser said (he was the senior Martin Marietta official present). "Just look for the tall poles, the problems that really stick out."

Simpson got a kick out of that line. He carefully read the document looking for Charlie's "tall poles." The men did not have to search very hard before realizing that the document appeared at some major points to be substantially different from the terms agreed to the day before. Or perhaps, to be more accurate, the points that had remained open on Thursday, by Saturday afternoon had been rendered to UTC's advantage.

"I never even heard about this liquidated damages position," Simpson said, referring to a point that called for Martin Marietta to pay $2 million to UTC to cover their expenses in the event Marietta walked away from the agreement.

"Yeah, and there's more," Larrabee said, making notes.

The men ticked off a list of almost a dozen "tall poles."

The most substantial area of concern was the Bendix fuel

controls business. But there was another problem involving the Elliott company, which UT wanted to "put" or sell to Martin Marietta. The whole package was worth $600 million. Each component had its own value.

"This makes it sound like the price for the Bendix fuel controls business is a fixed price—three hundred million dollars," Menaker said.

"Tom told me that was an approximate price," Leithauser said.

"Well, this says three hundred million dollars, no ifs, ands, or buts."

They turned to the second sticky point.

The Martin Marietta management team had hoped that they would have in effect an open hunting license to examine Bendix and buy what they wanted. The document made it clear that if UTC and Marietta could not agree, UTC had the right to decide what Marietta would or would not buy and for what price.

"This document does not reflect what Tom told the board," Menaker said.

"I think it's important that we regard this as a negotiating position that UTC is taking," Larrabee said.

It looked like Harry Gray had decided to play hardball.

"Oh, boy," Leithauser said.

"Everybody in the pool," Fullem said.

On Sunday, the Martin Marietta team assembled at Wachtell, Lipton to review the agreement. Charlie Leithauser had his "tall poles" written down on a sheet of paper. Principally he and Menaker would speak for the company. Ed Large did most of the negotiating for United Technologies. As a lawyer and a businessman, Large was capable of straddling the conversations between the managers from Martin and the lawyers. The two companies met in conference room No. 1.

"I must say that we have some trouble with several points," Leithauser said. "Perhaps most notable is the fixed three-hundred-million-dollar price for the Bendix fuel controls business. Our understanding was that the price would vary if an independent evaluation pointed to some other figure."

"That's not as we understand it," Large said with no smile.

"You're not going to be arbitrary about this, are you?" Menaker asked.

"It's not arbitrary. We feel it is appropriate."

"We have a problem with the way this is written," Leithauser said.

"The three-hundred-million-dollar figure is a good deal for you guys."

"For the moment, we are not disputing that. Our problem is that our understanding of the conversation between Tom and Harry was that these prices were adjustable rather than fixed."

"No, those are hard figures."

After several hours of back and forth, it was obvious to both sides that they were not making progress. Ed Large was not offering any indication of backing off the document. While both sides were protecting against allowing their positions to harden, there was a shared perception that they were not talking on the same wavelength. Part of the problem was that the two teams were offering different versions of the same agreement—originally negotiated between Harry Gray and Tom Pownall. It reached the point where it was obvious that the principals would have to talk again.

Ed Large reached into his pocket for Harry's number. He knew that Gray was on Nantucket, staying at Stillman Brown's house. Large thought that perhaps Gray would be out sailing. But he gave him a try.

Stillman had a long extension cord on his telephone. Harry and Stillman were outside in the backyard, in casual clothes, enjoying the sun.

"The three hundred million dollars for fuel controls is a real problem for these guys," Large told Gray. "Their understanding of the agreement lets that figure be a parameter. They don't want a hard figure."

"Well, I talked to Tom Pownall, and he knows damn well what I said," Gray told Large. "That three hundred million dollars is the price of the business and we can justify it on the earnings. That was an agreement I had with Tom. It was clearly understood, and I don't understand why they're having difficulty with it."

"They also are having trouble with the other three hundred million dollars, like what would happen if we can't mutually agree on businesses to make up that figure."

"What the hell is going on with those guys?" Gray said.

"I told them that in order for this agreement to work, we

have got to have an agreement to agree. If we can't settle with them, then we'll put businesses to them at fixed prices."

"Who are you talking to?" Gray demanded.

"I'm talking to Leithauser," Large said.

"Well, goddamnit, Ed, don't tell me what Leithauser is saying! I never made any deal with Leithauser! Give Tom Pownall my phone number, and if he's got a problem, tell him to call me."

Not long after that, Tom Pownall called Harry Gray from an office at Wachtell, Lipton. Pownall had been attending the sessions but allowed his staff to take the lead in hammering out the details. It would not be appropriate for Pownall to negotiate with anyone but Harry Gray.

"I'm getting hell from my people," Tom Pownall said to Harry. "My finance people are saying that we can't set a price that way. They want an appraisal of the businesses. Something independent that I can show the board."

Gray was losing his patience.

"Tom, as far as I am concerned, what Large is telling your guys is what we agreed to. I want you to know that we are still willing to stay in there and help you if you want us. But I'm not changing the agreement."

When he emerged from the office, Pownall had a grim expression on his face. Simpson, Menaker, and Leithauser stood waiting for news.

"Harry's set on the three hundred million dollars," Pownall said. "Either we work with this or we don't have a deal."

Given Gray's intransigence, Pownall was now faced with a new problem: UTC was asking for $300 million for a company that Tom Pownall knew next to nothing about.

"We've got to find out what the damn thing is worth," Pownall said.

When the teams got together again, both sides were operating on the same assumption: UTC had prevailed. The fixed figure would stand. The issue then became whether Martin Marietta would accept the figure. Tom Pownall and Charlie Leithauser were not the types—no matter how badly they needed the deal—to buy any business unless they knew what they were buying and what it was worth.

"How did you evaluate the fuel controls business?" Jim Simpson asked, adding, "I mean, Ed, did you come up with the figure off a boxtop?"

"We can't ask our board to approve the three-hundred-million-dollar purchase price without putting data in front of them that would justify the price," Leithauser said.

"We can show you what it's worth," Large said.

"Well, get it out," Simpson said.

United Technologies had in fact utilized inside information to come up with the $300 million price tag. The UTC company Pratt & Whitney sold almost $3 billion a year worth of jet engines to the U.S. government and other friendly countries around the world. The most successful engine in P&W's military engine programs was the F-100 engine, which provided twenty-five thousand pounds of thrust to the U.S. Air Force's premier fighters, the twin-engine F-15 and the single-engine F-16. Over twenty-seven hundred F-100 engines were in service.

For its advanced engine, Pratt & Whitney bought fuel control devices from the Bendix energy controls division in South Bend, Indiana. P&W and General Electric were Bendix's biggest customers.

Knowing the success of the F-100 engine and its long life, and the amount of business P&W gave Bendix each year, the UTC financial team had worked up the $300 million price tag. All that remained was to convince Martin Marietta that the figure was fair.

To accomplish that, Ed Large got in touch with Irv Yoskowitz, the UTC general counsel. Yoskowitz was asked to put together a group of experts from Pratt & Whitney who could come to New York and parade their facts before the Martin Marietta team.

For their part, Martin Marietta was determined to find an independent appraisal of the worth of the business. Public documents could tell them only so much. And while they had confidence that UTC would share their orders from Bendix, Tom Pownall and Charlie Leithauser still could not put their arms around the business.

Pownall had the team calling everybody they could think of in the engine business.

"Ask a lot of questions," Pownall said.

Marty Siegel was working late at his office on the problem. A cunning man with broad contacts, Siegel had several ideas. On Sunday night he was also watching the time.

Marty and his wife, Jane, who was a bond trader at Kidder, Peabody before she became pregnant with Jessica Grace, their six-month-old baby, planned a lavish party at their cedar and glass home on the shore of Connecticut.

In keeping with his successful career, the house was spectacularly equipped with a small gymnasium, pool, tennis court, and a sprawling view of a private beach.

For the party, Siegel had invited a lot of the big mucky-mucks from the office, including Kidder's president, Ralph D. DeNunzio. Knowing that commuting by car or train was too time-consuming, Siegel chartered a seaplane to pick him up at the dock at Thirty-third Street and fly him to his house.

Siegel loved dramatic entrances.

The cost of the flight would be billed to Martin Marietta.

FOURTEEN

Harry Gray was not the only man on Nantucket Island interested in buying the Bendix Corporation.

Thirty miles off the mainland of Massachusetts, Nantucket was once an important whaling port, and the quaintness of its tree-lined, cobblestone streets and classic New England gabled architecture owes its origins to those days. Since the turn of the century, the island has been a favorite vacation spot for people who choose to avoid the hubhub of nearby Martha's Vineyard. The amusements are simple. A bike ride. A walk by the shore. Or window-shopping. The galleries are expensive, but the wind and the sun are free. The Yacht Club bristles with boats.

Tucked into a slip over the Labor Day weekend was a large, powerful, motorized yacht called *Bethabelle.*

On board was a tall, purposeful man with a broad forehead, and thin, combed-back dark hair, gone gray from his long sideburns to his temples. On the man's mind was the Bendix vs. Martin Marietta drama.

"Ed, want a cold one?" a companion asked.

Edward L. Hennessy, Jr., reached out his hand.

At fifty-four, Hennessy was the chairman of the board and chief executive officer of the Allied Corporation, a huge international diversified giant with annual sales of well over $6 billion.

On Sunday, Hennessy went ashore to play some tennis.

On another court was Harry Gray from United Technologies.

The relationship between Ed and Harry had been a favorite of Wall Street wags for years. The scuttlebutt had it that they were "at odds," even "bitter enemies."

From 1972 to 1979, Hennessy worked for Harry Gray—the last two years as chief financial officer, group vice president, and executive vice president. Both men denied any ill feelings toward each other. But they circled each other socially like prize fighters. It was only a matter of time before they would meet in the business ring.

Some wags said Harry owed a measure of his success to Hennessy.

Others said Hennessy soured on Gray when his own rise at UTC was stymied.

Their respective staffs whispered about each other.

The men were competitive, perhaps too much alike.

Both men were hard-headed, blunt, ready to go it alone.

Within days of becoming president of Allied on May 1, 1979, Hennessy had assembled an acquisition task force. Within five months, Hennessy had decentralized the company, laid off seven hundred people, and saved the company $30 million in corporate overhead.

Hennessy did not win many friends around the Morristown, New Jersey, headquarters. He received some threats. For several weeks, Hennessy was shadowed by bodyguards. He never broke his stride.

Soon he made his first acquisition—paying $598 million for the Eltra Corporation, a divisified firm that manufactured automobile batteries, electronic equipment, and Converse athletic footwear. Hennessy later chewed up Eltra, keeping what he wanted and selling off Converse and other parts of the business.

Hennessy also sold off portions of Allied—selling a natural-gas pipeline in Louisiana in 1980, and its Canadian oil and gas subsidiaries in 1981.

By March 1982, Allied under Hennessy's leadership had acquired more than fifteen companies; purchases included $347 million for Bunker Ramo, an electrical manufacturing firm; $311 million for Fisher Scientific, a laboratory equipment manufacturer; and a $714 million joint acquisition of Supron Energy Corporation with Continental Group.

Hennessy had been interested in Bendix Corporation for several years. When he worked for Harry, Hennessy worked with and respected the Bendix energy controls division, which made fuel controls for the F-15 and F-16 fighters and the C-130 military cargo plane.

Hennessy was involved in targeting Bendix as a potential acquisition candidate for United Technologies. He also knew the antitrust problem because of the overlap in business between a UTC company, Hamilton Standard, and the Bendix energy controls division.

When he first joined Allied, the company was too weak to consider tackling the financially robust Bendix Corporation. Hennessy kept his eye on Bill Agee. Hennessy's time would come.

Harry Gray did not see Ed Hennessy on the tennis courts. He was told offhandedly that *Bethabelle* was in the harbor.

While Gray was on the phone with his team in Bethesda, Hennessy was conceiving a plan of his own. Ed tried to phone John Gutfreund, the cochairman of Salomon Brothers in New York. Hennessy could not get Gutfreund but did manage to get ahold of Jay Higgins.

"I see you are involved with Bendix," Hennessy told Higgins. "Tell John to give me a call."

Gutfreund later returned Hennessy's call.

"I just wanted you to know that I'm watching the situation," Hennessy told Gutfreund, "and if there is anything I can do to help, just give me a call."

"Thanks, Ed. The situation is well in hand, but I will keep it in mind."

Gutfreund passed the intelligence on to Bill Agee.

On Sunday, Andy Samet was in his office at the Bendix headquarters in Southfield. He sat before his bookcase of legal volumes with one of his assistant lawyers—Dick Sanderson, a young man with a black moustache and an eager disposition.

"Barron wants me to come to New York," Sanderson said.

"What are they looking at?"

"For the board meeting on Tuesday, Agee wants us to draft some golden parachutes for a bunch of Bendix people," Sanderson said.

With Bendix attacking Marietta, and with Marietta coming back at Bendix, this situation seemed like an escalating arms race to Samet, a deliberate man, well liked, but known to put secretaries to sleep with long, erudite dictation.

"So first Martin Marietta got parachutes," Samet said, "and now I guess its the senior executives of Bendix."

"Barron thinks it's a good idea," Sanderson said.

"Yeah."

With Sanderson sitting in front of him, Samet got on the phone and called New York. He spoke with Hal Barron, his boss, and John Cooke, VP for human resources and a member of the regular eight-man chairman's council. Samet wanted to make a point.

"John, I just want to say that Sanderson's client is the Bendix Corporation. He cannot be put in a position of representing the interests of specific individuals."

"That's clearly understood," Hal Barron said. "We know that Dick is the lawyer primarily in charge of the Bendix plans, and his assistance would be appreciated in drafting language."

"He'll be there tomorrow," Samet said.

Kathy Kress, thirty-four, was a secretary in Al McDonald's office. McDonald utilized two secretaries—like Bill Agee. McDonald's main secretary was Martha. Kress provided backup support. The personnel department at Bendix ranked employees according to levels. A new secretary would be a 13. Kress was a 16—senior administrative. Martha was a 20—executive secretary.

With Martha headed for a long-planned vacation in Canada, Kress was asked to go to New York.

A perky woman with a pleasant figure and short, permed hair, Kress seemed more like a girl reacting to the chance to go to New York.

"Don't get too excited," Martha told her before she left, "they are probably going to put you up at the Barbizon Hotel. No great shakes. The one good thing is you can walk to work."

Martha told a funny story. One night, at the Barbizon, she was sitting on her bed, with her head down, brushing her hair. She was startled to see under her bed a pair of men's shoes.

Martha also told Kathy about Al McDonald getting caught in the rain.

They shared a mischievous laugh.

"He never asked me to call him a cab!" Martha said with delight.

On Labor Day morning, Kress flew on the Bendix Jetstream to New York with a large group of company officers, including Al McDonald; Don Kayser, the chief financial officer; Bernie Winograd, the treasurer; and John Cooke.

Dick Sanderson from the legal department also came along.

Kress sat in her seat, eyes forward. She was nervous about the limousine reservations she had arranged, especially since McDonald was present. He made her nervous. There was something about the man that seemed cold and distant. When he gave her work to do, his attitude was "take this and don't ask me any silly questions." Many times Kathy would sit at her desk and try to solve the riddle, afraid to ask for clarification.

On the plane, McDonald surprised Kress.

"Hi, Kathy, how are you?" McDonald asked.

He was very pleasant and obviously in a good mood. The whole Bendix group was feeling positive. Over the weekend, an important deadline had passed—the proration period for the Bendix offer to buy Martin Marietta.

To qualify for the $43 per share offered by Bendix, Martin Marietta stockholders had to "tender" their shares to the Bendix depositary by midnight on Friday.

On Saturday, Bendix representatives were at Fidelity Union Bank in New York counting the number of shares tendered to the offer.

By Sunday, word had spread that the Bendix offer was oversubscribed. More than 58 percent of the shareholders of Martin Marietta stock had tendered their shares into the Bendix proration pool. The arbitrageurs, insurance companies, pension funds, and a myriad of other institutional investors as well as individuals had decided to get in line to sell their stock for $43.

The shareholders still had the right to withdraw their shares.

But assuming that remote possibility did not occur, at a minute after midnight on September 17, the Bendix Corporation would by law be allowed to purchase the Martin Marietta Corporation.

In New York, McDonald planned to work with Bob Meyers to draft a press release and to review the final text of an ad that was scheduled to run in *The Wall Street Journal* on Tuesday.

In the ad, Bendix would thank Martin Marietta shareholders

for their "overwhelming vote of confidence"—over twenty million shares had been tendered. Everything was going according to plan. McDonald had good reason to feel relaxed as he chatted with Kress.

"Have you ever been to New York?" McDonald asked.

"No—well, yes, once," Kress said.

McDonald smiled.

"I remember seeing ladies on the way to work wearing running shoes and carrying their high heels," Kress said. "And all the tall buildings."

"When I worked for McKinsey and Company," McDonald said, "my wife loved New York. She used to say 'I never want to leave.' We had a small baby at the time. And our apartment had a balcony. One day, my wife found the baby crawling on the balcony, and that made it easier to leave."

At the airport, the group split up, with McDonald and Sanderson and several others heading downtown in one limousine to meet with the lawyers. Kathy Kress found herself riding alone in the other limousine with Donald Kayser to the Helmsley Palace, where she waited in the lobby by her bag until Bob Meyers arrived and gave her instructions.

Bill Agee was going to be in his suite during the day, holding a series of meetings. Kress was placed in a room across the hall just in case Agee needed secretarial support. There was a typewriter and a telephone.

The ornateness of the Palace was exciting to Kress. It was the most beautiful hotel she had ever been in. When she was told that at the end of the day she would check into the Barbizon, Kress was ticked.

"Imagine leaving this beautiful room empty to sleep at the dumb old Barbizon," she said on the phone.

Marty Weinstein, the head of the Salomon Brothers four-desk arbitrage department, was in the backyard of his home in the Riverdale section of the Bronx when he got a call telling him of a meeting in a couple of hours in Ira Harris's suite at the Regency. Weinstein dreaded leaving his barbecue. His kids were in the pool. It was a gorgeous New York day, eighty-two degrees.

He threw his cigarette into the glowing coals.

Ira Harris had wound up his vacation in Hawaii and returned

to New York on Saturday. Agee had been on his case to come back and get involved. Harris kept trying to get Agee to accept the advice of Jay Higgins. Agee damned Higgins with faint praise.

"He's a good guy but you're the pro at Salomon," was the best Agee could muster in his conversations with Harris. It was also obvious to Harris that Higgins was getting frustrated with Agee. Harris spoke with Higgins every day, as a rule, even when Harris was on vacation.

"The guy is not dealing with me straight," Higgins said to Harris about Bill Agee. "He says one thing and does another."

Harris was not exactly certain what Agee wanted from him, but he agreed to a meeting. But first he would hold a meeting of his own at his suite at the Regency at Sixty-first and Park.

Harris invited the Salomon team—Jay Higgins, John Gutfreund (the cohead of the firm), Harold Tanner, and Marty Weinstein. Art Fleischer, Agee's outside acquisitions lawyer, was also invited.

Harris and Higgins both knew that the arbitrage side of an investment banking house often has the freshest contacts with the street. Weinstein was asked his opinion of where things stood.

"It's great that the proration pool is oversubscribed, but that's not the story. I think we need to make a conditional increase in our bid," Weinstein said, noting that the street already expected Bendix to boost their offer publicly to coax Martin Marietta into submission.

"Well, Marty, I've got to disagree with you," Art Fleischer said. "In my experience, until the target company's management expresses some interest in negotiating price, a conditional raise never works."

"Has Bill heard from Pownall?" Harris asked.

"Not a peep."

"What did you have in mind?" Harris asked Weinstein.

"I'm not saying we go soft, but what I am saying is that we should say to them, 'Look, we're buying at forty-three dollars and that's where we are gonna buy you, but if your board agrees to a friendly transaction, we'll pay fifty dollars.'"

"Why fifty dollars a share? That's a big jump. Why not forty-seven or forty-eight dollars?"

"It just seems to me that seven dollars times the number of

137

shares, thirty-six million, that's a quarter of a billion dollars. It's got that magic ring to it. I think the pressure on them would be heavy."

"That is not something I can support at this time," Fleischer said.

Fleischer's dissent squelched the conversation.

Harris and Higgins thought the increase in price was a good move but decided not to press the issue with Fleischer.

They would just have to move it to the right forum at the right time.

Following their meeting at the Regency, the group went by cab to the Helmsley Palace to meet with Bill Agee. They took the special elevator up to the suite on the forty-fifth floor.

Mary answered the door.

She graciously led the men into the living room of the suite.

Marty Weinstein, still thinking of his barbecue in the Bronx, went to a window. The view out the windows was over the shoulder of St. Patrick's Cathedral. A *Newsweek* magazine neon sign. There was a glimpse of Rockefeller Center. In the distance, a sliver of the Hudson River.

Bill Agee and Al McDonald were on the couches set at right angles.

Surprised to see so many men, Agee spoke briefly to McDonald.

"Let's break this meeting down into groups, shall we?" McDonald said. "My suite is nearby, and Don Kayser, Mike Rowny, and Bernie Winográd are over there."

"Marty," Harris said to Weinstein, "why don't you wait over there."

In the other suite, it was obvious that everyone was waiting.

The Bendix execs were there just to be available if needed.

"Do you mind if I turn on the TV?" Weinstein asked, looking for something to do.

"Not a good idea," one of the men said, concerned about appearances if McDonald or Agee should happen to walk in. Weinstein found the remnants of the Sunday *Times* and sat down with the crossword puzzle.

"So what are you working on?" McDonald asked the Salomon contingent.

"We have been discussing raising the bid," Harris said.

"Raising our bid?" Agee asked, feeling confident.

"A conditional raise—to send the right signal," Higgins said.

"To get Tom Pownall to sit down and talk," Harris added.

Fleischer repeated his doubts about the plan. The men talked about the concept without reaching any particular decision. It was an option to be considered. As is his approach, Harris cut right to a critical question.

"Bill, would you sell Bendix?"

"First you want us to raise our price and now you're asking if we want to sell the company?" Al McDonald asked incredulously.

"That is not my objective," Agee said, flatly.

"Do you have something in mind?" McDonald asked.

"I want to know the options you would consider, Al," Harris said.

Harris had no great love for McDonald.

The things Higgins was telling him made Harris think McDonald should go back to Harvard, where he belonged.

Agee did not mind planting the possibility of selling the company in Ira Harris's mind, but he did not want Jay Higgins scouring the earth looking for candidates to buy Bendix.

"We're not on the block, but I will examine all options," Agee said.

Bill wanted Ira to come to him with ideas.

Agee regarded his job with an unusually rational eye. He did not have particular prejudices. He admired any solid financial transaction.

On a beautiful, sunny Labor Day in New York City, while the Bendix advisers were meeting with Bill Agee, the Martin Marietta team and their lawyers assembled again at the Wachtell, Lipton offices on Park Avenue a few blocks away.

Having worked on the agreement between United Technologies and Martin Marietta for days, energies were beginning to lag. Almost everyone could think of something—almost anything—they would rather be doing than poring over the fine print of documents.

Ed Large had delivered on his promise of more information.

A group of business and technical people from UT's Pratt & Whitney company trooped through the proceedings, detailing their knowledge of the Bendix energy controls division in South Bend, Indiana.

And they knew a great deal from direct experience. Because Bendix was a crucial supplier to the F-100 engine, Pratt & Whitney quality control engineers had physically gone to South Bend over the years, talking with the Bendix personnel, inspecting the plant, and talking with the union labor leaders.

In their summary to the Martin Marietta management group —Pownall and Leithauser principally (Larry Adams, the chief operating officer, was in London at the Farnborough Air Show) —the Pratt & Whitney specialists quoted their recent orders from Bendix and made projections.

"You know about the labor problems in South Bend?" a P&W man said.

"Just what I've seen in the papers," Leithauser said.

"On August 26, about thirty-six hundred hourly employees —from United Auto Workers local nine—held a wildcat strike on the shop floor."

Leithauser looked at Frank Menaker.

"They didn't show up for the first shift," the P&W man added.

"Are there still labor problems?" Leithauser asked.

"Well, Bendix planned to move the business—or at least new orders—to a new plant in North Carolina because of the labor expense in South Bend. Next to Notre Dame University, Bendix is the largest employer in town. People are very concerned about the effects of the move on the local economy."

Leithauser and the Martin Marietta team listened carefully to a long parade of facts and figures. Menaker took notes on a yellow legal pad. The men occasionally broke the discussion so that the Marietta people could meet alone in Dick Katcher's office.

And then they were back with more questions.

Marty Siegel was taking a different approach to try to find the value of the business. Like a private detective, Siegel was calling around to former Bendix employees, looking for someone to talk to about fuel controls. It was plain knowledge that Bill Agee had lost a lot of friends in Southfield following the reorganization of the company.

Bill Panny, the president of the company, had been fired after he lost out in a power struggle with Agee. Panny was not very flattering about the impact that Mary had had on Bill.

Jerry Jacobson, the Bendix strategic planner, also fell out of favor because of his announced intention to act as a consultant to both Bendix and the Burroughs Corporation. Jacobson was asked to resign. Agee's old mentor turned nemesis, Mike Blumenthal, the head of Burroughs, took Jacobson in.

Bob Purcell, a former senior statesman on the Bendix board, also ran amok of Agee and his allies. Purcell resigned and took his story public in an interview with *Fortune* magazine. Purcell laid his animosity toward Agee on the table.

Joseph Svec was the head financial guy at Bendix before he was asked to leave by Agee because of "disloyalty."

Marty Siegel tried very hard to track down anybody he could get who would know the value of the business.

Siegel had in fact the day before gotten Joe Svec on the phone at his home in the Detroit suburb of Bloomfield Hills. Siegel had known Joe Svec for several years. Although not close, the two men had developed a working relationship during the Bendix acquisition of Warner & Swasey.

Siegel presented Warner & Swasey to Bendix.

Not yet working after having resigned in February his position as executive VP and chief financial officer of Bendix, Svec was interested in what Siegel had to say.

Svec had a lot personally at stake.

Svec had a holding of Bendix stock.

If Martin Marietta succeeded, he could make a nice nest egg.

Svec was also wary of Siegel, knowing the bitter struggle that was emerging. He did not want to be caught in the middle.

"Joe, let me come to the point," Siegel said. "Would you consider being a consultant to Martin Marietta?"

"What are they looking for?"

"We are examining several businesses of Bendix and would appreciate your input. In particular, we are interested in knowing more about the fuel controls business in South Bend, Indiana."

"What about it?"

"What it is worth . . . what kind of business it is . . . what the financials look like."

"I have to be careful," Svec said.

"It would be a straight consultant relationship, and I can guarantee you that no one would ever know."

Svec was already a consultant to Bendix.

He was making $15,834 a month through January 31, 1983.

He did nothing actively for the salary. It was part of the payoff he got when he resigned.

"Marty, look, I wouldn't mind helping you," Svec said after a long pause on the telephone. "I just don't think I can do it."

"Can I call you again?" Siegel asked.

"Sure."

"Thanks, Joe. I'll stay in touch."

"You know there are other people who might be more able to help," Svec said. He knew in fact there were more than a few. He had bumped into purged ex-Bendix guys more than once. The subject of bitter conversation was sometimes Agee and McDonald.

"I've got a couple in mind," Siegel said.

Time was running out on Tom Pownall. Despite the parade of experts and financial information provided by United Technologies, Pownall was unconvinced.

Harry wanted him to pay the $300 million up front for parts of Bendix that were of undetermined value. Pownall was trying to make rational business decisions, and the situation was asking him to throw his caution to the wind.

"To hell with it," Pownall said to his advisers during the early afternoon on Monday. "Unless we get more information, I'm just not prepared to go ahead. I'll walk away first."

The mood among the Martin Marietta management team was doom and gloom. They had worked so hard to put it together but if the CEO wouldn't bite, then that was it. The game was up.

Charlie Leithauser thought Tom was right to balk.

That left Charlie in a box with his discussions with Ed Large.

The positions of both sides were polarizing. Pownall did not want to go forward, and Harry Gray's man Ed Large had no new instructions. To maintain the workers' enthusiasm, Pownall did not share his doubts with anyone beyond his inner circle.

The Martin Marietta and UTC lawyers were in another conference room planning a lawsuit to be filed in Maryland by UTC if a deal was struck. United Technologies, at the suggestion of their bankers, had planned to publish advertisements in national newspapers such as *The Wall Street Journal* announcing their tender offer for Bendix.

As the 4:00 P.M. deadline for cancellation at the *Journal* drew near, the problem could not be held back any longer. UTC reps put out the word: Cancel the announcement of the UTC offer for Bendix.

As the teams were milling around the Wachtell, Lipton offices on the thirty-sixth floor of the high-rise on Park Avenue, Marty Siegel emerged from Dick Katcher's office very excited.

"We got him!" Siegel said. "We got a guy to talk!"

Tom Pownall, Charlie Leithauser, and Dick Katcher moved into the office. Katcher sat next to the window, Siegel in the chair behind the desk. Pownall took a seat on the couch. Leithauser stood. Siegel put the former high-ranking Bendix employee on the speaker box so that everyone in the room could hear the conversation.

"I know you have gone to considerable trouble to speak with us," Marty Siegel said, "we appreciate it and you can be sure that this meeting will remain confidential. I have several people in the room with me here—Tom Pownall, the CEO of Martin Marietta, and his chief financial officer, Charlie Leithauser. We would like to ask you some questions about the South Bend operations."

"Go right ahead," the man said.

Siegel and Leithauser then asked the informer a series of questions about the business: What kind of business is it? What kind of return does it throw off? Expenses? Does the value of the business justify a $300 million acquisition price? Is it a free-standing facility, or does it share space with other Bendix operations? Do they have shared computers? Why are fuel controls being moved to North Carolina? What is the labor situation? What is the pay scale like in comparison? What are the DOD contracts? Who are the key guys?

The list of questions continued to grow, and the answers continued to come back. Dick Katcher, who listened rather than participated, watched darkness fall on Park Avenue. Lawyers—Larrabee and Fullem and others from the Martin Marietta team —passed the door, poked their heads in, and drifted off to continue work on the assumption that a deal could still be struck with UTC.

The informant answered Charlie Leithauser's tricky financial questions. And everybody in the room assumed—knowing the man's former title at Bendix—that he was "someone who should know."

When Siegel hung up, he turned to Pownall, who was thinking intently.

"When did he leave Bendix?" Pownall asked.

"About a year ago," Siegel said.

"I think we can factor what he said and be reasonably up to date," Leithauser said.

Tom Pownall smiled.

"Neat," he said, baring his teeth.

He had enough information to proceed with the agreement on United Technologies' terms. He would stamp management approval on the package and lay it out for the board the following day.

FIFTEEN

In the morning, Tom Pownall awoke in his suite at the Waldorf-Astoria. Sunlight was warming the long drapes, casting the room in soft colors. He had been up so late the night before that he decided to stay over in New York. Whenever possible he went home to Marilyn, his wife of thirty-six years. The couple married just after Tom's stint during World War II and several years before his naval tour of the Korean peninsula.

Pownall was a soft touch with his family.

At sixty years old, Pownall was a vigorous grandfather. His thirty-one-year-old daughter Fuzzie had three children, including an eighteen-month-old boy, Eric. Pownall called the precocious little boy "LeRoy." And LeRoy called his grandfather "Weef." For a while, Pownall thought the little guy was trying to say "Chief."

During the past two weeks, Pownall struggled with his responsibilities as chief executive officer. In an odd way, Pownall began with almost no personal feelings about the situation. But once the directors voted to reject the Bendix offer, he had a mission. The takeover game was all so new, he worked very hard to get up to speed.

In his worst moments, once late at night at the bar with Larry Adams, Pownall said he didn't really give a damn what happened to him personally. If Agee won, he'd quit and spend his time with his grandchildren. He wanted to teach LeRoy how to spit and drive a tractor.

This new deal with United Technologies was seen by Pownall and his advisers as their best chance to stave off defeat.

"The street thinks Gray is a finisher. When the UTC bid is announced, the price of Bendix stock will go up to here," Siegel said, holding his hand above his neatly combed head during a morning prep meeting. If the stock market believed the Martin Marietta and UTC agreement had a chance, the price of Bendix stock would climb as investors bought up Bendix stock in the expectation that Harry Gray would strike a deal with Bill Agee.

Charlie Leithauser was looking at it another way.

"Martin Marietta and Bendix are going to be put together," Leithauser said, "maybe this will give us parity in negotiations with Agee."

That line got a smile from Pownall. It was like the U.S.A. vs. the Soviet Union. Our Pershing against their SS-20. Negotiations were the only way to get out from under the palisades of missiles.

The thirteen-man board of directors had been assembled for hours behind closed doors in the conference room at Dewey, Ballantine when lawyer Dick Katcher slipped out of the meeting and placed a call to his partner Marty Lipton, who was in Hartford with Harry Gray.

"Marty, the deal has been accepted. Pownall will call Harry on the conclusion of the board meeting."

Less than twenty minutes later, Pownall made his call with Dick Katcher at his side in a corner office at Dewey, Ballantine.

"My board has given its go-ahead," Pownall said to Gray after an exchange of pleasantries.

"Fine, Tom. I'll get my board to approve. We're on our way. Just one day off schedule."

"Harry, I've got some space reserved in *The Wall Street Journal* tomorrow and if you want, you can have it," Pownall said, remembering the dark moment in the negotiations when UTC was forced to cancel their announcement space in the *Journal.*

Gray thanked Pownall but did not mention that he had already reserved space on the hunch that Martin Marietta would come around.

"Are you going to come sign this thing?" Pownall asked Gray.

"Tom, Ed Large is already down in New York staying at the Essex House. Just send the papers over to Ed and he'll sign for me."

> 12:22 PM EDT SEPT 7-82
> HARTFORD CONN—DJ—United Technologies Corp. said it is commencing a cash tender offer for up to 11,900,000 shares of Bendix Corporation at $75 a share. . . .
> United Technologies said the offer is conditioned on Bendix terminating its tender offer for Martin Marietta Corp. without having purchased any shares and on Bendix not adopting the charter amendments which are to be considered by Bendix stockholders at a special meeting on Sept. 21. . . .
> If Bendix terminates its tender offer for Martin Marietta without purchasing stock the agreement says Martin Marietta will similarly terminate its tender offer for Bendix leaving United Technologies' offer as the only tender offer for Bendix.

Within a minute, trading in Martin Marietta and Bendix stocks was suspended on the New York Stock Exchange, pending the full dissemination of news. Trading of these shares did not resume for the rest of the day. The volume of Bendix stock trading in the morning had been light. With the price closing at $56, it was still disastrously short of Martin Marietta's offering price of $75.

At 3:36 P.M., the summary story from Dow Jones staff reporter Tim Metz crossed the wire:

> CONFUSION REIGNS IN WAKE OF UNITED TECHNOLOGIES' BENDIX BID
> NY—DJ—Wall Street professional investors are scratching their heads over the import of United Technologies Corp.'s plan to offer $75 a share for 50.3% of Bendix Corp.'s shares.
> Some professionals such as money manager Kazi Hasan of Hale Associates figure "this puts Bendix under an awful lot of pressure. Before people were saying that Martin Marietta's offer for Bendix wasn't serious. It sure looks serious now" he said.

However the United Technologies move could add impetus to Bendix' quest for Martin Marietta. One professional takeover trader noted that as previously reported United Technologies' offer is conditioned upon Bendix not buying control of Martin Marietta. "Presumably if Bendix does forge ahead and buy the Martin Marietta stock United Technologies would drop its offer," the takeover stock trader speculated.

With the third Bendix board meeting scheduled for 1:00 P.M. on Tuesday at the Bendix International offices on the twenty-first floor of the GM Building, directors were already beginning to arrive through the glass and gold bar double doors when the story of United Technologies' announcement was clacking noisily over the teletype machine Dick Cheney had had installed in the Bendix offices. Agee and McDonald were quickly alerted.

After reading the 260-word story, Agee settled his composure and walked briskly into the waiting area outside the boardroom. He chatted with Jack Fontaine. Agee intended to bring up "golden parachutes" for key Bendix employees at the day's meeting. Fontaine would manage the discussion.

Fontaine also wanted to talk with Agee about another subject.

"I talked with Dick Cheney," Jack said. "He reminded me that Marty Lipton is involved with Gray in this new development."

Bill Agee's eyes searched Fontaine's face.

"He may come after me or Mary the way he tried on the RCA deal," Agee said.

"We could prepare something," offered Fontaine.

"Good idea."

Dick Cheney knew a private investigator named Jules Kroll. Cheney knew him to be reputable. One of his men was the principal investigator for Ed Koch; another one was a former assistant DA. They could look around a little at Gray and UTC just in case.

"Just as an insurance policy," Cheney had said.

Word spread quickly through the ranks of the assembled directors that Harry Gray from United Technologies had made a bid. Only Professor Cohen from Texas and General Thomas Stafford were missing. The eleven present directors filed into the boardroom after indulging in soft drinks and dry sandwiches.

With the UTC bid adding fuel to the fire, Agee thought that this was a good time to unfurl management "golden parachutes." It had been discussed earlier, even before the Martin Marietta counteroffer, but at that time Agee, in discussion with Fontaine, decided that it was unnecessary and perhaps tactically unwise. Now there was nothing to hold back.

"We have a crowded schedule for today's meeting," Agee said after greeting the directors, who took their regular positions at the board table. William Tavoulareas sat next to Hugo Utyerhoeven and across the table from Donald Rumsfeld and Jack Fontaine. Director Jewel Lafontant sat next to Fontaine. The inside directors were toward the other end of the table.

"As a first order of business, I would like the board to consider employment contracts for key Bendix employees. As I am sure you are aware," Agee said in the direction of Tavoulareas, an experienced hand in takeover battles, "guaranteed contracts will go a long way in reassuring Bendix employees and maintaining a steady approach to our businesses. We have considered the issue carefully and with the assistance of the lawyers have prepared sample language and terms for a group of individuals. We are looking for board approval to proceed and formulate these contracts."

"Gentlemen," Agee said, sliding back his chair.

With that McDonald, advisers Hal Barron and Don Kayser, and the inside directors—Bill Purple, Fred Searby, and Paul Hartz—withdrew from the boardroom to allow the outside directors to hold an executive session to discuss the "golden parachutes." Jack Fontaine moderated the discussion. He opened a folder to examine his notes.

"The contracts call for a continuation of the executive's base salary and incentive compensation for a term of three years," Fontaine said. "The executive would keep company benefits such as health insurance as well as stock options. The triggering device is if there is a change of control of the company."

"It seems to me," Rumsfeld said, "that the number of people covered should be kept down to a handful of main people like Bill and Al and some of their people."

Rumsfeld had been chairman of the compensation committee but after earlier discussion he relinquished the responsibility to another director. Rumsfeld did not like controversy, and in his mind the whole Bendix vs. Martin Marietta battle was beginning to create a problem.

"But other people are affected, too. Why not cover all the officers of the company? They are all to some degree visible," a director said. "The list provided by management includes most of the officers. I think it should be all of them."

"One thing is for sure: I would rather see a shorter list than the one we've got here," Rumsfeld said. "But if all these guys are going to be included, then I think the term of Bill Agee's contract should be changed. If these other contracts are going to be three years, I think Agee's contract should be five years. He should not be hurt by doing this deal for Martin Marietta. And God knows with Harry Gray coming in if this thing does fall down, it may take him that long to find another job!"

The board voted to authorize the company to enter into contracts with the people on Agee's list, which included himself, McDonald, Hal Barron, John Cooke, Bill Purple, and four VP group executives from aerospace, Mike Rowny, Andre Laus (the new president of Fram Corporation, a Bendix subsidiary), Fred Searby (head of the industrial company), Don Kayser, Larry Hastie, and J. W. Weil. The term on Agee's contract was changed from three years to five years.

Following the executive session, Bill Agee and other executives returned to the board meeting, and R. W. Pogue, the lawyer from Jones, Day in Cleveland, was invited in to address the board of directors on the issue of their responsibilities concerning the SESSOP issue and the participants' rights to tender to the Martin Marietta offer. As the plan stood, the participants could not tender to the offer.

"I would like to say," William Tavoulareas began, "Jack Fontaine and I, at Bill's request, met with Dick and representatives from Salomon Brothers on Friday to review this issue. We decided at that time that a special board meeting before this meeting was not necessary and that more than likely the board would not be forced by legal considerations to amend the plan."

Dick Pogue distributed to members of the board a memorandum entitled, "Fiduciary Responsibility Under ERISA." Pogue was dressed very conservatively in a brown suit and restrained tie. His approach was objective, above the fray.

"One of my partners prepared this memo and I think it is instructive. The main issue at hand is the Salaried Employees

Savings and Stock Option Plan. As it stands, the plan participants cannot tender their shares to the Martin Marietta offer."

"That could make somebody mad—I mean, Martin Marietta
is offering seventy-five dollars in cash, and where is the stock
now?" a director said.

"Around fifty-six dollars," Agee said.

"Of obvious concern is the possibility that the board could
be sued by a participant because of the terms of the plan,"
Pogue continued. "A claim could be made that substantial financial damage was suffered by a participant in not being allowed
to tender his shares to the Martin Marietta offer. That potential
liability could run into the millions of dollars. However, it is the
opinion of my firm that the board would not be acting unreason-
ably and should therefore be immune from liability if the board
decides not to amend the plan to allow tenders to the Martin
Marietta offer."

After discussion, the board agreed not to give up their hold
on the SESSOP participants. The plan would not be amended.
Martin Marietta would be deprived of 23 percent of the company's stock. The feeling was that Marietta would go hungry on
Thursday at midnight when their proration deadline for Bendix
shares would expire.

"I would suggest that the chairman send a letter to the participants explaining the situation," Pogue said. Several directors
nodded their agreement.

"Yeah, at least tell them what they can't do," Rumsfeld said.

"What about the UTC offer?" another director asked.

Agee signaled Hal Barron, who went to the boardroom door
and invited Art Fleischer, Jay Higgins, Harold Tanner, and Mike
Rowny into the meeting. The men quietly took seats as Agee
began speaking.

"As you are all aware," Agee said, holding a piece of paper
in his hand, "the Dow Jones broad tape carried the announcement of an offer for Bendix just minutes before the beginning
of the board meeting. I would like to distribute to the board
copies of the UTC press release.

"In light of this UTC move, I feel it is imperative that we take
steps necessary to maintain our offer. We haven't actually seen
the filings yet—but I want to present to the board the option of
raising our price for Martin Marietta shares. Jay, why don't you
address this point."

"At this stage, it is very important to show strength on the street," Higgins said, speaking forcefully. "There could be withdrawals from our pool if the arb community loses confidence in our ability to weather the storm. To dramatize our staying power, Salomon Brothers is recommending that the price be raised to forty-eight a share from the current forty-three dollars."

"What am I gaining?" Tavoulareas asked, unfolding his hands.

"We're demonstrating our strength."

"Yeah, but we are bidding against ourselves. Why raise the price?"

"In the opinion of Salomon Brothers—"

"Jay, I don't mean to interrupt you, but frankly you've said that before, and I am looking for more than a slogan. What is this thing going to cost . . . what, maybe seventy-five or a hundred million bucks?"

"If we buy what we originally asked for, it's seventy-nine million dollars," Higgins said flatly, with a trace of irritation.

"So we're paying that money for what?"

"Salomon Brothers has a great deal of experience in negotiations of this sort. We feel a price rise is required."

Higgins seemed to be stepping over the line—almost challenging Tavoulareas by repeating the opinion of Salomon Brothers.

Jewel Lafontant, sitting across from Tavoulareas, was paying close attention. This was the first time she had really noticed Higgins out of the stream of advisers Agee brought in. She thought, "Egads, what's his problem?"

"Tav," Agee said, trying to separate the two men before a heated exchange, "as you can see from this press release, the UTC offer is conditioned on us not buying the Martin Marietta shares. I feel we could gain some ground with Wall Street by showing right off the bat that we are still determined to buy and that the UTC offer isn't going to affect us anyway. If their conditions are as stated, then they may back off when we buy Marietta, and raising the price is the best signal we can send."

Agee tried to smooth it over with Tavoulareas and felt uncomfortable with Higgins' power play. Agee would do something about Higgins soon.

The board was then canvassed, and the proposal to raise the price to forty-eight dollars was accepted. It was the way that

some of the directors slowly raised their hands that made Agee
realize the strain was beginning to show. The minutes prepared
by Hal Barron would read that the proposal was unanimously
approved.

Agee then read to the board a letter he intended to send to
Tom Pownall. It concluded with a third request to meet.

> Dear Mr. Pownall . . .
>
> I think it important that you and I meet promptly to
> discuss our revised proposal in a spirit of understanding
> and with a view to achieving a sensible, business-like
> solution in the best interests of the shareholders of both
> companies.
>
> Very truly yours,
> William M. Agee

After the meeting, Bill Agee was sitting in his office, with the
door shut. He had given instructions to one of his secretaries,
Marie, to hold his calls.

Agee wanted an uninterrupted minute to make a decision.

His phone buzzed, momentarily breaking his concentration.

"Mr. Agee, this is Barbara. I'm sorry. A Mr. Rohatyn is on
the line."

"Okay, put him through."

"Bill, I just wanted you to know that Harry would like to talk
to you about this situation," Rohatyn said.

"That's one hell of an offer," Agee said sarcastically.

"I could set up a meeting between you and Harry," Felix
said.

"You can tell Harry I don't think much of his price. What did
Harry expect me to do when he came out with an offer with so
many conditions attached? What has he got in mind?"

"Bill, I really think Harry can answer you better than I,"
Rohatyn said.

"Fine, I'll be willing to talk to him sometime."

"When?"

"Let's talk about it later in the week."

Although Agee sounded curt on the phone, in fact, he appreciated the call from Felix. If only Tom Pownall would pick
up the telephone, Agee thought. He had tried twice before to

get Pownall to talk. The letter made it three times. The man was being inflexible. At least Harry understands, Agee thought. Deals like these were meant to be talked out, face to face.

"Barbara?" Agee said to his intercom. "Tell Al to come in."

Agee wanted to talk with McDonald about Jay Higgins. After Higgins' emotional performance at the board meeting tangling with Tavoulareas, Agee wanted to make a change.

Fortune magazine in its September 6 issue ran a piece on the investment banking firm of First Boston Corporation, under the banner "The High Rollers of First Boston." The company's chairman, George Shinn, fifty-nine, was pictured in a plaid kilt marching on the lawn of his New Jersey home playing the bagpipes.

The article was a glowing puff piece on the explosively successful company. The litany of victories included helping DuPont stage a gigantic takeover in 1981—the $7.8 billion purchase of Conoco. First Boston got a fee of $14 million. Then came First Boston's repping of Marathon and another $17 million in fees. Then the score of the Cities Service deal.

Another photo pictured Bruce Wasserstein, from the mergers and acquisitions department, strolling down the carpet in a dark hallway at First Boston's headquarters in a skyscraper that rises behind the Racquet & Tennis Club on Park Avenue.

In the article, written by Lee Smith, Wasserstein was described as a "whiz kid, a brilliant architect of complex deals, although a little egotistical." For his labors, Wasserstein earned more than $1 million a year.

With Al McDonald, Bill Agee revisited his short list of investment bankers. Every major firm not already involved had been actively soliciting business from Bill Agee for days.

Among those pumping for a job was Bruce Wasserstein.

"First Boston has seen a lot of action," Agee said, thinking it over.

At his instruction, Mike Rowny gave Bruce Wasserstein a call.

"We are interviewing a number of firms," Rowny said. "Would you care to compete for being an adviser to Bendix as a supplement to Salomon Brothers?"

"When and where can we meet?" Wasserstein asked with elation.

"We would like to see you tomorrow morning at our offices in the GM Building on Fifth Avenue."

"Will Bill Agee be at that meeting?" Wasserstein asked.

"No. I will be there with Don Kayser, our chief financial officer. If the interview is to our satisfaction, you should expect to come back later in the day to meet with the chairman and Bendix president Al McDonald."

Leonard Larrabee was in the downtown offices of Dewey, Ballantine during Tuesday afternoon. He had decided to rent a car rather than take a taxi home to New Rochelle that night, as was his usual practice. As he walked through the black and white tiled waiting area, the receptionist called to him just as he was preparing to enter the elevator. A man was standing next to the receptionist's desk.

"Mr. Larrabee, this man has just delivered a letter for you."

"Oh, thanks," Larrabee said, walking back to receive the letter. The man nodded and departed. Larrabee opened the letter and began to read. It was Bill Agee's letter to Tom Pownall raising the price to $48 a share.

"Geez," Larrabee said out loud. He walked briskly back into the offices and headed straight for Bob Fullem's office. Fullem was at his desk.

"Bob, I just got this letter. Agee is raising his price. Will you deal with this, and I'll be right back in an hour. I got this rental car downstairs. . . ."

Fullem got on the telephone and called Dick Katcher at Wachtell, Lipton. Fullem read the letter over the telephone, with Katcher taking notes on a yellow legal pad. The tone of the letter riled the two lawyers.

"Listen to this," Fullem said, quoting the letter: " 'Your offer contends that it is probable that, for legal reasons, Martin Marietta will be able to exercise control over Bendix before Bendix can exercise control over Martin Marietta. I trust that your Board is not relying on this sentiment as a basis for continuing your offer. We believe that the analysis underlying this contention is faulty.' "

"We need to write a nose-tweaker back to these guys," Fullem said.

"Let me talk with Siegel."

"I called him and told him. Call me back."

Before he could dial Siegel's number, Dick Katcher's phone rang. His secretary said it was Siegel on the line.

"Don't you think we should respond immediately?" Siegel was talking very excitedly. "Can we have an immediate board meeting from a legal point of view?"

"Yes and yes."

"Let's get everybody together over at Dewey and put together this thing over the phone," Siegel said.

"I'm scheduled to go to California on a seven P.M. plane on other business, but I'll get somebody there," Katcher said.

By the time Larrabee got back with his rented car and returned to the office, Tom Pownall and Frank Menaker were waiting. Don Rauth was also there, as was Marty Siegel. John Hanigan, chairman of Genesco, was one of the few directors still in New York. The rest had scattered after the morning board meeting. Rauth and Pownall's secretary were trying to locate the directors for a telephonic board meeting. They were lucky. Most directors had gone home, and Rauth was able to reach them. One director was caught at a restaurant.

"Gentlemen," Rauth said, once the board members had all been patched in. The Martin Marietta management team and its advisers were seated in the conference room at Dewey, Ballantine. "Tom received a letter from Agee that we feel demands immediate attention by the board. Tom, why don't you read the letter."

Pownall then read the letter, noting the price rise to $48 and Agee's request for a meeting with him or the board.

"He says in the letter, 'Martin Marietta's Board is distinguished and experienced. I am certain that they are all well aware of their fiduciary responsibilities to all of your stockholders, including the decisive majority who have demonstrated their desire that our proposal be effected.'"

"I don't need Bill Agee to tell me my fiduciary duties," former Attorney General Griffin Bell said in his elongated southern drawl.

Pownall continued to read Agee's letter:

"'We have just had the opportunity to note the proposed offer by United Technologies Corporation for Bendix. We have requested our financial and legal advisers to carefully review the offer from all aspects. From the published reports, however, it is immediately apparent that the financial consideration proposed by United Technologies is even less than that proposed by Martin Marietta which our Board . . . determined was grossly inadequate.

" 'I have also noted that the United Technologies offer appears subject to a variety of conditions which raise questions about its commitment to the transaction. Finally, the entrance of United Technologies, with the concurrence of your company, confirms the judgment of our Board that Martin Marietta did not have the financial capacity to acquire Bendix and its offer was diversionary in nature.' "

"What the hell is Agee up to?" a director asked.

"He's saying that he won't be scared off," Bob Fullem said.

"But why the raise to forty-eight dollars? Who's he competing with?" Frank Ewing asked.

"I don't understand it," Jack Byrne said.

"The United Technologies announcement ads are coming out tomorrow," Marty Siegel said. "Agee is obviously trying to steal the thunder, and that's why it is imperative that we react strongly. Our feeling at Kidder, Peabody is that the price is inadequate at forty-eight dollars."

"Why are we getting worked up about a five-dollar price increase? I don't think it is really worth considering. Damn right it's inadequate," Griffin Bell said, sounding irritated for being bothered at home.

"Are you going to meet with him, Tom?" Jack Byrne asked.

"Not with a gun to my head," Pownall said. "Besides, I think the price increase is so small it's not worth talking about."

The board voted unanimously to reject the Bendix price increase.

After the meeting, Tom Pownall, at the insistence of his advisers, wrote a response to Bill Agee in which Pownall registered the company's rejection of the terms proposed by Bendix and a touch of the indignation felt by the board of directors:

Our Board of Directors, who are well aware of their responsibilities, are indeed distinguished and experienced, as you correctly observed in your letter to me of this date. Upon consideration of your revised offer, that Board has voted unanimously tonight to reject it on grounds of inadequacy and as being contrary to the best interests of Martin Marietta shareholders.

I can find no useful purpose to be served by a prompt meeting with you on the basis that you requested. . . .

We also find it puzzling that Bendix is pursuing its attempt to alter Bendix's charter in order to prevent the Bendix shareholders from deciding for themselves what is in their own best interests. . . .

You should by now clearly understand that we intend to achieve the objectives which we have established, either through our acquisition of Bendix or our agreement with United Technologies.

Very truly yours,
Thomas G. Pownall

SIXTEEN

The thought of Bendix passing the defensive charter amendments at a special stockholders' meeting was more than "puzzling" to Tom Pownall and the Martin Marietta team. It was ominous music.

Bill Agee had created a new battleground.

Leonard Larrabee found it hard to believe.

What made matters worse was that the SEC and the NYSE were cooperating with Bendix, allowing the normal proxy solicitation time frames to be drastically slashed.

A tireless worker, Larrabee tried to get some satisfaction. He instructed several lawyers from Dewey, Ballantine to go to Washington to meet with the Securities and Exchange Commission.

"Try to find out what the damn amendments look like," Larrabee said to the lawyers. "Tell the SEC we need to see the Bendix amendments. How can we prepare materials in opposition if we don't know what the hell they are saying?"

Larrabee wanted the SEC to stretch its rules and allow Martin Marietta to see the language of the Bendix amendments as soon as the amendments had been rubber-stamped by the SEC.

From his downtown office, Larrabee decided to call the New York Stock Exchange. He phoned Dick Grasso, the head of the stock lists department at the NYSE.

"What the heck is going on over there?" Larrabee asked Grasso. "I thought you guys had rules."

"What can I do for you?" Grasso asked, knowing he was going to get his ear chewed.

"How can Bendix get a clearance from you for a ten-day solicitation period? Your rules call for at least thirty days!"

"Thirty days are what's recommended. Bendix came to us a week ago and explained the situation and they've got a right to hold a meeting and try to pass amendments and if they're going to do that, the time requirement had to be shortened."

"It's outrageous!" Larrabee said, his nasal voice cracking as he got excited. "What about the poor bastards who want to get the seventy-five bucks that Martin Marietta is offering for Bendix shares? If these amendments pass—and how the hell can we fight effectively in a goddamn week?—if these things pass, there goes the seventy-five bucks! I mean, it's a given that if those proposals are adopted, Martin Marietta won't be around."

"We don't want to get involved in this mess," Grasso said.

"Are you going to let them flaunt the guidelines?" Larrabee shouted.

Grasso stuck to his guns. The Bendix stockholders' meeting would be allowed to proceed as scheduled on Tuesday, September 21.

On Wednesday morning, September 8, Arthur Fleischer got a call from his Washington partner Harvey Pitt, who was responsible for ferrying the Bendix amendments through the maze at the Securities and Exchange Commission. Pitt knew the system well—from 1975 to 1978, he was the general counsel of the SEC. At thirty-seven, Pitt was a well-known lawyer and author. A portly man, usually dressed in a conservative three-piece suit, his beard well manicured, Pitt had exciting news for Fleischer.

"I just got a call from Brian Cooney, the staffer I've been working with at the Division of Corporate Financing," Pitt said. "He said they have no further comments. The amendments have cleared the SEC!"

"Outstanding," Fleischer said.

Pitt had jockeyed the amendments through at a record speed.

The Bendix plan was unfolding smoothly. With the materials cleared by the SEC, the Bendix staff and hired consultants prepared to mail a white voting card and instructions to each Bendix stockholder.

A "yes" vote would crush the plans of both Martin Marietta and United Technologies.

Larrabee heard the SEC news, too.

He delivered it to Bob Fullem, who was in his office on a chilly, overcast day. Clouds seemed to hang heavily on the shoulders of the skyscrapers outside Fullem's floor-to-ceiling window.

"The SEC has cleared the Bendix proxy materials," Larrabee said, glumly. "And they still won't show us even a draft. They say we're gonna have to wait like everybody else until Bendix puts the cards in the mail."

"We won't have to wait long," Fullem said, adding, "besides, if we don't get some action from Wall Street in the next thirty-six hours, nobody is gonna give a damn about the meeting. Bendix won't need it!"

"How is it looking? Are the Bendix shareholders tendering their stock to Martin Marietta?" Larrabee asked.

"The bankers say the response is anemic at best," Fullem said.

"Didn't the price of Bendix stock go up?"

"Yeah, but not near enough. The arbs still don't have much faith that Martin Marietta is going to succeed. So nobody's tendering their stock."

"Will we get fifty percent?" Larrabee asked.

"Not a chance," Fullem said.

"Oh, jeez," Larrabee said, pacing the room.

With few Bendix stockholders getting in line for the $75 promised by the Martin Marietta offer, both men suspected the war was nearing a decisive battle.

"Len, you better start writing some rosy press release to explain all this come Friday morning."

Next to Bank of America, Citibank was the largest private financial institution in the country. In 1982, headed by Chairman and CEO Walter B. Wriston, Citibank was a sprawling multibillion-dollar bureaucracy with two committee chairmen, three vice chairmen, sixteen executive vice presidents, forty-two senior vice presidents, and a veritable army of line vice presidents.

Citibank was in an unusual position in the Bendix and Martin Marietta fight. The commercial side of the bank was loaning Martin Marietta $140 million. In addition, Citibank was the depositary for the Martin Marietta offer. All Bendix stock tendered to Martin Marietta would be tabulated and controlled by the bank office at 111 Wall Street.

The investment side of the bank was the trustee of the Bendix SESSOP. The importance of that large block of Bendix stock held by the Bendix employees was not lost on anyone at Bendix or Citibank.

A trustee agreement governed Citibank.

The Bendix position was that the bank could not—under the terms of the agreement—tender any Bendix stock to the Martin Marietta offer. That position was confirmed by two different vice presidents of the bank.

But there were details to handle.

"What are we going to do with all this tender offer paperwork that Martin Marietta dumped on us?" Ed Smith, a bank VP, asked. "They want us to deliver it to the SESSOP participants." He was talking with a Bendix attorney, Dick Sanderson.

"Well, you guys should write a cover letter and send the whole package out," Sanderson said.

"What should we say?" Smith asked.

"Say that the enclosed materials are for your information only. Tell the Bendix employees that the bank doesn't have the power to tender to the offer."

"Dick, I've got to talk to my people—the lawyers—and get them involved in drafting the letter," Ed Smith told Sanderson. The two men knew each other on a collegial first-name basis since having worked closely together on Bendix business in 1981.

Smith called the institutional investment division lawyer, Jamie Long, another Citibank vice president. Smith and Long worked together with Dick Sanderson, his boss, Andy Samet; and Hughes, Hubbard lawyer Bob Enright on the procedural aspects of sending the materials.

Both Ed Smith and Jamie Long passed the word on at Citibank.

The decision climbed higher and higher. Long called his boss in the general counsel's office, Robert Dinerstein, who in turn contacted Paul Collins, the executive vice president in charge of the capital markets group. Collins was on the top floor of the bank's corporate offices on Park Avenue—just down the hall from the chairman of the bank, Walter Wriston.

Meanwhile, having passed the problem higher, the line guys —Ed Smith and his lawyer Jamie Long—were continuing their discussions with Dick Sanderson at Bendix.

"Are you sure that Bendix is not going to amend the plan?" Smith asked the Bendix team. "Has your board of directors considered amending the plan to allow us to tender?"

"Our board has considered amending the plan and they decided not to in regard to the Martin Marietta offer," Dick Sanderson said.

"What about the United Technologies offer?"

"The board plans to meet on Friday to discuss it."

"Okay," Long said. "I guess that's it."

Through conference phone calls, the Bendix and bank lawyers drafted a transmittal letter from Citibank to the participants. Once the language was agreed upon, the letter was sent to the company's printer on Wednesday. By return messenger, the Bendix team was sent a printer's copy.

The two-paragraph letter concluded:

> We as Trustee cannot tender shares held in trust under the Plan since the Trust Agreement, absent of amendment, does not permit the Trustee to sell any Bendix shares except as necessary to facilitate cash withdrawals from the Plan by participants. Accordingly, this material is being furnished to you for your information only.
>
> Very truly yours,
> Citibank, N.A., Trustee, The Bendix Corporation
> Salaried Employees' Savings and Stock Ownership
> Plan.

Doris Rush was at her desk at Martin Marietta headquarters. She was on the phone with her boss, Frank Menaker. It was their first discussion since before the Labor Day weekend.

"Frank, I think I know how to pry loose the Bendix SESSOP shares. At least I have a good chance."

"That's the good news. What's the bad news?" Menaker asked.

"I can't do it through Dewey because they don't agree with the theory—and I admit this area is gray and legally undecided —but I think something is there."

"Did you talk with the Dewey people?"

"Briefly. I don't think they're interested."

"So what's next?"

"I'm going to shop for an opinion," Rush said.

"Uh-hmm," Frank said unenthusiastically. With the deadline for tendering to the Martin Marietta offer only a little more than thirty-six hours away, shopping for a legal opinion seemed like a waste of time. But looking at the determined expression on Rush's face, Frank knew that Doris was serious.

"Do you know where to go?"

"I've got some ideas."

Doris had only one name to call—Maureen Donovan, a skilled lawyer with ERISA experience from the firm of White & Case. She was a friend. Maureen was in and out of meetings all day. Doris caught her briefly. There was a problem. The firm had a new client committee. It would take time.

"And Doris, we represent Citibank on a bunch of things. I don't think this would fly politically," Donovan said.

"Who can I call?" Rush asked.

The first name on a short list provided by Donovan was Arthur Sporn of the law firm of Barrett, Smith, Schapiro, Simon & Armstrong. Doris reached Sporn at his office at about 11:00 A.M. on Wednesday, September 8.

As she got on the phone with Sporn, former Martin Marietta general counsel Jim Simpson peeked his silver-haired head into her office. She waved him in, indicating a chair.

"Mr. Sporn, this is Doris Rush of Martin Marietta. How are you? Your name was given to me by Maureen Donovan of White & Case. I have a fiduciary problem I would like to discuss. I assume you've been following what's going on with us in the papers?"

"Yes, I have."

She went on to explain the Citibank situation, her approach to solving the problem, and her legal thinking and rationale of fiduciary responsibility.

"I think Citibank has the legal responsibility to tender the SESSOP shares to our pool. Do you agree?"

"I do."

164

"You do?" Rush asked again.

"I do."

"Great. Could you write an opinion to that effect for delivery to Citibank?"

"Well, yes, I think we could do that, but it's not the kind of thing that can be done in twenty-four hours."

"Who said anything about twenty-four hours?" Rush said excitedly. "I will be in your office in two hours. I'll come prepared to help you. All right?"

"Well, fine."

Hanging up, she turned her attention to Jim Simpson, who was leaning over her desk to deliver several pieces of paper.

"I talked to Frank and he said you were working on the SESSOP situation," Simpson said. "Several days ago I talked to my niece, who works at the Department of Labor. I think maybe we should try to get them involved. Here are my notes from my conversation with her and her phone number. If we could get the government to lean on Citibank, it could help."

"Wonderful," Rush said. "Are you taking the noon flight to New York?"

"Yes."

"I'll go with you."

Doris had figured on the phone with Sporn that it would take her twenty-five minutes or so to get to Dulles International Airport outside Washington, and then the Martin Marietta G-2 jet would get them to Newark Airport in about forty-five minutes and then it would be another thirty minutes to Manhattan. She was cutting it close. But the schedule was tight. Tonight she had to attend a meeting of the banks, scheduled by Mendenhall. Tom was trying to line up a second loan agreement, per Charlie Leithauser's instructions. Mendenhall was looking for another $400 million in loans.

Grabbing her suitcase left by the door of her office, Doris headed out with Jim Simpson. They were joined on the flight to New York by Menaker, Leithauser, and Pownall, who did not talk about where they were going. Respecting the secrecy of some of their proceedings, Doris did not ask.

After instructing the limo driver where they wanted to go, the Martin Marietta people were divided into groups based upon their destinations. Doris was put in the limo with Tom Pownall and Frank Menaker.

"How are you doing Doris?" Pownall asked.

"I think I've got a live one with the SESSOP shares."

"Is there anything new?" Menaker asked.

"Well, it's just shaping up. I think we can come on pretty strong. After all, Citibank is supposed to be the trustee. They're supposed to do everything for the sole benefit of the participants, and here you have a case where the participants are trapped. Nobody can act for them. They can't act for themselves, so if Citibank doesn't act for them, who will? Nobody is looking after their interests. That's not what ERISA requires.

"And the clincher is not just the fiduciary responsibility argument. Citibank has everything to gain and nothing to lose. If they tender, the shares could still be withdrawn. But if they don't tender, then the Bendix plan participants will get the lower back-end price. Citibank could be liable for one hundred million bucks!"

"Sounds good," Pownall said as he and Menaker stepped out of the limousine. Doris looked out of the car at the surrounding high-rises, wondering where they were going. Downtown, there were hundreds of places.

The offices of Barrett, Smith, Schapiro, Simon & Armstrong were located at 26 Broadway, at the tip of Manhattan, easy walking distance from the Federal Court House, an imperial building with enormous columns.

Arthur Sporn, fifty-five, was a Harvard man all the way. He received both his undergraduate and doctoral degrees from Harvard, *magna cum laude*. He was also editor of the *Law Review* there and a member of Phi Beta Kappa.

Doris Rush met Sporn in his office at 2:00 P.M. as promised. She found that Sporn was curious about her plans. He had been following the Bendix and Martin Marietta story in the newspapers and was just a touch excited to be getting involved.

Rush explained to Sporn the timetable. At midnight tomorrow—September 9—the proration period of the Martin Marietta offer would expire. That meant that if at least 50 percent of the Bendix stock was not tendered to the pool, the Marietta offer would die a quick death.

"We need those SESSOP shares. I want a legal opinion delivered to Citibank early tomorrow," Rush said.

"You realize that means I'm probably going to have to work half the night to get it in shape?"

"Yeah, I know that, and I expect to pay for it." Doris looked at her watch. "I have a meeting uptown at 8:00 P.M. It's a little after 2:00 P.M. now. What say we start."

Rush and Sporn talked for more than five hours, devising an outline for the legal opinion on why Citibank should tender the Bendix shares it held in trust. Doris mentioned the conversation with Ivan Strassner at the Department of Labor; Strassner agreed very strongly with her approach because the plan was structured so that the participants had no opportunity to tender their shares. Rush and Sporn had several problems, not the least of which was they did not have a current copy of the trust agreement between Bendix and Citibank.

"I'll be in your office tomorrow morning at nine A.M. to go over the final draft," Doris said as she left to go to Tom Mendenhall's bankers' meeting.

One advantage to sending Tom Mendenhall a telex promise to lend money was that it got you a ticket to the dinner buffet planned for Wednesday night at the Dewey, Ballantine midtown office at 101 Park Avenue. A cold prime rib roast beef buffet was served in a conference room. It was preceded by a cocktail hour that deliberately ran long.

Doris Rush mingled with the bankers before she was called away by a phone call. Mendenhall began the proceedings.

"As I'm sure you know, we are going to put together another agreement for somewhere between three hundred and five hundred million dollars. We want to put it together in the next week to ten days. It will be based upon the agreement that you have in your hands. I know you have a lot of questions about our intentions. We will try to be diligent and answer them all. I would like to introduce Larry Adams, the chief operating officer of Martin Marietta."

Calm and collected, Larry Adams smiled at the bankers and then launched into a general summation of the company's position and financial requirements.

Mendenhall felt relieved that Adams had agreed to address the bankers. He was perfect. A straight shooter, direct and methodical, Adams was just the right guy for the job. He could wave the flag and let the bankers know that someone was still running the company, that the Bendix mess had not swallowed up every officer, leaving the company's customers to twist in the wind.

The bankers had dozens of questions.

What about the Bendix shark-repellent amendments?

Can Martin Marietta win the proxy battle?

Doug Brown from Kidder, Peabody attended the meeting. Brown had a wry sense of humor. He passed out Xerox copies of a cartoon showing a chairman addressing his board of directors.

The cartoon chairman said, "Gentlemen, I was afraid this might happen. After one of the most vicious and expensive proxy battles in the history of our industry, I now discover that we have succeeded in taking over ourselves."

None of the bankers laughed.

With Bendix planning on buying Martin Marietta and Martin Marietta threatening to buy Bendix in retaliation, the joke too painfully resembled the truth.

The phone call Doris Rush received during the cocktail hour of the bankers' meeting was from Frank Menaker. Tom Pownall was with him. Doris found a quiet side room to speak freely.

"Frank, what's up?"

"Doris, I'm going to put you on the speaker phone so we can all talk. We've just come across a letter that Agee has written to all plan participants."

"What's it say?"

Menaker read from a letter dated September 7 from Agee to the members of the Bendix SESSOP:

" 'As described more fully in offering materials being forwarded to you by Citibank . . . Martin Marietta has made an offer . . . to purchase up to eleven million nine hundred thousand shares. . . . That offer as it presently stands set forth a proration date of September 9 . . . the offer expires September 28.' " Menaker paused to add emphasis. " 'Under the Plan, withdrawals of Company stock by you can be made only as of the last day of a calendar month (e.g. September 30) and shares would not be received in time to make an effective tender under the Martin Marietta offer.' "

Rush was ecstatic. She thought, Oh, my God, Agee has hung himself!

"Frank, that's beautiful, that's absolutely beautiful. It's the best thing that could have happened!"

"I thought you'd like it," Menaker said.

"He's actually telling them they're trapped and can't do anything about it! Frank, you've got to get that over to Arthur Sporn at Barrett, Smith. Look, it's after hours, but you're just going to have to make sure the messenger has got to put that letter in Sporn's hands."

Rush gave Menaker the address and floor number.

"You got it, Doris," Frank said. "Call me tomorrow after you've seen the opinion. We want to take a look."

Shortly before 11:00 P.M., Bruce Wasserstein and his associate Tony Grassi from First Boston Corporation were ushered into Bill Agee's suite on the forty-fifth floor of the Helmsley Palace Hotel. Al McDonald was also present for the meeting with the bankers. Mike Rowny, who had met with both men earlier in the day, made the introductions. The men engaged in precious little small talk before getting down to business.

"We would like you to consider our response to the United Technologies offer," Al McDonald said.

"What are your ideas?" Agee asked, turning to Bruce in a friendly way. "I'd like to get your best thinking on the subject."

Wasserstein knew this first meeting with Agee would be a dog-and-pony show, with each man maneuvering for position. As the new adviser, Wasserstein was looking for more information, while Agee was trying to detect if Wasserstein had any pearls of wisdom from his takeover battle experience.

Wasserstein was a large man. His suit jacket bulged. With oversized round glasses, wiry hair, a lumbering gait, and an intensity that never failed him, Wasserstein seemed more an absentminded professor than a Harvard M.B.A. turned lawyer turned investment banker.

Bill Agee had a way of appearing innocent that made Wasserstein do a double take. Agee asked simple and direct questions. For his part, Agee had a natural distrust of advisers, be they bankers or lawyers. They are always looking over their shoulder for the next deal, Agee thought. After two weeks of living through this battle with Martin Marietta, Agee knew that the outcome would affect his entire business career.

"Are you replacing Salomon Brothers?" Wasserstein asked.

"No, we're not," McDonald said. "We are simply adding to the team."

Bill Agee knew that being asked to come in and supplement Salomon Brothers was heady stuff for Bruce Wasserstein. Unless First Boston totally screwed up, this would be a big boost for the firm's rap on the street. Agee listened carefully as Bruce Wasserstein discussed the possible alternatives available to Bendix. Agee was impressed with Wasserstein's decisiveness. The decision to hire First Boston had already been made. The session was to allow the men to make adjustments to each other's expectations.

"The worst thing that could happen is to sell the company at the effective price of the UTC offer," Agee said emphatically. "How do you see the blended price?"

"Around sixty-two dollars. It's a lowball bid."

"I agree."

"The main thing to do at this point is not to do anything rash. You have to very carefully think through the options you've got and you've got a lot," Wasserstein said. He ticked off a series of possibilities. "What has Salomon done in terms of research?" he asked.

"They have basically done a series of analytical papers," Al McDonald said, thumbing a set of documents in his hand. "We do not think that Salomon has properly prepared a framework of likely options—we do not have what I would call a central decision tree. They have a tendency to react on a day-to-day basis. We want to be able to see as far ahead as possible."

"Can you work with Jay Higgins?" Agee asked. "I'm looking for a synergy between you guys."

"That's no problem. We've been called in like this before. It won't be a problem."

After the meeting at the Palace, Bill Agee and Al McDonald were impressed with Bruce Wasserstein. Agee thought his experience would be a valuable addition to the team. And both men saw something in Wasserstein that was missing in Salomon Brothers—an unquestioned leader. Jay Higgins was never more than a day-to-day man in the minds of Agee and McDonald. Gutfreund and Ira Harris had the stature and experience, but neither man was stepping forward to shoulder the load.

Having decided to add Bruce Wasserstein and First Boston Corp. to the Bendix team, Agee was then faced with integrating the efforts of his two bankers. Both Agee and McDonald knew that it was not going to be easy to smooth things over with Salomon Brothers. Egos are bruised easily on Wall Street, where reputation is your next meal ticket.

"I'll call Gutfreund," Agee said.

"I'll talk to Harold Tanner," Al McDonald said. Tanner and McDonald were old school chums from Harvard Business School.

Agee telephoned John Gutfreund, the cohead of Salomon Brothers, and informed him that Bendix was planning to retain First Boston.

"John, look, I've got multiple law firms and multiple PR firms. I think I should have multiple investment bankers. First Boston will be supplementing your efforts."

"That's not the way it is going to look to the street."

"John, I have great respect for your firm. This is not going to affect Salomon's compensation. We think Jay has done a fine job. I want you guys to work together with First Boston."

Al McDonald got a stiffer response from Harold Tanner.

"We don't like it one damn bit," Tanner said.

The mergers and acquisitions brain trust of Salomon Brothers—Ira Harris, John Gutfreund, and Jay Higgins—had a late-night conference call on the problem.

"I want to resign the account," Higgins said. He was very angry. He snapped out his words like bullets.

"The guy is two-faced," Higgins said. "Agee tells me one thing and then turns around and does something else. And he won't even let me talk with Marty Siegel! He's in over his head! He and McDonald blame me for the fact that Martin Marietta came back at them. McDonald was at the meetings in August before this whole thing started. I told him then that Martin Marietta could conceivably come back at Bendix. And he got on his high horse and told me, 'Oh, Jay, that's impossible! Oh, that would be totally inappropriate on their part! No board would okay such a disastrous move!' And now he's blaming the whole thing on me!"

"No matter how impossible the client is," John Gutfreund said, deciding company policy, "we're not going to resign the account when that client is under fire."

On Thursday morning, September 9, Doris Rush woke up early in her hotel room. A lot was on her mind. Midnight tonight was the proration deadline for the Martin Marietta offer. If a substantial number of Bendix shares were not tendered to the "pool," the battle was lost. Doris dressed quickly, wearing a neat blue suit and a blouse with a ruffled collar. She roughly brushed her platinum hair, checked the mirror, applied her lipstick and blush and repacked her purse as she left the room.

The meeting at Barrett, Smith with Arthur Sporn was scheduled for 9:00 A.M.

Sitting in Arthur Sporn's office, Doris read the thirteen-page letter slowly, taking in each point. Sporn had done a very good job. He had captured the essence of what Doris was looking for. He had also incorporated the damning portions of Agee's letter to the SESSOP holders.

"This is great," Doris said. "I think I found one typo. I wouldn't change a word!"

It was ready to be delivered. Last night, Doris had promised Frank Menaker that he would see the letter before it was delivered. She called him over at Dewey, Ballantine.

"Doris, I want you to bring a litigator from Barrett, Smith over here when you come," Frank Menaker said.

"What's up?"

"We're thinking of announcing this morning that if Citibank does not tender tonight, we're going to enter a lawsuit against them."

"Yeah, but Frank, to do that you need standing. Only employees who are participants in the plan or the Department of Labor has got standing to sue."

"We've got a current Bendix employee who is willing to sue," Menaker said. Doris was shocked.

"Jesus, Frank, does the person know that if this goes to trial, he will have to go public?"

"He was told and it doesn't seem to faze him."

Doris Rush left with the opinion letter to Citibank and headed by cab to Dewey, Ballantine. Arthur Sporn was to follow with his litigation partner Michael Finkelstein.

Frank Menaker read the letter. He asked Doris her opinion. Agreeing with her, he said it looked good.

"Doris, I spoke with Fullem about why we went to an outside law firm on this one," Menaker said in passing. "I told him that they had never responded and that we were running out of time. But I want Bob to read this."

Doris smiled and acknowledged. There were politics involved, some of which Rush did not understand. She thought Len Larrabee was the main Dewey, Ballantine lawyer, but by

172

Frank's tone, it was obvious that Fullem was the key strategist.

"Is it ready to send?" Menaker asked.

"Sporn will be here momentarily with the ribbon copy."

When Sporn arrived with Michael Finkelstein, the lawyers huddled with Menaker. Their drill was to draft a complaint against Citibank for not tendering the Bendix SESSOP shares to the Martin Marietta offer. The Bendix employee would be the one actually to sue.

Fullem, Larrabee, Menaker, Rush, Sporn, and Finkelstein sat in Fullem's office and talked with the Bendix employee, who was on the telephone. Fullem had it set up on the speaker so that everyone could listen. After thoroughly discussing the implications of the lawsuit on his career at Bendix, the employee was ready to go ahead. He was dissatisfied and gave the impression he would not be at Bendix long in any event. The lawyers took notes and thanked the man.

"Well, you know, what do you think? Do you think we should really bother with this?" Fullem asked Menaker after reading Sporn's letter to Citibank. He was concentrating on the lawsuit planning. He left the room momentarily.

"I want you to work with Finkelstein on drafting the complaint for the lawsuit," Menaker said to Rush.

"Frank, if we could just get that letter over to Citibank, maybe we won't even have to do the lawsuit."

"Yeah, we intend to do that. Wait till Bob comes back."

Doris was getting more and more concerned. She had thought that the letter would be delivered in the morning, giving the Martin Marietta team of lawyers time to go over to Citibank and sit down with the Citibank lawyers. In the hall, Rush expressed her impatience to Tom Mendenhall.

"Doris, you've got to learn to be more firm with your boss. We've got to get that letter over there, and Frank's letting Fullem sidetrack him on ten other things." Doris thought Thanks a lot, Mendenhall. I'm sure you do that with Bob Powell. Doris returned to the office none too certain how to proceed.

"Bob, you talked to a Citibank lawyer, is that correct?" Menaker asked Fullem upon his return.

"Jamie Long. Yes, I talked with him earlier and asked them if they were going to tender and he said "No, we can't. We don't have the authority to.' As I understand it, a letter is at the Citibank printers to that effect as of last night."

"Well, we really should deliver this opinion letter over to them."

"All right," Fullem said, buzzing his secretary. He dictated a two-line cover letter that said "Attached is a legal opinion which Martin Marietta has obtained. If you would like to discuss this, please contact us."

The letter was finally on its way.

SEVENTEEN

Duuring the day on Thursday, September 9, Fred W. Searby, president of the Bendix industrial group, was in Chicago at the International Machine Tool Show. He was dogged by a *Washington Post* staff writer, Mark Potts, who wanted a comment on the latest development in the takeover struggle, the entrance of United Technologies.

Searby, forty-eight, was brought to Bendix by Al McDonald from the Cleveland office of the management consulting firm of McKinsey & Company, McDonald's old alma mater. A dark-haired executive, Searby was the newest member of the Bendix board of directors.

He spoke with Potts at the trade show and predicted that the board would "come out swinging" in regard to the UTC offer.

Potts also talked to Searby about the SESSOP situation and the fact that the plan did not allow the Bendix participants to tender their shares to the Martin Marietta offer to buy Bendix stock at $75 a share.

"The Bendix SESSOP participants may want the seventy-five dollars, but [if they sell that may] change the character of the company and cost them their jobs."

Meanwhile, the Bendix publicity machine was turning out a press release on Thursday to counter the Martin Marietta argument that Bendix was preventing Bendix employees from tendering their shares to the Martin Marietta offer.

> NEW YORK—Bendix today charged Martin Marietta with spreading misinformation about the Bendix Salaried Employees' Savings and Stock Ownership Plan. Bendix said employees under that plan can withdraw their stock and tender it following the end of any month after giving notice on the 15th.
>
> Bendix said, "Martin Marietta, in its haste to counter tender with a front-end loaded scheme, did not take the month-end provisions of the plan into account when it set its 10 day cash proration period. Now it is attempting to cover up its bad timing by accusing Bendix of coercing employees.
>
> It is logistically impossible to allow participants in the plan to tender for cash in the 10 days allowed by Martin Marietta."

Tom Pownall was sitting with Larry Adams, his chief operating officer, in a side room at the Dewey, Ballantine downtown law offices. Lawyers and other Martin Marietta executives were coming in and out with messages and updates. Pownall got up to stretch his legs, tired of the seemingly endless processions of meetings. He adjusted the waistband of his trousers.

"From what this says," Pownall said, holding a sheet of paper in one hand, "there is a damn good chance that come midnight tonight we're gonna look pretty skinny."

Pownall was looking at a summary sheet of stock tendering to the Martin Marietta offer. The projections from the bankers were not optimistic.

Pownall was tired. He dropped the sheet onto the desk and used both hands to rub his face.

"Tom, let's just think about this from Agee's perspective," Adams said. "What would you be doing right now?"

"Probably planning how I was going to run the combined company."

"Yeah. And I bet he has an operational plan that includes you and Caleb Hurtt [head of aerospace] and maybe some other guys. I bet Agee thinks he can get the company and the people. I think he's in for some surprises."

"It just ticks me off thinking of Agee running our programs,"

Pownall said. "That *Business Week* article is on the money. It says Agee sees himself as a wily financier. What the hell is going to happen to the MX and the Pershing and the whole list in the hands of a guy like that?"

"Well, if he does buy us, I'm not going to stick around," Adams said.

"No?" Pownall asked.

"Agee's got McDonald. What are my chances? Besides, I may enjoy an early retirement."

Pownall did not need to say a word. The two men understood each other.

"That's the flaw in Agee's thinking," Adams said. "He expects that the men he really needs to run the company are going to stay."

By shortly after 2:00 p.m., Citibank receipted the hand-delivered opinion from Arthur Sporn of Barrett, Smith. While Doris Rush was at Dewey, Ballantine working on the Bendix employee complaint against Citibank, the countdown had begun. Tabulations were being run at Citibank about the numbers of shares that had been tendered by Bendix stockholders. Rush called Doug Brown.

"Look, Doug, I'm going to stick to the bitter end here at Dewey. Can you keep me posted on how it's coming in?"

"Sure."

"How does it look now?"

"You don't want to know. We've got less than five percent."

"Oh, my God!"

"It's still early," Brown said. "Citibank may tender SES-SOP."

"They have to!" Rush said.

Frank Menaker was debating tactics. The problem was how to use the proposed lawsuit against Citibank to exert maximum leverage on Citibank. The Martin Marietta lawyers had been trying to get through to the Citibank lawyers, but they were not having much luck. How could they threaten if they couldn't even get them on the phone?

Frank Menaker knew that trust departments were layered like insurance companies. By the time one exec reported to his boss who reported to his boss who reported to his boss, it would be too late. He had to find a way to red-flag the issue.

"Tom," Menaker said to Mendenhall, "call your people on the commercial side of Citibank. Tell them what we're planning."

Mendenhall got on the phone and called the two account people—Mary Docherty and George Moyer—who had been responsible for ferrying the $140 million loan through the bureaucracy.

Normally, for propriety's sake, the commercial side of the bank was not involved in the affairs of the trust side. Mendenhall had to find a way to get the two sides talking.

"George, hello, this is Tom Mendenhall. Look, I'm at the Dewey, Ballantine offices and we're gonna file papers in federal court by five P.M. or whenever the clerk's office closes and we're gonna sue you for two hundred million dollars. I think you oughta understand that."

"Tom, could you just tell me what you're talking about?" Moyer said, slightly flabbergasted.

Mendenhall explained the situation. That midnight was the deadline. That the trust department was looking at the SESSOP issue. But that it was taking too much time.

"Tom, that is a trust department problem."

"George, I know there is this Chinese wall at the bank. I understand that but I can't get any attention. Your people won't return our lawyers' phone calls. The only word we get back is that the problem is being looked at. If this thing gets screwed up with some bureaucrat in your trust department, we're gonna be mad as hell, and you're gonna get sued! I mean, this is crazy. You are our depositary, for God's sake!"

"Tom, I don't know what I can do."

"Who can handle it for me?"

"Oh, this goes way up there. I mean, this is for the big boys."

"George," Mendenhall said flatly, "give me Walter Wriston's phone number!"

"You're kidding."

"No, I'm not kidding, George. I've got to talk to someone! Give me Wriston's number, or his secretary, or his administrative assistant."

"I'll call you back," Moyer said.

"I think we got their attention," Mendenhall told Menaker, hanging up the phone. Everyone knew the commercial side could move quicker than the trust department. It was in the nature of the beast. Besides, if you threaten to go high enough, you can cross over the Chinese wall.

Later, Moyer called back.

"Tom, look, I can't tell you anything, but I talked to the lawyers. I can tell you this is getting attention at the highest levels of the bank. A decision will be made."

"George, that's all I wanted to hear," Mendenhall said. "We won't promise not to sue you, but at least we know you're working on the problem."

At around 4:30 P.M., Jamie Long from Citibank called over to Hughes, Hubbard to speak with the Bendix team. Andy Samet and Dick Sanderson were in Bob Enright's office. Enright put the call on the speaker phone.

"Jamie," Sanderson asked, "what can we do for you?"

"I wanted to ask you a question. Just to have all the relevant facts. The trust agreement as it now stands says that withdrawal rights can be triggered by notification in the middle of the month and then the shares can actually be withdrawn at the end of the month. Correct?"

"Correct."

"What is your latest thinking about SESSOP in relation to the United Technologies offer? Their offer does not appear to expire until October 5."

"What's the problem?"

"I just wanted to know if you had looked at that. It would appear the UTC offer fits the terms of withdrawal rights from the plan."

The lawyers talked back and forth. Long was friendly, apparently on a mission to gather facts. He said he would call back if any other questions arose. Within a half hour, Long was back on the line, this time with another Citibank VP, Charles Bisset.

"Gentlemen," Bisset said, "have you thought about amending your plan to allow tendering to Martin Marietta in light of the United Technologies offer?"

"Yes," Andy Samet said, getting familiar with the tone of their questions. "The board has thought about it in connection with the Martin Marietta offer. You may not know, but the board has hired outside counsel to examine the issue, and they have made a determination that amending the plan is not required."

"What about the UTC offer?"

"The board will consider it again in connection with the United Technologies offer."

"When is the board planning to meet to consider that," Jamie Long asked.

"My understanding is that the board will meet tomorrow."

"Thank you. That answers our questions," Bisset said.

Doris Rush was working at Dewey, Ballantine on the Bendix employee complaint, checking periodically with Doug Brown, who was getting reports from the depositary. Doris was keeping her own tab on a piece of scratch paper. By 7:00 P.M., with barely five hours left before the expiration of the proration period, the pool was struggling to get to 10 percent of the Bendix shares.

Despite soaring $6.00 to $62.75 yesterday on the news of the United Technologies offer, the price of Bendix stock had actually fallen by more than $1.00 today. Marty Siegel had been on the phone all day checking with the depositary.

It was not looking very promising for Martin Marietta.

Frank Menaker and Tom Mendenhall decided to leave Dewey, Ballantine. Rush thought they were looking a bit down in the mouth.

"It's gonna work," Rush said, referring to the opinion letter. "They are going to tender."

"Yeah," was the halfhearted response. Doris felt like she was the only cheerleader left.

"Did you see this?" Menaker asked, handing Doris a court paper. "The Michigan Department of Commerce issued a cease and desist order this afternoon, telling both Martin Marietta and UTC to immediately stop their 'tandem illegal tender offers' for Bendix."

"Oh, no," Rush said.

" 'Oh, no' is right. What are we going to say to Wall Street? 'Gee, sorry, our tender offer is good everywhere but Michigan, where a hell of a lot of Bendix stockholders live'?"

"What are we going to do?" Rush asked.

"We're going to fight them in court," Menaker said with resignation.

The team went home. Mendenhall and Menaker left Rush their home phone numbers. Menaker said, "Call me if it's not too late."

Doug Brown was also in touch with other members of the

team. Dick Katcher had taken his wife, Susan, to see the U.S. Open Tennis Championships at the National Tennis Center in Flushing Meadow. They had taken a limo from Dick's old apartment and arrived at about 7:30 P.M. to see Vitas Gerulaitis and Tom Gullickson. The matches were unexciting. Katcher excused himself and called Brown every hour. Dick tried to contain his anxiety being "newlywed conscious" with Susan after their three-month separation. Brown's reports were not making it any easier.

"We're hurting," Brown said.

Sitting in an office at Dewey, Ballantine, Doris suddenly realized that she had her suitcase with her. She had checked out of the Waldorf that morning and had no place to stay that night. Frantically she scrounged around until Larrabee's secretary offered to help. A room was found at the Vista.

Doug Brown was on the phone.

"I just want you to know," Brown said to Doris, "I've just made a couple of calls and taken a walk and I can tell you that the secretary who would be there if something was going on is there."

"What, are you teasing me?"

"All I'm saying is don't give up hope. They're burning the late-night oil over at Citibank. The lights are still on."

Doug Brown was right. In a conference room on the thirty-seventh floor of the Citibank tower at 399 Park Avenue, a team of Citibank businessmen and lawyers was meeting, working over the problem. Robert Dinerstein, the senior in-house lawyer handling the situation, was missing his fifteenth wedding anniversary. Other participants included Earl Huplits, the senior man in the institutional investment division. Another VP, Charles Bisset, was there. And Ed Smith.

Robert Dinerstein had come up with a recommendation.

He made a call to Paul Collins, an executive vice president.

Collins talked with Citibank chairman Walter Wriston.

The approval came down.

"Okay," Dinerstein said, hanging up the telephone, "the bank is going to tender the four million, four hundred eighty thousand shares of Bendix stock it holds in trust to the Martin Marietta offer."

The procedure was handing a piece of paper from one hand

of the bank to another. A professional from Ed Smith's institutional investment division on Park Avenue took the required documents to the stock transfer department at 111 Wall Street and approached the window. The tender was notarized.

Dinerstein decided that it would only be courtesy to notify Bendix. A letter would be sent to the Bendix chairman, Bill Agee. Another letter was drafted to be sent along with the Martin Marietta materials being mailed to the SESSOP participants.

"Charlie, you call Agee," Dinerstein said.

From the conference room, Charles Bisset called Hughes, Hubbard. It was almost 10:30 P.M. The call went into an interior conference room, where litigator George Davidson was working late.

"I would like to speak with Bill Agee of Bendix," Bisset said.

"I'm sorry. Did you say you're from Citibank?"

"Yes, and I would like to speak with Bill Agee."

"Mr. Agee is not here in the offices. Let me check if I can determine how to reach him."

Davidson roamed the offices looking for signs of life. He found Jack Fontaine just back from a late dinner at Harry's at the American Stock Exchange. Jack talked with Bisset and gave him Hal Barron's number at the hotel. Bisset talked with Barron and sent over a messenger. Barron was outraged when he read the message. It was difficult for him to call Bill Agee and inform him what had happened.

Only hours before, Hal Barron had passed along the appraisal of his legal team that everything was running smoothly. A letter from Citibank to the participants of SESSOP was at the printer. It was to be mailed tonight. Now—for unknown reasons —Citibank had done a perfect pirouette.

Bill Agee was in his suite at the Helmsley Palace. Al McDonald was with him. Agee had throughout the evening been monitoring the Martin Marietta stock pool, and he was optimistic. As best as his team could determine, the Martin Marietta offer would be undersubscribed, perhaps gaining only 28 percent of the Bendix stock. Agee and McDonald were feeling very up—it was looking as if the marketplace was about to crush the countertender. Tom Pownall and his board would certainly come to heel when the results were published.

At close to 11:00 P.M., Bill Agee took Hal Barron's phone call.

"Citibank has tendered SESSOP," Barron said grimly.

"What?" Agee said, completely dumbfounded.

"I just received a message for you from Citibank that they tendered the goddamn stock! They threw in the whole lot! Everything!"

The first thought that raced through Bill Agee's mind was that there must have been a mistake. This afternoon everything was fine. The lawyers said the letter was at the printer. He just couldn't believe it.

After Hal repeated again that there was no mistake—Citibank had tendered—Agee's thinking swung around to a more disturbing realization.

"My God, somebody caused this to happen."

Al McDonald was mad. He was exasperated. He and Agee paced the room, throwing out scenarios and invectives.

"Those bastards," McDonald said. "They completely disregarded the trust agreement. Nowhere does it say they can do this!"

"I want to know how this happened," Agee said with cooler anger. The only explanation the two men could come up with was a conspiracy. They knew that Harry Gray was on the board of Citibank and that Bill Spencer, the Citibank president, was on the board of United Technologies.

"It's outrageous!" McDonald said. "We should sue the bank!"

McDonald's face was turning red with anger. He punched a fist into his open palm. "Those bastards!" he repeated. Agee controlled his feelings. He let McDonald's anger wash over him.

Alone with Mary later that night, Bill Agee felt himself headed for his lowest emotional point in the battle. He tried hard to not let himself surrender to the situation. It was like riding a bicycle. If you slow down too much, you fall off.

Doris Rush was still at Dewey, Ballantine, awaiting news. Around midnight, she called the Kidder, Peabody rep who was standing by at Citibank.

"They tendered," he said matter-of-factly. He had known for some time. Doris's voice took off like a skyrocket.

"Are you positive? Is there any chance it's not there? Are you sure? I don't want to wake my boss up if you're not sure!"

Moments after she hung up, Doug Brown called her back.

"Doris, congratulations, you've saved the company!" Brown

said. "It's there, they're still counting and recounting, but it looks like we got 72.5 percent of the Bendix stock."

"Yahoo!"

The first call Doris made was to Tom Mendenhall. He was obviously asleep when the phone rang.

"Are you ready?" Doris said.

"For what?" a groggy Mendenhall asked.

"Citibank tendered. We got seventy-two and a half percent of all their stock!"

There was dead silence on Mendenhall's end of the phone.

"Hang up. I've got to call Powell," Mendenhall said, hanging up on Doris. Stunned, she dialed Frank Menaker. His wife, Sharon, answered. Frank was put on the phone. This time Rush waited until Frank was awake.

"Jesus Christ God Almighty, I'll talk to you in the morning," was Frank's reaction.

Having made her promised calls, Doris returned to the office where she was drafting the complaint against Citibank with the litigators from Barrett, Smith. Doris reached for a draft on the table.

"We're not gonna have to file this! They tendered!" she hollered, ripping the paper and throwing it into the air like confetti.

At the elevator on the forty-fifth floor, she saw Len Larrabee going home. It was the middle of the night.

"We did it! We did it!" Doris said. She dropped her bag and gave Larrabee a big kiss on the cheek.

"I know. I just heard." Larrabee was reserved.

"How can you be so calm and collected when we just got over seventy percent?"

"Well, Doris, don't misunderstand. I'm absolutely delighted. It's just I know in this business it's up one minute and down the next. I guess I'm just waiting for the other shoe to fall."

Doris overslept the next morning, her first good night's sleep in quite a while. But she awoke with a start, showered, dressed, and checked out of the Vista International Hotel. Unable to flag a cab, she walked with her case to the Dewey, Ballantine downtown offices.

The offices were jumping with activity, but Doris found an empty office next door to Bob Fullem, where she could make her calls to Bethesda to find out what was happening.

Mendenhall was all revved up. The mood had changed drastically from twenty-four hours earlier. Now Mendenhall was convinced that Martin Marietta was going to take over Bendix. He wanted Doris to bring Bendix documents in Larrabee's possession at Dewey, Ballantine back to Bethesda.

"And my wife wants to know who is this woman who makes me do an Indian war dance in the middle of the night."

Doris called Frank Menaker to find out what was going on.

"I understand I owe you a great deal of money," Menaker said. Doris at first could not figure out what he meant. She thought somehow she had gone overboard on her expense account.

"Doug Brown and the other Kidder people have been calling me, and they called Pownall and they called Leithauser and they are telling everybody that you literally saved the company! I was told that I owe you the biggest raise you have ever had in your life!"

"I'll drink to that!"

In the background, Doris could hear another assistant general counsel, Bruce Deerson, chiming in, "Go get 'em, Doris!"

"When are you coming back?" Menaker asked.

"Well, I guess anytime. The treasury people want me to bring some papers back."

"Okay. We really want to give you a hero's return," Menaker said. "I'm going to put Mary Lou on and we'll arrange for the limousine to pick you up at the airport."

EIGHTEEN

T he previous night, on the forty-fifth floor, by the elevator, when Dewey, Ballantine lawyer Leonard Larrabee told Doris Rush he was "just waiting for the other shoe to fall," he was talking in puzzles. In her excitement, Doris had no idea what the red-faced lawyer was talking about. She was ready to celebrate. Martin Marietta had won! Even Bill Agee's shares were tendered to the Marietta pool!

Larrabee was talking about the list.

The "other shoe" was the list of names of Bendix stockholders.

In eleven days, the Bendix Corporation was going to hold a meeting of its stockholders at the Southfield, Michigan, headquarters. Larrabee expected perhaps a hundred people to attend—a tiny fraction of the more than twenty-nine thousand Bendix stockholders.

The vast majority of stockholders—be they individuals or banks or insurance companies—would vote by mail. They would vote by proxy. If Martin Marietta did not establish personal contact with these people before they marked their ballots, Larrabee knew the game was up.

No one would remember the victory of the Citibank tender, if come September 21 at 10:00 A.M., the gavel came down in

Southfield and the "shark repellent" amendments were declared passed.

To organize a telephone campaign in opposition to the proposed amendments, Martin Marietta needed the list of names.

"We've got to get that list," Larrabee repeated to Frank Menaker.

It had been a frequent topic of discussion among the lawyers since the moment Martin Marietta had decided to fight with a tender offer of its own.

Under federal proxy rules, Bendix had two choices: It could either supply Martin Marietta with a list of Bendix stockholders, or Bendix could mail the Martin Marietta materials themselves.

Frank Menaker made his first request for information about how Bendix would handle the situation in a letter dated August 31 to Hal Barron, Bendix's general counsel.

A couple of days later, Bob Powell, the Martin Marietta treasurer, sent Barron a letter with five demands, among them the stockholder list on magnetic computer tape and the most recent stock transfer sheets showing the up-to-date names and addresses of persons who had made recent purchases of Bendix stock.

On the same day, Hal Barron had a letter hand-delivered to Frank Menaker. Bendix would hold on to its trump card and handle the Martin Marietta mailing.

There was another problem.

Neither Martin Marietta nor United Technologies knew the actual language of the Bendix amendments. Without a copy of the Bendix proxy solicitation materials, they were working in the dark.

By Thursday, Marty Lipton, the UTC lawyer, was going crazy.

"I have a copy of the Bendix proxy materials in front of me," Tim Metz said on the telephone. Metz was a key reporter from *The Wall Street Journal.* Lipton and Metz spoke frequently.

"Yeah, how's it look?" Marty Lipton said. He was steaming inside. Here Bendix had already begun solicitation by servicing the media, and the United Technologies side had not yet even finalized the language of their proxy solicitation materials!

A cagey lawyer with thick eyeglasses and curly hair, Lipton did not want to let on to Metz that UTC was behind in the fight.

He cut the phone call short and slammed his hand onto his intercom.

"Neff, get in here!"

Dan Neff, a twenty-nine-year-old associate, had an office several doors down. He came into Lipton's office in a hurry.

"The Bendix materials are on the street. Get me a copy!" Lipton said.

"What would you—"

"I don't care how you get them. Just get them!"

Neff went back to his office and called Peter Harkins at Georgeson & Company, United Technologies' soliciting agent.

"We gotta get this thing," Neff said, feeling the heat.

"I'll do what I can," Peter Harkins said.

Peter Harkins, a sharp, hard-driving twenty-seven-year-old solicitor with prematurely graying hair, was well aware of Neff's problem. The SEC had declined to let Martin Marietta or United Technologies see the Bendix proxy materials before they were released to the public. This left Harkins hanging. He needed to know the simplest of things—such as the color of the Bendix proxy card—to avoid confusion with his own. He had messengers all over town waiting at the offices of arbitrage friends. It became apparent that Bendix would deliberately hold off supplying the arbitrage community until about 6:00 P.M. to gain as much of a jump as possible.

Harkins knew from Lipton's conversation with Metz that Hill & Knowlton was supplying materials to the press. Peter got one of his associates, Carl Spofford, to act out a ruse. Harkins instructed Spofford to call Hill & Knowlton and pretend he was a reporter from a Long Island newspaper. Harkins figured that Hill & Knowlton may not have known the writers by name.

"Hello, my name is Carl Codyre," Spofford said, using Harkins' middle name as an alias. "I'm a reporter at *Newsday* and I'm working on a story about the Bendix and Martin Marietta situation."

It worked. Harkins got a copy of the Bendix materials.

Dan Neff met Peter Harkins at United Technologies' printer, Bowne of New York City, at 345 Hudson Street, downtown. They made the selection of color and decided all the small issues that were so important. Their attention to detail became harder as the night wore on. But the two men did their job and finally gave the go-ahead. Fifty thousand proxy cards were printed by

United Technologies in opposition to the Bendix amendments.

Although Bendix would physically mail the Martin Marietta and United Technologies materials to the Bendix stockholders, Harkins and the Marietta proxy solicitor still desperately needed the list of names to conduct a telephone solicitation campaign. Frank Menaker sent another letter to Hal Barron demanding— pursuant to Section 220 of Delaware Corporation Law—that Martin Marietta reps be allowed to inspect and copy the Bendix stockholder list. Bendix delayed as long as the law would allow.

At about one o'clock on Friday morning, a Bendix lawyer called Neff at the printers.

"Okay, it's been cleared," Ed Kaufman said. "We're giving access to the list to Martin Marietta and you guys. The time has been set for noon today in Southfield at Bendix headquarters."

"Eleven hours from now, right?"

"Right."

"What are the instructions?"

"Just ask for a lawyer at Bendix—Dave Young. He'll handle it for you. And Dan, I've been told that from now on any questions about the list or the mailing procedure should be addressed to Harvey Pitt, a lawyer with Fried, Frank in Washington. His number is 202-342-3500."

"Thanks," Neff said.

Neff and Harkins huddled to figure out what was next. Harkins knew from experience that "access" to the list did not necessarily mean a copy of the list. And the Delaware statute being invoked by the lawyers to get access mentioned only "access." They would have to be prepared to photograph the list.

Harkins tried continually to reach Carl Spofford at his apartment. It wasn't until almost 5:30 A.M. that he finally got him.

"Carl, look, I'm coming over to your house to pick you up. You've got to fly to Detroit on the next flight."

Harkins jumped in his car and headed for Spofford's apartment. He stopped briefly at Citibank to use the automatic teller to withdraw some cash. He would also give Spofford his American Express Card.

"I really don't have much time to explain the situation to you," Harkins said. "I just want you to go to the front door of Bendix and say, 'I'm Carl Spofford of Georgeson & Company, Inc., agent of United Technologies, and I'm here to claim access to the Bendix stockholder list under the Delaware State statute.'

Okay? You'll go with some representatives of Martin Marietta."

Carl Spofford traveled on a commercial flight to Detroit with Barry Bigger from Dewey, Ballantine and Chris Cole from Martin Marietta's solicitor, Morrow & Company. When they got to the airport, they rented a car and drove to the sprawling three-story Bendix headquarters on Civic Center Drive in Southfield.

At the arranged hour, upon making their identities known, the group was met by Dave Young, an in-house Bendix lawyer. Young was a tall man, with dark hair, black-framed glasses, a tight-lipped disposition, and a predilection for Hush Puppies. He escorted the group to a room that contained four large cartons of computer paper.

"You may begin," Young said.

The Martin Marietta and UTC team spread out, casually examining the four cartons as the photographer set up his equipment. He had come prepared with his own power source in the event that Bendix would not allow him to plug into wall outlets. He had enough film for thousands of pictures.

When Spofford opened a carton, he was shocked. Each page of the computer paper had only several names. Instead of running a program that would simplify their job, Bendix had obviously run the list to slow them down.

"Let's get to work," the photographer said, realizing that he had literally a small mountain of paperwork to photograph.

At 8:35 A.M. on Friday, court was convened at the Federal Building in Detroit before Judge Anna Diggs Taylor. After the clerk stated the case, Judge Taylor leaned forward to scrutinize the lawyers before her.

"The court received a call from counsel for United Technologies at six P.M. yesterday evening requesting a hearing concerning new developments which apparently have occurred. Will you state your appearances, please?"

The new development Judge Taylor alluded to was an order issued by E. C. Mackey, the director of the Enforcement Section of the Corporation and Securities Bureau for the state of Michigan. Bendix had convinced Mackey to issue a "cease-and-desist order" against Martin Marietta and United Technologies "in connection with their tandem illegal tender offers for common stock of the Bendix Corporation."

Mackey ordered the Marietta and UTC tender offers stopped in Michigan.

From day one, Michigan had been a problem for the Martin Marietta lawyers. On Monday, August 30, the day of the Martin Marietta decision to countertender, Leslie Fleming from the Detroit law firm of Butzel, Long, Gust, Klein and Van Zile had requested on Martin Marietta's behalf a hearing on the constitutionality of the Michigan takeover statute.

The state law threatened to derail their offer.

It was normally routine that such restrictive state laws were set aside since the U.S. Supreme Court decision in the *Mite* case in June 1982. Bendix had had a whole slew of such laws set aside —in Maryland, Louisiana, Nebraska, Oklahoma, South Carolina, and Utah.

When Martin Marietta launched their countertender, they attacked the laws in Delaware, Michigan, Missouri, and New Jersey. Most of the state laws fell like dominoes.

In Michigan, the case was assigned to Federal District Judge Anna Diggs Taylor, a fifty-year-old black woman appointed to the federal bench in 1979 by Jimmy Carter. She was the ex-wife of former Congressman Charles Diggs, who was convicted of shaking down members of his staff in 1978.

In her chambers on that first day, she was blunt.

"Your motion for a temporary restraining order against enforcement of the Michigan State takeover law is denied," Judge Taylor told the Martin Marietta lawyers.

Martin Marietta and United Technologies attorneys asked for the session on Friday morning to again seek a temporary restraining order against the Michigan takeover law and to block enforcement of the cease-and-desist order.

Two New York attorneys took the morning flight to Detroit to explain to Judge Taylor that it was a big world out there. Her decisions were affecting the outcome of an enormous financial struggle.

"Good morning, Your Honor," Russell Baite, a forty-four-year-old lawyer from Dewey, Ballantine, representing Martin Marietta, said. "I appreciate your allowing us to break into your morning like this. . . . I don't propose to talk about a lot of cases because there's been an enormous amount of discussion of cases, and I think we can all read law books as well as anybody else, but what I would like to do is talk a little bit about the tender offers. . . .

"Now, litigation situations like this usually end up with a great deal of bumping and shoving between companies. One wants to make a tender offer. The other, frankly, doesn't want to have it made. There's no question about the fact that Martin Marietta didn't want Bendix to make a tender offer for it. And the plain and simple fact is, as you can see, that the Bendix lawyers would like our tender offer for Bendix to go away.

"It would be a mistake to think that this is something solely in the interest of the Bendix stockholders who live in Michigan and the Michigan stockbroker community and Michigan commerce, because it isn't. . . . We can't carve out the state of Michigan and the Michigan shareholders. . . . That's all a ruse, Your Honor. Whatever is done here affects a nationwide tender offer for almost three billion dollars to thousands upon thousands of shareholders around the country. . . ."

Russell Baite talked for twenty minutes before Louis Barash, a twenty-seven-year-old attorney from Wachtell, Lipton, took his turn on behalf of United Technologies. Barash was quick to point out that Bendix had successfully sought injunctive relief against enforcement of state takeover statutes in six states.

"Your Honor, Bendix can't go around in several courts in other states and try to throw out the state statutes and then come in Michigan, where it happens to have its place of business, and say, 'Oh, gee, we want to try to enforce the Michigan statute.' This is duplicitous. They have argued that these statutes ought to be enjoined, that they are invalid on its face when they're on the offense. Now, United Technologies, some larger company, comes along and does to Bendix what Bendix was going to do to Marietta, all of a sudden the statutes that were clearly unconstitutional, Bendix, in its home state, wants to try to resurrect. . . .

"Now here, Bendix believes it has some home-court advantage with the state of Michigan commissioner, with the state of Michigan courts. That's why it's essential that this federal court, which has the responsibility to uphold the supreme law of this land, intervene here and stop these proceedings and this action by the Michigan commissioner. . . ."

Judge Taylor listened patiently to the New York lawyers demonstrate their persuasive tactics. She then turned down flat their motion for a stay order.

She smiled at the men standing before her.

"We would like to make an emergency appeal to the Sixth Circuit," a flustered Louis Barash said.

The Michigan "problem" was getting worse.

MERGER

Bill Agee was sitting in the living room of his suite on the forty-fifth floor of the Helmsley Palace on Madison Avenue. Clean-shaven and neatly dressed, Agee was thinking. A glass of grapefruit juice was on the table in front of him. The previous night, he suppressed his emotions about the Citibank tender of the Bendix SESSOP shares to the Martin Marietta offer. Al McDonald was the one who threw out oaths, damning the unseen hand behind the move.

Agee barely slept all night.

Mary was there when he needed her.

But even with Mary, Bill could not completely let down.

This morning, in a little more than three hours, Agee had to address the Bendix board. The company's situation had changed for the worse. Just hours ago, the Martin Marietta offer was doomed to failure. Now Pownall had an important psychological victory.

"It won't change the outcome," McDonald said last night, trying to see beyond his own anger. "What was an asset has become a liability, but it won't change the fact that we can buy first, and once we own them, Martin Marietta management will be forced to come to terms."

This morning, Agee was thinking about another player.

Bill was thinking about Harry Gray.

Harry Gray was out of town. He was in Wyoming at a gathering of the Conquistadores del Cielo Club, an invitation-only club of aerospace executives. The meeting, held at a ranch, offered the CEOs of many large aerospace outfits a chance to unwind and socialize in the rarefied air away from the hubbub of their day-to-day calendars.

The ranch has 135 beds. The club meets twice a year. Harry Gray had been a member since 1974. He was in the company of friends. Among his acquaintances in attendance were "Brizz"— John Brizzendine, who ran Douglas Aircraft; Sandy McDonnell; Bob Anderson from Rockwell; Roy Anderson from Lockheed; Dave Garrett from Delta; Ed Myer of TWA; Tex Bouillon of Boeing; and Al Casey of American. Gray had known Casey since Casey had been in the newspaper business on the West Coast.

At this gathering, fierce business competitors came together without the glare of publicity to swap stories and enjoy the great outdoors. The ranch had a range of activities such as fishing, hunting, horse riding, rodeo, and many organized games—pistol fast draw, knife throwing. These men of industry donned boots and spurs and hats and became cowboys for a couple of days a year.

No one from Bendix was a member of Conquistadores.

Tom Pownall was the president of its forty-sixth meeting.

He was a day late in arriving. The large group was sitting down for dinner in the ranch house. A man leaned over to Harry Gray for a word.

"Hey, I think I see Pownall on his way over," the man said.

Harry got up from his seat and went out to greet Pownall. The two men came into the dining hall, arm in arm. They received a prolonged ovation from the aerospace executives.

Later that night, in Pownall's room, the two men had a chat.

"Agee wants to talk with me," Tom Pownall said, "but I haven't got anything to say to him. You know, he didn't talk to me before he put his offer on the table. So why should I talk to him?"

"I'd like to talk with Agee," Harry said.

"Please do," Pownall said.

"You know, something funny is going on. Agee passed along a message a couple of days ago that it is important that we talk. He said it was 'urgent.' "

"What could that be about?" Pownall asked.

"Doggone if I know—but anyway, so I call him back and get his secretary, Barbara somebody, and she says she's unaware of any urgent request from Agee to speak with me. I ask her to check it out. No call comes back. So in a couple of hours I call back. Then she says she got in touch with Agee and he doesn't want to talk with me. He knows nothing about any urgent message."

The two men look at each other in puzzlement.

On Friday morning, Harry Gray and Tom Pownall were sitting down to an early-morning breakfast when a cook came out of the ranch kitchen. He found his way over to Harry Gray.

"There's a man on the telephone gotta speak with you," the cook said. "He says it's an emergency. Says he is Mr. Agee."

Harry and Tom looked at each other.

"Now, isn't this silly," Gray said to Pownall. He looked down at his plate of scrambled eggs and sausage.

"Hey, see if you can keep these warm," Gray told the cook. "Where's the phone?"

"In the kitchen."

With all the noise and clutter of the kitchen, Gray had a hard time hearing himself think, let alone talk with Agee. Harry found a little glass-enclosed office where the chef made up his menus and took the call in there.

"Harry, I hope I'm not disturbing you?" Agee said.

"No, Bill. What's up?"

"I'd like to have a chance to talk with you. It's important that we be reasonable about this. How about tomorrow?"

"I'm out in Wyoming," Gray said. "You've got me a little confused. I asked to meet with you earlier in the week before I came out here. You didn't want to meet. And then I hear from Clark McGregor that there is an urgent message to call you. And your secretary tells me you don't want to talk."

"There must have been a misunderstanding," Agee said.

"What changed?" Gray said.

"There must have been a misunderstanding," Agee repeated. "Lookit, I work on Saturdays. How about meeting with me tomorrow?"

Bill Agee wanted to hear the UTC deal straight from Gray.

"Bill, this thing lasts until Sunday morning. I'll be back late Sunday night. We could meet on Monday."

"I've got a conflict on Monday," Agee said.

"Let's make it Tuesday," Harry said.

"Okay, give me a call when you're back in New York," Agee said. "We'll make it Tuesday. I look forward to our meeting."

"Me too, Bill."

NINETEEN

The fourth Bendix board of directors meeting since it had started its attempt to take over Martin Marietta began at 10:00 A.M. on Friday at Bendix's New York offices on the twenty-first floor of the GM Building on Fifth Avenue. For the first time in the battle with Martin Marietta, all of the Bendix directors were present—with the exception of Coy Eklund, the CEO of Equitable Life, who had permanently excused himself from the outset.

Equitable owned 1,141,500 Martin Marietta shares. The Bendix offer promised Eklund's company a profit of $25 million. But Coy had to be careful to avoid charges that he inappropriately used insider information.

Agee missed Eklund at the board meetings. Throughout previous struggles with the Bendix board and the "Mary situation," Eklund had proven himself a valuable ally.

Agee was several minutes late for the board meeting. While the directors waited, Bill was huddled with Al McDonald in a side room after being alerted by PR chief Bob Meyers that a story was crossing the Dow Jones newswire teletype machine. Meyers ripped it off and showed it to the two men, who said nothing. The headline read: "MARTIN MARIETTA SAYS 75 PERCENT OF BENDIX SHARES TENDERED TO IT."

Bill Agee walked sharply into the boardroom, offered a shallow smile to the directors, and began the day's business.

"I would like to request an executive session of the board," Agee said.

Al McDonald stood by the door, and as the other inside Bendix directors filed out, he turned and exited, closing the boardroom door. That left seven men and one woman in the room. Director Jack Fontaine sat with a yellow legal pad to record the minutes of the executive session of the board.

"Our first order of business is to continue considering the employment contracts first discussed by the board during the last meeting," Agee said.

"Bill, did you see today's *New York Times?*" a director asked, holding the newspaper in his hand. "They don't waste any time. Look at this headline: 'BENDIX SAFEGUARDS EXECUTIVE BENEFITS.' Did you see the first paragraph?" the man asked, reading, " 'In a sign that some Wall Street analysts viewed as weakness . . .' "

"Yes, I have seen the article and I might add that our disclosure of the existence of the contracts was routine and required in our proxy filings," Agee said, his voice firm and clear.

"Jack, would you review where the board stands on the issue," Agee said to Fontaine, who turned to a stack of papers he had brought into the room. Fontaine summarized the status of the last meeting, during which sixteen Bendix executives were guaranteed salary and bonus for three years with the exception of Bill Agee, whose $805,000 annual salary and bonus would be guaranteed for five years in the event of change of control of the company.

"I have with me a list of seven more individuals who I feel should receive employment contracts," Agee said. "The list includes six vice presidents in the aerospace business and Bob Meyers, the corporate communications executive director."

"Why add more people?" Donald Rumsfeld asked.

"I received several comments from Bill Purple that he thought it was tough to exclude any of his vice presidents, especially since our aerospace operations appear to be of considerable interest to Martin Marietta."

"Well, how many aerospace VPs are there?" Rumsfeld asked.

"Ten. The board granted contracts to four last week. It is my feeling after talking with Purple that we should extend the coverage to his six other VPs," Agee said.

Rumsfeld said nothing. He shrugged his shoulders.

"There is also another matter I would like to bring up, regarding my own employment contract, which I feel needs clarification. As Jack has reviewed with you, there is a clause regarding any subsequent employment.

"If, in the event of a triggering of my contract, I invest my own money in an operation run by myself or with my family, I would not want to see my salary and benefits reduced by any salary I might give myself."

The executive session of the board after discussion voted—with Bill Agee abstaining—to exempt the chairman from the offset provisions of the employment contracts and also authorized director Hugo Uyterhoeven on behalf of the corporation to execute Agee's employment contract and the other fifteen agreed to on September 7. Agee was further authorized to enter into similar contracts for the aerospace vice presidents and the PR director. That brought to twenty-three the number of Bendix executives protected.

"Come on back in, fellas," Agee said through the open doorway to the other Bendix executives. Agee nodded to Bill Purple, the white-haired head of Bendix aerospace. Also invited into the meeting was special outside counsel Dick Pogue and his associate J. S. Leavitt.

"As I am sure we are all aware," Agee began, "Citibank last night around ten-thirty tendered the employee shares to Martin Marietta. It came as a complete shock to management. Our own shares were tendered in direct opposition to our wishes. Our people had been in touch with Citibank throughout the week to guard against such a reckless move, and we were told in no uncertain terms that Citibank had no intention of tendering. They recognized that the provisions of the plan do not allow tendering. And then abruptly last night, they reversed their position. What happened in those few hours I can only guess, and none of it is flattering to the bank."

"What about this connection between the Citibank board and Harry Gray?" a director asked.

"There is a connection," Agee said, controlling the tone of his voice. "Gray sits on the bank board along with William Simon and Bill Spencer, who sit on the UTC board. I'll tell you last night, when Al and I were at the hotel and heard the news, the thought ran through our minds."

"It's just unbelievable! Somebody put heat on the bank," a director said.

"Sons-of-bitches," Rumsfeld said with a smile for director Jewel Lafontant, who smiled back. Jewel was used to Rumsfeld's "naughty language." She thought Rumsfeld was the "bad boy" of the board. He liked dramatic profanity. Once, disregarding decorum, he propped his feet on the boardroom table.

"And remember that in addition to being the trustee on SESSOP, Citibank is also the designated depositary for the Martin Marietta and United Technologies tender offers. They're getting paid by everybody," Agee said.

"Could we sue Citibank?" director Jewel Lafontant asked.

"That has been considered and we decided it would just be a sidetrack," Agee said. "It would be a waste of our time. But we do have an approach to solve the problem. Dick Pogue will tell you about the possibility of amending the plan to force Citibank to withdraw."

"What I would say," Dick Pogue began, "is that while this area of law is far from clear, one thing is clear, and that is that the trust agreement with Citibank as it is now written does not allow them to sell stock except in routine circumstances. This action last night was unauthorized by the board and in excess of the powers bestowed on Citibank through the trust agreement.

"The board has several options," Pogue continued, launching into a description of the board's responsibilities in light of the applicable government regulations. He also described how the board could amend the plan and require Citibank to withdraw the tendered shares.

It seemed simple enough.

The board voted to amend the plan to force Citibank to withdraw the SESSOP shares from the Martin Marietta pool and then put back only the shares that Bendix employees individually instructed the bank to deliver to Martin Marietta.

"How many shares would that be?" Jonathan Scott, a Texas-based real-estate developer, asked. It was one of the few times Scott had asked a question during the whole affair.

"Not many," Agee said. "A trickle."

With Jay Higgins from Salomon Brothers and Art Fleischer and several other lawyers invited into the meeting, Agee began the discussion of the United Technologies offer to buy Bendix Corporation.

After reviewing a handout from Salomon Brothers and listening to Jay Higgins call the UTC offer "inadequate," the board voted unanimously to reject the United Technologies offer and on the recommendation of Art Fleischer to authorize legal action.

"As you have already heard," Agee said, "the UTC offer is loaded with conditions, among which is the requirement that Bendix terminate its tender offer for Martin Marietta without having purchased any shares. It is obvious to me that the UTC offer is not a serious offer and that we can most directly rebuff the offer by demonstrating our determination to buy Martin Marietta. It is in that regard that I propose to increase the number of Martin Marietta shares we intend to purchase from fifteen point eight million to eighteen point five million."

"It will demonstrate to the street that we are determined to assume control of Marietta," Higgins said.

That phrase "demonstrate to the street" made Agee flash back to the tangle between Higgins and Tavoulareas at the last board meeting. It must have triggered the same reaction in Tavoulareas.

"How does that affect the total price tag?" Tavoulareas asked Higgins.

"It increases the cash purchase by one hundred thirty million dollars."

Tavoulareas smiled and folded his hands. Agee had already informed him about his plan involving Salomon Brothers.

The board then was polled and voted in favor of notching up the deal.

"I would like to say in conclusion," Agee began, "that I have decided to add another investment banking firm to our team— First Boston Corporation—and that I have complete confidence in Salomon Brothers and the advice rendered by Jay. My feeling is that another banker—particularly in light of the UTC offer— could provide additional needed insights."

Director Jewel Lafontant could almost feel the tension from Higgins, who sat calmly with a screwed-down smile.

"Oh, and one last thing," Agee said. "Last night, our proxy solicitation materials were put into the mail for the stockholders' meeting—scheduled for a week from Monday."

"What are the latest predictions?" Tavoulareas asked.

"We continue to be optimistic that the two amendments will gain shareholder approval," Agee said.

The Bendix shareholders had the power to stop Martin Marietta.

A Bendix stockholders' meeting. On the dais (closest to the camera), Harold S. Barron, vice-president, secretary, general counsel of the Bendix Corporation; Alonzo L. McDonald, president; at the podium, William M. Agee, chairman and chief executive officer. In the front row, from right to left (after the stenographer): members of the Bendix board of directors, William C. Purple, executive vice-president of the corporation, president of the Aerospace/Electronics Group; Jewel S. Lafontant, lawyer, partner in Lafontant, Wilkins & Jones; John C. Fontaine, lawyer, partner of Hughes, Hubbard & Reed; Paul F. Hartz, vice-president of Bendix, chairman of Bendix company, Fram Corporation; Frederick W. Searby, president, Bendix Industrial Group; (partially obscured) Thomas P. Stafford, Lt. General (ret.), Gibraltar Exploration.

William M. Agee, chairman and chief executive officer of the Bendix Corporation, at a stockholders' meeting at Bendix Southfield, Michigan, headquarters.

Mary E. Cunningham

Arthur Fleischer, Jr., lawyer, Fried, Frank, Harris, Shriver & Jacobson, chief legal counsel to Bill Agee

Thomas G. Pownall, president and chief executive officer, Martin Marietta

Martin Marietta

Martin Marietta

Frank H. Menaker, Jr., vice-president, general counsel, Martin Marietta

Martin Marietta

Charles H. Leithauser, senior vice-president and chief financial officer, Martin Marietta

Doris M. Rush, assistant general counsel, Martin Marietta

Martin Marietta corporate headquarters, Rockledge Drive, Bethesda, Maryland

Thomas W. Mendenhall, assistant treasurer, Martin Marietta

Bruce Wasserstein, investment banker, First Boston Corporation

The takeover of the Bendix special stockholders' meeting held September 22, 1982. From left to right, standing: three lawyers from Richards, Layton & Finger, Martin Marietta's Delaware law firm; (partially obscured) Bernard E. Kury, lawyer, partner, Dewey, Ballantine, Bushby, Palmer & Wood; Bob D. Mannis, associate, Dewey, Ballantine; (at the podium) James D. Simpson, vice-president, Martin Marietta; at the extreme right is Andrew B. Samet, Bendix associate general counsel.

Martin A. Siegel, vice-president and director, Kidder, Peabody & Co., Martin Marietta's investment bankers

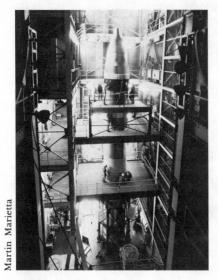

Martin Marietta Aerospace is a high-technology company involved in the design, development, and manufacture of major space and defense systems, including the Pershing II deployed in Europe.

Martin Marietta Aerospace is principal contractor to the Air Force for assembly, test, and system support of the Peacekeeper (MX).

Space and strategic-missile systems developed by Martin Marietta Aerospace include the Titan series of heavy-capacity space-launch systems and Space Shuttle's giant external tank manufactured by the company at NASA's Michoud Assembly Facility, New Orleans.

Edward L. Hennessy, Jr., chairman and chief executive officer of the Allied Corporation

Harry J. Gray, chairman, president, and chief executive officer of United Technologies.

John J. Byrne, Martin Marietta director, chairman and chief executive officer of Geico

L. Robert Fullem, lawyer, partner of Dewey, Ballantine, Bushby, Palmer & Wood

Leonard P. Larrabee, Jr., lawyer, partner of Dewey, Ballantine, Bushby, Palmer & Wood

The Honorable Joseph H. Young, U.S. District Judge, Baltimore, Maryland

TWENTY

Harry Gray was not the kind of man to pass over an opportunity or fail to exploit an advantage. He thought he was in a good position. Tom Pownall and Martin Marietta needed him for credibility, and Bill Agee appeared to be softening his opposition to the UTC bid.

Gray wanted to tighten his grip on Bill Agee.

Two of Gray's main strategists—investment banker Felix Rohatyn and lawyer Marty Lipton—thrashed through options, and an idea had fallen out of the conversation.

"The point is," Rohatyn said, "if Agee buys the Martin Marietta shares, he will have spent a billion dollars—and, as a result, he's going to be worth less to Harry."

The two men in conjunction with the UTC camp of executives came up with an interesting strategy. The concept was to shock Bill Agee by publicly announcing on Monday or Tuesday that if Bendix continued in its pursuit of Martin Marietta and actually bought the Marietta shares on Thursday at midnight, United Technologies would press ahead with its tender offer for Bendix, but at a lower price.

"He thinks we're gonna walk away if he buys Marietta," Rohatyn said. "This would turn it around—we would still buy him, but at an even lower price."

"It could work," Lipton said.

The pressure on Agee to avoid a lowball bid would be enormous.

This secret strategy was worked on by the Lazard Frères and UTC financial staffs on Saturday. There was a lot of analysis and paperwork to complete for the proposal to be announced early in the week.

Harry Gray reviewed the plan over the telephone from Conquistadores.

"That will give Agee forty-eight hours to think it over," Gray said.

Having prepared an aggressive strategy, Harry Gray wanted to have a carrot ready for Bill Agee. A way out with honor. While he was at Conquistadores, Gray and his advisers formulated the idea of offering Bendix another $100 million on top of the deal already on the table.

"I want to have this two-track thing worked out by Monday before I meet with Agee," Harry said. "Then I'll lay it out for him. My bet is that he will want to work something out."

Gray was a brilliant businessman.

He had a stick and a carrot for Bill Agee.

He turned to the man who needed him most—Tom Pownall —to finance the deal. Gray took Pownall aside at Conquistadores.

"Tom, I think I can work out a deal with Agee. It may take some help from you," Gray said.

"How can I help?" Pownall asked. He knew Gray was a master at this kind of game.

"Remember I talked about upping the bid for Bendix? Now is the time. I'm thinking of bumping up the price for Bendix by about a hundred million dollars," Gray said, telling Pownall about the carrot but not the stick. "But if I do up the price, we got to work out an add-on to our agreement."

"What, increase our six-hundred-million-dollar pledge to seven hundred million dollars?"

"Something like that."

"Let me talk to my guys," Pownall said.

"It may be your ticket out of this," Gray said, smiling.

Tom Pownall had a telephone installed in his room at the Conquistadores ranch. It was a special phone. When he picked it up, it gave him a dial tone in Martin Marietta headquarters.

He called Charlie Leithauser to talk over Harry Gray's plan. He then decided to call New York to talk with Marty Siegel, his investment banker.

"Marty, Harry wants to add a hundred million dollars to our deal. What do you think?"

Marty Siegel had to be careful. He knew that Gray and Pownall were close. He did not want to say anything impolitic. Siegel was worried. It looked to him like Harry Gray was trying to outmaneuver Martin Marietta and in the process take a shot at landing both Bendix and Marietta. But to tell Pownall that, Siegel thought, would be indiscreet. He would propose another idea.

"Tom, I don't think that's to our benefit. Our problem with Agee is not going to go away by Harry increasing his offer. Agee still thinks he can buy us first and then beat Harry on antitrust grounds. We've got to make a move that shows him we are for real."

"What's your idea?"

"We've got to do something dramatic," Siegel said.

"Like what?"

"It would have to be something that would really get his attention."

"Marty," Pownall said impatiently.

"I think we should drop the conditions to our offer. Tell the world that we are committed to buying Bendix no matter what unless they back off and don't buy our shares."

Pownall was silent. "Talk to the lawyers and let's get together tomorrow night in my office," he then said.

On Sunday, Doris Rush was home in Bethesda. Planning to putter around the house all day, her only goal was to get ahold of the Sunday newspapers. She had on old pants and a shirt and after a flick of her hairbrush just slipped her bare feet into shoes and jumped into the car to pick up the Sunday *New York Times*. The store was out of papers. She was just about to turn home when she remembered that the PR department at the office received all the newspapers. She decided to stop by the office.

The Sunday edition of the *Washington Post* carried a broad banner over four columns and a close-up photograph of Bill Agee. The banner read "AGEE AND THE PROSPECT OF DEFEAT—BENDIX CHIEF CARRIES ON WITH APLOMB."

Doris Rush read with fascination.

Agee, 44-year-old chairman of Bendix Corp., triggered a wild tag-team merger battle last month with a surprise move to take over Martin Marietta, the aerospace and construction-materials company based in Bethesda. And it looked for the first week as if Agee and Bendix couldn't lose.

Now, after a week of sudden reverses, he is on the defensive in a two-front struggle against Martin Marietta and its 11th-hour ally, United Technologies Corp. of Hartford, which are trying to take Bendix out of Agee's hands and split it up between them.

A week ago, analysts were calling Agee a genius for springing the attempt to take over Martin Marietta. . . . Now analysts are faulting Agee and Bendix for not building a better defense against the kind of counterattack Martin Marietta launched with United Technologies' help.

"Somebody didn't do their homework," Joseph S. Phillippi of Dean Witter Reynolds said last week.

The article went on to tell the encapsulated version of Agee's career. Almost a third of the article was a summary of Bill Agee's relationship with Mary Cunningham and the controversy that surrounded the couple.

Doris Rush could identify with Mary.

She thought it was horrible the way Mary had been savaged by the press. She was quick to note that Mary was the one who was forced to resign her position at Bendix—even though it takes two to tango.

Doris knew enough about sexism to see the double standard being applied to Mary's actions.

"Mary's big mistake," Doris thought, "was meeting Bill Agee!"

Padding slowly along the empty halls in the building, Doris thought it was almost ghostly. There didn't seem to be another soul around. Confronted by a mound of paper on her desk, Doris began rooting through her notes, trying to determine how best to attack the issues of the day. She slipped off her shoes, stretched out comfortably. She wandered back and forth between her office and the law library with a thick book spread in her hands. In the otherwise empty building, Doris spotted down at the end of the hall Tom Pownall, just back from Wyoming.

"Doris, Doris!" Pownall said, walking toward her.

Rush wanted to turn and run. Here she was wearing the lousiest clothes she owned and was barefoot, with no makeup.

"I just wanted to congratulate you. I think that was just such a super thing, a brilliant legal strategy."

The more Pownall praised Doris the lower she tried to sink to make her pants cuffs cover her bare toes.

As Pownall walked away, he turned and gave her a thumbs-up, "Just neat, Doris. Neat!"

During the day on Sunday, Bill Agee was expected at the Hill & Knowlton offices at 420 Lexington Avenue, near Forty-third Street. It had been decided that Bendix's efforts to solicit proxies in support of the charter amendments would be backed up by a videotaped message from the chairman to be delivered over the Bendix Video Network to salaried employees across the country who were members of SESSOP.

Writing the speech to be given by Agee had been difficult. So many hands had to touch it. Drafts were run through the Bendix PR operation in Southfield, through Dick Cheney's organization, past Al McDonald and Bob Meyers, the lawyers, and finally to Bill Agee, who handed the script to Mary Cunningham for her comments. One of Mary's responsibilities at Bendix had been directing the press area.

Rippling like a skip rope, the script went from the bottom to the top and back again. By Sunday, last-minute changes were still being made.

The TV studio at Hill & Knowlton was on the tenth floor. Bill Agee arrived with his wife and briefly socialized with the executives gathered for the session. Agee brought Mary because he trusted her implicitly and knew that she had no hidden agendas. Throughout, next to Al McDonald, she was his closest adviser.

Mary was shy around the cameras.* In early August, she was interviewed by Barbara Walters for an upcoming special on successful working women. During the interview, Mary discussed her role two years before as a strategic planner at Bendix. Without naming names, she cautiously discussed "The Acquisi-

---

*Bill Agee informed the author that Mary's "fears and anger . . . brought on by reporters carrying cameras" had prompted her to seek help from "numerous counselors."

tion Strategy." It was obvious that Mary knew Bendix was about to make a move.

Dick Cheney had a big smile on his face when he greeted Bill and Mary, but inwardly, Cheney was just a touch concerned about Mary's presence. She was not a Bendix employee. What was she doing here? Watching the two of them together, it was obvious that Bill looked to her for counsel. She was vocal about several phrases in the script. Several modest changes were made.

After Bill positioned himself for the taping, Mary talked with Bob Meyers about her husband's appearance. She was concerned that his hair and tie be neatly arranged. "Bill hates makeup," Mary told Meyers.

"When is this going to be distributed?" Agee asked.

"Probably tomorrow," Bob Meyers said.

"Do I look all right?"

"Fine, Bill," Mary said.

"I want to speak to you for a minute about the special meeting of Bendix shareholders to be held on Tuesday, September twenty-first. We recently mailed proxy materials to you notifying you of the meeting. I feel it is especially important that you, as employee shareholders at Bendix, have a clear understanding of the two proposals you are being asked to vote on. The first proposal is designed to assure—oh," Agee said, checking the script, "I screwed that up. Do I start again?"

"No, that was fine, we just do a pickup," the director said. "Start with the second paragraph."

Agee continued reading the four-hundred-word message, concluding, "I ask you to vote for both of these Bendix proposals by signing, dating, and mailing your Bendix proxy card today. The proposals are in your best interests as both shareholders and employees. They will protect the value of your Bendix stock. They will protect your rights as Bendix shareholders. And they will help us continue to work together to build a strong, secure company.

"Thank you."

By Sunday afternoon, the Martin Marietta and United Technologies solicitation teams were hard at work analyzing the computer tapes delivered by Bendix lawyer Dave Young at minutes after twelve noon. Young delivered the list of Bendix nonemployee stockholders as late as legally allowed.

In New York, Peter Harkins, United Technologies' solicitor from Georgeson & Company, used the Bendix computer tapes to run a statistical analysis of the Bendix stockholders. He broke down the list of individual holders into divisions classified by the size of the holding. He discovered that the majority of holders were individuals who controlled small numbers of shares. He also found that 164 holders controlled 67 percent of the outstanding Bendix shares.

Something had to be done fast.

A total of 10,190 Mailgrams to all Bendix stockholders with more than three hundred shares were delivered to the post office. The Mailgram was a short message advising the stockholders that United Technologies was opposing the Bendix management attempt to pass the "shark repellent" amendments. The letter advised the shareholder to wait until he or she received the United Technologies proxy materials before voting.

Dan Neff, Peter Harkins, and lawyer Ed Herlihy were sitting in Neff's office on the thirty-sixth floor at Wachtell, Lipton on Park Avenue.

"The SESSOP situation is a major problem," Harkins said. "We don't have a way to contact the SESSOP participants. Sure, Bendix is mailing our materials to them, but they're also calling the people on the telephone in opposition, talking to them at work, putting signs up on the bulletin boards at plants. If we can't find a way to get to the Bendix employees who own stock, we're going to be writing off almost twenty-five percent of the votes from the get-go."

"What about some kind of union organizing tactic?" Herlihy said. "We could have people show up at the Bendix plants and hand out leaflets."

"Oh, geez, c'mon, Big Ed," Neff said.

"Maybe television ads or radio ads," Herlihy volunteered.

United Technologies planned to run a $450,000 national newspaper advertising campaign in opposition to the Bendix amendments. Radio spots in Detroit would be added.

Sunday, September 12, was the hottest day of the month in New York City, with the mercury topping eighty-eight degrees under sunny skies. It seemed considerably warmer than that on the tennis courts of the Metropolis Country Club in Westchester. Dick Katcher and his wife, Susan, played doubles with their friends David and Marilyn. Dick and Marilyn won.

At about 3:00 P.M., when Dick and Susan returned home to their house on Fairway Drive in Mamaroneck, Dick received a call from Doug Brown at Kidder, Peabody.

"How would you like a fun-filled, all-expenses-paid trip to Bethesda, Maryland?" Brown asked.

"Terrific," Katcher said with an obvious lack of enthusiasm.

The Martin Marietta jet took off from the Butler terminal at LaGuardia at a little after 6:00 P.M. with Marty Siegel, Doug Brown, Peter Woods, and Dick Katcher.

Tom Pownall—back from Conquistadores—was waiting in his office with Larry Adams, Charlie Leithauser, Frank Menaker, and Roy Calvin.

"Where do we stand?" Pownall asked Siegel.

"Well, the perception on the street is that Bendix thinks that if they buy first, they will win. That we will blink before we buy back."

"So what are we going to do?" Menaker asked.

"As it is set up now, once Bendix buys, we're the ones who are going to have to make the decision on whether or not to buy them. And that's a tough spot to be in. There is going to be considerable heat from all quarters. We will be using our own equity to buy our own assets. That is not going to go over well."

"Tom, as you know," Charlie Leithauser said, "I had hoped that all of our moves to date would give us parity with Agee. If we had to put the companies together, we'd do it on equal footing, with some kind of parent umbrella over all our heads. But nothing's worked—now Agee is saying he's not gonna just buy forty-five percent of the company, he's gonna buy more. Parity is out the goddamn window! The guy wants it all."

Pownall looked at the men.

"Tell me again," Pownall said to Siegel.

"My idea is to turn the tables on Agee and put the weight on his shoulders. Our offer now has a bunch of conditions that give our board of directors a bunch of ways out in the event that Bendix takes down our stock Thursday at midnight. We know that. Agee knows that. The street knows that.

"After Bendix buys, the board is going to have to take a vote on whether to accept Bendix as the owner of the corporation or whether to pursue the Martin Marietta offer to buy Bendix and then fight to see who can control whom first. Agee has on Friday already said that he's going to buy a clear majority share with cash. The pressure on the Board to concede in light of the block owned by Bendix will be horrendous."

"Bendix will own us," Leithauser said.

"But not yet control," Dick Katcher interjected.

Pownall nodded to Katcher and then looked to Siegel again.

"If we drop our conditions," Marty continued, "we can send a clear signal that if Bendix buys, we are legally forced to buy. It will take the decision out of our hands and force Agee to make the decision."

Tom Pownall knew that the "decision" was a nightmare no matter who made it. The net result could be financial disaster. The idea of forcing Agee to make that decision appealed to Pownall.

"So what would be my options?" Pownall asked.

"We're removing your options," Siegel said.

"If he buys, we buy."

"Right, and we tell the world in advance. Everybody will be looking to Bill Agee to prevent this from happening."

Pownall was looking down, thinking. It did seem like a way to put the heat on Agee. The strategy was also incredibly risky. If Agee did not back off, the result was something Pownall found hard to visualize. If Bendix owned Martin Marietta and Martin Marietta owned Bendix, how would anybody get anything done?

Pownall knew he needed something. And fast.

"Are you ready to present this to the board tomorrow?" Pownall asked.

"I don't think we have much choice."

"Shouldn't we have some outs?" Menaker asked. "What about the Bendix 'shark repellent' amendments? What happens if they pass?"

"Where's Bob Fullem?" Katcher asked.

"I've been talking to him," Menaker said.

"Don't let him come into this cold tomorrow."

The two lawyers huddled briefly and decided to call Fullem to discuss the extent to which Martin Marietta should waive its conditions.

They went off to Menaker's office and found Bob Fullem at

his home. Menaker updated him on the discussions about waiving conditions. Fullem was in favor. He thought it was a good idea to put the burden of the decision on Bendix. Katcher had some doubts that all conditions should be waived.

"Jesus, shouldn't we have a litigation out?" Dick asked. "I mean, what happens if when we want to buy, they get some court to enjoin us?"

Katcher also related the experiences of Gulf + Western and the A&P case. "They got stuck by doing this," Katcher said.

"Ah, hell," Fullem said enthusiastically, "let's do it!"

"I'm going to meet with Harry Gray on Tuesday," Bill Agee said casually to Arthur Fleischer. The two men were in the Helmsley Palace suite. Fleischer stopped pouring himself a drink. He set the pitcher down and turned.

"Bill, we are attempting to fend off United Technologies on antitrust grounds in court. I can't see how this will help. And it certainly will not strengthen our position vis-à-vis Martin Marietta. If the meeting was disclosed in the press, we would be slaughtered. Unless you want to make a deal with Harry Gray, don't have the meeting, Bill."

"I just wanted to hear him out," Agee said.

"It would be a mistake," Fleischer said. The tall lawyer adjusted his glasses. His firm expression, wrinkled only slightly by the beginnings of a smile, conveyed his understanding of the situation.

Pownall would not talk. At least Harry would talk.

"He's going to call me tonight to confirm," Agee said, without committing to scuttle the meeting. A subtle strategy was unfolding in his mind. Bill Agee considered it his job to scour the waterfront, mindful of the interests of the Bendix stockholders. He considered his early conversations with Felix Rohatyn not to be tactical blunders, as he was hearing from the street and seeing in the newspapers. In Agee's mind, that was planting a seed.

Whether in his office at the GM Building or in the suite at the Helmsley Palace, Agee was searching for options, taking scores of calls from the investment banking community, talking to people who could provide him an edge. He would tell almost everyone something, key people most things, and no one everything. Agee knew well a principle of power: By being the only one capable of piecing together all the shapes of the puzzle, he maintained control.

Al McDonald and Mary joined Fleischer in the living room. The phone rang. It was Harry Gray.

"Harry, how are you?" Agee asked. He still had not made up his mind whether or not to meet as planned with Gray. Bill listened for several moments to hear what Gray had in mind.

"Lookit, Harry, if we meet at the Metropolitan Club, my God, we might as well announce the meeting on the loud-speaker. At least at the Palace, we won't be disturbed."

Again Agee listened.

"What do you mean the Palace is probably bugged?" Agee asked incredulously, looking over at Al McDonald. Gray sounded in a roused mood.

The thought of someone bugging suite 4509 at the Palace was not considered farfetched by the Bendix team. Big money could be made from overheard conversations. From day one, Jim Armstrong, the Bendix exec in charge of such things, was instructed to sweep the suite periodically. Listening to Gray explain his reservations about meeting at the Palace, Agee made a mental note to have Jim come up and go over the rooms again —just in case Harry was right.

Harry said something else that got Bill Agee's attention.

Bill thought Gray was waving the presidency of United Technologies in his face. From Gray's words, it sounded as if Bill could have a "good place" at UTC in the event of the merger of the two companies. Bill knew the No. 2 spot was open at the enormous corporation. It was an attractive idea—and with Harry only two years away from sixty-five . . .

"We both know there are serious antitrust problems in your offer," Agee said, adding a moment later, "and Harry, your price is way too low."

The two men continued to talk.

"In any event, Harry, my lawyers tell me that it is inadvisable for us to meet," Agee said, acknowledging the advice of Arthur Fleischer.

If only Pownall would call me, Agee thought.

TWENTY-ONE

Sunday night was the first scheduled working session between Agee and the new Bendix investment banker—Bruce Wasserstein from First Boston Corp. Michael Rowny had been working the contractual problem all during the week, meeting with Wasserstein and talking to him on the phone. Rowny also talked extensively with Wasserstein's attorney.

Agee's instructions had been to structure the deal with First Boston on the same footing as the deal with Salomon Brothers. That was proving difficult.

"Look, Michael," Jay Higgins had said, "we've been working on this acquisition since July, and now Wasserstein wants to come in at the last minute and earn the same fee as Salomon? It's a joke, to be honest."

Wasserstein had his own comeback.

"Mike, time hasn't got anything to do with these kinds of deals. Salomon Brothers has not done its homework. I don't care if they've been working on this since Christmas! We're coming in to square things up. I think, frankly, we deserve more than you're talking."

Rowny got back to Agee at each turn in the negotiations, relaying what the bankers wanted. Both Agee and Rowny were amazed at the price tags. Agee rejected certain formulas that would have seen the tabs crash well beyond the $6 million mark. Rowny and Wasserstein painstakingly worked out a fee ladder that included a range of formulas in the event of different outcomes in the transaction.

On Sunday, Mike Rowny was down in Maryland. He had tried placing calls to Wasserstein but couldn't reach him. Michael left his number, and during the afternoon, Wasserstein called.

"Where are you?" Rowny asked. There was a lot of background noise.

"I'm out getting one of my kids an ice-cream cone," Wasserstein said. In calmer times he spent weekends at his second home in the Hamptons on Long Island with his two kids and his wife, Chris, who was a psychotherapist. With the big meeting coming up, he was staying in the city. Wasserstein was talking to Rowny from a phone booth in Manhattan.

"I just wanted you to know that I've worked out those last-minute points. We'll be ready to execute an agreement," Rowny said.

"Great," Wasserstein said, competing with the cars honking on the street.

Wasserstein grew up in New York City. By sixteen, he was attending college at the University of Michigan. At nineteen, he was off to Harvard. During his summers, he worked on Ralph Nader projects and a War on Poverty program. Whatever he did, Wasserstein was a hustler.

He brought an associate, Tony Grassi, to the meeting with Bill Agee in suite 4509 at the Helmsley Palace. Al McDonald also was present.

Wasserstein, as was his nature, could not comfortably chitchat. Like a wound-up top, he had to start rolling. Agee respected Wasserstein's decisiveness.

"Look, Bill, we don't really have any stake in this business deal. We're coming in at the last minute. Let me tell you where we think this deal is."

"That's why you're here," Agee said.

"We think this deal is in big trouble. Frankly, we think the values of Martin Marietta were not correctly analyzed. We have yet to see any information from Salomon Brothers that analyzed Martin Marietta on an asset-by-asset and section-by-section basis. . . ."

"Did you ask to see the Salomon materials?" McDonald asked. "I thought your staff people were going to be in touch with the research people at Salomon."

"Al, all I can tell you is we haven't seen quantitative analyses. In any event, the first thing we'd like to do is go through what we have prepared regarding the values of Martin Marietta."

Wasserstein and Grassi ticked off the different components of the Martin Marietta business—as had Salomon Brothers during the preceding months. Bill Agee examined Wasserstein. He appeared slick, with a starched shirt, cuff links, stylish glasses. But his reddish, curly hair was slightly unkempt, and as he pondered, Wasserstein played a sprig of hair between his fingers.

"Looking at it from our analysis, we think that the correct values for Martin Marietta are between fifty-two and sixty dollars a share," Wasserstein said.

"Bruce," Agee said, sensing that the dynamics of the situation were encouraging Wasserstein to paint a dark picture, "you have to understand that I have an idea of what Martin Marietta is worth, and in fact my ideas are not so different from what you're saying. I place the worth somewhere in the fifties. What do you propose we do?"

"Well, I would like to continue," Wasserstein said. "In terms of strategy, there is another issue. This whole situation of the difference between the state laws in Delaware and in Maryland. We've talked with the lawyers, and nobody really seems to have a solution to the problem."

Agee felt vulnerable about this timing issue. On the one hand, he believed Art Fleischer that no matter what the nuances of the law said, whoever bought first would come out on top. On the other hand, Agee was irritated that he was not aware of the problem sooner. Art said it had been mentioned in meetings. Agee felt certain it had not been red-flagged.

"Fleischer feels strongly that he will be able to get a court in Delaware to prevent Martin Marietta from voting any Bendix shares they buy," Agee said.

"Even if that's true, you won't know for sure until it's too late," Wasserstein replied. "And besides, who knows what could happen? Maybe they could sell the shares to someone who could vote the stock. Bill, this is a hell of a situation, and the answers are not all there."

"So what do you propose?" Agee asked, acknowledging Wasserstein's interpretation of the situation.

"Let me ask you first. Have you done anything about arranging people to make an investment in Bendix?" Agee was shaking his head calmly from side to side, so Wasserstein continued. "How about sale of assets? Refinancing your bank lines? White knight lists?"

It looked to Wasserstein that Bill Agee's answers were no, no, no.

"Bruce I have not asked for that sort of work to be done."

Wasserstein had come prepared with what Agee had asked for: a decision-making tree, which he unrolled ceremoniously. Basically a "what if" map of one week's alternatives, the document had more than a hundred alternatives. Agee and McDonald had wanted First Boston to look ahead—beyond the next move—to determine the end game. A week was about as far as First Boston could put on paper. The variables were so complex. It became a sort of mind game.

"Bill, you're not going to win this unless you crack the Martin Marietta board. It's very similar to a problem we had with American General, and it worked there. You must make a conditional raise and do it in an elegant way. A way that gives the board the room to accept the offer. You can't do that when there is always a twenty-four-hour-fuse mentality. You've got to approach these guys as gentlemen and offer them a full price."

"What is your idea in terms of how many seats we should give to Martin Marietta on our board?"

"Bill, that's not going to satisfy them if you don't offer a full price."

"Now, wait a minute," Agee said, getting excited, "I just raised unilaterally to forty-eight dollars, and now you're telling me I should raise again?"

"Well, why did you do that in the first place? What made you think that was a good idea?" Wasserstein was also getting excited.

"Whether you think it was a good idea or not, that decision has been made."

"Bill, my point is this: Raising to forty-eight dollars had no effect because it's not a price to crack the Martin Marietta board. The shares were going to come in anyway—where were they going to go? It goes back to this issue of values, and that's what their board is looking at."

"I will consider that," Agee said. It was clear to Wasserstein that the answer to his proposal for a conditional raise was no, at least for now.

"What do you think Martin Marietta's next move is?"

"They are obviously looking for someone to buy a position in the company to try to throw off the Bendix timetable. But what I think is most important is to analyze the way they are thinking. It is very important at this stage to open up communications with them. I know Marty Siegel. I know we can talk."

Agee was interested in pursuing all angles. But he also knew just as firmly that the investment bankers could not negotiate this deal. He had to be personally involved. He hoped Tom Pownall would see the situation the same way. The bankers always had one foot in the present deal and another looking for a place to step. Agee knew that he and Pownall would carry the result of this battle around with them for the rest of their careers.

"I can tell you that Siegel has given Martin Marietta a lot of analysis of the situation. That's the way Kidder, Peabody works. We have to analyze the consequences of what happens if we buy and then if they buy. Siegel may be saying to them that the debt will be manageable. From our rough cut, it looks like that may be their perspective. And if that's the case, then it may be viable for them to buy despite the fact that you bought first."

"What's your feeling about the United Technologies bid?"

"You've got to take that threat seriously. You have got to start work immediately on possible white knights to buy the company if it comes to that. We need authorization to begin contacting people first with an eye to possible investment candidates to throw off the timetables of the Martin and UTC bids."

"Who do you have in mind?" Agee asked.

Wasserstein produced a list and showed it to Agee.

Jay Higgins had mentioned several of the same names.

"You can contact the top two," Agee said. That meant Allied Corporation and Esmark Corporation.

"And the conditional raise?" Bruce asked.

"On hold for now."

Bill Agee, looking relaxed, was silent for a moment.

"Let's set this discussion with Siegel in motion," Agee said.

"Warren, help me understand the role of a board member." Martin Marietta director Jack Byrne was on the phone with

the businessman he respected the most. Byrne considered Warren Buffett—a private investor from Nebraska—to be his mentor. Buffett's company, Berkshire-Hathaway, owned 35 percent
of Geico, the huge insurance carrier that Byrne ran.

"I take it this Martin Marietta and Bendix thing has got you
thinking?" Buffett asked.

"Yeah. Getting sued for breach of duty has a way of marvel-
ously focusing the mind," Byrne said, referring obliquely to the
Bendix lawsuit charging the Marietta board of directors with
dereliction of duty.

A mathematician by training, Jack Byrne was a gregarious
man, somewhat overweight, who preferred loafers to pointed
dress shoes, a cardigan sweater to his three-piece business suit.

In the enormous outer waiting area of his corner office on
tree-lined Western Avenue in Washington, D.C., memorabilia
from different Presidents lined the walls. His office had a green
rug, a rust-colored couch, and a blue chalkboard.

Jack Byrne was standing at his chalkboard, a piece of chalk
in one hand and the telephone in the other. He was writing
numbers and drawing lines and circles with exaggerated emphasis as he talked with Buffett.

Whenever Byrne was really stuck, he called Buffett. Most of
the time, they talked about money. Today it was philosophy.

Sensitive to secrecy, Byrne did not go into the details of his
problem.

"How do I best represent the interests of the stockholders?"
Byrne asked.

"Jack, you couldn't find a grayer gray area," Buffett said.

Looking back on the first crisis meeting of the Martin Marietta board of directors, Jack Byrne was troubled. The scene
was vivid in his mind. He was sitting next to Lee Everett—
another man with a deep financial background.

When Tom Pownall broached the idea of the countertender,
Jack could hear Lee Everett pull in his breath. Byrne was equally
taken aback.

"Oh, my God," Everett said, "think of the financial implications!"

"We're gonna be digging a great big black hole!" Byrne said.

Frank Ewing also voiced concern. A tough financial guy,
Ewing knew the numbers never lie.

Byrne and Everett in their positions dealt with investment

bankers on a daily basis. Therefore, both men took the enthusiasm of Marty Siegel with a grain of salt. Siegel was working on
a deal. But this could be the single most important decision Jack
Byrne made as a member of the Martin Marietta board of directors.

Byrne listened very closely to Charlie Leithauser.

He respected Leithauser and his conservative approach.

"Charlie, you're gonna have something like an eighty-five
percent debt-to-equity ratio," Byrne said incredulously.

"I know," Leithauser said. "I've looked at this very thoroughly. It's a stretch, but in my view, we can live with it and work
it out."

"Remember," Marty Siegel interjected, "we're dealing with
this decision on two levels—one, a tactical level, and two, a
financial level. I don't think we will actually borrow the money,
because I think the tactic will work. Bill Agee will back down."

Okay, Byrne thought, it's never gonna come about. It's just
a tactical ploy. If it does come about, I've done my duty. Leithauser says it can be done. It's tight, okay.

No one needed to explain to Byrne two days later the meaning of the fall in Bendix stock price.

Siegel's tactic did not work. Strike No. 1.

Then Byrne was staring at the possibility that Martin Marietta would actually borrow $930 million for the avowed pur-
pose of buying Bendix. Where that would lead, Byrne had no
idea—just a deep sense of dread.

How could he explain the decision to an average stockholder
—perhaps an old lady in Omaha? Her stock on the NYSE was
worth $33 a share before the Bendix offer. And Bill Agee pro-
mised to give her $48 a share.

How could Byrne make her understand why she should not
sell?

The company is worth more was the easy answer.

But was the company worth destroying to save it?

And then came the entrance of United Technologies. Harry
Gray was supposed to save the Martin Marietta offer. Byrne
could still visualize an ebullient Marty Siegel.

"The price of Bendix stock will go up to here," Siegel said,
holding his hand above his head during the board meeting.

Strike No. 2—the tactic had not worked.

"Don't worry," Warren Buffett said on the telephone,

"you're gonna find in this situation that the professionals—the Wall Street types—will take it right out of your hands."

Monday morning was sunny and hazy in Washington, a light wind from the south doing little to relieve the humidity. The directors of Martin Marietta gathered at the corporation's headquarters in Bethesda to consider their next move. The meeting was held in the conference room on the third floor of the executive wing.

The boardroom had a long wooden table skirted with perhaps thirty chairs. The walls were covered with dark wood wainscoting all the way around. At one end behind a curtain was an audio-video area. The ceiling was dotted with rheostat lights. A long bed of windows looked out onto the atrium.

"Gentlemen," Tom Pownall said, "at midnight on Thursday, the withdrawal period of the Bendix offer expires, and Bendix is free to buy our shares. And as you know, on Friday, their board increased the number of shares to eighteen point five million.

"We've tried several ways to send Agee a message—through our countertender and the agreement with Harry. It appears that nothing we have tried to date has worked. The market continues to treat us with skepticism. And as you remember from Agee's price increase to forty-eight dollars, he appears adamant. I have been discussing our situation with the bankers and the lawyers. It appears that this is the critical moment to send Mr. Agee another message."

The directors were attentive. Jack Byrne sat next to Lee Everett. At fifty and fifty-six, respectively, Byrne and Everett were young men in comparison to directors Eugene Zuckert, a seventy-year-old Washington attorney, and seventy-one-year-old John Hanigan, the chairman of Genesco, a Nashville-based manufacturer of apparel and footwear. Among the fourteen men on the board, there were over five hundred years of experience in the worlds of business, government, and the military.

The decision Tom Pownall was laying on the table was unnerving.

"The thinking of management," Tom Pownall said, "is that the board should at this time reevaluate the conditions attached to our offer to purchase the Bendix Corporation and remove all conditions that could be interpreted as giving us an 'out' against Agee. It is time to put it all on the line."

Pownall relied on his advisers—Marty Siegel from Kidder, Peabody and Bob Fullem from Dewey, Ballantine—to lay out the plan of action to waive the conditions.

Fullem reviewed Section 15 of the Martin Marietta offer, which included nine conditions under which the corporation would withdraw its offer to buy Bendix.

"What we are proposing," Marty Siegel said, looking fresh and confident, "is that the board eliminate all conditions but two. The only remaining conditions under which Martin Marietta would drop its bid to buy Bendix would be one, Bendix withdraw its offer; and two, Bendix pass the proposed 'shark repellent' amendments that would directly challenge our offer. With only those two conditions left, the entire burden will be put on Bill Agee's shoulders for the consequences."

Director Jack Byrne was worried. He remembered Siegel's last two tactics—neither of which had achieved the desired result. Could this be strike three and you're out? Byrne thought.

"We will be telling Agee," Siegel said, "that we are legally committed to buying his stock if he proceeds as planned and buys us on Thursday night. It will make him think twice before pulling the trigger."

"It's the only way to convince Agee that we're serious," said Bob Fullem. "He is gonna have to make not one decision but two decisions, number one being to buy our stock and number two, after he owns us, he'll have to turn around and buy his own stock."

"Will that hold up in court?" Gene Zuckert asked. The Martin Marietta board was invisibly divided into areas of expertise. When the issue was financial, Jack Byrne, Lee Everett, and Frank Ewing were the powerhouses. When the issue was legal, Griffin Bell, Mel Laird, and Gene Zuckert commanded the most attention.

"We can't say for certain," Fullem said. "But I can advise the board that the opinion of Dewey, Ballantine is that it will stick."

"Let's keep in mind our goal," Pownall said, "and that is to convince Bill Agee to go away."

"What happens if we waive our conditions and he doesn't go away?" Ewing asked.

That brought the room to silence. The directors were looking to Tom Pownall to supply the answer.

"It would be a highly undesirable situation, but from the financial reports presented by Charlie and Marty, I think we've seen that we could live with the result," Pownall said grimly.

"But if we look at this from Agee's perspective," Fullem said, "I mean, he is a rational man. If we withdraw our conditions, under those circumstances, it is hard to conclude that a rational man would continue and buy our stock. I mean, he's intelligent. He's rational. Look at his options. If he buys us, we will have already publicly announced our intentions and obligation to buy. He'll know the consequences. But we're giving him the chance to just back off. He will have to conclude that the financial burden if avoidable should be avoided.

"But I want to make one thing perfectly clear to the board: By considering waiving the conditions, the board is basically deciding now whether or not to buy the Bendix stock on the twenty-second at midnight."

The mood in the room was deadly serious. All the directors and the Martin Marietta management team knew that this decision was an ominous portent of uncertainty ahead. They could be committing the corporation to a massive expenditure of funds to in effect buy itself.

"Jesus, it's like détente," a director said. "The only thing that keeps Agee from sending up his missiles is knowing that we will send up our missiles!"

When the maneuver was fully understood on Wall Street, it was nicknamed "the Doomsday Machine"; Siegel himself called it "the dead man's trigger." Whatever the name, the potential for disaster was the same.

Several board members were unsettled by the development of this mutual-destruction approach. There were worries that something unforeseen could find the board unable to act.

"What happens if Agee comes along next week and offers sixty-five dollars a share? Then what do we do?" a director asked. He mentioned that price because it would be obvious to all members of the board that they should recommend a merger at that kind of price, $30 above market value.

Jack Byrne's "sell" price was $61.

"Well, if he comes in with a price like that," Bob Fullem said, "then we both agree to withdraw our tender offers—fulfilling the remaining conditions—and we agree to a friendly merger."

"Sure," Marty Siegel said, "if the board gets to the point of wanting to do a friendly merger, it can work. But that is not the issue. And Agee is not going to offer sixty-five dollars a share. If we want him to back off, we've got to put a guaranteed bad situation in front of him and let him decide what he wants."

There was give and take on the language of the remaining conditions. Griffin Bell suggested several changes from the drafts prepared by Dick Katcher and worked over by the other lawyers.

"How will this affect Harry?" a director asked.

"UTC is not in a position to help us," Fullem said. "They continue to be useful in the proxy solicitation and the court cases, but Harry Gray is not going to make a deal with Bill Agee."

"Hey, before we take this step," Frank Ewing implored, "isn't there anything else we can do?"

Ewing was a self-made millionaire, a man who had worked hard his entire life to reach the top. At sixty-seven, he remembered the hard years and the value of a dollar. To tie the corporation to a strategy that hoped for the best and could deliver the worst of financial repercussions cut across Ewing's grain. He was used to the time-honored traditions. This plan seemed desperate.

What was on the minds of several board members was never said.

No one wanted to say to Pownall "Tom, go talk to Agee about merging the companies."

"We've got to do this now," Marty Siegel said. "If we don't, fold the tent on Thursday at midnight."

"Marty, if you'll pardon me," Byrne said, "you've been wrong twice before. Should we really think you're gonna be right this time?"

While the vote would be registered as unanimous in the minutes taken by Frank Menaker, the board clearly was divided. The time for flag-waving was over. The time for reading the poetry about shareholders' value was gone. The decision was made: Fight Agee no matter what the cost. And pray he would retreat.

At 12:30 P.M., the story hit the Dow Jones wire that Martin Marietta had withdrawn all but two of the conditions to its offer. Peter Jaquith, a cigar-chomping partner of Felix Rohatyn, was sitting in his Lazard Frères office on the thirty-sixth floor at One

Rockefeller Plaza, practically a stone's throw from the Helmsley Palace. Jaquith smoked five or six cigars a day, just enough to leave a permanent haze in his office. To accommodate his wife, he never smoked on weekends.

In his office Jaquith had several computer terminals that constantly supplied the latest market quotations and news items. When the news crossed that Martin Marietta had waived all but two of its conditions, Jaquith almost choked on his cigar.

"What the fuck is Marty Siegel up to?" Jaquith yelled.

He immediately knew the implications. By waiving the conditions, Martin Marietta was guaranteeing the Bendix stockholders that they would purchase Bendix stock at $75 a share —thereby completely blowing out of the water the United Technologies secret strategy to announce publicly a lower price for Bendix if Agee went ahead and bought Martin Marietta.

There in the wire story, Pownall was quoted: "We want it explicitly understood that Martin Marietta intends to purchase 11.9 million Bendix shares on terms of our tender at the earliest time possible even if Bendix may have earlier purchased Martin Marietta shares under the terms of its tender."

Jaquith was immediately on the phone with his partner. The word spread like wildfire through the offices of Wachtell, Lipton. Marty Lipton was aghast. All the paperwork had been completed on the United Technologies move. It was to be announced tomorrow. Later, Lipton went into partner Dick Katcher's office.

"Why the heck did you do that?" Lipton asked.

Katcher shrugged his shoulders and said "Chinese wall."

The executives at United Technologies were astounded. Ed Large thought it was incredible that Tom Pownall had not called to talk the thing over before launching such a drastic move.

"Apart from torpedoing our tactics, this is outrageous. It's unbelievably reckless," Peter Jaquith said in conversation with his contacts at United Technologies. "Jesus Christ, they've taken away any decision-making by the board. They're totally locked in to whatever action Agee takes."

Jaquith's analysis was correct—and exactly what Marty Siegel wanted the world to think. The burden would be on Agee.

Harry Gray was in his corner office atop the "Gold Building" in downtown Hartford. Tom Pownall was on the telephone.

"Can I come up and talk with you, Harry?" Pownall asked.

"What's going on?" Gray asked.

"Let me come up and talk with you."

When Gray told Ed Large that Pownall was on his way to Hartford, Large was not impressed. "That's an apology trip, Harry," Large said. The damage had already been done.

Pownall arrived accompanied by Frank Menaker and Charlie Leithauser, and as Ed Large had surmised, Pownall figuratively had his hat in his hand. The men were escorted into Harry Gray's office. Harry sat at his desk, behind him heavy gathered drapes and a bronze statue of an eagle on a writhing snake. It was a gift to Gray from the employees of Pratt & Whitney on the tenth anniversary of his ascension to chairman of United Technologies—the largest employer in New England.

In one corner of the office was an American flag, in another the yellow flag of colonial South Carolina. Among the other artifacts was a precious collection of porcelain soldiers. Out the twenty-sixth-floor windows was a panoramic view of Connecticut.

"Let's sit there," Gray said, gesturing to a small cherry and glass table. The men took their places.

"Harry, we thought it was really the best thing that we could do," Tom Pownall said.

Harry didn't say anything. He got up from his chair and walked over to his English hunt desk and poured himself a glass of water. Without turning, he began to speak.

"Tom, I don't think we'd have advised you to do that. Incidentally, why didn't you call me?"

"Harry, I've got more advice than I know what to do with. We decided on this in a very short period of time. I didn't think it would make any difference to you."

"It makes a great deal of difference," Gray said, turning back sharply. Still wearing a smile, Gray then explained to Pownall his two-track strategy to put pressure on Bendix.

"Harry, what can I say?" Pownall said, chagrined. He claimed that he did not know what United Technologies was planning. Gray knew Rohatyn had made mention to Siegel; that was all he knew.

"Ed, what do you think? If Agee buys us, will the courts stop us from pulling the trigger and taking down the Bendix stock?" Pownall asked Large, a businessman and a lawyer.

"I don't think so."

"We hope Agee reads it the same way," Menaker said. "He'll have to back off."

"Maybe," Large said. Pownall looked tight-lipped. This was obviously not easy for him. Large knew that Pownall was wise enough to realize that if Bendix did not back off and Martin Marietta bought anyway, that would leave a very, very weak company—combined after buying out their own equity with their own assets.

"If we do end up pulling the trigger and we end up owning Bendix, would you be willing to buy some of Bendix from us?" Pownall asked Gray.

"It's possible we would put some money in. But frankly, Tom, it does not look all that attractive," Large said.

"Tom, you fellas have to be the guardians of your own future," Gray said, putting his hand on Pownall's shoulder.

Having received the go-ahead from Bill Agee to open a line of communication with the other side, Bruce Wasserstein prepared himself for the call to Marty Siegel. There were three options Wasserstein wanted to explore.

First and foremost was at what price Martin Marietta would agree to sell their company to Bendix; the second course was to convince Marty Siegel that Agee—if he wished—could bully the deal to completion; the third tactic was perhaps the most novel; it involved arranging that all three companies—Bendix, Martin Marietta, and United Technologies—would simply stand down from the battlements and agree to forget the whole thing.

A fast thinker, Wasserstein ticked off the tactics and probable responses. His desk was strewn with paper. His tie knot poorly made. His shirt tails peeking from his pants.

Within minutes after the announcement crossed the Dow Jones wire that Martin Marietta had waived all but two of the conditions to its offer, Wasserstein was on the phone to talk with Siegel. He was not in the office. Wasserstein left a message. Later in the afternoon, Siegel—just back from Bethesda—returned the call.

"Bruce, how are things going with you guys?" Siegel asked. "Are you working with Higgins on this?"

"First Boston is handling the discussions now," Wasserstein said.

"Agee is like George Steinbrenner," Siegel said.

"Hey, Marty," Wasserstein said, getting down to his three options, "I got three things to talk about. I got bribery, I got war, and I got peace. Which do you want?"

"Well, I guess bribery and peace are the only two I can control."

"What's the number, Marty? What's the dollar sign that will get your guys to accept a deal?"

"Make me an offer and I'll take it to the board," Siegel said, evasively.

"Think about it," Wasserstein said. "I want to know at what number would Kidder, Peabody recommend acceptance."

"These guys in Bethesda are not going to give up easily," Siegel said. "Let's talk peace. Would Agee drop his bid if we dropped ours?"

"I'm not saying we're not gonna buy, Marty. I want to know your responses. I do know that Agee won't do anything if United Technologies is left staring us in the face. Can you arrange to get Harry Gray to take a walk?"

"Let me check it out," Siegel said.

After hanging up, Siegel was excited. He thought the fact that Wasserstein had mentioned the "peace" option was positive news. Perhaps Agee was taking the waiving of conditions seriously and realized he had to walk away to avoid a financial nightmare.

"The market will tell us," Charlie Leithauser said to Tom Pownall.

During the day on Monday, the price of Martin Marietta stock began to fall, dropping ¼ within minutes followed by another ¼ and then another and another. Volume was light, but by the close, the price of Martin Marietta common stock had tumbled 3⅞ to $33.63—the lowest level since Bendix began its attack.

The sinking price meant that demand for Martin Marietta stock was also down. The stock-market professionals were having second thoughts. If Agee also had second thoughts and backed down, the arbs stood to lose a bundle.

The news was greeted with excitement in Bethesda.

Maybe this time the tactic was working! The street obviously believed that Martin Marietta was serious—so serious that the value of the company was likely to be impaired.

Likewise, the price of Bendix stock began to move—up—as the investing community tried to come to grips with the new developments. Bendix common started up by ⅛ and then another to close up slightly at $59.25—still drastically short of the $75 offered by Martin Marietta.

Investors—gambling that the Martin Marietta threat was real —were buying Bendix stock and driving up the price.

Leithauser hoped that on Tuesday it would go higher.

The bad news was quick in coming. Almost from the opening bell, the price of Martin Marietta stock began to rise, and the price of Bendix began to fall sharply. It would close off $2.00.

Wall Street had thought it over and was not buying the tactic.

"It's still up to Agee," Siegel reassured Tom Pownall.

TWENTY-TWO

The federal tender offer rules as envisioned by Congress and amended by experience contain a myriad of legal crawl spaces that allow skilled and well-counseled companies to extricate themselves from precariously tight spots.

Martin Marietta had their lawyers looking closely at one such rule—as a last-ditch effort to throw another obstacle in the path of Bill Agee. The Securities and Exchange Commission rule stated that any new offer for more than 5 percent of a target company's stock would automatically change the timetable of all offers for the company's stock.

In the language of Wall Street, it's called an "extender" or a "mini white knight."

Use of such tactics was but one of the tools of investment bankers.

Marty Siegel had been preparing for this eventuality since day one.

As soon as Martin Marietta was attacked, Marty Siegel and his team from Kidder, Peabody—notably Doug Brown—scoured the Martin Marietta books looking for assets that could potentially be sold to another company and thereby grant Martin Marietta a temporary reprieve from Bendix's noose.

Unversed in such intricacies, Tom Pownall and his key people listened patiently in late-night meetings, over sodas and sandwiches, learning the Wall Street tricks of the corporate take-over game.

Larry Adams, the chief operating officer of the company, was called upon to look at his companies and pick a self-contained, marketable asset that represented from 5 to 10 percent of the value of the company.

Doug Brown and Marty Siegel did their job.

They quickly surfaced potential candidates to buy Martin Marietta assets: W. R. Grace was interested in Marietta's chemical operations; Holderbank, a Dutch company, was interested in Marietta cement.

As is the case in any transaction being noisily conducted in public, every investment banking firm on Wall Street spent considerable amounts of energy trying to figure out how to get into the deal and the lucrative commissions. Bankers contacted their clients to determine possible interest.

William Morris, a partner at the firm of Lehman Brothers, thought he had a live one. He called Marty Siegel. Morris had worked closely over the years with LTV Corporation, a sprawling Dallas-based conglomerate that owned Vought Corp., a major defense contractor. Almost 55 percent of LTV's sales were in military aircraft subcontracting, with another 25 percent in the missile and space business.

During the day on Tuesday, discussions were swirling, with people from Kidder, Peabody talking with W. R. Grace and Holderbank. Time was a problem, and the depressed state of Marietta's chemical and cement operations made matters worse. Larry Adams knew he could never get what he thought they were worth. He had to look for something that was turning a good profit. That meant some operation in the aerospace division.

It didn't take long for Adams and the rest of Martin Marietta management to center on their Baltimore division. The Denver operation was out of the question. It was real bread and butter. That's where the work was being done on the Space Shuttle's external fuel tanks and the assembly, testing, and support for the MX missile. The Orlando operation handled the Pershing missile and a whole array of other missiles for the military.

Baltimore was a neater package. Not too big but not too small. They made CG6-80C jet aircraft engine thrust reversers for DC-10's and Boeing 747's as well as horizontal and vertical stabilizers for the B-1 bomber.

Paul Thayer, the chairman of LTV, was a friend of Tom Pownall. And a member in good standing of the Conquistadores Club. The two men had seen each other in Wyoming and had had some relaxed chats.

LTV—like Bendix—subcontracted on a variety of projects handled by Martin Marietta.

The Baltimore operation of Martin Marietta was a nice fit for LTV, which also had a subcontract from Rockwell International to build fuselage sections of the B-1B bomber. In addition, they made horizontal stabilizers for the DC-10 and tail sections of the Boeing 747 as well as rocket systems.

A deal was attractive to both Tom Pownall and Paul Thayer.

Pownall would sell Thayer the Martin Marietta Baltimore operation.

Thayer thought he could possibly pick up some assets at bargain prices, and Pownall would gain a temporary reprieve from Bill Agee's pursuit—possibly enough time to work out a more permanent solution.

By late morning on Tuesday, the Martin Marietta G-2 jet had gone to New York to pick up members of the LTV and Martin Marietta adviser teams. The negotiations would be held in secret in Bethesda.

"You better tell some of the guys," Tom Pownall told Larry Adams.

"Mr. Hurtt?" Adams asked. Pownall gave him the nod.

Caleb Hurtt was the fifty-one-year-old newly named president of Martin Marietta Aerospace. He had come up through the ranks of the Denver facility.

"Hey, Caye, we're gonna offer to sell Baltimore to LTV," Adams said.

"You're gonna do what?"

Adams explained the extender situation to Hurtt.

"You guys gotta get with it and cooperate," Adams said. "We're bringing Bob Kirke and his men from Vought down here today. And by the way, they want to go up and tour Baltimore."

"How in hell am I going to do that?"

"I don't know, that's your problem, but a couple of guys are going to be up there and they want somebody to go with 'em, preferably you or Jim Martin. Be sure to show it in its best light."

It wasn't long before Jim Martin, who ran the Baltimore outfit, was on the phone with Adams.

"Hurtt tells me we're selling Baltimore!" Martin said incredulously.

"Not yet. I don't want you to get everybody riled up. Vought is coming in to take a look."

"Whoa."

"Look, Jim, that's the way the old ball bounces."

"We'll do what we can," Martin said, obviously downhearted.

"Hey, look, as far as you're personally concerned, don't worry about it. You got a contract and you got a golden parachute. Just make nice with these guys."

LTV's investment bankers—Lehman Brothers and their lawyers from Davis, Polk—had drafted the terms of an agreement. LTV would tender for approximately 10 percent of Martin Marietta stock and swap the stock for the Baltimore division. After boarding the Martin Marietta plane at the Butler Aviation terminal at LaGuardia, Phil Coviello from Dewey, Ballantine examined the draft with Doug Brown from Kidder, Peabody and Jack MacIntyre from Davis, Polk.

LTV had sent its own corporate jet from Dallas with Vought head Bob Kirke and his chief financial officer and several operational staffers.

The LTV team was gathered in a conference room on the third floor of the aerospace area in the Martin Marietta headquarters. The doors in the office wing were closed to everyone except those with special clearance. Many people working in their offices were aware of activity but did not know what it meant. And they were careful not to appear too nosy.

Two men on the Martin Marietta team—Tom Quinn from the treasury department and Mark Bennett, vice president of finance in aerospace—were frantically assembling the necessary financial projections.

The two teams of lawyers and bankers continued to thrash out the contract, but it was obvious that what was missing was a critical determination by the businessmen on exactly what the Baltimore operation was worth.

"Here we go again," Quinn said. "Charlie wants to know what it's worth."

What made it hard was that the real value of the operation was not fixed assets but cash flow—derived from government contracts. That granted both sides considerable leeway in interpretation.

Doris Rush was in her office, working over plans for a lawsuit to be filed against Citibank and Bendix to prevent the withdrawal of SESSOP shares from the Martin Marietta pod. She was also thinking ahead to another possible lawsuit. Bendix was just a little more than forty-eight hours from being able to buy the Martin Marietta shares.

It seemed like years ago to Doris that she felt the flush of victory when the Bendix SESSOP shares were tendered to the Martin Marietta offer by Citibank. By her calendar, it was four days.

Rush concocted a lawsuit that claimed that neither company should be allowed to purchase stock until the state law timing difference issue was resolved. If Bendix buys, the argument ran, then Martin Marietta is legally obligated to buy, and the result would be a tragic waste of corporate assets.

Rush had run the argument by the Dewey, Ballantine team earlier in the week, and the response she got was, "Yeah, we're working on it." A day later, Rush talked to Fullem.

"Oh, by the way, what about the motion requesting an injunction if all else fails?"

"Yeah, we're gonna do that."

On Tuesday night, Doris called Fullem on another matter but turned the conversation to the planned motion.

"Is it ready?" Doris asked. "I mean, Bob, Thursday night Bendix is going to buy us if we don't have something to stop them."

"Oh, you can forget it, it's all over. Thursday's not the deadline," Fullem said cheerfully.

"What do you mean, 'it's all over'?"

"Where are you now?"

"In my office."

"Well, right down the hall from you in the conference room, your guys are making a deal with LTV. They're going to tender for ten percent of Martin Marietta stock and then we'll swap it for the Baltimore plant."

This was all news to Doris.

"Are you sure?"

"Yeah, the deal's almost done. We're gonna get an automatic ten-day extension."

* * *

It was a warm night in Bethesda—still in the seventies.

Something happened on the way to the party—the business-men were trying to agree, but the numbers kept coming up wrong. There were four evaluations of the Baltimore operation —one by Kidder, Peabody; one by Martin Marietta; one by LTV; and another by its investment banker. The values of the two sides were almost 30 percent apart.

Tom Pownall and Paul Thayer were on the telephone shar-ing with each other the opinions of their respective sides. The two men saw the problem but agreed to take another crack.

Larry Adams, Charlie Leithauser, and Doug Brown from Kidder, Peabody sat down in the conference room to go over the figures again. At the outside, Leithauser could agree to shaving 10 to 15 percent from their original estimate. They reported to Tom Pownall in his office at about 9:30 P.M.

Hearing the bad news that a substantial gap still existed, Pownall wanted opinions from his advisers.

"When we look at these appraisals by Kidder and then their offer, could the board of directors legally accept their bid?"

"I don't know if we can answer that," Menaker said. He had discussed it with Fullem.

"Well, is the damn thing going to work? Will we get the extension?" Pownall asked.

"Maybe yes, maybe no," Menaker answered, chagrined.

"It's a fifty-fifty thing," Dick Katcher said. "The courts have not looked favorably on straight stock for assets extenders be-cause it really looks like a sham transaction. And if the price being offered is lower than what Bendix is offering, you got a whole other set of problems."

"Well, damn it, and Charlie, you're telling me the price is practically a giveaway. I'm not gonna give it away on a hope and a prayer that the extender will work," Pownall said in frustra-tion.

He got back on the telephone and called Paul Thayer. The two men acknowledged that the deal could not be put together.

"Good luck," Thayer said.

"I'm gonna need it," Pownall said. In forty-eight hours, un-less the lawyers could pull something out of the bag, Martin Marietta would be owned by the Bendix Corporation.

And that would pull Marty Siegel's deadman's trigger.

* * *

"If we've got a chance to stop them in court," a cool Frank Menaker said to Tom Pownall, "it will be in Baltimore, and George Beall will be the guy to do it."

A handsome, silver-haired, forty-five-year-old Miles & Stockbridge lawyer and former U.S. attorney for Maryland, George Beall was a man with a reputation. In 1973, Beall had initiated the investigation and developed the factual case against Vice President Spiro Agnew that led to Agnew's resignation.

Beall commanded respect in the federal courthouse in Baltimore.

Beall had been working on the Martin Marietta case practically from the minute he heard the late-breaking news on the radio while sunning himself on Jetty's Beach on windswept Nantucket.

That was three weeks and several court appearances earlier.

At 2:15 P.M. on Wednesday, September 15, Beall was standing in his office in downtown Baltimore. Pictures of his pretty blond wife, Caroline, and his two boys and two girls were on the credenza behind his desk. One picture was from Rainbow Bridge in Arizona; another had Old Faithful as a backdrop.

Beall walked over to the federal courthouse on Lombard Street on the shore of Chesapeake Bay. A light wind from the southwest was in his face. It was a beautiful day, with the temperature in the low eighties.

Courtroom 5B was the Honorable Joseph H. Young's courtroom. A forceful man in his fifties who wore his black judicial robes with distinction, Judge Young sat with his back to a giant bronze dial mounted on the wall. The ceiling was a series of wave forms to perfect the acoustics of the room. Young thought the acoustics were too good. He ordered a hushing system that emitted a sound like constant surf to allow counsel to approach the bench with confidence.

This afternoon, there was no jury.

Only a smattering of spectators were seated in the long pews behind the attorneys' tables. George Beall looked around. He saw a familiar face—that of Tommy Houston*, a local attorney. Beall suspected that Houston represented a New York arbitrageur.

Beall was correct.

By reputation, Houston was usually mysterious about his

---

*Not his real name

clients. He did not dress the part of a successful attorney. Instead, Houston wore Hush Puppies, a garish tie far too wide to be stylish, and a worn pair of trousers and a jacket that did not quite match.

Houston sat quietly, waiting for the proceedings.

Court was convened at 3:00 P.M.

"The case now pending before this court is ·Civil Number Y-82-2560, Martin Marietta Corporation, a Maryland Corporation, versus the Bendix Corporation."

The clerk went on to introduce the seven attorneys assembled at the counsel tables in courtroom 5B. Martin Marietta attorney George Beall was joined by Bob Myers, the head of the litigation team from Dewey, Ballantine.

Bendix attorney John Henry Lewin was joined by New York attorneys Marc Cherno from Fried, Frank and Gerald Goldman from Hughes, Hubbard, the two day-to-day architects of Bendix's legal strategy, which now employed 140 lawyers.

Both sides knew this was the beginning of the showdown.

"Gentlemen," Judge Young began, "this hearing is basically on the challenge of Martin Marietta . . . against the Bendix offer to purchase [Martin Marietta] and the request of Martin Marietta for injunctive relief. Before we get to the merits, let me say something that is appropriate in this case.

"The public and judiciary are frequent to criticize the lawyers for not doing the job they ought to do. If there is a case that there should not be criticism, this is the case. All of you have done an outstanding job in a short period of time. I thank you for that. The issues are not easy. . . . Many of the issues that would otherwise have given counsel of lesser abilities problems to resolve them, you have been able to resolve them leaving only one to be resolved."

"Your Honor, we appreciate your kind words," George Beall said. "Let me just acknowledge your willingness to go beyond the ordinary time schedule to receive our papers after hours and in unusual place. . . ."

"I read this when I was high, about thirty-five thousand feet," Judge Young said. He had just returned from a meeting in Seattle of the American Cancer Society. Young was a member of its national board. Beall had his papers sent by messenger to Seattle. "But let's get down to the issue. The way I see it, your basic challenge is to the language of paragraph eleven."

"That's it. That is the only challenge," George Beall said.

Martin Marietta's case was long on theory but somewhat short on facts. The Williams Act, enacted in 1968 as an amendment to the Securities Exchange Act of 1934, was designed to close a significant gap in the disclosure requirements of the federal securities laws by requiring an offeror to make full and fair disclosure to shareholders faced with a tender offer so that informed investment decisions could be made.

Martin Marietta claimed that Bendix violated federal law by not disclosing its intention to sell off the Martin Marietta cement and aluminum businesses upon completion of the merger. To attempt to prove their point, Martin Marietta lawyers had been taking the depositions of Bendix employees for ten days at the Dewey, Ballantine offices in New York. Among those deposed were Bill Agee, Al McDonald, and Mike Rowny, as well as board members and outside advisers such as Jay Higgins from Salomon Brothers.

Documents were demanded and provided under the intricate procedures of the discovery process. The Martin Marietta lawyers scoured handwritten notes and personal notebooks of Bendix officials, looking for a "smoking gun."

"I think that it is clear that Bendix had under study for a significant period of time—for a year, in fact—a plan to dispose of the nonaerospace assets of Martin Marietta," George Beall said. "If you are, for example, an employee and shareholder of Martin Marietta working in the aluminum company, you want to know where you're going to be six months from now. Bendix has not properly disclosed its intention to sell off Martin Marietta's aluminum business.

"Bendix has failed to fulfill a legal obligation. . . . That failure is the kind of failure that has to be cured. We are not asking Your Honor to enjoin this tender offer forever; all we're asking Your Honor to do is force Bendix to cure this omission."

"That could be forever in this case, can't it?" Judge Young said, sensitive to the timing of tender offers.

"We don't see this particular issue today as something that is going to stop Bendix in its tracks. It is something, however, that should delay the offer," Beall said, downplaying the impact of the proposed order.

"Isn't that the sort of delay which Judge Friendly was concerned about in his comments?" Young said, noting another case. "He talked about how no tender offer can be perfect, just like no trial can be, and that there should be no unrealistic requirements that would place it in sort of a laboratory environment. These disclosure requirements should not be a tool that management can use to delay a takeover. Isn't that the ultimate result here? Thank you, Mr. Beall. Mr. Cherno?"

"Your Honor, Marc Cherno, and I will be making the presentation for Bendix. . . . In order to find for Martin Marietta, you have to find that every senior management personnel at Bendix who testified in this issue were telling an untruth."

"That is not right," Judge Young retorted.

Judge Young looked down from his seat to Cherno, a wiry attorney, his hands nervously working over papers, his graying hair disobeying its part. The man was all energy and argument.

"Your Honor, Mr. Agee testified unequivocally that there is no intention, plan, proposal, or any word you might want to use to divest Martin Marietta assets. Mr. McDonald, the president of the company, the same unequivocal testimony. Mr. Kayser, the chief financial officer, the same unequivocal testimony. There was a whole slew of staff memoranda. Some talk of divestiture possibilities, some talk about other things. It was the type of staff memoranda that are generated in every responsible takeover."

"The law requires that anything that is material to the shareholder in making his decision, he ought to have access to," Judge Young said.

"Mr. Cherno makes much of the fact the decision has not been made to divest the nonaerospace aspects of Martin Marietta," George Beall said when given his turn to speak. "But nowhere is there any statement to that effect in the offering materials. If that decision has been made, as Mr. Cherno suggests, why haven't the shareholders been told that?"

"I can't follow that," Judge Young said. "If they did that and the economic situation turns around and they suddenly decide to do it, there would be lawsuits galore. To say a decision, I find nothing to indicate that Bendix has made a plan. . . ."

George Beall continued to turn his argument to meet the need.

Beall took his time exploring subtle nuances of language and definition, trying to snare the logic of the moment and sway Judge Young to Martin Marietta's defense.

"All right," Judge Young said, closing debate, "To enable either of you the maximum amount of time to do whatever further things you feel necessary, when is the latest you wish to have an opinion?"

"We're free to purchase, Your Honor, at midnight tomorrow," Marc Cherno said.

"I am thinking whichever way it goes, is tomorrow morning too late?"

"No, if Your Honor please, I would suggest, either way it goes, we will probably be contacting one of the judges upstairs," Beall said.

"It will go up to the ninth floor, I suppose," Judge Young said, referring to the Court of Appeals. "I will have a written opinion for you tomorrow morning at ten o'clock. That will give you time for a full day to do whatever you have to do or need to do."

Before the attorneys could leave their tables, arb rep Tommy Houston was in the aisle and headed for the telephone in the lobby. Houston was as much spy as attorney. His job was not to interpret events, only to report the developments back to New York.

He gathered information by monitoring court sessions. By skillfully using his contacts in the clerk's office. By talking with the press. By keeping his ear to the ground. His job was to have Baltimore covered for his client—arbitrageur Ivan Boesky.

While George Beall and the other attorneys filed out toward the elevators, Houston was on the phone, talking to Perry Cohen, the research director for Ivan Boesky in New York.

Cohen was the one to figure the news into the scheme of things—each twist and turn in the courthouse would affect the discounting of Martin Marietta and Bendix stock in New York.

"Okay," Cohen said. Houston was huddled over the phone, talking discreetly. "Call me the second he decides."

"Will do," Houston said, hanging up.

On Wednesday night, Bill and Mary were returning from a late-night dinner. Frank Maloney, a retired New York policeman, was the Bendix chauffeur. He drove the 1982 Navy blue Cadillac Fleetwood up to the curb in front of the Helmsley Palace. Mary was quietly listening to a tape of Lionel Richie. Bill was on the telephone to Al McDonald. The three planned a nightcap in the Agees' suite.

In the hallway on the forty-fifth floor, Bill and Mary headed for their suite. Bill noticed a man—tall, in nondescript dark clothes—walking slowly behind them. Bill glanced over his shoulder. The man appeared to pretend to stop at a door and look for a key in his pocket. Bill hurried Mary into the suite and took one last look. The man was still in the hall.

"Call security," Mary said to Bill.

A while later, there was a knock on the door.

Bill opened the door cautiously to find Al McDonald.

"Hey, Al, we thought you were security."

"What's up?"

"We just saw some weird guy walking around in the halls, and you never know with this thing in the papers so much, some crazy could think we've got a lot of money up here."

At 9:00 A.M. on Thursday, September 16, Bruce Wasserstein met with Al McDonald and Bill Agee in Agee's corner office in the GM Building. Out the window, the sun was casting long shadows between the high-rises. Arthur Fleischer had called. He was delayed by traffic.

Wasserstein was reporting his conversations with Marty Siegel.

"I asked him for a dollar sign," Wasserstein said, referring to the price at which Siegel would recommend to the Martin Marietta board of directors that they agree to sell the company.

"What did he say?" Bill Agee asked.

"Marty said he would present to the board any figure you wanted to offer," Bruce said, easing his large frame down into a chair. "He wants to know if you'll agree to walk away if Pownall can get Gray to walk away."

"Can he get Gray to walk away?" Agee asked.

"Yeah. In Marty's words, Pownall and Gray are good buddies."

"When did you talk to him last?" McDonald asked.

"This morning. He confirmed that Gray would join a three-way laydown."

Bill Agee was not saying much. He removed his glasses and set them carefully onto his desk.

"Bill, there appear to be three basic options," Wasserstein said, using his fingers for impact. "And I think we should ask the board for authorization to pursue these three approaches. One, a raise of our offer to fifty-two dollars. Tonight, before we buy, we have our greatest leverage with these guys, and a raise of four dollars per share may tip the balance. Two, I've talked to Marty, and this three-way peace settlement is a viable option—Gray will go along."

"And three, we buy as planned," Agee said without waiting for Wasserstein to finish.

"Yeah," Wasserstein said.

"What do you think of this peace proposal?" Agee asked McDonald.

"We oughta think about it," McDonald said slowly. Al was the classic backroom adviser, capable of a straight face, ready to go either way. This time it was obvious to Agee that McDonald was not advocating peace.

"Bill, a laydown is a victory for Martin Marietta. That puts us back at ground zero," McDonald said.

"Should I continue to talk peace with Siegel?" Wasserstein asked.

"Sure. Find out what's there. I want to know all my options," Agee said. "What do you think are the chances that Siegel is going to line up an extender for Martin Marietta?" Agee was concerned that the midnight deadline when he could begin buying shares would disappear as the day wore on.

"Marty told me yesterday that they were not looking for an extender, but I understand from my people that Lehman Brothers is representing LTV in negotiations with Marietta."

"What's that tell you about Siegel?" McDonald asked with distaste.

Wasserstein shrugged his shoulders. Agee was also uncertain about Marty Siegel's credibility.

"Arthur says if we buy first, we will win," Agee said.

TWENTY-THREE

While Bill Agee was being briefed by his advisers, Bendix and Martin Marietta and Citibank lawyers were standing at tables a cab ride away, at the United States District Court for the Southern District of New York.

The courthouse commanded lower Manhattan's Foley Square.

At 9:00 A.M., the court clerk brought the proceedings to order while the judge made his way to his position at the bench.

On the previous day, Michael Finkelstein, forty-nine, a senior litigation partner at Barrett, Smith, the law firm contacted by Doris Rush, filed a lawsuit on behalf of Martin Marietta in federal court. Marietta was suing Bendix, the individual members of its board of directors, and Citibank.

Martin Marietta was requesting an injunction against Bendix and Citibank and a declaration striking down the recent amendment of the SESSOP by the Bendix directors.

Before Citibank tendered the Bendix SESSOP shares to Martin Marietta, Bendix claimed that tendering was logistically impossible under the withdrawal provisions of the plan. Once the tender was a *fait accompli,* Bill Agee and the Bendix board of directors had changed course. The SESSOP was amended to allow participants first to withdraw from the plan and then to tender to the Martin Marietta offer.

The catch was that first Citibank was instructed to withdraw all shares tendered to Martin Marietta and then to await instructions from the individual employees—all sixteen thousand—as to their desires.

And the employees had to offer their instructions within six days.

If no instructions came, Martin Marietta got no shares.

It was a cunning and skillful move.

To cap it off, Bill Agee sent a letter to the SESSOP participants advising them of the procedure—but warning them of serious "consequences" if they actually tendered to Martin Marietta.

At 3:52 P.M. on the previous day, the court clerk stamped the official seal onto Martin Marietta's complaint. Finkelstein, a pleasant man, short in stature, balding, and his associate, David Frankel, a young lawyer with reddish hair and a moustache, handed copies of the complaint challenging the Bendix move to George Davidson, the Bendix lawyer.

The attorneys stood around tight-lipped but trying to be pleasant while the court clerk used the time-tested method of random selection of the judge who would preside over the case. The clerk spun the wheel and pulled up the name of District Judge David N. Edelstein. While the clerk assigned the case a number (6135), Finkelstein and Davidson exchanged a concerned glance.

Neither Davidson nor Finkelstein had argued a case before Judge Edelstein—but they certainly had heard the stories. At seventy-two, Judge Edelstein was legendary for presiding over the thirteen-year boondoggle known as *U.S.* v. *IBM.*

Later that afternoon, ten attorneys representing Bendix, Martin Marietta, and Citibank assembled in Judge Edelstein's courtroom for a quarrelsome debate of the issues.

Martin Marietta requested immediate action by the court.

"This thing becomes obnoxious," Judge Edelstein said with irritation. "Here it is ten past five, you didn't arrive in the courtroom until almost four-thirty. How much time are you giving me?"

A new hearing for this morning was squeezed into Judge Edelstein's busy schedule.

"Your Honor," Michael Finkelstein began, "right now the Bendix SESSOP shares are in the Martin Marietta proration pool because Citibank protected their interest by tendering. Then Bendix amended the plan. If the participants don't get back to Fidelity by next Wednesday, they lose the benefits of that pool, which is about twenty dollars higher than the price of Bendix stock."

"Your Honor," Bendix counsel George Davidson said, "the events in this courtroom have a significance beyond in terms of market activity in the stock, and any appearance that the court will order something or has required that Bendix or the trustee do something can be used in the press and other forums to make things appear as they are not. . . ."

"Let me see if I can remove some of the uneasiness and pressure that you feel," Judge Edelstein said, noting the time. "It is clear to me that I cannot hear you all today. It is my intention to adjourn my other trial tomorrow and start with you again early in the morning and listen to you and hope to come to a resolution. I don't possibly see how I can really do very much more between now and ten o'clock. I certainly don't want to hold the jury in my tax-evasion case. They are here, some of them have come from places as far as Newburgh. . . . We will resume this discussion tomorrow at nine o'clock."

"Your Honor," Finkelstein interjected, "could I raise one point?"

"Yes."

"Today is the day, at twelve o'clock midnight, tonight. After that date Bendix can start buying the shares of Martin Marietta that have been tendered to it. That will change the whole situation here. The situation is about to change."

"I am going to ask that the status quo not be changed in any fashion whatsoever," Edelstein said, glowering. "And unless I have that assurance I am going to enter an order to the effect that the status quo will be maintained until I reach a resolution. Nobody is going to dissuade me from that point."

George Davidson went almost sheet white.

A status quo agreement would prevent Bendix from buying Martin Marietta at midnight. That would alter the company strategy completely.

"Your Honor," Davidson began, thinking fast, "Bendix has commenced the tender offer for Martin Marietta, which is not involved in these proceedings in any way. There is no relief sought with respect to that tender offer at all!"

"I follow you," Judge Edelstein said, "I am ready to follow you clearly or understand all the points. . . . I am trying to do the best that I can . . . but I am not going to give you the opportunity to take advantage of this indulgence by changing the status quo. . . ."

Davidson showed nothing outwardly but he was beginning to panic. The Martin Marietta lawyers could not believe their good fortune. Judge Edelstein sounded like he wanted to stop the whole shooting match!

"All I am saying, Your Honor," Davidson continued, holding his voice in check, "I have no problem with Your Honor entering into whatever order Your Honor feels is appropriate with respect to the issues in this case. But to enter an order with respect to other issues which are before other courts on an expedited basis that involve tremendous consequences—"

"I am merely suggesting," Judge Edelstein said, "that you be reasonable and enter into a standby agreement so the effort I am making to hear all of you will not be thwarted, will not become moot, that's all I am asking."

Davidson wanted to get out of court before Edelstein did something rash. The Bendix lawyer remembered the stories from the IBM case. The judge was known to take matters into his own hands. Davidson decided to change his tactics.

"Very well, Your Honor, I will be happy to suspend now, and I will work out with Mr. Finkelstein something that would be acceptable."

"Why don't you proceed to do that? I won't hear you any further, and we'll resume again tomorrow at nine o'clock."

Finkelstein and Davidson met in a conference room. Both men left frequently to use the telephone. In light of the mood of Edelstein, Davidson was inclined to go along with Finkelstein's original arguments about the SESSOP situation. For his part, having been thrown a new bone by the judge, Finkelstein was determined not to let go of the chance for a freeze on the tender offers.

When enough time had passed to give the impression of best efforts, Mike Finkelstein contacted Judge Edelstein's clerk and requested an immediate meeting. Tomorrow morning would be too late.

"You called this conference, Mr. Finkelstein?" the judge said.

"Yes, I did, Your Honor."

"Very well."

"We have been unable to reach an agreement on any stipulation . . ." Finkelstein said.

"Your Honor, I did offer a stipulation to Mr. Finkelstein, as Your Honor had requested, responsive to the relief which he sought in this action from Your Honor," George Davidson countered, adding, "unfortunately, that was not satisfactory to Mr. Finkelstein, who has continued in his desire to pull into this case a wholly separate tender offer, which is the subject of litigation before Judge Young in the Federal District Court in Maryland who has before him voluminous papers on the Bendix offer for Martin Marietta, which is not involved at all in this lawsuit and is nowhere mentioned in Mr. Finkelstein's papers.

"I would like permission to hand up to the court—unfortunately, this is handprinting—the substance of the stipulation we offered Mr. Finkelstein. He sought that Bendix be directed to make certain communications to the sixteen thousand Bendix SESSOP participants. . . . That is quite a job to communicate with sixteen thousand people. We have had recent experience with it, we will grind that procedure all up again, get the envelopes, and other materials prepared so that the minute the court would order anything, it could go out promptly and the mechanical delays would be avoided."

"Mr. Finkelstein," the judge said.

"Your Honor, we have gradually come to Your Honor's suggestion that was made this morning about freezing the status quo in this tender offer fight.

"Now as you know, there are two tender offers. The timing of those two offers is very critical. Each has so far received tenders of more than fifty-one percent of the other, and there is a struggle now brewing over which one is going to get control first. So that the last thing in the world that maintains the status quo is something that moves one tender offer and not the other."

"Well, clearly I had no prior jurisdiction or authority to do anything about the Bendix tender offer," Judge Edelstein said.

"I think, Your Honor, you may have. Because the party who is making the offer is before you, and you have jurisdiction over that party. . . . It appears clear now that it would be very difficult, if not impossible, for the court to order an appropriate correction in the communication by Bendix with its shareholders.

. . . There is no way that those employees are going to be able to receive that communication and get back to Fidelity by noon on Wednesday. Not possible. So the whole thing will have gone by default. And employees who don't receive that communication from Bendix will be deprived of an opportunity to tender their shares.

"What we would propose for a temporary restraining order is a freeze, a true freeze that freezes both tenders for a period of time sufficient for this court to consider the merits and make a decision and then Bendix to communicate with its shareholders to correct the prior communications, which we say are erroneous and violates the Williams Act."

Finkelstein approached the bench and gave the judge an order drafted for his signature.

"Let me pose this question to both of you," Judge Edelstein said. "Let's assume for whatever reason I enter an order to grant Mr. Finkelstein's client all the relief that they request about recommunicating with the Bendix shareholders. Could that be accomplished before the deadline?"

"I don't think so, Your Honor," Finkelstein said.

"Then am I to accept an order which is null and void and of no effect? I am not criticizing the postal service, but I think it can generally be accepted that it is somewhat less than quick. If I entered an order which practically tells me by logic and experience that it could never be given effect before the deadline."

"That is why we are asking for an extension," Finkelstein said. "Your Honor, let me tell you as an added twist to that, it is not only just getting the letter to the participant."

"And the return," Edelstein said.

"And not only the return. But if you read the letter—the Tuesday, September fourteenth letter from Bill Agee to the participants—it contains reference to tax consequences. They urge employees to—"

"I don't think it can be done," Judge Edelstein said.

"I don't think so, either," Finkelstein seconded.

"So where do I stand?" Judge Edelstein asked. "Even if I were to agree with you and grant you all the relief that you request in your application for preliminary injunction, it would be a nullity. That's correct, isn't it?"

"I believe so. That's why we asked for an extension."

"I am not going to allow any of you here to turn me into a

Don Quixote," Judge Edelstein said loudly. "I am afraid I am going to have to intervene, and I am going to have to insist upon a freeze."

"Your Honor," George Davidson said, jumping to his feet, "there's another actor in this corporate takeover, that is, United Technologies Corporation, which is not before this court. . . . If you enter such an order there is every likelihood that you will cause Bendix to fall into the arms of United Technologies based upon a complaint which really is without substance."

"The last thing in the world I want to do," the judge said, "is emphasize any balance which will give any suitor any advantage. . . . You want me to look at your papers? I will be glad to do that. Then at least to this extent I would enter a freeze order which would embrace all of today and at least all of tomorrow up until five o'clock. Otherwise I will not spend any time doing that.

"Now I give you two options: I will enter my freeze order, or you go out and cooperate and come back and compromise and negotiate your own freeze order. But have no doubt about it, I am going to enter a freeze order. That's it!"

"Your Honor," Davidson said, on his feet.

"I am not going to be dissuaded, sir, by any further argument. I am going to have a freeze order, and the status quo is going to be maintained."

"Your Honor, we communicated with our shareholders in a very brief period just a few days ago. We can do it again. We are not going to have any nullities here. We'll get this stuff to the people in time, they will have their chance. . . . Without any papers on our tender offer before you, Your Honor, you are tipping the balance on the respective matters that were fully briefed and argued before Judge Young in Maryland, and if Your Honor was disposed to call Judge Young—"

"If you think I am tipping the balance, that's your perfect right. . . . I will be available again later on today."

Court was recessed.

Marc Cherno and John Lewin were enjoying a light lunch of sandwiches and sodas in Lewin's office in the Mercantile Bank and Trust Building in downtown Baltimore. They had been able to report great news to Art Fleischer in New York and Bendix's general counsel, Hal Barron.

Marc Cherno, knowing that Judge Young was going to issue his opinion in the morning, decided to stay over in Baltimore rather than return to New York. He had dinner with John Henry Lewin, who checked him into the new Hilton, within sight of the Federal Building. Cherno went to sleep confident that Young would rule in Bendix's favor in the morning.

By 10:00 A.M. as promised, Judge Young produced in his chambers a twenty-two-page "Memorandum Opinion and Order" with thirteen footnotes. His law clerks had obviously worked practically through the night to prepare the document from Judge Young's notes. Attorneys from Bendix, Martin Marietta, and United Technologies were invited over to Judge Young's chambers to pick up his decision.

Martin Marietta's motion for a preliminary injunction was denied.

In his order, Young said, "The denial of a preliminary injunction permits the three antagonists to continue their struggles according to their own self-imposed timetables."

George Beall, assuming that would be Young's decision, drew from his briefcase a formally drawn "Notice of Appeal," which he intended to sign and file with the court clerk.

"See you on the ninth floor," Beall said to John Henry Lewin as he left the judge's chambers.

Over lunch with Art Fleischer on the speaker phone, Lewin and Cherno basked in victory. Within a matter of hours, Bendix would buy control of Martin Marietta, and the whole damn thing would resolve itself in a meeting of the minds among the businessmen.

In the middle of lunch, a frantic call came in from George Davidson, the Hughes, Hubbard lawyer defending Bendix in the case brought by Martin Marietta in New York before Judge David Edelstein.

"Tell that to me again so Marc can hear," Lewin said, putting the call on the speaker phone.

"Judge Edelstein is threatening all kinds of things. He's talking about imposing a freeze—a standstill—on the tender offers! I mean, it's totally crazy. I told him that our offer has nothing to do with the matters before him, but he's adamant about imposing a freeze! And the Martin Marietta lawyers are egging him on."

"Hey, George, we're gonna close tonight. I think your SES-

SOP case up there is the tail wagging the dog. Give him anything reasonable to placate him. Let's not stick on points that may end up hurting us in terms of whether we get to buy tonight. I want to get this offer through!" Cherno yelled.

"The Martin Marietta guys are telling him he has the power to stop the offer."

"Well," Cherno said, "it's inconsistent of them to argue that we shouldn't litigate against them in Michigan and then they turn it around and litigate against us in New York. Their whole argument was that the substantive tender offer issues should be in one court, before one judge."

"In light of the fact that Judge Young enjoined the Michigan case, maybe he would get upset if he knew a judge was end-running him in New York. Can you bring what's happening here to Young's attention?" Davidson said.

"No problem," Lewin said.

The situation gave Cherno a bad feeling in his stomach. He had just won a victory before Judge Young this morning; he didn't want to push his luck. But with Edelstein threatening in New York, he did not see that he had much choice.

"Now, look," Cherno said to Lewin, "just call Judge Young's office and check if he's around in case we need him."

There was a lot to prepare. Marc Cherno was off working on his notes for the meeting scheduled in the afternoon before Judge Harrison Winter of the Fourth Circuit Court of Appeals. Winter, whose offices were on the ninth floor of the federal courthouse in Baltimore, four floors up from Young's chambers, had agreed to hear the appeal. Beall wanted a stay order against Young's denial of Martin Marietta's motion to stop the Bendix tender offer.

While Cherno was working on the appeal preparation, Lewin phoned Judge Young's office.

"Hello, this is John Henry Lewin. Is Judge Young available?"

"This is Judge Young."

"Judge Young, oh, Your Honor."

"What can I do for you?"

"I wanted really just to know your availability."

"What is the problem?"

"Well, it seems we may have a problem in New York, Your Honor. There may be a situation that may require some relief.

It seems in contradiction to your earlier order consolidating this case before Your Honor, Martin Marietta has pursued another issue in New York, but Judge Edelstein is mentioning the possibility of freezing the tender offers."

"He's going to do what?"

"I have spoken with Bendix counsel in New York and he informs me that Judge Edelstein is preparing to issue a freeze, delaying the tender offers."

"I will be available."

Judge Young immediately got on the telephone and called Judge Edelstein in New York to find out for himself what was going on.

TWENTY-FOUR

Judge Edelstein was obviously in a bad mood when he started the afternoon session in the federal courthouse on Foley Square in New York City.

"Do you have a report to make?" he asked flatly.

"Yes, I do, Your Honor," Mike Finkelstein said. "We have met with counsel for Bendix and Citibank on the question of a freeze to give Your Honor a chance to hear the preliminary injunction motion, and we cannot seem to reach agreement with them."

"Your Honor," George Davidson said, rising, "I have been asked to convey certain developments to the court which have happened since we appeared before you this morning."

"Were you the one or somebody on your behalf who called Judge Young?" Judge Edelstein did not restrain his anger. The judge's face was flushed.

"Your Honor, I believe that Judge Young was called—"

"I am aware of that," Judge Edelstein said coldly. "Judge Young called me and discussed what was happening before him. He advised me that a call had been made, and I advised him what was occurring before this court. . . .

"I specifically told him and underscored that I have asked for some cooperation between counsel for a standby, and that cooperation was not forthcoming in any great degree. So both of us are aware of precisely what has occurred in each of our respective courts."

"Your Honor, I will not further address that point," Davidson said sheepishly. "My associates and I spent the lunchtime talking with Bendix officials and have learned that it would be possible by means of the electronic mail system that connects the Bendix work locations to send any communication virtually instantaneously. . . . Any order Your Honor would be disposed to make . . . by way of additional disclosure could be effectively accomplished well within the time frame that is contained in the Marietta offer."

"I have prepared a proposed order which I am prepared to sign. . . . I will be happy to read it to you."

Judge Edelstein then read his order. George Davidson was listening intently for the word "freeze." It never came.

"Your Honor, that order is satisfactory to us and we believe it preserves the status quo," Davidson said loudly, jumping to his feet. He felt an enormous burden fall from his shoulders. Bendix was not going to be stopped from buying Martin Marietta at midnight.

"May I have one moment, your Honor?" Mike Finkelstein said, wanting to review the terms of the order more closely. What Edelstein had ordered was actually more than Martin Marietta had requested. They did not get the freeze, but they did get something else.

Judge Edelstein had ordered that Citibank not withdraw any of the SESSOP shares from the Martin Marietta offer—except where Bendix employees had specifically asked to have them withdrawn. And in the absence of instructions, Citibank was ordered not to withdraw any stock.

Judge Edelstein had turned the situation on its ear!

The entire burden was now on Bendix, which had only six days to get sixteen thousand people to withdraw their stock from the Martin Marietta offer!

"Your Honor, that order is satisfactory to us," Finkelstein said, amazed at his success.

It would be a couple of hours before George Davidson realized the impact of Judge Edelstein's ruling. Bendix had seventy-five locations in the United States as well as divisions, subsidiaries, and affiliates in twenty-two countries. Plants across the country would post new instructions for the sixteen thousand Bendix salaried employees who participated in SESSOP. The office intercoms would blare directions on how to withdraw from the Martin Marietta pool. Supervisors would lean as hard as necessary to get the job done in the time available.

Overseas was another matter. The trickiest people to contact would be the members of the Bendix Field Engineering Corp. Among the contracts handled by BFEC was a $337 million fifty-year deal for personnel and technical services for the Saudi Arabia Air Traffic Control System. Bendix employees were located at thirty-one sites in the deserts of Saudi Arabia.

With money no object, a plane would be chartered to fly around the Saudi Arabian deserts to collect the signatures of BFEC employees withdrawing their shares from the Martin Marietta tender offer. Another plane would go to Ascension Island, south of the equator in the Atlantic Ocean. A truck would drive into the hinterlands of Korea. Through government contacts, the Air Force would send a plane to the Aleutian Islands in Alaska to collect more signatures.

With the opportunity to buy a majority share of Martin Marietta at midnight that night, the fifth Bendix board of directors meeting since the start of Bendix's attempt to take over Martin Marietta, scheduled for 2:00 P.M., was shaping up to be decisive. Agee was well rehearsed and prepped by his advisers. He had the facts at his fingertips. But he was tense.

He was seen by the secretaries walking sharply from his office into McDonald's office and back again—as if just stretching his legs.

As was their custom, when the directors arrived for the meeting, they first gathered in a small room adjoining the boardroom that was stocked with donuts, coffee, and soft drinks. Al McDonald was outwardly calm, exchanging pleasantries with the directors.

"Hi, Paul, how was your flight?" McDonald asked Paul Hartz, the sixty-year-old chairman of Fram Corporation, a subsidiary of Bendix. Hartz was also a Bendix vice president.

"Fine, Al. How are you holding together?"

"No problem," McDonald said.

Within ten minutes, after circling the room and chatting with other directors, McDonald again reached out his hand to Hartz.

"Hi, Paul, how are you?"

Embarrassed, Hartz responded as if it was their first meeting of the day.

Many of the directors were talking about the latest development. It was a headline in that morning's *New York Times:* "UNITED TECHNOLOGIES IN PEACE BID TO BENDIX."

The article was written by financial reporter Bob Cole. The article detailed an offer by Harry Gray to increase his bid from $75 to $85 per share if Bill Agee and the Bendix board would agree to a friendly merger.

> Wall Street professionals said they felt that while United Technologies' latest proposal might apply considerable pressure on Bendix to accept, they did not expect Bendix's response to be favorable—unless Mr. Agee and Mr. Gray, both exceptionally strong personalities, could find a way to resolve their individual needs. One leading professional . . . reasoned that Mr. Gray, who will be 63 in November, could be so eager to land Bendix that he might be willing to make a deal with Mr. Agee, who is only 44, for the Bendix chief to become an important executive in United Technologies for the time being and possibly even its head once Mr. Gray steps down.

"Did Bill get a letter from Harry?" a director asked McDonald.

McDonald nodded. "And Harry called."

"Gentlemen," Bill Agee said, emerging from his office, "let's begin." The directors moved into the boardroom. Donald Rumsfeld and Jewel Lafontant were absent. Jewel was in Anchorage, Alaska, preparing for a trip to Japan.

"Since our last meeting there have been several developments. As I am sure you have seen in the papers, Harry Gray wrote me a letter yesterday. I'd like to read it to you and then bring in some of our advisers to discuss the adequacy of the offer."

Agee outlined Gray's proposed increase to $85 a share from $75 for 11.9 million shares of Bendix common stock.

"I talked with Harry yesterday. He called me. I told him that the increase was not sufficient. And that the blended price—considering the low back end—was just not realistic."

Art Fleischer was invited into the meeting by Michael Rowny, who slid back his chair and went to the door. Jerry Shapiro, the antitrust lawyer from Hughes, Hubbard, was also invited.

"As you know," Agee said, "Jerry Shapiro has been examining the antitrust implications of our offer and the offers of Martin Marietta and United Technologies. He has gone to Washington and talked with the Justice Department concerning the situation. He correctly predicted that our offer would not receive a second request for information from Justice. At our last meeting, the board decided not to respond to the UTC offer until a thorough study had been completed. Jerry, what do you say now about the UTC offer?"

"Well, to start with, on Tuesday, William Baxter, an assistant attorney general, issued his report that the Justice Department will not block any merger between Bendix and Martin Marietta. In our ongoing discussions with Justice, we have highlighted the market overlaps between Bendix and United Technologies. Based on the kind of questions we are getting back, I think that UTC is going to get a second request from Justice and that will delay their offer for Bendix."

"You've been right up until now, let's hope you're right again," Jonathan Scott said.

When Agee reviewed the kind of conditions remaining in United Technologies' offer, the directors felt that the raise to $85 was more a bluff than an inducement.

"They don't want us to buy Martin Marietta tonight," Bill Agee said.

Bruce Wasserstein and Jay Higgins were invited into the meeting to give their advice about the financial implications of the UTC offer. While the two men sat side by side at the table, it was obvious from Higgins' tight-lipped demeanor that he was uncomfortable. Normally First Boston and Salomon Brothers were competitors. With Agee obviously drawing more heavily on First Boston, Higgins felt like the girl sitting out the dance. Both men gave their opinions. The United Technologies' offer was inadequate. The board voted to reject both the original offer and the latest increase.

"Do you think Martin Marietta is going to have somebody to

buy five percent of their company tonight and delay our offer?" Professor Uyterhoeven asked.

"There have been rumors that LTV is preparing to jump in," Agee said.

"If between now and midnight they get an extender," said Scott, removing his clear plastic glasses and setting them carefully on the table, "it's a whole new ball game."

"If they get somebody, are we going to get somebody?" Tavoulareas asked.

"Tav, I can get one if I need one," Agee said. He did not mention that tonight he was planning to meet with Ed Hennessy of Allied Corporation. Agee knew Hennessy was interested. Getting Allied involved would be a backup plan.

"Art, why don't you tell us the legal situation," Agee said.

There was something about Art Fleischer that the board of directors liked. He was widely seen as a heavy hitter, among the best in the business. But his gentlemanly, nonhype approach ingratiated him to the directors. He impressed them by presenting his opinions and analyses not as facts but merely as tools to facilitate the board's decisions.

"There has been a recent development," Fleischer said, combing back his gray hair with his hand. "This morning, my partner Marc Cherno, who is in Baltimore, informs me that Judge Young has denied a Martin Marietta motion for an injunction against our offer."

Fleischer shared a smile with the directors.

"So we're free to go ahead tonight and buy?" Tavoulareas asked.

"Let me say that so far we are free to buy. Cherno also tells me—and he is probably arguing right this moment—that Martin Marietta has appealed to the Fourth Circuit. The decision could be overturned."

"Oh, God," General Stafford said.

"However, if we look at the broad issues, I think we are in good shape. The critical issue is one of control. Assuming that they buy after we have already bought—as their PR efforts are claiming they will—the issue is who can take control first. From a legal point of view, it comes down to the wording of the Delaware statute dealing with subsidiary voting rights. Maryland also has similar statutes. However, based upon the language of the Delaware statute—where we are incorporated—I think we will win the Delaware case. I think if we buy first, we will be able to take control first and remove the Martin Marietta board of directors."

"Do they think they can beat us based on the Maryland statute and remove us?" Tavoulareas asked.

"I think that's their assumption," Fleischer said.

"Well, then maybe we should consider golden parachutes for the outside directors of Bendix," Tavoulareas said with a straight face. A laugh rippled around the room.

"I think the Delaware court will prevent them from getting control," Fleischer said.

"Let's hope it doesn't come to that," Hugo Uyterhoeven said.

Agee then reviewed for the board the action by Martin Marietta to waive all but two conditions to their offer. Only if Bendix backed off or passed amendments to its bylaws would Martin Marietta not buy Bendix.

"How is the vote going on the two amendments?" a director asked.

"We continue to be optimistic," Bill Agee said. "We are ahead."

In fact, a memo prepared by the stock transfer department showed that with 20 percent of the vote tabulated, the count was 2,227,070 votes for; 356,862 votes against; and 34,331 abstentions. Bendix was winning by a landslide. However, as the experts had informed Agee, voting in proxy fights typically began with a surge of support for management.

The final results could not yet be predicted.

Agee turned the meeting to the central question: In light of the Martin Marietta threat, should the Bendix Corporation buy the Martin Marietta Corporation at midnight tonight?

Agee canvassed his financial advisers for opinions. Sitting to Wasserstein's right, closest to Agee, Higgins was to go first. He passed out materials on the two companies and the resulting balance sheet. He mentioned the impact on the shareholders and ways to improve the debt-to-equity ratio.

"Salomon Brothers is not going to tell the board to buy or not to buy. We will talk about the options," Higgins said. "If you buy and the legal strategy of Arthur Fleischer works, then it will be a real coup. Bendix will successfully acquire Martin Marietta on some negotiated basis. Blocked in court, they will have no other option but to settle. However, you will have to take the enormous risk that if the legal strategy does not work and they do buy our shares, then in the worst-case scenario they may take control of Bendix first. Or at the very least, the debt ratio of the combined company would be enormous."

Bruce Wasserstein began his discussion without notes or handouts. His energy was a stark contrast to Higgins' low-keyed approach. Wasserstein was slick by comparison. He was an unusual sight: His wiry hair shooting in different directions. His white pressed shirt heavily wrinkled at the elbows. He wore a bow tie and had removed his jacket—following Bill Agee's lead.

"I do not think we can assume that Martin Marietta is bluffing in their announced intention to buy Bendix if we buy them tonight. Marty Siegel is telling Tom Pownall that the thing is doable.

"What we need is the flexibility of several options tonight depending on the legal situation and the attitude of Martin Marietta. The board can force through the deal already offered, or raise the price to induce an agreement, or walk away in a settlement negotiated with all parties. We must be prepared to react to the events of the evening."

"In this regard," Agee said, "I think it would be appropriate for the board to appoint a special committee to review the situation again tonight. I would like to suggest myself, Al, General Stafford, Scotty, and Tav."

Agee had spoken to the men before the start of the board meeting after first hearing the suggestion from Wasserstein in the prep meeting. The board voted to accept the committee and authorize it to make decisions on behalf of the corporation until the next board meeting.

"I would just like to get a sense of the board," Agee said, "assuming we do not have a consentual agreement tonight or some legal development that blocks us. Is the board willing to go ahead and buy?"

There were affirmative nods from the directors.

As the meeting was breaking up, Paul F. Hartz, the inside director who was in charge of Fram Corporation, approached Bill Agee about his personal employment situation. Planning to retire in January, Hartz was scheduled to remain a Bendix consultant. Agee had already given his handshake to the deal. But he had also promised something in writing.

266

Distracted, and strapped for time, Agee cut short the discussion but said, "Paul, if I get shot tonight, Al knows about your deal."

As the board members exited from the conference room, Al McDonald called out above the noise of the office:

"I have been advised that there are all sorts of press people and legal processors in the hallways and the main lobby of the building. We have arranged for you to be escorted from the building to the limos. Please follow the security guards."

Under guard, the directors who were in a hurry to get to their planes, were led down the service elevators and through the subbasement of the building, where they crept out in twos to waiting limousines.

Flying home in a company jet at sixteen thousand feet in smooth air, director Paul Hartz almost fell out of his seat when the plane hit a very hard bump.

"What was that?" he yelled up to the pilot.

"Jet stream from the Concorde."

At shortly after 3:00 P.M., Judge Young's clerk Harold Kahn called over to John Henry Lewin's office. Lewin and Cherno were working on defending against Martin Marietta's appeal to be heard momentarily before Court of Appeals Judge Winter. The two Bendix attorneys did not understand why Judge Young's office was calling.

"Judge Young wants to see you in his chambers at four P.M.," the clerk said. Lewin took the call and was puzzled. He spoke with Marc Cherno.

"What the hell does he want?" Lewin asked.

"I don't like it. What did you tell him about Edelstein?"

"I told him that we wanted to know his availability and that we may need relief because of what Martin Marietta was doing in New York."

"Well, we're due over there before Winter now," Cherno said. "We've got to split up. I'll go handle the appeal, you wait on Judge Young, and I'll get there as soon as I can."

George Beall, Martin Marietta's counsel, had arranged the appeal before Judge Harrison Winter. While the Court of Appeals for the Fourth Circuit actually had its seat in Richmond, Winter's office was on the ninth floor of the Federal Building in Baltimore. Beall was seeking a stay order nullifying Judge Young's order issued earlier that morning blocking Martin Marietta's motion against Bendix.

Beall did not get very far in his arguments before Judge Winter. Marc Cherno found the judge receptive to his arguments that Judge Young had done the proper thing in blocking the Martin Marietta move.

"Time is of the essence in takeover situations, Your Honor," Cherno said. "As Judge Young notes in his opinion, there would be irreparable harm imposed on Bendix if the timing of its offer were delayed by an injunction. The marketplace is the proper arena to resolve these kinds of disputes."

Winter said that the Martin Marietta claim of illegal incomplete disclosure by Bendix did not hold water. He said he even had trouble with the few doubts raised by Judge Young in his opinion. Winter denied the appeal.

The whole process took less than an hour.

"One down, one to go," Cherno said optimistically.

George Beall and Marc Cherno boarded the elevator and went down four floors to Judge Young's chambers. They were on time. Cherno shared Judge Winter's decision with John Henry Lewin—just loud enough so that the other attorneys would hear. A quick survey of the room would divide the lawyers into winning and losing camps. Broad smiles from the Bendix lawyers were contrasted with blank expressions from George Beall and Bob Myers and United Technologies' attorney Frank Burch.

Judge Young came into the small conference room attached to his 5B office, quickly drawing the attention of the assembled lawyers. Since they were all unaware of what the judge had in mind, they were more than a little curious.

"Gentlemen, this situation seems to grow in complexity practically by the hour," Judge Young said. "I understand proceedings are happening in other districts that affect the cases before me. I would like to hear from counsel."

"Your Honor," John Henry Lewin began, "Martin Marietta has brought suit against Bendix and the trustee of the employee stock plan, Citibank, in New York, as I know you are aware. I understand from counsel in New York that Martin Marietta counsel is encouraging Judge Edelstein to issue a stand-still order against all our tender offers. I find it rather puzzling that Martin Marietta sought to prevent us from litigating in Michigan —an approach agreed to by Your Honor, who declared our claim to be a compulsory counterclaim that must be heard in this jurisdiction—and then they proceed in New York in direct contradiction."

"Your Honor, if I may," Bob Myers said, waving to his partner George Beall, "we had no choice but to file in New York because of the bank venue statute. We had to sue in New York."

"Citibank would have consented to move the case down here," Lewin said.

"We have the right to go to any forum we choose," Bob Myers said testily.

"Gentlemen," Judge Young said, waving off the discussion, "I really think this is getting out of hand. I have tried everything I could to accommodate your demands. But this is impossible. You are also making similar demands on other courts. This has obviously become a confusing state of affairs. We have three tender offers. We have three sets of timetables. There is a profusion of litigation in many jurisdictions that threatens to affect the interests of these corporations as well as the investing public. I mean, there are suits in Michigan, here, people are running to New York and God knows where else. We need a cooling-off period. I have discussed the situation with Judge Edelstein. This imposition on the courts has got to be stopped. Therefore I have decided to issue a ten-day hold on all the offers."

Everyone in the room was completely flabbergasted. No one had petitioned for such relief. George Beall and Bob Myers could hardly believe their ears—or their good fortune. Marc Cherno and John Henry Lewin were stunned.

"Just wait a minute," Cherno said, dropping all formalities as he got excited. "Look, all we've done is make a perfectly legal tender offer. There's hardly anything confusing about that. You've just held this morning that it was legal. If there's any confusion, it has resulted from the unprecedented defensive tactics employed by Martin Marietta. You can hardly lay those at our doorstep. You should hardly enjoin our offer because they have tried to confuse the marketplace with these unprecedented defensive tactics.

"You just ruled in the state takeover case that we're entitled to proceed with a legal tender offer under the Williams Act time periods. That's all we're doing! How in the world can you do this now? We have done nothing!"

"The purpose of the Williams Act is to protect investors against having to proceed with inadequate information," Judge Young said sternly, having made up his mind. "A ten-day hold is the only fair way to work this situation out."

Cherno was fumbling through the papers in his briefcase.

"Let me read your own opinion . . . ah, 'this is particularly true where, as here, Bendix' tender offer is legal and an injunction would at the very least delay the offer and might possibly kill it forever. . . .' That's the opinion you issued this morning! If you issue a ten-day hold, that's what is going to happen! Nothing is going to get unscrambled. If you permit this delay, Martin Marietta will think of some new defensive tactic that no one's even thought of yet! They've already come up with one that's pretty new. How can you say that because they created confusion, our tender offer has to be delayed?"

Judge Young was a man with strong opinions—once found, rarely shaken. He listened impassively to Cherno's plea.

"Your Honor," Lewin tried, relieving an obviously over-heated Marc Cherno, "this really puts us behind the eight ball. We have just come from Judge Winter's office, where he supported your decision this morning, allowing us to proceed with our offer. We are scheduled to buy the Martin Marietta Corporation tonight at midnight. I agree with you that this is a complicated situation with three major corporations bashing heads. But frankly, Your Honor, I question whether you have the authority to issue a hold on our legal tender offer."

"Whether or not I have the authority, that's what I am going to do," Judge Young said, drawing an order out from his pocket. "Here it is, and now I am going to sign it."

Judge Young glanced at his watch and noted the time—4:45 P.M.—on the 1½-page stay order before affixing his huge, looping signature.

From a telephone in the courthouse, Bob Myers called his partner at Dewey, Ballantine, Bob Fullem—who, after Martin Marietta had waived its conditions, he teasingly referred to as "Darth Vader at the controls of the Death Star."

"Bob," Myers said very excitedly, "Young just issued a ten-day stay order!"

"What?"

"Young just a couple of minutes ago signed a ten-day stay."

"On what grounds?" Fullem asked incredulously.

"I can't tell you what grounds," Myers said. "Basically, he thought there was confusion in the marketplace and our opening up the New York case kind of capped it. He wants the dockets put into some kind of rational shape and everybody's claims brought together."

"Outstanding! This changes everything!" Fullem's voice was piercing over the telephone. When he was excited, Fullem's voice almost broke into falsetto.

"Cherno and Lewin are taking the decision up to Judge Winter in the Appeals Court," Myers said.

"What is the chance of him overruling?"

"Both George and I think Winter will probably overrule. He didn't think much of our arguments this afternoon. The Bendix arguments seem to have the inside track with him."

"Well, do whatever you can to keep the stay. This is just outstanding!"

TWENTY-FIVE

In the late afternoon, Marty Siegel was having his deposition taken at the Fried, Frank offices near Battery Park. The session broke abruptly. Siegel found out from his attorney that Judge Young in Baltimore had just imposed a stay order of ten days on the tender offers. It seemed to Siegel that the Bendix lawyers just ran from the room.

When Siegel got back to his office at Hanover Square, a stack of messages were waiting for him. He sat in his chair with his back to the huge glass windows looking down on a skyscraper canyon. The sun was clipping the tops of the buildings, but it was shadow below.

There was a message from Jay Higgins. And there was a message from Bruce Wasserstein. Siegel decided to call Higgins first. In an odd way, Siegel felt sorry for Higgins. He thought he had been sandbagged.

"Hey, Marty," Higgins said, "thanks for returning my call. Look, this is unofficial. I didn't even call you, okay? I just want your number in case my client needs to get to you tonight. Where are you going to be?"

Siegel gave him a number.

"What do you think of this peace thing?" Siegel asked. With the stay order, Seigel thought he would never have more leverage for peace.

272

"I'm thinking about recommending it," Higgins said.

"I think if I'm given about twelve hours, I can get the agreement. We can all walk away. That's acceptable to my side. Why don't you see what Agee has to say?"

"Are you getting anywhere on price with the guy?" Higgins asked, referring to Wasserstein.

"He wants me to give him the price," Siegel said.

A skilled negotiator, Siegel knew there was no love lost between Higgins and Wasserstein. Sensing that Higgins and Wasserstein were not talking, Marty could play both sides of the street. Siegel had heard the reports that the Bendix board was surprised by the Martin Marietta counterbid. How was Jay to know he would pull such a bold move? Siegel reasoned.

"Watch out for these guys," Higgins said.

After the board meeting and a brief get-together with the special committee, Bill Agee, accompanied by Bruce Wasserstein, headed over to the Helmsley Palace. Bill took the private elevator to suite 4509. Having lived at the Palace for weeks, he recognized the elevator operator. Wasserstein waited in the lobby for Ed Hennessy from the Allied Corporation to arrive.

Hennessy was in New York that night to attend a fundraising dinner for Senator Strom Thurmond. Ed was co-chairman of the event. Around the cocktail hour, Hennessy arrived at the Helmsley Palace and was met by Bruce Wasserstein, who accompanied him up to the suite. Mary answered the door and ushered the men in. After Agee greeted Hennessy, Wasserstein left.

Bill and Mary were sitting in the central living room, drinking champagne. Agee offered a long-stemmed glass. Hennessy accepted. The two men had known each other for some time. Both were members of the Business Round Table.

Bill excused himself to take a phone call.

Hennessy chatted with Mary. The two had several things in common—Mary was a Catholic by training. Hennessy had once served as an altar boy. What they did not know at that time was that Hennessy had actually received religious instruction as a boy from Father Bill, the priest Mary considered her surrogate father.

Agee was smiling when he got off the phone.

"Good news?" Hennessy asked.

As Agee sat down to talk, Mary excused herself.

"Ed, I want to be frank with you," Agee said. "We are more

than likely going to take down the Martin shares tonight. It's being worked on now in the courts. There are several distinct possibilities. At some point, I may be looking for a minority investor to get an extension. If Pownall does not see his situation and presses forward, I may need you."

"What about Gray?" Hennessy asked.

"UTC has an antitrust problem. My people tell me Justice will stop Harry."

The two men continued to talk about Harry Gray. Agee was struck by the tone of Hennessy's remarks. It sounded as if Hennessy were afraid of the man.

"Well, Bill, I want you to know that we're here," Hennessy said.

"Ed, at this point I am exploring all options. Allied could be a strong candidate if we need help. I think our people should stay in touch. I would like to have an approach in place if we need you next week. Allied could make a tender for a ten percent stake of the Bendix shares and then we'd do an exchange of the stock for assets."

"We'd like to participate. I could put the minority thing in front of our board," Hennessy said.

"I'm going to Michigan this weekend, but let's get our people together to work out a minority position. It could work for both of us."

Bruce Wasserstein walked back to his Park Avenue Plaza office near the corner of Fifty-second Street. The air was cool, almost wet in midtown. Back at his glass-walled office, Wasserstein participated in a partners' meeting to review the situation. The stay order issued by Judge Young changed the whole complexion of the night. Wasserstein wondered if Agee knew.

Peace was discussed at the partners' meeting. Wasserstein was in favor. The one problem was that knowing Bill Agee, the peace had to be "honorable"—meaning that Martin Marietta would at least have to appear to make concessions in the settlement. In addition, the deal would have to be structured to avoid enticing some other company from coming in and making a lowball bid for Bendix. It would have to be confirmed that Harry Gray would stay in Hartford and not pull any tricks.

Wasserstein left the meeting to take a call from Marty Siegel.

"Did you hear about the stay order from Young?" Siegel asked.

"Yeah, I hear we're appealing," Wasserstein said flatly. "Look, Marty, I think we should open a line of communication."

"What do you want to talk about?" Siegel said coyly.

"Where are you on the three options?"

"Bruce, you should tell me what your expenses are. I think we should make a settlement here. With the courts involved, this is getting very messy. God knows where it is going to end up. Why don't we just work out a peace agreement. My guys will buy back the stock you already got—the 1.6 million shares—and we'll pay the expenses of the Bendix bankers and lawyers."

"What about UTC?"

"I gotta find out what their expenses are. We can work this out."

"Marty, Agee wants to buy you guys. I just want you to be prepared because if the court comes our way, then at midnight I may say 'Would you like to sell the company at fifty-two dollars?' and if you say 'No,' then I may ask you 'What's your best peace offer?,' and if that price isn't right, we're going to take down the shares at forty-eight dollars. So you got a lot of decisions to make."

"When are we going to talk again?" Siegel asked.

"Look, I'm going to call you every hour, okay? I'll talk to you at 6:00 P.M."

At 5:30 P.M., Bendix lawyers Marc Cherno and John Henry Lewin were taking the beaten path from the fifth floor to the ninth floor to see if Court of Appeals Judge Winter was still available. Cherno carried Judge Young's stay order in his hand. Neither Lewin nor Cherno had prepared a formal notice of appeal. The paperwork would have to wait. Events were unfolding too fast.

The two men walked down the modern white hall of the Federal Building in Baltimore to Winter's office and asked his clerk to speak with His Honor. George Beall and Frank Burch arrived. Winter came out moments later to the small waiting room.

"What can I do for you?" Judge Winter asked. Having already ruled in Bendix's favor that afternoon on Martin Marietta's appeal, Winter was surprised to see the lawyers.

"Judge Young has signed a ten-day stay," Marc Cherno said, holding out the order for Winter, who immediately looked quite confused. He read the 1½-page order before speaking.

"I don't understand this. He just ruled today that your offer was legal. And I backed his decision on appeal. It seems curious that he is doing this now."

Judge Winter still had a look of puzzlement.

"We would like you to review this stay order," Lewin said, noting the obvious but trying to elicit further reaction from the judge.

"Well," Winter said, rubbing his neck, "this situation is somewhat different from this morning. I have jurisdiction to review a preliminary injunction order. But normally, I don't think I have jurisdiction to review a stay order. This is rather strange. Did Young say why he did this?"

"From our point of view, his reasons are unclear," Cherno said.

"We find this move to be an astute understanding of the confusion in the marketplace," George Beall countered. Frank Menaker from Martin Marietta was with Beall. He had driven the thirty miles from Bethesda as soon as he heard of Young's ruling.

"Again, gentlemen, although this order does seem strange to me, I question whether I have the jurisdiction. Is this order a follow order from which I can consider an appeal, or is this some sort of arbitrary order that I can't touch? I want you all to come back here at—say, 8:00 P.M.—and I am going to consider this jurisdiction issue between now and then and I want you all to consider this issue also. If I can take it I will, and you should be prepared to argue the merits of what Judge Young did."

With that the lawyers filed out of Winter's chambers, past the ragtag collection of interested onlookers that included arbitrageurs' reps such as Tommy Houston, and newsmen. The onlookers were asking a flurry of questions about what decision had been made.

"George, c'mon," Houston said. "Give me something."

"He wants us back at eight P.M.," Beall said, throwing a small bone.

Confronted with Winter's concern about his jurisdiction to hear an appeal of Young's stay order, the attorneys split into their respective camps on the steps of the courthouse and headed back to their offices: the Martin Marietta team returned with the United Technologies reps to the Miles & Stockbridge office in the Maryland National Bank Building on Light Street. Marc Cherno and John Henry Lewin returned to Lewin's office in the Mercantile Bank Building.

Both sides hit the law books, looking for precedents allowing or prohibiting Judge Winter from countermanding Judge Young's stay order. Both sides were on the telephone marshaling the staffs of their New York offices. The library in Lewin's office was a chaotic tumble of opened books, and lawyers calling to each other. Marc Cherno was on the telephone, with the Fried, Frank office in New York being posted regularly. He was on the phone with Gerry Goldman at Hughes, Hubbard. Cherno did not have time to hold hands with the client. Everyone understood. The decks were cleared for action.

Lewin thought he found a precedent in one of the books.

"Here's a case where some judge in the District of Columbia entered some crazy order, which he was without power to enter, and an appeal went to the D.C. Circuit Court, and they reviewed."

All the lawyers kept a steady watch on the time. When it was time to return to the courthouse, Lewin was almost through the doorway when he said to Cherno, "You know, we oughta at least have a piece of paper showing that we're in the right court." He sat down and wrote out a notice of appeal on a yellow legal pad —what he calls foolscap.

The lawyers in town who represented arbitrageurs knew each other—perhaps not well, but with tacit acknowledgment. They were secretive about their clients—as their clients insisted. In large financial transactions on Wall Street, the arbitrageurs were the unseen hand.

That did not preclude cooperative action at times among the Baltimore reps. While the Martin Marietta and Bendix attorneys were poring over the law books in their offices in preparation of arguing before Judge Winter, Tommy Houston and Robert Baker and Gordon Haines and several other arb reps were sitting in a small alcove outside Winter's chambers. That was as good a place to wait as any. Close to the action.

News is a precious commodity. Money is made off news. The slightest edge could mean the difference between huge profits and huge losses.

Periodically, Houston checked in with his contact man—

Perry Cohen, the research director for Ivan Boesky. Cohen was working late at the office in lower Manhattan. During the break imposed by Judge Winter, Cohen went home, leaving Houston his home number.

Houston also called Ted Shelsby, the financial writer for the *Baltimore Sun*. Nothing much was happening. It seemed everyone in New York and Detroit and Bethesda was waiting for Judge Winter.

Houston sat with the other arb lawyers, waiting for developments. The lawyers chatted among themselves to pass the time.

"Whichever way it goes, do you think either Bendix or Marietta will go to a higher court?" Houston asked. All the lawyers knew that meant going to the U.S. Supreme Court.

"Who on the High Court would be the circuit justice to hear an appeal?" one of the men asked.

"It's Warren Burger."

"How are we going to find out if something is happening tonight?"

"I drive by the Court on my way home," one of the attorneys volunteered. "It's not really out of the way. . . ."

"What do you say?" Houston asked.

"Yeah, okay, give me your telephone numbers, and I'll swing by after we're done here. If the lights are on, I'll give you a call."

Wasserstein went to dinner with Art Fleischer at the See Yang Restaurant, several doors down from the Helmsley Palace. Wasserstein was hungry and ate heartily. The two men were basically stalling for time. Wasserstein was planning to call Siegel. Fleischer was awaiting word from Baltimore on the status of the appeal to Judge Winter. Having heard a summary of the situation from his litigation chief, Marc Cherno, in Baltimore, Fleischer was calm and confident. He thought that Young's order would be overturned.

At 6:00 P.M., from a phone booth in the restaurant, Wasserstein called Siegel's direct-dial number.

"Have you thought about price?" Wasserstein asked.

"I can't speak for the board," Siegel said, couching his words, "but I think the number has got to have a six in front of it."

"You're gonna have to do better than that," Wasserstein said. "Where are the values for that kind of price?"

"Have you thought about peace?" Siegel asked.

"You're gonna have to get Gray to agree," Wasserstein said.

"How about we buy the one point six million shares from you for twenty-seven dollars per share plus expenses?"

"What about Gray?"

"I can get Gray."

"We're gonna buy you at midnight for forty-eight dollars," Wasserstein said, overstating his case. Winter had not ruled. "If it's peace, then you can buy back the shares at forty-eight dollars plus expenses."

At 7:00 P.M. there was still no word from Baltimore. Cherno had informed Fleischer that Judge Winter had questioned whether he had the jurisdiction to review the appeal. Fleischer was on the phone, directing traffic with his office to make sure that a position was constructed that backed up Winter's ability to hear the appeal. Cherno told Art that the judge wanted the parties back at his office at 8:00 P.M.

Wasserstein made his 7:00 P.M. call to Siegel.

"Have you found out what the Bendix expenses are?" Siegel asked.

"Yeah. Seven and a half million dollars."

"How much are you getting, Bruce?"

"It's two and a half for First Boston, two for Salomon, and three for the lawyers."

"Okay," Siegel said. "Look, I've talked with Marty Lipton and he says that United Technologies' expenses are five million dollars for the lawyers and the bankers. The way it will work is that Marietta will pay the Bendix expenses, but you guys have got to pay UTC's expenses."

"I still haven't heard a price that sounds reasonable for the shares. Last time you were saying a lousy twenty-seven bucks. I can't take that to Agee."

"We'll give you thirty-three."

At 8:00 P.M., Marc Cherno was talking with Judge Winter. But still no word. Wasserstein was still at the See Yang Restaurant.

"So Marty, what's the price to get Martin Marietta to lower the flag and sell the company to Bendix? Last time it was a bullshit sixtyish."

"All I can say is that it's at least high fifties," Siegel said, giving ground. "What about the peace price?"

"Marty, Marietta's stock was trading today for thirty-seven fifty, and you're offering me what, thirty-three?"

"I can go to thirty-five. Agee will make thirteen million on his investment."

"Marty, that's still below market. The damn stock is trading for thirty-seven fifty! How can you not even give me market?"

"Your cost was twenty-seven a share," Siegel said.

"Yeah. So what? Besides, thirty-seven fifty is the midpoint between twenty-seven and forty-eight."

The two men haggled like *shmatte* dealers. The gaps were narrowing. Siegel had shown some flexibility on price to sell the company. And there appeared to be a $2.50 difference per share on the peace price. From Wasserstein's tone of voice, Siegel thought he was leaning toward peace.

"Marty, look, I'll talk with Agee. I'll give you a call at ten P.M."

"Talk to you at ten P.M.," Siegel said.

By the time the lawyers reported back to the Federal Building for their meeting with Fourth Circuit Judge Winter, a small group of reporters and interested onlookers had gathered on the ninth floor outside Winter's chambers. Tommy Houston was there, representing the interests of Ivan Boesky. Also standing around were Robert Baker and Gordon Haines. The *Baltimore Sun* had a clutch of reporters, poised with pens and pads and small tape recorders. Frank Allen from *The Wall Street Journal* office in Philadelphia was present, as were reporters from other national publications.

Marc Cherno and John Henry Lewin were joined by George Beall, Bob Myers, and Frank Burch. Armed with the fruits of their efforts of the past two hours, the lawyers passed the onlookers and went into Judge Winter's chambers.

George Beall was dressed formally, in black tie. He had originally planned to attend the opening of the Meyerhoff Symphony with his wife. Tonight was the christening of the brand-new symphony hall. It was a major social occasion for Baltimore. Beall's wife went on to the hall. Beall went to the hearing. He would join her as soon as possible.

Before Judge Winter had been appointed a federal judge in

1961 by President Kennedy, he had been the lawyer for Baltimore City. Before that, he had been a member of Miles & Stockbridge, George Beall's firm. In the Baltimore legal community, everybody knew everybody.

When Judge Winter came into the small conference room in his chambers, he was accompanied by three of his clerks. It was obvious that just as the Bendix and Martin Marietta lawyers had been working feverishly since 5:30 P.M., so had the judge and his staff.

While he invited their comments, Judge Winter was quick to say that after reviewing the situation, he felt confident that he did have the jurisdiction to consider an appeal of Judge Young's decision.

"Frankly, gentlemen, I view Judge Young's stay order as having been cut from whole cloth," Judge Winter said. "I would like to hear the merits."

The lawyers argued back and forth. Marc Cherno passionately repeated his argument that the courts must not interfere with the legitimate functioning of the marketplace. He continued to hammer away that Bendix had launched a legal tender offer and that delay could mortally wound his client's legitimate business objectives. The judge listened intently.

"Would you all step outside for a minute and let me try to write an order," Winter said after both sides had stated their clients' point of view.

When the lawyers filed back in, one of Winter's clerks handed out a Xerox copy of his decision.

Judge Young's stay order was overturned. Bendix would be free to buy the Martin Marietta stock in less than three hours.

As the lawyers walked down the hall toward the elevators, the reporters and arbitrageurs' representatives were swarming like bees looking for honey. There was considerable commotion, with lawyers and reporters jockeying for position. Tommy Houston had his foot blocking the elevator door.

"Let it go," Cherno said.

"C'mon, can't you say anything? What did he rule?"

"Read the smiles," Cherno said.

Bob Myers and George Beall got on the telephone together this time to tell Bob Fullem in New York that Martin Marietta had lost on appeal and that Bendix was free to take down the shares. Fullem was disappointed by the predicted decision.

"So it looks like Bendix is going to buy Martin Marietta," Beall said.

"Not necessarily," Fullem confided. "Marty Siegel has been in touch with Bruce Wasserstein, and there has been considerable discussion about all three companies just backing away. Some kind of three-way laydown. They are talking now. It may happen."

When word came from Frank Menaker in Baltimore that Judge Winter had indeed overruled Judge Young, Tom Pownall was out to dinner. The broad hallway on the second floor of the executive wing in Bethesda was quiet. Occasionally a glum staffer would leave one office and enter another.

Doris Rush was eating cheese and crackers and drinking a Coke.

"I can't believe it; are they really going to buy?" Karen Barry, a young attorney, asked Doris, taking a cracker for herself and then discarding it uneaten into an ashtray. "Just think, in maybe three hours, we're going to be owned by Bendix."

Some people wanted just to go home and forget about it. Doris heard the phone ringing on Frank Menaker's extension—6125. With the switchboard closed, the only way to talk to anybody was to direct-dial an extension. Doris went to her secretary's desk in the hallway and hit the button to pick up the call.

"Who's this?" Tom Pownall asked.

"This is Doris." She recognized the voice. "Judge Winter has overturned Judge Young."

Pownall was silent.

"I'm on my way back to the office."

The hallway was a mix of people exhausted by disappointment. Winter's ruling had taken the wind out of their sails. It seemed all they could do was sit and wait for their company to be bought.

"What about the Supreme Court?" someone asked.

That was all Doris Rush needed to hear. Suddenly she had a project again. As she got excited about the possibility of getting a U.S. Supreme Court justice to overturn the circuit court, the pace picked up. However, no one knew how to contact the Supreme Court at this time of night.

"We've got to get a justice at home or something," Rush said. Just glad to have something to do, Rush and Karen Barry decided that they should check the phone book for justices' telephone numbers. First they had to brainstorm the names.

With some people pulling phone books out of the law library and another out of Menaker's office, the group thumbed for phone numbers.

"Don't forget to look in Montgomery County and northern Virginia. Some of them are bound to live there."

All they could come up with was the telephone number for Justice Potter, who had retired from the Court. Some of the treasury people called friends who had worked in law firms, looking for anybody who knew somebody who knew a Supreme Court justice. They succeeded in spreading the word that they were looking for a justice, but they never found a justice. The effort fizzled out, and again the depression spread.

"You know, this is really a shame," Rush said. "I mean, Young was overturned because he had no basis for his stay order. I mean, there wasn't even a motion before him."

"Well, is there anything we can do about it?" Bob Powell asked.

"Wait a minute! What about that motion that Fullem was going to work on?" Doris said. "I've got to talk to Fullem."

While Doris was desperately trying to get through to Dewey, Ballantine's offices in New York to speak with Fullem, Karen Barry across the hall had him on the line. Someone came in and told Doris.

"What about that motion?" Rush asked Fullem. "I mean, all Young wants is a reason to put a stay order on this thing. He did it all on his own and got overruled. But maybe if we give him a reason. Can we do that in three hours?"

Fullem was not particularly optimistic that anything could be accomplished with Young after Winter had already overruled. But Rush was on her horse, and nothing was going to stop her. After hanging up with Fullem, she sat down with Karen Barry and tried to figure out how to draft an order for a temporary restraining order. Not being a litigating lawyer, it was a lot harder than it looked.

"We've got to get to Miles & Stockbridge," Rush said. Suddenly there was a new project. Doris had a directory of telephone numbers for Miles & Stockbridge. They had the same kind of phone system. If you didn't have a direct-dial number, the switchboard would not answer. Rush and Bob Powell assembled people at any available desks. Everybody got on the phone and called a dozen different Miles & Stockbridge extensions. When no one answered immediately, they let the phones just ring and ring.

Finally someone got through, and Doris got on to speak with Frank Menaker.

"Let me put you on the speaker so everybody here can hear," Menaker said. He was with George Beall and his people from Miles & Stockbridge as well as Bob Myers from Dewey, Ballantine.

"Well, Frank, we were thinking. All Young really needs is a motion to be put in front of him. He ruled with nothing before him. No wonder Winter overruled," Doris said. She was sitting at her secretary's desk, with Steve Smith and Bruce Deerson from the legal department leaning over as if to hear the conversation.

"I'm going to put the call on the speaker here," Deerson said to Rush.

Both offices were now connected with open speakers at both ends. Rush was explaining to the team at Miles & Stockbridge the idea of putting a motion before Judge Young.

"What kind of motion would it be?" someone in Baltimore asked.

"It should be an injunction on the grounds of waste of corporate assets," Doris said. "You know, I talked to Fullem about this nearly a week ago. I asked him to have something ready. But he tells me nothing is ready."

"Well, it's a little late to be trying that now," someone in Baltimore said. It was obvious that no one was very impressed with the idea.

"Yeah, but the only reason Young got overruled was because he didn't have anything before him. Isn't he likely to say 'Yes' to any motion?"

"We could call Young and sound him out," someone in Baltimore volunteered.

With Bob Powell, Tom Mendenhall, Bruce Deerson, Steve Smith, Karen Barry, Janet MacGregor, and others all facing the speaker phone, no one noticed when Tom Pownall came into the crowded office. He stood at the back, listening.

Rush was trying to convince the team in Baltimore, without much luck.

"Yeah, but this is no time to give up," Bruce Deerson said, getting worked up. "At least we could try. What the heck have we got to lose?"

"Well, we could maybe call the judge, but I really don't think it's gonna do anything," someone in Baltimore said.

"Frank, this is Tom. For pete's sake, can't you guys out there show some signs of life? At least try. Let's not give up yet! They're right on this end. At least try!"

When Doris heard Pownall's voice, she was terrified. Menaker will kill me, she thought, he will absolutely have my head. Doris thought it must have sounded to the people in Baltimore that Pownall was there all along and that they were being set up to look like jerks to Pownall. Doris wanted to crawl into a hole and hide.

No light would be lit at the U.S. Supreme Court that night.

TWENTY-SIX

After each phone call with Bruce Wasserstein, Marty Siegel was back on the phone giving status reports to Tom Pownall and the team in Bethesda. Siegel was also talking with Marty Lipton to stay in touch with the United Technologies side of the equation. And he was also calling over to Dewey, Ballantine to talk with Bob Fullem to find out the status of the court case in Baltimore.

Siegel felt increasingly optimistic as the evening progressed. Noting the amount of time he and Bruce had devoted to the details of the peace agreement and the fact that Bruce had talked the dollars and cents of peace, Siegel was able to give positive reports to Pownall.

After the 8:00 P.M. call, Siegel called Pownall again.

"Tom, it seems to me that Wasserstein wants peace," Siegel said. "He has finally brought down his asking price for you to buy back the shares. I was saying thirty-five and he's now saying thirty-seven fifty."

The difference between the two figures was only $4 million.

"Well, hell, we'll go to thirty-seven fifty if that will do it," Pownall said. Against his better judgment, he was allowing Siegel's optimism to raise his spirits. Perhaps this nightmare would end. The past twenty-two days had seemed like years.

"Bruce said he's gonna call me back at ten P.M., Siegel said.

286

By 10:05 P.M., Bruce had not called, and Siegel was getting itchy. Then 10:10 P.M. and still no call. What made Siegel feel even worse was that Wasserstein had never told him where he was. He had no number to reach him. Fullem was on the phone wanting to know how the call had gone.

"He didn't call," Siegel said, exasperated.

"Oh, no," Fullem said.

By 10:45 P.M., still no call. Siegel was now hearing from everyone—Tom Pownall, and the UTC team over at Wachtell, Lipton. They all wanted to know what went wrong. Where was Wasserstein? Siegel called over to the First Boston offices and got ahold of Tony Grassi, Wasserstein's associate.

"Hey Tony," Siegel said, trying to sound calm, "I was supposed to hear from Bruce. We were gonna talk at ten P.M."

"I'll tell him you called and have him call you back," Grassi said.

Tony Grassi tried the See Yang Restaurant. Wasserstein was no longer there. After his last call with Marty Siegel, Bruce Wasserstein and Art Fleischer had walked to the Helmsley Palace. From the lobby phone, Bruce called up to the forty-fifth floor. Agee invited both men up to the suite.

Bill was there with Mary and Al McDonald.

"How are our friends at Martin Marietta?" Bill Agee asked. He knew Wasserstein was talking with Siegel.

"I'm talking the three options with Marty," Wasserstein said.

"Has there been any movement?"

"On the buy side, he started out at sixty and is now talking maybe in the high fifties."

"They're not taking us seriously," McDonald said.

Neither McDonald nor Agee knew the intensity of Wasserstein's negotiations with Siegel. In their minds, Wasserstein had not been authorized to enter such negotiations. His job was to outline the options.

Fleischer was wanted on the phone. He sat on the couch and spoke into the phone in a low-key but firm tone of voice. Bill was watching Fleischer out of the corner of his eye.

"Winter has overruled Judge Young," Fleischer said calmly.

"Fantastic!" Agee said. Mary congratulated both Bill and Al McDonald. Fleischer stayed on the telephone, nodding acceptance of Agee's enthusiasm.

Now it was Wasserstein's turn. There was a call from Tony

Grassi. Wasserstein paced as he spoke, the telephone cord stretched to its maximum extension.

"It's after ten P.M. Siegel is expecting a return call," Wasserstein said. "He is expecting us to come at him with a proposal."

"We just got cleared by the court to buy," Agee said.

"Sixty dollars is completely unreasonable," McDonald said, trying to understand what was behind Wasserstein's advocacy of his discussions with Siegel.

"If we can't agree on a price for a friendly transaction, you still have the option of settling. Marty has Gray in agreement to a laydown. Martin Marietta will pick up the Bendix's expenses and buy back the shares you own at a reasonable price."

"What kind of price?" Agee asked.

"I think they'll go to thirty-seven fifty."

"This is ridiculous," Al McDonald said. "I don't know what you've been saying to Siegel, but it sounds off-base to me. They're just playing around with you. They're stalling. They're trying to find any way possible to keep us from buying!"

"There is a rumor that they may try tonight to get Warren Burger on the Supreme Court to sign an order," Fleischer said.

"See!" McDonald said. "Siegel's got a credibility problem."

McDonald and Wasserstein went back and forth, with Agee listening intently. Bill had no interest in the laydown—now that the courts had given him the room to purchase a majority share of the Martin Marietta Corporation.

From what he heard from Wasserstein, Agee thought the two investment bankers were just fishing—looking for any way to make a deal. And that was not the way he operated. Bill Agee was the only one to make the deal. Skillfully, Agee let McDonald and Wasserstein argue the issues—reserving his own opinion as the deciding one.

The fundamental question of whether to buy absorbed Bill Agee. He was at a critical crossroads. One way or another, he knew, things would never be the same. He had told the world that he wanted to build a better Bendix Corporation. He had launched a stunning attack on Martin Marietta. The courts had gone to the brink of intervention and then pulled back. The decision came down to Bill and what he wanted. In the back of his mind was the threat from Tom Pownall that Martin Marietta would buy Bendix if Bendix bought the Marietta shares tonight.

Bill looked at the men standing in the hotel room. Fleischer seemed to have a knowing look in his eyes. Bill excused himself and walked into the bedroom. Mary followed.

Alone together in the bedroom, Agee went through the scenario in his mind again. He turned over and over the options. When Bill and Mary emerged, Bill was outwardly calm.

"I've decided we're going to buy."

After a pause, Wasserstein said, "Bill, even if you're going to buy, you've got to carry this thing through. At midnight, we have the greatest leverage over them. Let me see what I can come up with from Siegel. I should make the phone call I promised him."

"I'm offering forty-eight dollars a share," Bill said. "Siegel has talked to you about some number in the sixties. That is off-base. I frankly think, Bruce, that Siegel has been playing with you. Let's stop the communication."

"That's a mistake," Bruce said.

"Bruce, you were not empowered to negotiate this deal. And from what I hear, Siegel is not talking in good faith."

"I should call him," Wasserstein said.

"Look," McDonald said, getting agitated, "Bruce, forget it. We do not want you to make any calls. You are sequestered. You're impounded!"

"I have a courtesy problem," Wasserstein said.

"All you care about is courtesy to these other guys on Wall Street!" McDonald shouted. "Just tell Siegel after midnight that your client said you couldn't make the call."

"I told him I'd give him a call," Wasserstein insisted.

"Bruce, we told them we intend to buy their company. There is nothing to negotiate at this point in time. We're committed to buy and we're going to buy!" Bill Agee said.

At 11:15 P.M., Siegel called Grassi again.

"Tony, what's up?"

"He'll get back to you," Grassi said.

Hanging up, Siegel felt somewhat relieved. He thought that Agee and Wasserstein were playing the mind game to its limit. They were just putting on the pressure, Siegel thought.

At about 11:30 P.M., Siegel called Marty Lipton.

"I think the lines of communication are open again. Bruce is supposed to call me. I think they're playing the time for all it's worth."

"I hear a rumor," Lipton said, "that the press has been called to the GM Building for a big announcement."

Both men knew that meant only one thing—Agee was going to buy.

"I can't believe that they'd do that without even talking to us," Siegel said.

At around 12:30 A.M., Siegel got a call from Wasserstein.

"Marty, I want to apologize. My client had me sequestered and wouldn't let me return the call. What do you think about the idea of getting Agee and Pownall to sit down and talk this over?"

"I'm sure Tom will talk to Bill if we can work something out."

"How about next week?"

"Well, wait a minute. What did Agee feel about the peace price?"

There was a pause. Wasserstein had no idea that Siegel had not heard.

"You know we bought," Wasserstein said incredulously. Siegel had no response. "Marty?"

"He's a fool," Siegel said.

Tom Pownall was waiting for word in his office. Larry Adams was with him. Leithauser was around. Roy Calvin was in and out, always with a cigarette in one hand. After Wasserstein disappeared without making the 10:00 P.M. call to Siegel, everything seemed to go into slow motion. And Pownall and everybody in his office could see the roundhouse punch coming. But there was little they could do but wait.

Roy Calvin picked up the report from a newspaperman that Bendix was scheduling an announcement at the GM Building. That was enough for Leithauser. He went home. Pownall stayed in his office—as if he were going to go down with the ship. Bob Powell wandered in at one point. Tom was on the phone with Harry Gray, passing the time.

At 12:45 P.M., Siegel called his client.

"They bought," Siegel said. "I just heard from Wasserstein. I've got some stuff to talk to you about, but I guess it can wait until morning. I hear Agee is planning to buy up to seventy percent."

Tom Pownall took the news stoically. Only the sound of his raspy breathing revealed the strain. The 70 percent business made matters worse. It was obvious that Agee felt confident that if he bought an overwhelming majority of the company, Pownall and the Marietta directors would acquiesce. But looking at the situation as Pownall did, the two companies were now inevitably going to be put together, and Agee's move to take down 70 percent meant he was spending almost $300 million of the combined companies' money needlessly.

Pownall and Larry Adams found it hard to believe that Agee had bought the stock without first trying to talk to them. They expected him to take another crack at negotiating a friendly deal. From Adams' point of view, there was a chance Martin Marietta would have accepted a midnight deal.

Tom Pownall was on his way to the elevator to go home. A core group of staffers was left in the offices—Doris Rush, Tom Mendenhall, Karen Barry, Janet MacGregor, Steve Smith, Bruce Deerson.

"I just got word, they bought," Pownall said to the group. He was calm. He smiled. It was very quiet. "I wonder if I should call Agee," he said almost as an afterthought.

Everyone in the group—following Pownall to the end—shook their heads and said "No."

"Don't worry, we'll get 'em," someone said to try to cheer up Pownall. He smiled.

At the elevator, after pressing the button, Pownall turned around.

"I want you all to know how grateful I am for all your efforts. I know how hard you all tried."

With that he was in the elevator and gone.

TWENTY-SEVEN

Bill Agee was having breakfast with Al McDonald and Arthur Fleischer in the suite at the Helmsley Palace on Friday morning. A white-uniformed waiter had delivered coffee and tea with a silver service, and a tray of toast and danish. Bill had specifically requested grapefruit juice.

After months of planning and a tough three weeks of public push and shove, Bill Agee felt refreshed and confident. He had reached a major objective: The Bendix Corporation was now the majority stockholder in the Martin Marietta Corporation.

Arthur Flesicher also was in a good mood. The securities lawyer had orchestrated a legal battle with his partners that prevented Martin Marietta from achieving in court what they could not win on the battlefield.

The phone rang. Al answered, listened, and hung up.

"It just ran on the tape," McDonald said. "The headline is 'BENDIX BUYS CONTROL OF MARIETTA, TO SEEK 70 PERCENT STAKE.' That should shake them up in Bethesda. Wasserstein says the whole world will tender to us today."

"I think it's time that these guys in Bethesda wake up and start dealing with reality. We own them now," Agee said powerfully, turning to Fleischer.

"Here's the letter to the Martin Marietta board that we discussed," Fleischer said, pulling several pages from his briefcase. He handed it to Agee, who silently began reading.

"Yeah, I like this: 'Bendix hereby demands.' That's good."

"We start off each of the three points that way," Fleischer said.

"Okay, so the Martin Marietta directors are instructed to resign; and the immediate termination of the Marietta offer and agreement with United Technologies; and Marietta agreement not to vote any shares of Bendix common at our special stockholders' meeting—good."

The penultimate paragraph included a threat: "Bendix will seek in its litigation to hold each member of the Marietta Board fully and personally responsible for all damages which Bendix, Martin Marietta and their respective shareholders may sustain as a result of the Board's failure to comply with Bendix' demands in this letter."

"Excellent," Agee said.

"Oh, Arthur," McDonald said, "Bruce says the meeting with the Allied people is now set for two P.M. at First Boston."

At Agee's get-together last night with Ed Hennessy after the reception for Strom Thurmond, Bill and Hennessy hammered out the framework for a minority investment by Allied in Bendix. When called upon, Hennessy was to make a tender offer to purchase 10 percent of Bendix common stock at a price of $80 per share. Agee in turn would create and sell to Allied for $175 million a new series of convertible preferred stock.

That was Agee's backup plan in case Tom Pownall would not listen to reason. If by next Wednesday it appeared Pownall was still adamant about spending $1 billion for the Bendix shares, Agee would spring the Allied deal—thereby delaying Pownall for at least ten days.

"Are you going to attend today's meeting with Allied? I understand Hennessy will be there," Fleischer asked, using his linen napkin.

"No, I've got other plans," Agee said. "You and Bruce handle it."

Having successfully bought the Martin Marietta Corporation, Agee planned to concentrate today on setting up a meeting with Tom Pownall.

Tom Quinn, an assistant treasurer in charge of planning for Martin Marietta, was in the office looking at numbers. With a stack of papers in his hand, he went into Tom Mendenhall's office. Mendenhall was working on the mountain of paper on his desk.

"What's up?" Mendenhall asked. Quinn was absolutely in the dumps.

"I've been looking at this they buy us, we buy them stuff. It's just unbelievable. I mean, it looks like Agee is going to buy us two hundred percent. There's no way our board will go for this and buy Bendix. I mean, it's just obvious from the look of it. We'd look irrational. We'd look crazy, you know?"

"What'd ya mean?" Mendenhall didn't need to hear this gloom. The offices were ghostly quiet—it was the silence of people wondering about their jobs and mortgages. Would Bendix fire everybody in the corporate headquarters building?

"Bendix already owns us," Quinn said. "We're now the same goddamn company. So what is the board going to do? Spend a billion dollars just to get even? People would think we had lost our minds."

Quinn succeeded in making Mendenhall depressed.

"I'm not gonna hang around if Bendix gets control," Mendenhall said.

"Aw, you're crazy," Quinn said. "You gotta live to fight tomorrow."

Now Quinn was trying to cheer up Mendenhall.

"No, there's no way," Mendenhall said. "It's a style thing. I'm just not gonna do it."

"Aw, you'll change your mind. You better get used to the idea."

In his low moments, Mendenhall had given it some thought. Several of the banks had even told him not to worry. "We'll find you a place," one of the loan officers had said.

But now Mendenhall had something else on his mind. He went in to see his boss, Bob Powell, the treasurer of the corporation.

"Bob, I think we should borrow the money now," Mendenhall said.

"How so?"

"Look, if it were me, if I were Bendix, the first thing I would try is to get an injunction to prevent Martin Marietta from borrowing the money to take down the Bendix shares."

"I think you're right," Powell said.

"There's a twenty-four-hour-notice provision in the agreement with the banks. I think we ought to give the banks notice today."

Bob Powell and Tom Mendenhall went in to talk with Charlie Leithauser, the senior financial executive.

"The money's not going to do us any good if we can't get it when we need it," Leithauser agreed.

Tom Mendenhall had the cost of borrowing the $930 million down to a science. It would cost $267,000 a day in interest; $11,125 an hour; $185 a minute; $3 a second.

The first step was for Tom Mendenhall to call the lead bank —Bank of America. He tried to reach Tom Tegart. Tegart was on vacation. Mendenhall reached Tegart's boss, Lynn Vine.

"Lynn, this is Tom Mendenhall at Martin Marietta. We're planning on taking down the money a little early. We'd like you to give the banks notice and have them forward the money."

"Tom, what's up?" Vine asked.

"We'd like to line up the money in a demand account."

"Are you serious about this? You want to borrow the money now?"

"Just as soon as we can get it," Mendenhall said.

"Tom, I'm going to have to take this up with my boss," Vine said.

"I understand," Mendenhall said, feeling a moment of panic. Holy cow! he thought. What if they decide not to fund? It would blow us out of the water!

Knowing that it was a sensitive subject, Mendenhall did not pressure Vine. Instead, Tom suggested to his boss, Bob Powell, that he have a boss-to-boss discussion with Lyle Krapf, the senior vice president for North American operations of Bank of America.

"I think these bank guys are wondering if they're holding on to an amputated foot," Mendenhall said to Powell. "I think you should talk to Krapf."

"The mandate hasn't changed," Powell said to Krapf. "We want the money sitting in an account with our name on it ready when we want it."

"Bob, it looks bad for you guys," Krapf said.

"Yeah, it may look bad, but we know what we're doing. We said we were going to buy, and that's what we're going to do."

"I never thought you'd actually take down the money," Krapf said.

"To tell you the truth, neither did I," Powell said.

"If you want it Monday, I'm going to have to give you a fixed higher rate on the twenty-four-hour turnaround."

"Yeah, we know," Powell said. "Don't worry, we're good for the money."

"Okay, I'll have my people send the telexes to the banks today. You'll have the money at nine A.M. on Monday."

As the assistant treasurer in charge of cash and banking at Martin Marietta, Mendenhall was responsible for the actions of Dorothy Hamm, the assistant cash manager. As the money markets had deteriorated in the recent months, Mendenhall had insisted upon a strict set of parameters governing Dorothy's investment of the company's cash.

Once he heard that the company would have the money, Mendenhall knew that come Monday, he would have $930 million to invest. He went in to talk to Dorothy Hamm.

"Dorothy, I've just talked with B of A and we're taking down the nine hundred thirty million as of Monday. And it has to be invested."

Hamm went completely white.

"And not only that, it has to be invested according to my guidelines."

"Oh, Tom!" It was more than the woman could stand.

"I'm only kidding, Dorothy. We'll all be working on this one, too."

"Tom, you'll have to excuse me," Hamm said, regaining her composure, "but lately it's been so difficult to tell 'only kidding' from reality."

"Amen to that," Mendenhall said.

In his September 17 *Newsbreak* feature on CBS Radio, Charles Osgood, as was his custom, launched into a convoluted rhyming story, interrupted by a commercial in true teaser style. When he returned, he finished his story about the Bendix vs. Martin Marietta vs. United Technologies battle by saying:

Is it big, is it brutal, is it complex?
If Bendix runs Martin and Martin runs Bendix
the resulting confusion is simply horrendix.
The corporate law books up there on the shelf
say certain things one can't do to one's self.

Will the giants arrive at some kind of accord?
Which board of directors will swallow which board?
Which directors will stay?
Which ones will be pruned?
We'll know before long
So fight fans stay tuned.

Jack Byrne, of the Martin Marietta board of directors, was in his office at Geico Corporation. He had heard the news from a somber Tom Pownall. Now he had another phone call from a lawyer—a mutual friend of Bill Agee.

"I think you and Bill Agee should talk," the man said. "If I can set it up, will you take his phone call?"

"Yes, I will, Sam," Byrne said. "I'm on my way to the University of Chicago now—for one of those business school seminars."

Later in the day on Friday, during his presentation to the one hundred executives gathered for the seminar, Byrne was approached at the podium by an embarrassed dean of the business school. The man whispered to Byrne that Bill Agee was on the phone and would like to talk to him.

"Tell Bill that I will call him back in ten or fifteen minutes," Byrne said. "That's all I've got left."

The dean retreated, only to reappear moments later, clearly agitated.

"Mr. Agee says this can't wait."

Byrne turned to the students and asked to be excused.

"Bill, this is Jack Byrne."

"Jack, I appreciate you taking the time to talk to me. I've heard such good things about what you've done at Geico. It's super what you've been able to do."

"Thanks, Bill. What can I do for you?"

"Jack, I've written Tom Pownall two letters. I called him when this whole thing started. I think I've made it clear that I want to talk with him. Why hasn't this man called me?" Agee asked.

"I told Tom before that I thought he should talk to you. I guess his advisers are advising him against it."

"Jack, this is ridiculous. Bendix owns seventy percent of the company, or will soon, and the chief executive officer won't talk to me?"

"Don't underestimate Pownall and those guys at Martin Marietta. They don't think the fight is over yet. They intend to buy as advertised."

"This is ridiculous, Jack. It doesn't make any sense that these two companies are on a collision course."

"It's too bad it's turning out that way," Byrne said.

"I want to meet with Tom. I'll meet him over the weekend or on Monday, but we're gonna have a meeting. I've told Gutfreund and everybody else to spread the word on this one. I would appreciate your help. You tell him. Just tell him."

Word came back through the investment bankers. Tom Pownall agreed to meet with Bill Agee Monday morning at the Dewey, Ballantine offices at 101 Park Avenue.

"Monday," Agee said to Mary on the phone.

"That's wonderful," Mary said. She had thought all along that if Bill and Tom Pownall could sit down together in the same room, the issues could be resolved.

"Let's go home for the weekend," Mary said.

Home for Bill and Mary was their condominium in Orchard Lake, a suburb of Detroit. Bill bought the condominium in April, a couple of months before marrying Mary. He paid cash. The small pond on the grounds reminded Bill of his place in Idaho. Mary decorated the condo in soft pastels—yellow, peach, and green. A jacuzzi was in the basement. The familiar surroundings would be a welcome relief from the Helmsley Palace, which doubled as an office for constant after-hours meetings.

"It's important that you stand back. The rest will do you good," Mary said.

Mary was tired of New York. She never really considered it home. At the condo in Orchard Lake, Mary felt the urge to cook and clean and decorate. In New York, there was nothing but business.

Bill decided to go after hearing the developments in the stock market. Mike Rowny had delivered the latest tallies.

"How's it look?" Agee asked. He knew it looked good.

"Marietta didn't open until eleven-thirty A.M. because of an imbalance of orders, and right now, they are up over nine dollars per share, to around forty-seven dollars per share. We couldn't ask for much more. Almost two and a half million shares changed hands! And the market is treating us well: Bendix is down more than three dollars on weak volume."

With the Bendix stock price falling, it was obvious that investors did not believe that Martin Marietta would press ahead and pay seventy-five dollars per share in five days. Agee thanked Rowny for the good news. The Wall Street professionals were crowning the Bendix victory.

For the first time in weeks, Bill Agee could relax.

Agee had a favorite phrase he picked up from McDonald. Agee talked about "the end game." Like a master player of chess, the takeover strategist had to see beyond the day's events to the upcoming challenges.

Every morning when Agee awoke in the hotel, he would ask himself, "What would happen if? . . . Where should I be this time tomorrow? . . . How can I close the deal?"

Both Bill and Mary thought that "the end game" was going to be the greatest moment of Bill's career.

At 3:12 P.M. on Friday, Tom Pownall sent Bill Agee another message—this time in the form of a story on the Dow Jones wire.

MARTIN MARIETTA SAYS AMENDMENT
CONDITION STILL STANDS
Bethesda, MD—Martin Marietta Corp. said the only remaining condition under which it won't be obligated to buy tendered Bendix Corporation shares is if Bendix holders adopt either the two charter amendments to be voted on at a special meeting of the Bendix holders at 10:00 A.M. on Tuesday, September 21.

Three times on Saturday, a van from the Bendix headquarters mailroom went to the Southfield post office to pick up the sacks and trays of mail addressed to P.O. Box 5060.

For the past week, the proxy solicitation teams from Bendix, Martin Marietta, and United Technologies—supported by a blitz of advertisements in *The Wall Street Journal, The New York Times,* and regional papers around the country—fought hard for the votes of the 29,197 Bendix stockholders.

That meant a mountain of work for Claudette Berard, the manager of the stock transfer department in Southfield, and the men from Corporation Trust—the vote tabulators.

The personnel department had assembled a team of eighteen secretaries at Claudette Berard's request. Some managers had grumbled over losing their secretaries. After all, they said, we still have to run the business. But staying on top of the proxy fight took precedence.

Claudette, a dark-haired, petite woman, had established a system.

First, the boxes or mail sacks were opened with the envelopes stacked and sent through a mechanical slitter. One worker handed the opened envelope and its contents to another woman across the table, who would stamp a number onto both the letter and envelope. Another women would stack them up. The men from Corporation Trust checked each proxy to be sure it had been properly executed and signed. The proxies were stacked and delivered down the hall in EO West to data processing, where three women sat at terminals all day long to keypunch in the voting results.

While the computer department was generating reports for Hal Barron, who reported to Bill Agee, the white proxy cards were stacked again and taken under guard to a series of rooms known to Berard as "Alpha Control," where the women alphabetized the cards. It was mind-numbing work. Everyone got so sick of the word "alphabetize" that Berard eventually just said "Okay, the other room" when it was time to go to Alpha Control.

"I heard Bob yelled at you today," Berard said to one of her workers, referring to the secretary's boss.

"Yeah, I guess everybody's on edge. I think I took it out on my husband last night," the woman said.

Berard thought she was lucky not to have a husband under conditions like these. When she got home after working an eighteen-hour day, she had nothing left to give.

Throughout the weekend, Tom Pownall, Larry Adams, Charlie Leithauser, and practically anybody else they could buttonhole were on the telephones, calling the key Bendix stockholders, looking for "no" votes against the two proposed "shark repellent" amendments.

Karen Barry, a young Marietta attorney, had organized the calling from Martin Marietta headquarters. Barry knew that 164 people each owned more than ten thousand shares of Bendix stock. The Marietta executives would concentrate on sending a message to these influential stockholders.

Tom Pownall was in his office on Sunday, looking out his window at the greenery of Montgomery County, Maryland, and calling a woman in Florida.

"Mr. Pownall, I am a widow. My husband bought this Bendix stock over the years. With this crazy mess going on, I have a stack of paper on my kitchen floor that is just death-defying. I don't know how I'm going to get it out of the house. What would you suggest I do about the situation?"

"I see you have forty thousand shares," Pownall said, knowing that the Martin Marietta offer was worth a $1 million profit to the woman. "Have you voted in the Bendix special stockholders' meeting?"

"I haven't."

"Well, if these amendments pass, then there is no way you will be able to enjoy that premium afforded by our tender offer to buy the Bendix Corporation."

Frank Menaker, Marietta general counsel, was hoping to take the pressure off by scoring a victory in court. He was awaiting word from Delaware. On Friday, September 3, Martin Marietta had filed a lawsuit challenging the validity of the amendments. Marietta counsel Frank Balotti, from the firm of Richards, Layton & Finger, had asked the court of Chancellor Grover C. Brown in Delaware to grant a temporary restraining order against the holding of the Bendix special stockholders' meeting scheduled for Tuesday, September 21.

During the morning on Sunday, Menaker, looking dejected, wandered into Pownall's office. Tom was just hanging up from a phone call, preparing to make another.

"I just heard from Delaware," Menaker said, "Chancellor Brown issued an interlocutory order denying our application for an injunction. The Bendix special meeting is still on."

"What's next?" Pownall asked without looking up from his list of phone numbers.

"We're going to appeal to the Delaware Supreme Court," Menaker said.

In the Sunday editions of *The New York Times,* the *Los Angeles Times,* the *Chicago Tribune,* the *Detroit Free Press,* and other metropolitan newspapers, Bendix announced in full-page ads that Monday, September 20, would be "Bendix Unity Day"—an event to be celebrated by worker rallies at dozens of locations across the United States and Canada.

After a leisurely morning of reading the newspapers and packing up clothes at their condo in Michigan, Bill and Mary were ready to tackle New York again. Mary was working on several interesting projects at Seagram's. Bill was preparing himself for the important meetings planned for Monday. He would meet with Tom Pownall in the morning, Ed Hennessy around noon, and then there was a Bendix board meeting in the afternoon. Over the weekend, Hennessy had called Agee to say that things looked good concerning the minority investment in Bendix by Allied.

When Agee arrived back at the Helmsley, there were messages waiting. From the suite on the forty-fifth floor, Bill called Ed Hennessy.

There was a lot of background noise. Hennessy explained that he was at his home in New Vernon and had several hundred people there as a benefit for a local hospital.

"Thanks for calling me, Bill," Hennessy said. "My lawyers tell me that we may have a problem."

"What kind of problem?"

"It's this antitrust situation with some of our businesses. I'm not sure that there is a problem, but you know the lawyers, and they are telling me that your guys are not coming up with the right answers to make this problem go away."

Agee thought the real problem was getting the Allied team up to speed, or perhaps Hennessy was trying to establish a negotiating ploy. Bill was firm and clear in his comments—wanting to stay on a heads-up, friendly basis with Hennessy.

"I'll talk to Fleischer," Agee said. "Let the lawyers thrash this out."

Ed Hennessy's lawyer was Morris Kramer, a young, determined man with piercing eyes and swept-back black hair showing gray. He was from the firm of Skadden, Arps, Slate, Meagher & Flom. Kramer had a small mole between his eyebrows and a reputation for skill and toughness. Along with his senior partner, Joe Flom, a "who's who" securities lawyer, Kramer had worked opposite Hennessy in the acquisition of Bunker Ramo by Allied in 1981.

The offices of Skadden, Arps were between Fifty-fifth and Fifty-sixth streets on Third Avenue. After hours of delays, Art Fleischer and Bruce Wasserstein arrived at the Skadden, Arps offices on the thirty-fifth floor at 9:00 P.M. Sunday. Morris Kramer was waiting with Ed Hennessy's investment banker, Eric Gleacher, from Lehman Brothers—one of the leading M&A firms.

Gleacher was a well-tailored, bright, streetwise man, with an office a stone's throw from the East River. He had an apartment on Fifth and Ninety-fifth; a house out on Wainscott, a little community in the East Hamptons; two big black dogs; and his wife, Annie, and their three kids.

Yesterday morning, on Long Island, Gleacher went to the golf course to watch his older son, John, hit some golf balls on the practice range. A chartered plane picked Gleacher up at the East Hampton airport and flew him to New Jersey. A Lehman partner, Bill Kearns, who lived in New Vernon and was a social acquaintance of Hennessy, drove Eric to the Morristown, New Jersey, headquarters of Allied for a day of meetings.

Gleacher had a sixth sense about deals.

This deal just didn't seem right.

Kramer led Gleacher, Wasserstein, and Fleischer into a conference room in the Skadden, Arps offices. The room was enormous—stretching the width of the building. Seated around a modest table, the group seemed lost in the gigantic room designed to accommodate meetings of hundreds of people.

Morris Kramer was seated opposite Art Fleischer, the merger and acquisitions expert. Kramer had a sneaking suspicion that Bill Agee, acting through Fleischer, was dragging his feet on handling the details of this investment deal. It seemed obvious to Kramer that Agee thought Allied was just one of his options.

Kramer was an emotional man, compact, almost athletic. Unlike Fleischer, who prided himself on cool detachment, Kramer seemed to enjoy getting mad. Usually his fuse was well burned before he showed his feelings, but when they came, he could be explosive. Almost from the start, it appeared that this would be a heated session.

"Arthur, look," Kramer said, "we've been working on this thing since Friday. Eric and I spent most of the weekend in Morristown in an airless conference room talking to the Allied people. Saturday night this antitrust problem with the electrical connector and spark plug businesses came up. We want to get past it. But every time one of my lawyers calls up one of your lawyers they say, 'Gee, I have to find out if we can get that information for you,' and then we still don't hear. Let me be frank with you: This is not the kind of cooperation I would expect from someone who wanted to do a deal."

"Morris, this is obviously a difficult situation. There are definite time constraints. From our examination of the documents, we don't feel there is an antitrust issue left to be resolved. What seems most pressing at this time is to resolve the terms of the stand-still agreement."

The stand-still agreement would prevent Hennessy from expanding his planned holding of Bendix stock. Agee wanted Hennessy, just in case. But he wanted Allied under control—not like a loose cannon on the deck.

Fleischer was looking for protection; Kramer wanted a deal.

"We'll get to that," Kramer said, getting heated, "but first I want to resolve these antitrust issues." He slid a sheet of paper over to Fleischer.

"C'mon Arthur, let's talk about it," Kramer said with a slight stutter.

"We are trying to get you the information."

"Do you want this deal?" Gleacher said, turning to Wasserstein.

"Hey, you and I are set," Bruce said. "It's up to the lawyers now."

"Agee is supposed to go to his board tomorrow," Kramer said, fiercely, "and my guy is supposed to go to his board tomorrow, and I can tell you that Ed Hennessy is not going to recommend a goddamn thing unless I tell him this problem no longer exists."

"We can solve it," Fleischer said, acting the gentleman.

At Bendix headquarters in Southfield on Monday, about two hundred administrative staff employees wearing "I Love Bendix" T-shirts and styrofoam boaters with the "blue banana" Bendix logo left work and gathered in the parking lot for an hour of popcorn, hot dogs, and soft drinks, and pep talks from company officials and local politicians. The participants were joined by a clutch of reporters from local and national newspapers as well as photographers and TV news crews.

"We got unity, yes we do. We got unity, how about you?" was the cheer led by Carol Warren, a personnel administrator with Bendix for twelve years. She and several other women were dressed up as cheerleaders complete with pompoms borrowed from Warren's twelve-year-old daughter. The women were photographed by a *New York Times* reporter.

Warren and the other cheerleader employees shouted the cheers as the Redford Union High School Panther marching band played the University of Michigan fight song.

At one point, as the crowd was led in a chorus of "Let's Go Blue" by Bendix vice president John Speyer, a plane towed an "I Love Bendix" banner above the parking lot. The mayor of Southfield and several city council members sang "America the Beautiful" with the crowd.

TWENTY-EIGHT

Monday was the coldest day of September in New York City. Temperatures barely broke out of the fifties. By 9:00 A.M., a drizzle of rain was falling from the overcast skies.

Bill Agee was standing without a topcoat under the entranceway of the Helmsley Palace. He was wearing a dark business suit, white shirt, and red striped tie. He was greeted by Arthur Fleischer and Bruce Wasserstein. The three men got into the 1982 navy blue Fleetwood Cadillac that Agee had waiting for him twenty-four hours a day.

"Frank, we're going to One oh-one Park Avenue," Agee said to the driver. It was a short drive—really just a matter of blocks.

The three men talked strategy.

"I think I'm going to go up alone," Agee said to his associates. "If I need you, I'll give you a call on the radiophone. I think Tom and I should meet alone."

The driver pulled the limo over to the curb and got out to open Bill Agee's door. Bill was already out before the driver got to the other side of the car.

"Stay with these guys," he said.

The meeting between Tom Pownall and Bill Agee was held in an empty corner office on the fortieth floor of the office high-rise on Park Avenue. Large windows provided a 180-

degree view of Manhattan from the East River to the Hudson. Rain was beading on the windows.

"Tom, good to see you again," Bill Agee said, extending his hand.

Agee and Pownall had met before, in Michigan. On the Sunday before the Republican National Convention began in Detroit, Bill Agee hosted a birthday party at his home for Representative Jack Kemp. Pownall was among the more than one hundred guests. Kemp had provided the list of politicians and businessmen he wanted invited to his forty-fifth birthday party. Pownall was on the list.

Both Agee and Pownall had an agenda for this meeting. Agee planned a mixture of hard numbers and "ego" solutions to present to Pownall. For his part, Tom Pownall wanted to be cautious. "Remember what happened Thursday night," Marty Siegel had told him during the prep meeting. "They said they would call—they never did. Agee may not be in control. Get whatever he offers in writing."

"Life has been tough these last few weeks," Agee said, breaking in the conversation. "I want you to know that when I started this thing, it wasn't my intention that it turn into such a mess."

"Yeah, I wish the hell we weren't in this position," Pownall said, adding, "Can you imagine what it would be like to run a company like this?"

"My original intention was to put these two companies together on a financially sound basis. I still want to do that. Tom, we own seventy percent of your company. Let's figure a way out of this."

"Bill, the last thing I want to do is to preside over a company that's financially crippled."

"Then we're agreed on that," Agee said. "I spent some time at Boise Cascade when they were in financial shape not nearly as bad. There is no way I am gonna let that happen to Bendix."

"Life is too short for this much trouble," Pownall said.

"I think we could work well together," Agee said. "I'm prepared to make you the second-highest-paid person in the combined company. Tom, you could be vice chairman."

"Bill, don't talk about me."

"Ah, well," Agee said.

"Don't talk about me. I'm not here dealing for me. I'm just here dealing for the company. To tell you the truth, I'm not interested in who's gonna run the thing after this. Bill, our guys at Martin Marietta take a lot of pride in the company. And they're the best damn bunch of guys imaginable. Once you bought our stock, there's no way for us to lay down. I'm telling you we can't deal with you on this basis. And your letter to our board was not well received."

"Tom, I'm prepared to offer you fifty-three dollars per share and that four of your directors will be appointed to the board. I would like to come to your next board meeting and talk with your directors. I am prepared to make these offers."

"How do you get yourself prepared to do that? Do you have your board's approval to do this?"

"Well, I've got a little committee I can go to. The board is meeting later today. Tom, you can't go through with your plan to buy Bendix."

"You haven't read the material," Pownall said in a friendly voice. "Our offer as it now stands insists that we do it."

"You don't have to do that," Agee said. "My lawyers tell me you don't have to do that."

"That's not the way we read it," Pownall said.

"So you think you have a legal problem?"

"Yeah," Pownall said.

"I can honestly tell you from my point of view," Agee said, "I'll do everything and anything I can to make sure that we don't commit financial suicide. We both want to put this together. My lawyers are telling me that it's not a legal problem. So unless there is something else here, maybe we ought to get that squared away. Let me get Arthur Fleischer in here. Let's get our lawyers talking to each other."

Agee stood up and went to the desk. He called down to the waiting limo. He asked Art Fleischer to come up.

Art Fleischer appeared within minutes, escorted by his counterpart, Bob Fullem, Tom Pownall's chief outside counsel.

"As you may recall," Fullem said, "when we waived our conditions just a week ago, we left two remaining conditions that would allow us not to fulfill our promise to buy the Bendix stock. The first was that Bendix not buy our stock. On Thursday, you removed that condition. The only remaining condition is if you get shareholder approval of the amendments to block our offer. Otherwise, Martin Marietta has a legally binding contract with the Bendix shareholders to buy their stock this coming Wednesday."

"If we dropped our offer," Pownall said, "my board would be open to being sued by every frustrated Bendix stockholder in the world. We told them we'd pay seventy-five dollars cash for eleven point nine million shares. I don't see how you can get around that."

"I'm sure we can resolve the problem," Fleischer said calmly.

"What do you propose?" Fullem asked.

"Indemnification," Fleischer said. "We propose to indemnify Martin Marietta and its directors against any and all lawsuits that may arise out of this. If you agree not to buy the Bendix stock, we will protect you from any liability."

"You could be talking hundreds of millions of dollars," Fullem said.

"We are aware of that," Fleischer said.

"We will be pleased to examine your idea," Pownall said. "But the board feels legally, morally, and ethically bound to this, and we have no intention of changing it unless there was demonstrated to us some other way. We'll have to think about indemnification."

"Gentlemen, we have a legal problem that needs to be solved," Agee said, looking at the lawyers. "You two are the experts. Solve it."

At Bob Fullem's suggestion, he and Fleischer left the room to discuss the indemnification issue.

"Tom, I would like to present my proposals to your board."

"Well, okay, I can't promise that the board will want to talk with you, but I'll express your interest to the board."

"When can we meet?"

"Tomorrow sometime," Pownall said.

"I'll be there. I'll be available."

"Bill, please bring a letter that I can show the board, because I don't want there to be any misunderstanding at this point about what you've said and what I've said. It has to be in writing, and it has to say that your board has authorized your proposals."

"See you tomorrow, Tom," Agee said.

After his meeting with Pownall, Agee wanted to walk to his next appointment. The rain had stopped. He was to see Ed Hennessy at Skadden, Arps. But first Agee, accompanied by Art Fleischer, walked uptown several blocks to meet Wasserstein back at First Boston. The cool air did Bill some good.

When they arrived at First Boston, Bruce Wasserstein was

nowhere to be found. Agee and Fleischer shrugged it off and proceeded to Skadden, Arps to meet with Hennessy.

Bruce Wasserstein was still sitting in the limo on Park Avenue waiting for Agee to appear from his meeting with Pownall. Bruce was checking his watch and getting agitated.

"What the hell are they doing up there?" he said aloud.

He continued to wait.

"I don't like this," Wasserstein said. Then he added, "What is this—some kind of setup?"

Frank, the driver, piped in from the front seat.

"Hey, I don't know if you know Mr. Agee, but that's not his style."

"Sure," Wasserstein said. "Look, will you get on the phone and find out where the hell he is."

Frank called Agee's secretary Marie Leonard, who informed him that Agee was already over at Skadden, Arps with Arthur Fleischer for the meeting with Mr. Hennessy. Frank drove the annoyed banker over to the meeting.

"Bill, how are you?" Ed Hennessy said. The two men shook hands.

Hennessy was accompanied by Skadden, Arps lawyer Morris Kramer, and Eric Gleacher, the banker from Lehman Brothers.

Bruce Wasserstein arrived at Skadden, Arps just in time.

Wasserstein was called on by Agee to summarize the state of negotiations between Bendix and Allied.

"The investment proposal as it stands provides that Allied will make a tender offer for up to two point six million shares of Bendix common stock at a price of eighty dollars in cash per share," Wasserstein said. "That's about ten percent of the Bendix common stock on a fully diluted basis.

"Bendix will sell to Allied in addition, two million shares of a new series of convertible preferred stock for a hundred seventy-five million dollars. I understand that there are some other points that we should discuss."

"I'd like Morris to review our concerns," Hennessy said.

"Well, it seems there are five open questions," Kramer began, reciting a series of issues that had not been resolved in his earlier discussions with Art Fleischer. They were sticky problems involving the stand-still agreement, which was planned to be a little over three years in term—and tied to Bill Agee's birthday, January 5. The stand-still agreement would hold Allied in check by not allowing them to acquire more than 27.5 percent of the total combined voting power of all Bendix securities.

Kramer took a considerable amount of time detailing the issues. It was obvious that the Allied team had adopted a "good guy, bad guy" strategy to the negotiation. Hennessy was staying above the fray, choosing to appear ready to make a deal once the advisers worked out the details. Kramer was the bulldog.

Bill Agee, instead of deferring to Wasserstein or Fleischer to respond, chose to answer Kramer's problems himself. After a lengthy dialogue by Agee, Kramer was ready to bite back.

"Bill, what you're saying to the five open questions is 'no, no, no, no, and no.' "

"You don't understand me," Agee said.

"Why don't you try me again," Kramer said.

Agee again recited how the problems were not really problems. He made some subtle refinements of his argument.

"Okay, so now you're saying, 'no, no, no, no, and three quarters no.' "

"Morris, that is not the case," Agee said.

Kramer turned to Fleischer.

"Arthur, I'm obviously having trouble understanding your client. Maybe you can explain it to me."

"Look, let Bill and I have a second," Fleischer said, standing up. He walked into the hall with Agee.

"Bill, let me work out the details with Kramer. That's not what you should be addressing. The Bendix board meeting was scheduled to begin in ten minutes. You're already late. Just press Hennessy and let me do the details."

When Fleischer and Agee returned, Bill was smiling. He appeared relaxed.

"Ed, look, my board meeting is gonna start in a couple of minutes, I really have to go. I'm sure Arthur can resolve these issues with Joe and Morris. But the point is either we have a deal or we don't have a deal. I'm gonna present it to my board in a few minutes. Are we in good shape?"

"I'll confirm right after my board meets this afternoon," Hennessy said.

Bill Agee shook Hennessy's hand and was gone.

* * *

311

The Bendix board meeting was scheduled for 3:00 P.M. in New York at the GM Building. Earlier, director Donald Rumsfeld was at his office at G. D. Searle & Co. in the Chicago suburb of Skokie. He was finishing up some business. The Bendix corporate jet was going to pick him up within the hour and fly him to New York.

Rumsfeld had joined the pharmaceutical company as president and chief executive officer after he left his position in the Ford Administration as Secretary of Defense. His office was decorated with the trappings of his years of public service. A model of America's strategic nuclear missiles stood on a bookshelf near the flag of the nation and of the Department of Defense.

A man with his hands in business and politics, Rumsfeld was known to have an ego and an ability to pick his way through tight spots. This Bendix vs. Martin Marietta situation was a sore point for Rumsfeld. It was not the kind of publicity he wanted. He could not see how he could gain.

Once on board the Bendix jet, Rumsfeld was dismayed to learn that the jet first was making a stop in Detroit before continuing on to New York. At Metropolitan Airport in Southfield, boxes were loaded onto the jet, and with minimal delay the plane was airborne again.

Rumsfeld wanted to know what was so important in those boxes that he had to be delayed. He asked one of the flight crew.

"Don't know, sir."

Rumsfeld went to the back of the plane and opened one of the cardboard boxes to examine the contents.

"Well, I'll be damned," he said, holding up a T-shirt that proclaimed Bendix Unity Day.

By the time the other directors began to arrive at the Bendix offices on the twenty-first floor of the GM Building, the T-shirts and straw bowler hats had been broken out among the staff. Michael Rowny was wearing both, looking somewhat sheepish. The secretaries were laughing, and he was playing along.

Several directors would not attend the meeting. Wilbur Cohen, the mild-mannered professor from the University of Texas, had a prior responsibility. William Tavoulareas of Mobil and lawyer-director Jewel Lafontant, a Mobil director, were out of town.

There was a scheduling conflict.

The Mobil Oil Corporation board was meeting in Anchorage, Alaska. Mobil chairman Raleigh Warner had also asked Jewel to fly to Japan to christen a new eighty-thousand-ton oil tanker, the *Mobil Reliant.*

On Monday afternoon, as the Bendix board meeting was about to begin, Lafontant was flying from Tokyo to Nagasaki, site of the christening.

The Bendix directors were all assembled in the conference room on the twenty-first floor, awaiting Agee. The meeting had been planned for 3:00 P.M.

At 3:45 P.M., Agee came into the conference room. To the staff members and directors who knew him best, the stress written on his face was obvious. Agee was giving the situation every ounce of energy he had.*

"Gentlemen," Agee said, "I would like to begin by recounting our status. As you know, at midnight on September sixteenth—last Thursday—Bendix began buying shares of the Martin Marietta Corporation. After a determination by myself and Art," Agee said, nodding to Fleischer, sitting at the long table, "I contacted the special committee and received authorization to purchase up to sixty-five percent of Marietta shares."

McDonald, Scott, Stafford, and Tavoulareas comprised the special committee.

"We purchased all of the nineteen point three million shares tendered to our offer and continued purchasing on a first-come, first-served basis at forty-eight dollars a share until we had purchased twenty-three point nine five oh million shares. When this total is combined with the five percent we owned prior to our offer, the Bendix Corporation now owns seventy percent of the Martin Marietta Corporation."

It was a moment to savor for Bill Agee. He appreciated the smiles from directors around the table. At long last, victory seemed within grasp.

"I would like to announce that I have been in negotiations with Tom Pownall and Martin Marietta. I met this morning with Pownall at his lawyers' offices. I have asked to address his board of directors tomorrow, and he has given his assent. Our goal

---

*During this period, Agee was examined by his doctor. He had lost ten pounds.

obviously is to effect a negotiated combination of the two companies."

"How did it go with Pownall?" Bill Purple, head of the Bendix aerospace operations, asked.

"He's receptive. He told me that he did not want to preside over the destruction of our two companies. I told him it was idiotic at this point to proceed with his plan to purchase our stock. There are several things I need authorization from the board to bring my discussions with him to fruit."

Agee repeated Pownall's insistence that Martin Marietta was legally committed to buying the Bendix shares and Pownall's fear of lawsuits from disgruntled Bendix shareholders if Martin Marietta dropped its offer. Agee requested authorization from the board to set up an insurance plan that would indemnify the Marietta directors and the company against the possible lawsuits.

"What would that cost?" a director asked.

"A worst-case scenario could be several hundred million dollars in damages. But I would like to point out that we feel safe in offering the indemnification. There are a variety of ways—and Art will address these if you're interested—in which we can blunt possible action against the company."

Agee turned the discussion to another issue.

"There is the matter of the remaining thirty percent of their stock not in our hands. In my negotiations, I want to be prepared to offer an exchange of stock worth in the range of fifty-three dollars per Martin Marietta share."

"How much does that add to the kitty?" a director asked.

"Only twenty to thirty million dollars more. It is a price move I anticipated earlier and am prepared to make."

After hearing from Bruce Wasserstein on the economics of the situation, the directors voted unanimously to authorize Agee to negotiate with Pownall utilizing the general terms he had presented.

Arthur Fleischer took the floor. From the early Bendix board meetings, Fleischer had grown in stature in the eyes of many of the directors. As opposed to the bustle and reputation of Wasserstein, Fleischer was low key.

"As you know, the special stockholders' meeting is scheduled for tomorrow morning at ten A.M. I would recommend that we delay that meeting," Fleischer said. "There are outstanding legal and tactical questions. I will let the chairman address our situation in the solicitation of votes for the two amendments to the charter that would effectively bar the Martin Marietta offer by their own admission.

"From a legal point of view, Marietta filed this morning in federal court in New York to block Citibank from voting any SESSOP shares at the special meeting for which it has not received instructions from the participants. That presents a problem."

"How do we stand on the vote?" Jonathan Scott asked.

"As I have been told," Agee said, "these sorts of solicitations typically begin with a surge of support for management positions from individuals and like a bell curve turn downward on the reaction of the professional investing community. I'm told it is close. We need a majority. I am not overly optimistic."

The totals Agee saw in the morning showed the tide was turning.

"But as you remember," Fleischer added, "with the chairman headed for negotiations tomorrow with Martin Marietta, the possibility of a victory in the vote is a potent weapon against their threatened purchase of our stock. From that point of view, postponing the meeting by twenty-four hours could keep the Martin Marietta team guessing."

"Are we continuing to solicit votes?" a director asked.

"Right up to the meeting," Agee said, smiling.

A vote was taken, and the directors approved postponing the meeting.

Fleischer left to make a phone call. When he returned, he addressed, as he had at previous board meetings, the key legal issue: the struggle for control.

Bendix had purchased 70 percent of the stock of Martin Marietta. The next step was to call a Marietta stockholders' meeting and vote the present Marietta board of directors out of office. By doing that, Bill Agee could elect himself chairman and take command of Martin Marietta.

The problem was that under Maryland law, Agee could not convene a Marietta shareholder meeting without written notice and considerable delay. In the meantime, Martin Marietta threatened to purchase a majority interest in Bendix and—aided by a more liberal Delaware law—immediately unseat Bill Agee.

Fleischer thought he could stop the Marietta plan in court.

"I am convinced that we will get a favorable ruling out of Delaware that will block Martin Marietta's ability to vote any shares of the Bendix Corporation that they may purchase.

"It is my impression that the possibility of not being able to vote the stock may dissuade their purchase. The best they could hope for legally is to get the Maryland court to block our ability to vote the shares we have purchased. That is a stalemate with consequences I'm sure they are aware of. Both companies will suffer while the courts addressed the problem. It could take years to resolve. As rational businessmen, they will have to take another look at their plan to buy on Wednesday. Their directors will have to ask themselves, 'Why?' "

"Thank you, Art," Agee said, impressed with Fleischer's arguments.

"One more important piece of business, gentlemen," Agee began, motioning to Hal Barron, who began distributing a two-page memorandum to the directors. "In the event that my discussions with Pownall are not productive, it is essential that we extend their purchase deadline. This memo before you is a term sheet for a proposal for a limited investment in Bendix by the Allied Corporation.

"What this proposes is that Allied make a partial tender offer for Bendix before midnight on Wednesday. That would effectively put off Martin Marietta's ability to take down our stock for ten more days—extending their withdrawal date to early November. By then we would be able to assume control and remove the Marietta board of directors."

Agee then reviewed the financial terms of the Allied package.

"I think some of you know Ed Hennessy, the chairman and CEO of Allied. Nice guy," Agee said.

"Do we need Allied?" Donald Rumsfeld asked. The situation seemed to be getting more and more convoluted.

"Rummy," Agee said, "we can't allow ourselves to be put into a situation on Wednesday at midnight where we have nothing to prevent Pownall from buying our shares. With no charter amendments and no Allied, it would be suicide."

Agee wanted to cover all the bases.

"I would also note that under the proposal," Agee added casually, "Hennessy and one of his people will join the Bendix board, and I will join the Allied board."

There was no mention of whether two of the directors would

have to resign their positions on the Bendix board to make room for Hennessy and his associate. A bylaw stipulated that the corporation would be run by fourteen directors.

"How optimistic are you of getting peace with Pownall?" Hugo Uyterhoeven asked.

"I am hopeful that they are reasonable men."

"If you are optimistic, then why go with the Allied deal and sell out twenty-seven point five percent of your stock?" inside director Paul F. Hartz asked. Trained as an accountant, Hartz could quickly penetrate the figures. The two men had a good working relationship. Agee respected the older man's experience.

"Peace is a high-risk deal, Paul," Agee said. "I hope it will come. I want it to come. I think Pownall wants it. But going out on a limb waiting for peace while they're preparing to take down our stock—that's a risk I am not prepared to take. The possible results if Pownall was that stubborn would be catastrophic. To stave off that possibility, I am willing to go with a minority-stock investor."

Bruce Wasserstein distributed to the board copies of Allied's 1981 10K and 10Q forms for the quarter ending June 30, 1982. Wasserstein reviewed each line of Allied's businesses.

"I have received other offers from companies and individual investors interested in a minority investment in Bendix," Agee said, careful not to mention names. "However, these offers are less attractive. In most cases, these outfits are trying to pick up some of our assets cheap."

When the board was asked to vote, the Allied proposal passed unanimously.

As the directors were sliding back their chairs, Agee remembered one small item on the day's agenda.

"The regularly scheduled board meeting for Thursday is canceled."

That board meeting, planned a year in advance, was a standard review of operations. As the directors departed, a director whispered to Paul Hartz, "He's so wrapped up in this, I wonder who's minding the shop?"

TWENTY-NINE

One of the members of Allied Corporation's board of directors was William R. Haselton, chairman and CEO of the St. Regis Paper Company. Hennessy called him and asked to use St. Regis's boardroom for an Allied meeting to discuss a possible business move. Haselton was pleased to oblige.

St. Regis Paper was located on East Thirty-seventh Street in Manhattan, just blocks from the United Nations headquarters on the East River. After the meeting with Agee, Hennessy went over to St. Regis, leaving Morris Kramer of Skadden, Arps to get together his papers and thrash it out for a while longer with Art Fleischer.

Before the Allied board meeting began, Bruce Wasserstein was on the telephone with Hennessy and his bankers, suggesting some changes in the agreement. There was a lot of give and take. Fleischer was also on the phone.

The Allied board meeting had already started by the time that Morris Kramer and senior partner Joe Flom arrived. As they were passing through the St. Regis reception area, Kramer heard the receptionist say "There's a call for Mr. Hennessy."

"Who's calling?" Kramer asked.

"A Mr. Agee," the receptionist said.

"Wait a second."

Kramer eased his way into the boardroom and discreetly notified Hennessy that Agee was on the phone. Hennessy excused himself from the beginning of a slide presentation being handled by Hal Buirkle, the senior VP of finance and planning for Allied.

"Bill, what can I do for you?"

"How is your meeting?"

"Well, we're just really getting started."

"I just wanted you to know that the Bendix board has approved."

"That's fine," Hennessy said.

"I was also thinking that in addition to the seat Bendix will have on the Allied board, we would want the right to buy up as many shares of Allied as you have of Bendix."

"That's not in our understanding," Hennessy said.

"Perhaps not totally as much, maybe only five percent," Agee said.

"We could discuss that," Hennessy said. He thought the deal was getting crazier and crazier. Listening to Agee, Hennessy did not know who was buying whom. "I've got to get back to my meeting," he said.

"Good luck. I look forward to working with you," Agee said.

Ed Hennessy was now losing enthusiasm for the whole concept of the minority investment in Bendix. But he wanted to be a player.

"I know you've seen this situation in the newspapers," Hennessy said to his assembled board members. "It's been spread all over the goddamn world. Here's what's happened that may offer Allied an opportunity to get involved."

The St. Regis boardroom had a large, oval-shaped table. Several members of the board were connected to the proceedings by telephone via a microphone system placed in the middle of the table. By speaking toward the center of the table, all the directors could hear and be heard. Roger Morley was in France. J. P. Cobb, president of California State University in Fullerton, was in California. Another director was in Ireland.

Hennessy had his financial staff present the numbers of the proposed minority investment in Bendix. Eric Gleacher, the banker, talked about the values. Kramer gave his appraisal of the antitrust situation. Flom gave a general strategic wrap-up.

On the way, the proposal ran into opposition from the board.

"Why should we tie up four hundred million dollars of our cash to help Bill Agee make an acquisition?" a director asked.

Paul Thayer, chairman of LTV Corporation, and an Allied board member, felt particularly close to the situation. He had earlier been negotiating with Tom Pownall about making a minority investment by LTV in Martin Marietta. That would have done for Tom what Bill Agee was now looking for from Ed Hennessy.

"Ed, this minority thing is tricky," Thayer said. "We don't know how Pownall and Martin Marietta are going to fare in their tender offer for Bendix. What happens if we have a minority stake in something they end up owning?"

The meeting went back and forth. The slide presentations were confusing. The presenter had to say continually, "Well, of course, that number is not right. It's been changed since then."

The minority-investment proposal was not put to a vote. It was simply decided by consensus that it didn't make sense for Allied to get involved with Bendix as a minority stockholder.

As the meeting was adjourned and the long-distance participants signed off, Ed Hennessy said to the departing directors, "I might get back to you in a couple of days. I'm gonna work on this, and if push comes to shove, maybe Agee will sell us the whole company."

"That'd be fine," several directors noted.

Bob Cole at *The New York Times* was an irascible man who had his finger in almost every big financial story. Cole prided himself on never being beat to a story (which was usually true) and on getting the story first (which was sometimes true). In the press coverage of this deal, Cole would be there first a couple of times.

Cole joined the *Times* in 1962 as a deskman in the financial news department. He wanted to be a reporter, not a copy editor. He soon found a way, and for almost twenty years, nearly two hundred days a year, the red-faced Irishman has written financial news for the *Times*. He was well known. Liked by some. Not liked by some.

Bob Cole was not the kind of reporter inveigled by press releases. As a rule, he did not like talking with PR men. To Cole, PR types in general were "NFG"—no fucking good. He did not like being sold a story. He dug for the story.

One of the people Bob Cole did not get along with was Dick Cheney of Hill & Knowlton, Bendix's outside PR firm. Cole and

Cheney had a long history. Cheney, normally a jovial, expansive guy prone to bow ties, turned serious thinking about Cole.

"Cole is a son-of-a-bitch," Cheney has said to friends.

"Cheney is NFG—he doesn't understand the *Times*. He hypes stories like they are billion-dollar deals when they deserve two lines buried in the financial section," Bob Cole has said to his friends.

One day, Cole read Cheney the riot act.

They hadn't spoken since.

On his desk on the third floor of the *Times'* offices at 229 West 43rd Street, Cole had drawers of dog-eared index cards with contact names. Over the years, he had built a large file of people he talked to daily. They knew his home phone number in Leonia, New Jersey, over the George Washington Bridge, and he knew their after-hours numbers. He knew the names of their kids, and the gossip about who is doing what to whom. But Cole was a man who protects his sources. When he talked on the telephone, he took notes on a yellow legal pad. He wrote in the margin whether or not a comment was for attribution.

On Monday, as usual, when Cole got into the office, he checked the Reuters stock market monitor for a list of all the stocks on the NYSE and the AMEX that had not opened for the day or had been halted, pending news. He also checked the Dow Jones newswire looking for "call indications"—indications that the stock was expected to go up or down.

Martin Marietta stock did not open on Monday, September 20, until 12:08 P.M. because of an imbalance of orders.

Bob Cole got on the phone. He had some angles he wanted to check out in the Bendix vs. Martin Marietta story. He'd been working on it since the beginning, turning out stories. He talked to Bob Meyers at Bendix and Bill Harwood at Martin Marietta and the bankers, the lawyers, the analysts, and the arbitrageurs. Today he was going to focus on the court developments. Bendix was seeking to block Martin Marietta in federal district court in Baltimore. And there were the developments in federal court in New York. And in Delaware.

Sometimes Cole called up his contacts and simply said, "Hey, let's talk." During the early evening, just before deadline, one of his sources said something new.

"Allied Corporation," the man said.

"What about them?" Cole asked.

"It was going to be a minority thing," the source said, "at

least ten percent, maybe up to almost thirty percent so that Agee would get an extension and stop Pownall from buying."

"Allied is going to buy into Bendix?" Cole asked.

"*Was* going to," the source said.

"Will you stop being so goddamn mysterious," Cole said. "What the fuck are you talking about?"

"Bendix was pitching a limited investment in the company to Allied. Agee wanted to put a stopper against Pownall."

"But it's not going to happen?"

"Don't think so. Ed Hennessy did not want to stop at thirty percent."

The headline on Tuesday's story was: BENDIX SEEKS TO BLOCK MARIETTA BID. The story was mostly about court developments.

But in the fourth paragraph, Cole wrote: "Other sources said they had heard that the Allied Corporation, a chemical company with big oil interests, might be coming to Bendix's rescue. Still other sources close to the situation said, without identifying any new bidder, that 'there's nothing imminent yet.' "

Cole had decided after checking around and not being able to confirm the Allied story told by one of his sources, that he would put it out there—the source was usually reliable —but that he wouldn't make it the lead. He wasn't sure yet what was going on.

"Ed Hennessy did not want to stop at thirty percent," the source had said.

Normally a Scrooge when it came to a story, Bob Cole let a golden insight slip through his fingers.

Jim Simpson, the silver-haired president of Martin Marietta's chemicals company and former general counsel of the corporation, took a commercial flight on Monday to Detroit and a cab to the Michigan Inn in Southfield, near the Bendix headquarters. Simpson met Bernie Kury and Bob Mannis, two lawyers from Dewey, Ballantine, for dinner. The three men were joined by four representatives from Martin Marietta's solicitor, Morrow & Company.

While the men discussed the upcoming Bendix special stockholders' meeting, across the dining room a large group of men and one woman were enjoying themselves over drinks.

"Bendix retainers," Simpson said, gesturing with his head to the group. "The hotel is full of them."

While they were at dinner, one of the Dewey, Ballantine lawyers went to the telephone to check with his office. Word came back. Bendix attorneys in New York federal court had advised Judge Edelstein at a late-afternoon session that the meeting would be delayed so they could argue against a Martin Marietta motion that Citibank not be allowed to vote the SES-SOP shares at the special meeting without instructions from the plan participants.

"Bendix put out a press release this afternoon saying that they are going to adjourn the meeting until Wednesday at ten A.M., Kury said.

"Now what do we do?"

"We'll go to the meeting tomorrow morning and watch them adjourn it," Simpson said.

After his board meeting, Bill Agee stayed at the GM Building, waiting to hear from Ed Hennessy. At 6:00 P.M., having heard nothing, he went over to the Palace. Mary was home from work at Seagram's. They had a drink together and waited to hear from Hennessy. Art Fleischer came by. Agee was sure there was a problem.

"Hennessy didn't even have the courtesy to call me," Bill told Mary.

Eric Gleacher, Hennessy's investment banker, was the one who passed along word of Allied's rejection of the minority investment. Bruce Wasserstein was the first one to know.

"It's a no-go," Gleacher told Wasserstein. "The directors just didn't like it."

"I understand," Wasserstein said, never rattled.

"Bruce, I told you Friday, Sunday, and today, Hennessy would like to buy the whole company."

"That's not where we're at."

"I'm sorry it's developed this way. I wish we could have helped you out, but it's so wide open with you and Martin Marietta, they just wouldn't go for it."

"Thanks, Eric. Maybe I'll get back to you, but no promises. There's a lot going on right now."

"Are you talking with Siegel?" Gleacher asked.

"I'm talking to everybody," Wasserstein said with deliberate vagueness. After hanging up, he called Agee.

"I can't believe it. They turned the deal down?" Agee said.

"They turned it down," Wasserstein said.

"No reasonable man could have said that deal would fail," Fleischer told Bill after he hung up the receiver. Fleischer had worked long hours to resolve the outstanding differences between Allied and Bendix.

Bill was angry. In his mind, Ed Hennessy had promised that he could "deliver" the Allied board on the minority investment.

Agee waited five hours to hear from Hennessy.

Finally, Agee called Hennessy at his home in Morristown, New Jersey. It was shortly after 10:00 P.M.

"It just wouldn't fly, Bill," Hennessy said.

There was a lot Agee could have said but he held back.

There was a more pressing concern. Having wasted several days on the assumption that the Allied minority investment in Bendix was a "done deal," Agee was now left without an extender to prevent Pownall from buying the company in forty-eight hours.

"Let's get a meeting set up with Donald Trump again," Agee said to his advisers.

Donald Trump, a young, dashing New York real-estate tycoon, was the centerpiece of another of Bill Agee's backup plans. Trump had a large holding of RCA stock. So did Bendix. Maybe a deal could be arranged. If Hennessy would not stop Pownall, maybe Trump would.

On Monday night at about midnight, Arthur Fleischer called a Fried, Frank partner, Stephen Fraidin, at his home in Chappaqua, in Westchester County. At forty-three, Fraidin had had a lot of experience in takeover cases. Art respected Fraidin, a tall, good-looking lawyer with brown, curly hair; his coolness under fire had proven valuable before. Except for the briefest of discussions, Fraidin had not worked on the Bendix case at all.

"Steve, sorry to call you so late," Fleischer said.

"No problem," Fraidin said.

"I need your help on the Bendix case. What I'd like you to do is meet with us at Bill Agee's suite at the Helmsley Palace tomorrow."

"What's up?"

"I can't really go into much detail now, but basically, Steve, we're considering making peace by offering to indemnify the Martin Marietta directors if they back off their tender offer for

Bendix shares. I want somebody at the negotiations who doesn't already have any adversary relationship with the guys on the other side. See you at eight A.M. at the Palace."

Steve Fraidin had met Bill Agee before. Fraidin had spent several frantic days working on a possible Bendix bid to buy the Lockheed Corporation; he had met intensively with Agee and Hal Barron and Art Fleischer. During those planning discussions, Fraidin, after listening to Agee's thinking, took Art aside.

"Somebody ought to take Agee and talk to him without an audience," Fraidin said, referring to the other players in the room. "I don't think he's been in a contested takeover situation before. Somebody should discuss with him his personal situation and how that could become a factor."

Everybody on Wall Street knew the stories of Bill and Mary Cunningham, and there seemed to be a whole earth catalog of ways to use that information against Agee.

"Go ahead and do it, Steve," Fleischer told him.

Fraidin did. It was obvious that Agee refused to be held hostage by the publicity that accompanied his relationship with Mary Cunningham.

"I've got nothing to hide," Agee said.

"I want your good mind today," Bill said to Mary in the dawning hours of Tuesday morning.

"You want me to come?" Mary asked. She was surprised by the invitation.

"I want an observer I can trust," Bill said.

From the beginning, Mary was the person who gave late-night summation to meetings and events of the day. She was perceptive about people. While allowing the experts to advise Bill on the subtleties of legal and financial events, Mary combined her acute analytical skills with a probing look at the personalities and chemistry involved. She thought all along that if Bill and Tom Pownall could only escape the grips of their advisers, a deal could be reached.

The morning meeting concerned the indemnification issue. Agee had requested that Bob Lee, the Bendix corporate director for insurance, join the discussion. There was also a representative from the underwriters. The consensus was that Bendix could write a program to handle the problem.

"This is gonna work," Agee said.

He was clearly optimistic. Agee was prepared to offer to Tom Pownall a price higher than Martin Marietta stock had ever been, plus indemnity against lawsuits. And when Agee looked at Pownall's only other option—buying the Bendix stock and bankrupting the combined company—it all seemed to make sense.

But Agee also wanted protection in case it failed.

He instructed McDonald to meet with Donald Trump on the partial-investment strategy. And Agee had a private conversation with Bruce Wasserstein.

"Gleacher says Hennessy wants to buy the whole company," Wasserstein said.

This was the first Agee had heard of the plan. Suddenly the resistance of the Allied board to the minority deal was making sense.

Agee nodded. "Let's have them ready just in case."

Wasserstein called Eric Gleacher.

"I don't know what's going to happen," Wasserstein said, "but you should go ahead and work up the papers for a one hundred percent transaction."

If worse came to worst, Bill Agee wanted to know that Ed Hennessy and the Allied Corporation were within reach—if he decided that was the only way to salvage an honorable deal.

"Okay, we gotta go," Agee said to the group.

Bill, Mary, Art Fleischer, Steve Fraidin, Bruce Wasserstein, and his associate Tony Grassi all collected their papers and boarded the gilded and red plush elevator and headed for the lobby. The limo was waiting at the curb.

At first look, it was obvious that everyone was not going to fit into the limousine. And the small Bendix jet waiting at the airport was only a five-seater. Those logistics became sidewalk conversation.

At Agee's signal, Mary ducked her strawberry-blond head into the limo.

"I think all we need here," Agee said, "is Art, Mary, Bruce, and myself."

"Steve's coming," Art said. This was the first moment that Fleischer realized Mary was going to Bethesda. That occurred to the others, too. There was an awkward moment of silence. Agee did not ask for opinions. None was forthcoming.

"I'd like Tony to come," Wasserstein said. Grassi had been in on the deal since the beginning.

"Fraidin's gonna come," Fleischer repeated, hanging on to

his strategy of having a fresh face on the Bendix team—somebody who wasn't already high on the Martin Marietta enemy list.

Fraidin climbed into the limo after Agee nodded. Grassi was left at the curb.

After a poor night's sleep at the Michigan Inn, Jim Simpson and the Martin Marietta advisers and solicitors arrived at Bendix headquarters at minutes before 10:00 A.M. on Monday. A printed sign was outside near the parking lot directing the way to the special meeting in the room known as "the disco" on the second floor of the Bendix headquarters building.

More than a dozen Bendix employees were seated at a long table handling credentials. Simpson and his team were greeted, their names checked off a list. They were issued red badges—Bendix reps were wearing blue, stockholders had white, and United Technologies people had gray.

To enter the meeting area, Simpson had a briefcase inspected, and he passed through an airport-type metal detector. Past that was a row of Bendix security guards dressed in uniforms with white scarfs at their necks.

Beyond that were coffee and donuts.

At 10:00 A.M. precisely, Donald G. Speyer, a Bendix vice president, took to the podium. He read the company press release and adjourned the meeting until the following day.

Jim Simpson had retained a local lawyer, George Martin, and the team returned to Martin's offices to talk over the next move. Bernie Kury from Dewey Ballantine was there with Bob Mannis.

"I think the reason for adjourning the meeting is a crock," Currier said. "It seems to me that if Bendix had the votes, they'd hold the meeting."

"Yeah," Kury agreed.

"What do you think is the count? What have they got?" Simpson asked the solicitors.

"It could go either way. They need a simple majority. Our best guess is that they've got something like forty-eight percent. They may figure that another day will put them over the top," a man from Morrow & Company said.

"What are we gonna do tomorrow if they try to adjourn?" Simpson asked. "Can they adjourn the meeting knowing they're gonna lose?"

"That's the only reason they would adjourn."

"Bernie," Simpson said to the Dewey, Ballantine lawyer, "can you check this out? Can you find out if there's some way we can stop them from adjourning?"

"I'll call New York," Kury said.

At 11:00 A.M., Marty Siegel, Doug Brown, Bob Fullem, Leonard Larrabee, and Dick Katcher were assembled in the Butler Aviation hangar near LaGuardia Airport, preparing to board the Martin Marietta Gulfstream jet on the tarmac. It was a forty-five minute flight to National Airport in Washington, where they would be met by cars and brought to Martin Marietta's headquarters in Bethesda.

Larrabee was walking through the terminal when he saw Arthur Fleischer on the telephone. Seasoned pros, neither man was really surprised. They waved. The Bendix jet sat on the apron barely a hundred yards from the Martin Marietta jet. Larrabee watched Bruce Wasserstein board. He recognized Bruce's portly profile.

"You just missed Bill and Mary," Bob Fullem said to Larrabee as the two men were taking their seats and buckling up.

"Oh, geez," Larrabee said. Now he was surprised. "Agee brought Mary?"

"I'm sure the guys in Bethesda will get a kick outta this," Katcher said.

"I wonder if they're bringing reporters?" someone asked.

All the men laughed. It seemed the pinnacle of innocence or idiocy for Bill Agee to bring Mary Cunningham along on such sensitive negotiations with the opposition.

"It does make you wonder who's calling the shots," Larrabee said to the team of advisers. The Martin Marietta jet taxied out to the runway, followed by the blue-and-white Bendix corporate jet. The whole situation struck Len Larrabee as bizarre.

On the Bendix jet, Bill Agee was in full form, commanding, optimistic that his plan for the merger of the two companies made perfect sense in light of the alternatives. He looked forward to addressing the Martin Marietta board of directors. He knew they were distinguished men. He was sure that they would be attentive and that his presentation would prevail.

"Okay, let's get down to it and put this letter together," Bill said to the small group of advisers. Agee was relaxed, not wearing a jacket. He ran his tie between his fingers and gestured with his hands.

Mary, with a yellow legal pad and a pen, sat next to Bill.

"I want it to be simple and direct," Bill said, already having a rough draft idea of what he wanted to say. "Dear Tom, the time has come for us to put any disagreements behind us. The original proposal for the merger between our two companies was intended to create a combined entity that would be financially stronger and more capable of servicing our national defense needs."

The letter made a restrained but impassioned plea.

"I believe that our proposal presents the most prudent course for your board. The benefits of a combination are obvious. The dangers of proceeding with the purchases of Bendix stock are, in our view, dramatic."

Agee listed five dangers, all ominous for both Bendix and Martin Marietta. From the airplane's telephone, Agee placed a call to the Bendix aerospace headquarters in Arlington, Virginia. He dictated the letter to a secretary, who was instructed to bring her typewriter and meet Agee and his advisers at the Marriott Hotel in Bethesda.

"So what do you think?" Agee asked his companions on the plane. "Is this going to work? What do you think, Art?"

"Well, Bill, I am not certain I can properly evaluate it. From a big-picture point of view, your approach makes a lot of sense," Fleischer said. "But they could challenge the enforceability of the indemnification plan."

"What do you think are the chances it will work?" Agee asked Fraidin.

"It is certainly a reasonable position for us to take. If I were representing Martin Marietta, I would tell the board that while it isn't a hundred percent certain that the indemnification would be enforceable, the board could find comfort in the odds of its enforceability. We can make it stick in court," Fraidin said.

"I think it's gonna work," Agee said.

At National, Agee and the others got into the Bendix limo.

"Jamie!" Bill said, recognizing the driver.

About a mile north of the Naval Medical Center, near the Beltway, was the sixteen-story Marriott Hotel on Pooks Hill Road in Bethesda. A corner suite on the second floor was already registered in Arthur Fleischer's name.

After the letter to the Martin Marietta board was retyped by the Bendix secretary and handed to a lawyer from Martin Marietta, Bill settled in to wait for the phone call asking him to address the board. Mary's presence was comforting.

Bill sipped on a soft drink and ate a sandwich to pass the time. "What's taking them so long?" he asked, checking his watch. "They've had three quarters of an hour to read the letter."

THIRTY

The directors of Martin Marietta were gathered in the boardroom on the second floor of the executive wing of the building. The curtains were drawn along one wall. The long table of polished dark wood reflected the recessed overhead lights.

Tom Pownall had already recited his conversation with Bill Agee from the day before, when the letter arrived. Marty Siegel had discussed the financial terms with Bruce Wasserstein earlier and reviewed them with the board. Siegel also highlighted the change in the situation as a result of Agee buying not just fifty-one percent of Martin Marietta but pushing Bendix's ownership to seventy percent. It just made the balance sheet look all that much worse. Horrible, in fact. But Siegel said and Charlie Leithauser concurred that the situation could be dealt with.

Siegel was fresh, his clothes unwrinkled, his dark hair perfectly arranged, his smile intact. Before the Marietta directors, he was perfectly composed. There was no sign of anxiety, despite the fact that of the three tactics Siegel had recommended —first the countertender; then the deal with Harry Gray; and finally, a week ago, the waiving of all but two conditions—had failed to force Agee to withdraw. While the tension of the battle was visible in the faces of Tom Pownall and many of his directors, Siegel was aloof and self-confident.

"Agee's over there at the Marriott," Pownall said. "He's got a bunch of his advisers with him—no one from Bendix, I understand. And he wants to address the board."

"Does he really have Mary with him?" a director asked.

"Yup."

"That guy is unbelievable," Griffin Bell said, adding, "Didn't Napoleon like meeting with the committees of the enemy?" That got a guffaw from several directors. It was hard to find much levity in Martin Marietta's situation. The prospect of meeting Bill Agee with Mary Cunningham on his arm was the only diversion any of the directors could conceive. Some were downright curious to meet this woman they had heard stories about.

Pownall distributed to the board copies of Agee's letter.

"Have you requested to address the Bendix board of directors?" director Griffin Bell asked.

"No," Pownall said.

"Well, I don't see why we should see him. What's he gonna say?"

"I'll tell you what he's gonna say," a director said. "He's gonna give us this silly sophomoric pledge of allegiance to the nation like this last paragraph in his letter—as if we're the ones that started this whole fuckin' thing."

It was obvious to Tom Pownall by a quick glance around the room that few directors were in favor of Agee addressing the board.

"He also wants to have his outside lawyer—Arthur Fleischer —address the board on the legal questions," Pownall said.

"We do not need his legal counsel to inform us of our responsibilities. We have our own counsel," Griffin Bell said indignantly.

"Well, just to cut to the heart of it," Pownall said, referring to Agee's letter, "the key provision seems to me to be this Number six on page five, which reads 'No shares of Bendix stock would be purchased under the Martin Marietta offer without Bendix' consent. . . .' To protect the directors and the corporation from an avalanche of lawsuits, he offers this indemnification plan on page three."

"Yeah, what it comes down to is Agee wants us to renege on our commitment to pay the Bendix shareholders seventy-five dollars a share," Gene Zuckert said.

"Tom, this is an ethical issue," Frank Bradley said. "We promised. We made a contract with these people. I don't see how we can put that aside."

The directors who had the most financial experience—Jack Byrne, James Lee Everett, and Frank Ewing—were struggling with the financial implications if Martin Marietta did proceed with its plan. Byrne had experienced the nightmare of bankruptcy at Geico. He never wanted to repeat that again. Ewing, a self-made millionaire, was the kind of man who did not spend money easily; the thought of spending $900 million for "ethical" reasons seemed to him almost obscene.

"Do we have any alternatives to get out of this?" Ewing asked.

"Yeah. Before we reject Agee out of hand," Byrne said, "can we work out a merger, or can we do something here that doesn't throw both balance sheets into such an awful disaster?"

Finally the phone rang. Agee picked it up before the second ring.

"Mr. Agee? This is Roy Calvin over at Martin Marietta. Tom Pownall wanted me to call you to say there has been some delay. The board of directors is meeting now."

"When will I address the board?"

"My instructions were to simply inform you that there has been a delay. I will get back to you."

Bill Agee and his advisers sat around the orange and yellow room at the Marriott and debated what was going on over at Martin Marietta headquarters. Agee was rehearsing his presentation to the board. Art Fleischer was on the telephone. When he got off, he had good news.

"I just heard from Marc Cherno, reporting the events in Delaware," Fleischer said. "The Delaware Supreme Court has issued its ruling. Martin Marietta's appeal to stop our stockholders' meeting has been denied."

"Excellent," Agee said. Steve Fraidin was anxious to hear the language of the ruling.

"And it goes beyond that. The court said that 'in seeking relief, Martin Marietta is in effect asking the Court of Chancery to assist it in a violation of its moral duty to its majority stockholder, Bendix,' " Fleischer read from his scratch notes.

"Outstanding," Agee said. "What was that—'moral duty'?"

"The Delaware Supreme Court says Martin Marietta has a moral duty to its majority stockholder," Fleischer said, quoting the opinion. "And listen to this: 'If the Marietta board trys to effectuate control of the Bendix board of directors, it will do so in violation of a moral duty to Bendix.' "

"That's it!" Agee said. "What can they do?"

"We should call over there and make sure the lawyers know about this," Fraidin said, referring to the Dewey, Ballantine team at Martin Marietta.

The implications of the ruling were a real boost to Agee and his team. They had discussed on the plane the problem that certain of the Martin Marietta directors felt a moral responsibility to buy the Bendix shares. Well, now the court ruling gave Bendix the "moral" edge.

"Yeah. Art, call over there," Agee said.

Fleischer dialed Martin Marietta and after waiting several minutes for the person who answered to direct the call properly, Fleischer spoke with Leonard Larrabee, the second-in-command Dewey, Ballantine lawyer.

"Leonard, have you heard the Delaware Supreme Court decision?"

"I have," Larrabee said.

"I wanted to bring to your attention that aspect which referred to the moral duty owed by the Martin Marietta directors to the wishes of their majority shareholder."

"That's dictum," Larrabee said, dismissing the language as not necessarily germane to the outcome of the case.

When Fleischer repeated Larrabee's response to Fraidin, the group had a chuckle. Larrabee had obviously been rattled.

"They're probably trying to assess the situation," Fraidin said.

"Let's offer them another buck," Bill Agee said. "The deal says fifty-four dollars. Why doesn't Bruce call up Marty Siegel and offer them fifty-five dollars?"

Until the remaining Martin Marietta stockholders sold their thirty percent interest in the company, the merger could not be completed. Agee thought the price hike would entice the holdouts.

Wasserstein placed his call. Siegel was unavailable. He would return the call. When the phone rang, Mary picked it up, and after identifying herself and saying hello to Siegel, passed the phone to Wasserstein.

"Marty, we'll go to fifty-five if you recommend to the board that the price is fair," Wasserstein said.

Marty Siegel came into the room and whispered to Tom Pownall.

"Agee has increased his offer to fifty-five dollars," Pownall said, allowing Siegel to detail the terms of the increase.

"Is this financial package really worth what Agee says it is worth?" Jack Byrne asked. He had some doubts about the package of securities.

"Marty?" Pownall asked Siegel.

"Agee is right. It's worth fifty-five dollars."

For Jack Byrne, fifty-five dollars per share was still out of the question. His minimum "sell" figure was sixty-one dollars. He had arrived at that number the day Tom Pownall called him and said Bendix had launched its bid.

"For fifty-five dollars we should tell him that we'll paddle our own canoe," Byrne said.

"The real issue," a director said, "is are we going to buy the goddamn Bendix stock!"

"Our decision to buy has already been made," Frank Bradley said. "We made a decision a week ago Monday when we waived our conditions. We have a contract with the Bendix shareholders. And Agee's offer of indemnification for us does not solve our ethical problem with those people if we back down."

"Tell me again why this indemnification thing won't work," Byrne said.

If the lawyers could reassure Byrne that Agee's indemnification plan could protect Martin Marietta and its directors from lawsuits by disgruntled Bendix stockholders who wanted the seventy-five dollars Tom Pownall had pledged, then maybe the board could find a way around its "moral responsibility." Jack Byrne had made some inquiries of his own about the indemnification idea presented by Agee. The response to Byrne was that it could work.

"Bob, why don't you address this," Pownall said to Fullem.

"Well, gentlemen, it seems to me we are looking at two issues: One do we have an alternative to buying, do we have an out? and two, if we don't have an out, can we rely on this indemnification plan?"

It was clear to Fullem that if the question of whether Martin Marietta should buy was put to a vote now, there would be dissenters. Frank Ewing more than likely would not agree to buy. He couldn't stomach the financial consequences. Jack Byrne also looked like he was having trouble. Lee Everett was also openly questioning the wisdom of the move.

"When the board decided to waive its conditions," Fullem said, "the message was clear. We would buy—period—unless Bendix either drop its bid, which it hasn't, or pass the charter amendments, which they haven't. Our solicitors feel that since Bendix has postponed its meeting by twenty-four hours, they are having trouble coming up with the votes. On September thirteenth, we made it perfectly clear to Agee that the choice was his. We were tying our decision to his decision. The board of directors, having made that decision and announced it to the public, is not culpable for the financial consequences.

"Having said that—that we do not have an out to restrain us from buying the Bendix shares—the next question is: If the board decides in any event not to proceed with the plan to take down the shares, can we rely on Agee's indemnification plan?"

"Are we at risk if we accept the indemnification?" Mel Laird, former Secretary of Defense and a prominent lawyer, asked, cutting through.

"I have received advice that it could work," Byrne interjected.

Bob Fullem, a genial but worldly-wise lawyer, chose his words very carefully in responding to Jack Byrne.

"You will have the better of the arguments, but I cannot describe it as a remote risk," Fullem said slowly, allowing his audience to measure his words.

Trained as a mathematician, Jack Byrne converted Fullem's statement into odds. He reasoned that by saying there was a "better" chance that the indemnification would work and hold up in court, the odds were better than 55 percent, but because Fullem said there was not a remote risk it would fail, the odds worked out to somewhere between 55 and 90 percent that it would work.

Byrne felt flushed thinking about the September 13 meeting when the conditions were waived and Marty Siegel's "dead man's trigger" was cocked. If he had the chance, Byrne would relive that meeting.

If the tactic had worked, Marty Siegel would be a hero.

Not now. Byrne thought Siegel was looking like the goat.

The three lawyers on the board—Mel Laird, Gene Zuckert, and Griffin Bell—all continued to probe Fullem's assessment of the risk. Under each challenge Fullem would elaborate but then return to his carefully chosen position.

"The odds are that Agee's indemnification plan will work, but there is not a remote risk that the indemnification plan will fail."

Byrne and Lee Everett also pushed Fullem hard, but the lawyer held his ground. It was obvious to the directors that Fullem was being very deliberate. The seasoned lawyer was rendering his most important advice.

Fullem was against Agee's plan.

"That's it," Gene Zuckert said, as if closing a book. Both Griffin Bell and Mel Laird agreed.

"If our counsel says that is the risk, there is no sense debating it because we cannot go forward," Laird said.

"You know," Griffin Bell said in his slow southern drawl, "it's one thing for a board of directors to stand in front of a judge and say that they did what their counsel told them to do, and it is a very different thing to say that they went beyond what their counsel told them to do."

Another call for Bill Agee came from Roy Calvin. Bill and his party had been holed up at the Marriott for more than an hour and a half.

"The board is still deliberating," Calvin said, adding, "I am not certain you will appear before the directors."

"You're not sure?"

"Correct."

"Well, if the jury is still out, make sure that the defendant has a chance to appear before the verdict is handed down," Agee said in a sweeping metaphor that at once revealed the vulnerability he felt. He had to talk to the directors. He had to convince them not to go through with this crazy scheme to spend almost $1 billion and take down the Bendix shares.

Frank Ewing and Jack Byrne were looking at each other.

"So this is fundamentally a legal decision?" Byrne asked.

"Our counsel refuses to endorse Agee's indemnification plan," Zuckert said. "Without that assurance, we would be reckless to abandon our prearranged course."

Mel Laird and Griffin Bell agreed with Zuckert.

Just as the board members perhaps listened more acutely to Ewing, Byrne, and Everett when they were discussing financial matters, now the directors listened for the comments of the three prominent attorneys on the board.

Jack Byrne thought "Well, who am I to judge levels of risk if Dewey, Ballantine and the former Attorney General of the United States and the Secretary of Defense say 'no go'?"

"I guess there is nothing left to talk about," Everett said.

"Before we do anything, Tom, you've got to sit down with Agee," an impassioned Frank Ewing said. "Try something."

"Look, fellas," Tom Pownall said, "we're having a board meeting tomorrow afternoon late. Your final decision about buying is not being put to a vote now. Tomorrow night we will review the facts."

"Hello, Bill, this is Tom Pownall."

"Tom, finally, how are we doing?" Bill Agee asked.

"Bill, why don't you come over here," Pownall said, not waiting to hear Agee's reaction. "The board is finished, but they have asked me to meet with you to see if we can't resolve this mess."

"You finished?"

"Yup."

"Did they consider the letter?"

"They did. Come on over. We'll talk about it."

Within minutes two limousines from Martin Marietta were at the entrance of the Marriott waiting for Bill Agee and his party to come between the glass doors. When Bill Agee hung up the telephone, his intense expression practically told the whole story.

"They decided not to see me," Agee said to Mary, Bruce, Art, and Steve Fraidin. There was no way to get around it. That was a bad sign. The team collected their briefcases and left.

During the drive to the Martin Marietta headquarters, Agee looked out the window at the tall pine trees, and as the car wrapped around Rockledge Drive, he caught sight of Martin Marietta—a low, sleek, three-tiered concrete building standing alone amid rolling lawns and willow trees along the banks of a man-made lake. The cars drove under the building, depositing

Agee and his team at an elevator inside the garage that lead directly to the executive wing of the building.

Tom Pownall shook Bill Agee's hand.

Pownall was outwardly calm, but his eyes darted back and forth. The Bendix team mixed with the inner circle of Martin Marietta executives—Frank Menaker, Charlie Leithauser, Larry Adams, Roy Calvin. And the Dewey, Ballantine lawyers—Bob Fullem, Leonard Larrabee. Marty Siegel shook Bruce Wasserstein's hand.

The atmosphere was cordial if perhaps stiff. Mary Cunningham was the only woman present. She shook several hands. But behind the professionalism, many members of the Martin Marietta team were amazed—even momentarily stunned—to see her emerge from the elevator. She looked just like her photographs in *People* magazine.

Without delay, the Bendix team split. Frank Menaker led Art Fleischer, Steve Fraidin, and Mary into the boardroom and encouraged them to get comfortable. Wasserstein went off to an adjacent office to talk with Marty Siegel. Bill Agee followed Tom Pownall down the long hall to his office. The two principals would talk alone.

"Bill, just so we have a place to start, I put together this letter as the response of our board to your letter," Pownall said, handing Agee a one-page letter. The two men settled into chairs in Pownall's clean and Spartan office. Out his window was a warm but overcast day.

Agee read the letter.

Pownall had no intention of striking a deal with Agee. His attitude was as leathery as his skin. Drilled in military tradition, Pownall had a mission: At 2400 hours tomorrow night, Martin Marietta was going to buy the Bendix Corporation. It was a matter of principle. Once he took down the shares, Pownall would achieve parity with Agee. Then maybe the two men could work something out—some kind of détente.

"You have a legal problem accepting my offer?" Agee asked.
"Yes."
"Okay, let's tell the lawyers," Agee said.

Agee oddly found that encouraging. He reasoned that if everything else in this gigantic transaction made sense, the legal issue could be overcome.

339

"With the businessmen talking," Arthur Fleischer said down the hall, looking at the lawyers gathered around the table, "I guess we should see if we can clear up the legal issues. We have several ideas on how to solve the problem."

"Art, if I could," Bob Fullem said, "let's see if as a preface we can state the problem."

"Well, it seems to me that the central problem is that the Martin Marietta directors are unwilling to drop their decision to buy the Bendix shares because of two factors: a sense of duty to the Bendix stockholders who have been promised seventy-five dollars for their stock; and second, a legitimate concern that if they did indeed drop the decision to buy, they—being the directors—would be liable for damages to those same Bendix stockholders."

"That's a good start," Fullem said.

Steve Fraidin had never met Bob Fullem, but he had heard very good things about this expansive, cigar-smoking, lawyer. The man had a reputation of being a big-picture guy—somebody who would not let the details get in the way. Fraidin had seen tougher legal problems solved.

The lawyers rehashed the issues and the law. Arthur Fleischer repeated his contention that if Martin Marietta did buy the Bendix shares, they would be prevented in the Delaware court from voting the shares at a Bendix stockholders' meeting. If that was the case, Martin Marietta never could take control of the Bendix Corporation.

"So why buy the shares in the first place?" Fleischer asked.

"We'll get in Maryland what you'll get in Delaware," an adamant Bob Fullem said. "If we can't vote, neither can you."

Both men knew that would mean a complete stalemate, with neither company capable of taking control of the other. The two giant corporations would be imprisoned in the resulting confusion.

"Why don't we focus on the issue of indemnification," Frank Menaker said. "Some of our directors feel that they've made a personal commitment that requires them to buy the Bendix stock."

The lawyers went around and around, doing what they are trained and paid to do—talk, reason, build persuasive arguments. Bob Fullem was getting tired. He slid back his chair and walked to the door. He turned to ask a final question of Steve Fraidin.

"Steve, can you tell us that there is no risk that this indemnity —or contract as you say—will be knocked out of court?"

"Of course I can't say there is no risk, but it strikes me as not an unreasonable risk."

Hearing the answer to his question, Fullem walked out, saying not a word. Fraidin was perplexed. It seemed Fullem was very rigid on the issue. He had made up his mind.

Bruce Wasserstein was sitting on his hands in one of the offices, waiting for the conclusion of the discussions between Agee and Pownall. Wasserstein had talked with Marty Siegel. But really there was not much to talk about. No one had made price an issue. Siegel seemed reasonable on that point. Maybe a dollar here or there. What it all came down to was a legal discussion.

Unless the lawyers blow it, Wasserstein thought, we might be able to pull this out.

People wandered around. Fleischer and Leonard Larrabee came in. Bob Fullem was in the hall. Steve Fraidin came in. The men chatted, really about nothing. They waited for word from the discussions between Pownall and Agee. Bob Fullem could not imagine what was taking so long. Larrabee was drinking a soda and munching on a sandwich when Mary Cunningham came into the room.

She introduced herself to Larrabee and Fullem—although she needed no introduction. After a brief moment of awkwardness the chitchat resumed, and Mary fell right in.

During the discussions between Agee and Pownall, the two men took periodic breaks to get out and stretch their legs and confer with their advisers. After one such break, several hours after the talks had begun, Agee shook his head at Bruce Wasserstein in the privacy of an office.

"This doesn't seem to be going anywhere," Agee said. "Stay in touch with Allied."

Bruce had been talking with Eric Gleacher on and off all day —almost from the moment the previous night when the minority-investment deal had gone sour.

At close to 4:00 P.M., Wasserstein called again.

"Where are you, Bruce?" Eric asked. The connection was fuzzy.

"I can't tell you."

"So where do we stand?"

"I am sympathetic to your interest," Wasserstein said, as if he were being careful with words. "Let's proceed and I will call you back at seven P.M. and tell you what's our feeling at this end."

Mary wandered alone into the office. She wanted to know how it was going.

"While I think of it, Mary, get Al on the phone," Bill said.

When McDonald picked up the telephone in his suite at the Helmsley Palace in New York, he was momentarily stunned when he found himself talking with Mary. He had not known she had gone to Bethesda. When she put Bill on, McDonald said nothing.

"How's it going with our friend?" Agee asked, referring to Donald Trump, whose interest in the RCA stock held by Bendix offered the promise of a deal to extend the Martin Marietta timetable. But Agee was not sure that a deal with Trump would stand up in court.

"The meeting went well, but I think we've got to talk some more," McDonald said. "Trump was surprised not to see you."

"Okay," Agee said, "I'll talk with you later. At the moment, I've got as many issues as I need. See ya, Al."

The discussions continued for another hour.

Bill Agee emerged from his meeting with Pownall and huddled briefly with Arthur Fleischer.

"Let's get going," Agee said to Mary and his advisers. They said their good-byes. The Bendix team got into the elevator and headed for the garage without saying what had transpired.

In the garage, Agee changed his mind.

"Art and Mary, let's go back up. I want to talk about one more thing."

Fraidin and Wasserstein were left standing in the garage.

"What the hell is going on up there?" Wasserstein said after twenty minutes.

Finally the elevator began making noise and Bill, Mary, and Art reappeared. The cars were pulled up. Bill and Mary got into the first limousine, with Bruce Wasserstein joining them; Art Fleischer and Steve Fraidin got into the next car.

"We went through it again and they're saying no but we're supposed to talk tomorrow morning," Fleischer reported to

Fraidin as the car pulled out of the building into the warm night, following the other limousine.

"It just seems ridiculous to leave under these circumstances," Fraidin said. "Fullem is stuck on this, but it just doesn't seem that the issue is really that impossible."

"What else could we say to them?" Fleischer asked, thinking.

Fraidin opened his briefcase and took out a legal pad, taking a pen from his suit jacket. He and Fleischer began throwing out ideas. Steve wrote them down.

THIRTY-ONE

On West Forty-third Street in Manhattan, Bob Cole was in his office, sitting at his small desk in the sea of cubicles on the third floor of *The New York Times'* building. While the entire news department was computerized, and Cole wrote his stories in takes on his desktop computer, a Remington manual typewriter sat on a large shelf like an icon.

On the phone, his balding head bent over, Cole scribbled on a yellow legal pad. He was talking with one of his "sources." On this Bendix deal, the man was proving to be valuable.

"I understand there've been big meetings today," Cole said, fishing.

"Yeah, Agee's having big meetings today," the man said. He would never tell Cole the whole story, just enough to keep him looking.

"Who was in the room?"

"Mary was there," the man said casually.

"Mary was at the meeting?" Cole asked.

"Yeah."

"What was she doing?"

"Nothing, really. She was just sitting there."

"Did she ask questions?"

"No, she just sat there."

"Why was she there?"

"She's Bill Agee's wife. Beyond that, you got me."

Cole sat at his desk, thinking the whole situation over after hanging up. He personally did not give a damn about Mary Cunningham. And the *Times* was not interested in a man's personal life. When the Bill and Mary story had boiled over the financial pages, Cole did the obligatory summaries. But as far as he was concerned, Mary was gossip column fodder.

But Cole sat there thinking. Here was a multibillion-dollar transaction going on, and Mary Cunningham was present at the discussions. She wasn't a Bendix employee. Her only connection was being Bill Agee's wife. Behind-the-scenes counsel was one thing, but she's going to goddamn meetings!

Cole sat at his keyboard and pounded out his story for the day. The headline in Wednesday's paper would read: TAKEOVER OF BENDIX ADVANCES.

Buried in the narrative, in the tenth paragraph:

> William M. Agee, chairman of Bendix, was understood to be conferring late yesterday with close advisors on what Bendix might do next. Mary Cunningham, who is Mr. Agee's wife and a former Bendix executive, was also understood to have participated.
>
> Sources said that Mrs. Agee had attended similar meetings in the past and attached no particular significance to her presence.

After finishing the long story, Cole electronically sent the story to an editor's desk. Word came back "See me."

Cole trudged through the swirling activity of the news department to the desk.

"What's this doing in there? It's gotta come out," the deskman said, pointing at the passage about Mary Cunningham. "What's that got to do with anything?"

"No, that's very important."

"It should come out," the deskman said. "You even say her presence had 'no particular significance.' "

"Jesus, don't you understand?"

Bob Cole held most editors in low esteem. They were the guys who butcher other people's hard-earned words. He rarely questioned the judgment of the senior editors, men such as John

Lee, the financial editor. But this deskman was another story. What a priggish little fuck, Cole thought.

"Nobody ever brings his wife to a billion-dollar takeover meeting," Cole said angrily. "I'm not making this news—it's the goddamn participants who are making this news. I mean, did I libel this woman? No. Did I say she's got a fat ass or bowed legs or crossed eyes? No. It stays."

Bill and Mary and Bruce in the lead car driving to the airport were not saying much. Having a Martin Marietta employee as the driver did not encourage open conversation. But words were said. It was obvious Agee was having a hard time letting go.

"Pull over at that gas station," Bill said to the startled driver. The second limousine followed their lead. Agee and the others walked away from the cars to talk. Bill was using his hands, gesturing vigorously as he spoke to Fleischer. Art and Fraidin reviewed some ideas. Bill went to a pay phone.

"Tom, I had to call you again," Agee said from the phone booth at the gasoline station. "I know we said the lawyers would continue to look at this and we'd talk tomorrow, but somehow I just think where there's a will, there's a way. My people have some thoughts about how this thing could be undone. Why don't we get the advisers together and see what they have?"

"Sure, come back," Pownall said, already tired.

Pownall went into an adjoining office, where his advisers were decompressing from the earlier discussions.

"Agee wants to come back," Pownall said noncommittally.

"What's he proposing?" Menaker asked.

"I don't know. He says he's got something."

"Well, let's hear him out," Menaker said.

"Besides, Tom," Marty Siegel said, "if Agee is here talking with you, he's not off talking to somebody else about extending the withdrawal rights of our offer."

The men smiled. It was not a planned strategy—that would be too cynical for tired men—but it did suit their purpose. Besides, maybe the ride toward the airport had given Agee some second thoughts.

When Bill and his team returned, all of the participants gathered in the boardroom. Bill and Mary sat at the long table next to each other, their backs to the curtained windows overlooking the courtyard. Fleischer and Fraidin and Wasserstein sat farther down. Mary had a pad in front of her, and as Bill began to speak, she started taking notes.

The Martin Marietta team was on the opposite side—Pownall, Leithauser, Menaker, Fullem, Larrabee, Katcher, and Siegel were seated, with others still filing into and out of the room.

"I suppose it is pointless to talk about how we got here," Bill Agee said, "but I think it is important that you understand what our motivations are. Our goal at Bendix is to make a combined company that would be financially stronger than either company alone. We want to work together with you. Martin Marietta would continue with its own board of directors. Naturally, Bendix would have a majority of the seats. But your headquarters would still be here. The price we are offering is fair. I have heard no arguments about that.

"You have mentioned repeatedly," Agee said to Pownall across the table, "that you have a legal problem and that the Martin Marietta board of directors owes a duty to the Bendix shareholders. We recognize the merit in your opinion, but the best legal advice available says that the problem is not insurmountable. We can work this out. The directors of Martin Marietta will not suffer.

"These two corporations are already destined to become one entity," Agee said. "It would be a tragedy for you to spend any more of the combined company's money."

Leonard Larrabee was having a hard time taking Agee seriously. Here he was talking about saving the company's money when he had just needlessly spent $300 million to buy an additional 20 percent of Martin Marietta. That hadn't changed anything. All it had done was speed the destruction of the company's cash reserves. Larrabee slouched down in his chair to hear out Agee.

"Take a look at who is really going to profit from you spending a billion dollars to take down our stock. We all know this is going to take a long time to settle. It's going to be in the courts, maybe for years. The Bendix shareholders aren't going to get seventy-five dollars. The arbs are the ones who are going to make the money! The arbs and the professional investors! If the Martin Marietta board owes a duty to anyone, it isn't the arbs. They owe that to the people who made Bendix, the employees who will withdraw their stock from your offer tomorrow. What about the Bendix employees?

"I believe we have an opportunity and an obligation to do

something in the best interests of our two companies, our share-holders, our employees, and really when you think about it, our country and our national defense. I believe—"

"Hey, why don't we dispense with that and get down to what proposals you have to undo our waiver of conditions," Menaker said interrupting. Frank had a hard time listening to Agee wax philosophically—especially after having already gone through a merry-go-round of discussions.

"All right," Agee said, never showing any emotion. "Arthur has several ideas to discuss with you to get us out of this dilemma. I guess, Tom, you and I can continue our discussions."

The fact that the Bendix team was invited back gave Bruce Wasserstein reason for optimism. While the lawyers met, Wasserstein found an empty office and made his promised call to Eric Gleacher.

"We're pounding out the numbers for a one hundred percent transaction," Gleacher said merrily, referring to the potential deal of Allied buying all of the Bendix Corporation.

"Look, I don't want to be responsible," Bruce said, "if you and Ed do all this work and then something else happens. If you want to, you should proceed."

Gleacher was baffled by Wasserstein's shift in gears. After having worked all weekend on the minority-investment deal that the Allied board rejected, and putting up with the last-minute changes proposed by Agee and then working with the lawyers on the papers for a 100 percent transaction, Eric was getting tired of the run-around. Damn, he thought, it takes two companies to make a merger.

Wasserstein was at best noncommittal under his quick cross-examination. When Gleacher hung up, he thought, that's it. He got on the phone to Hennessy in Morristown.

"He won't tell me where he is or what they're up to," Gleacher said, "and he's really jerking my chain about our next step. He didn't sound interested."

"He didn't give you any encouragement?" Hennessy asked.

"No."

"Well, we're not gonna spend time chasing our tail," Hennessy said.

"Here are some thoughts," Arthur Fleischer said to the Martin Marietta lawyers assembled in the conference room. He was examining the notes taken by Steve Fraidin in the limo. "I am not saying that any of these are certain, but maybe they all add up to something that can work. Here are the approaches. If a majority of your board of directors resigned and was replaced by directors from Bendix, the new board could voluntarily withdraw the offer; secondly, if you stopped soliciting and the amendment to our charter passed, you would have an out; and thirdly, the Martin board could amend the offer with some condition which Bendix could violate, thereby negating the obligation to buy."

The response was not positive.

"Wait a minute, Art," Dick Katcher said. "When we waived our conditions, we said the only out—other than your guys not buying—was the passage of the proposed Bendix amendments. Now you're saying we can get around that by just stopping soliciting proxies?"

"And you'll keep soliciting?" Larrabee asked.

"Right."

"In other words, Martin Marietta should just roll over?"

"It is an idea."

"Arthur, that won't even pass the red-face test," Larrabee said.

"I think you are wanted," Roy Calvin said, passing along the message to Art Fleischer and Frank Menaker. "In Pownall's office."

When the two lawyers found chairs, Agee began his pitch by leaning forward in his chair.

"Lookit, fellas, for you to spend nine hundred million dollars out of a sense of moral duty is a tragedy. You have the right to rely on the indemnification. To spend that money is a waste."

"I don't look forward to it," Pownall said.

"Let's be creative," Agee said. "You're not being creative enough. You are getting bad legal advice. You can do it. You can! Don't take down the stock."

"I don't know what I can tell you," Pownall said, exhausted.

"Let's hold the legal problem aside for a moment. Is there anything else? Is it price? Is it organization?" Agee asked Tom Pownall.

"Well, I have to give something else to my board. They just turned down your letter, Bill," Pownall said.

"Let's talk about the board," Frank Menaker said. "You're

offering us four directors out of fourteen. What about a split board?"

"Are these matters that are contentious as far as you're concerned?" Agee asked Pownall.

"No, it's a legal problem."

"Well is there anything else?" Agee asked, searching for hidden agendas. He had expected them to quote the legal problem, but he thought they also would eventually talk price and management structure. The impasse seemed all too clear. Their lawyer wasn't moving from his position, and Fleischer had given his best case. There was no meeting of minds. He had to ask again.

"Is there anything else?"

"What about a split board?" Menaker repeated.

"We own seventy percent of your stock," Agee said.

Agee looked at Fleischer.

"We'll move it up to six directors," Agee said. "Tom, look, if you knew my style of management, you'd know that I delegate authority. I don't want to run Martin Marietta. You'll run it. Your headquarters will still be here. Your contribution would be recognized. You would be vice chairman. We could even change the name of the new company to 'Bendix Martin.' "

"What about co-chief executives?" Menaker asked.

"Is this an issue for you, Tom? If this is, all right, but I'm not going to talk about this if this does not help the legal problem."

"That doesn't help my legal problem," Pownall said, tired of hearing his own voice.

"Tom, this will be in the courts if we can't settle this. I don't want some judge telling us how to run our business," Agee said.

Pownall looked at Menaker.

"We'll get another opinion about the indemnification," Menaker said.

"Good. Do that. We'll talk tomorrow morning."

Mary peeked into one of the offices. Charlie Leithauser was sleeping on a couch. She went next door and saw Roy Calvin, smoking a cigarette, with Bill Harwood, his PR associate. Calvin waved her in. Smiling, she sat down.

"How's your guy doing?" Roy asked gently.

"Oh, I just wish that Tom and Bill could be doing this by themselves without these batteries of lawyers and bankers. You know, Bill thinks the world of Tom, and I know Tom thinks the world of Bill. And they could just get so much done if they didn't have all these people hanging around and keeping them from acting naturally."

Roy smiled through the haze of his cigarette smoke.

"What do you think is going to happen?" Mary asked.

"Well, we're gonna buy the stock."

"That is really a shame," Mary said. "You know, this whole thing has just been blown out of proportion. I think there have been many regrettable actions. The tendering of the employee stock by Citibank was really quite outrageous. Can you imagine someone tendering your stock without your permission? No broker in the world could get away with that. You should have heard the anger of some of the people.

"I think it was quite a show of support for Bill when some fifty thousand Bendix employees turned out for Bendix Unity Day yesterday. It was a marvelous, spontaneous outpouring of loyalty and affection. Bill was touched by it."

Both Calvin and Harwood remained quiet. Harwood realized he really couldn't say anything without being rude. He had been getting calls from Bendix employees saying that they were being paid time and a half to help organize and participate in Unity Day. Some of them even asked for Martin Marietta T-shirts or caps, anything they could show in defiance.

Somehow to Harwood, Mary sounded like a phonograph record—her message was loud and clear but impregnable to a comeback.

When Agee appeared in the hallway and signaled to Mary, she smiled and said, "Nice talking with you."

After she had left, Roy turned to Harwood and said, "Either she wrote that Unity Day press release, or she memorized it!"

Bruce Wasserstein called Eric Gleacher at his apartment at Fifth Avenue and Ninety-fifth Street. Wasserstein could hear Gleacher's two huge black dogs barking in the background.

"Eric, I got another idea for a minority deal," Wasserstein said. Bruce knew that Agee had almost reached the end of his rope with Pownall and the Marietta team.

"What kind of deal?"

"The thought is that we pull the aerospace divisions of Bendix and Martin Marietta out of both companies and form a new company jointly owned by Allied and Bendix."

Wasserstein then began explaining the financial framework

of the deal when Bill Agee came to the door and waved him off the phone.

"I gotta go," Wasserstein said abruptly to Gleacher.

"Hey, Bruce, before you get off, look, you're gonna have to explain this to me. You're not making sense. I don't have enough information to talk to Hennessy about this."

"Look, I gotta go," Bruce said in an obvious hurry. "Talk to my people in New York." Then he hung up.

Gleacher called First Boston. He let it ring. Tony Grassi answered.

"Tony, I just had a strange hurry-up call from Bruce proposing a new minority deal. He said to call you."

"Can't help you," Grassi said after a moment.

"Well, look, where is he?"

"Can't help you."

"Get ahold of him and find out what the hell's going on, okay?"

On the plane on the way back to New York, there was lobster and champagne for everyone. Agee had hoped it would be a victory celebration. But he never let on that he felt defeat. He was on the phone talking with Al McDonald about the status of the negotiations with Donald Trump.

"I need an ironclad guarantee if I'm going to do this with Trump," Agee said to McDonald. Bill found the mimicking of Pownall's words a bitter taste. The Trump deal looked doubtful.

After he hung up, Agee was quiet. He tried to put his head back against a pillow. But he was quickly up again.

"We're gonna keep this thing going," he said. "Let's just proceed to the next step, and we'll see what happens."

In less than twenty-four hours, Martin Marietta would be free to purchase 11.9 million shares of Bendix stock. The disaster that Bill Agee said he would never accept was winding down around him.

A couple of hours later, back in New York, Bruce Wasserstein called Eric Gleacher again.

"Look, it's an interesting thought," Gleacher said after Wasserstein reviewed his proposed deal, "but I don't think Hennessy or the board is going to go for any kind of investment deal. It just won't fly." Gleacher did not tell Wasserstein his impression that the board did not want to do any deal with Bill Agee in the driver's seat.

"But, sure, I'll talk to Ed in the morning about it. I am not gonna wake him up to talk about a deal he's not interested in."

"Well, check it out," Wasserstein said.

"Okay."

Before dawn, Gleacher called Ed Hennessy at his home in New Jersey and ran down the deal that Wasserstein was pitching. Hennessy agreed with Gleacher's judgment of the situation.

"No way are we going to do that deal or any other investment deal. Make them understand," Hennessy said.

At 6:30 A.M., after Bruce had been up almost all night talking with Agee and trying to play all the cards, he called Gleacher.

"Let's talk," Bruce said, still running on nervous energy.

"Hey, you turned me off last night. We got nothing. Ed told me to make you understand. It's all or nothing. That's where it's gonna end up, and the longer you wait, the more complicated and difficult you're gonna make it. I mean, in what, seventeen hours?, they're gonna take you down."

"What are you thinking for price?" Wasserstein asked.

"Look, this is the deal we're thinking. Gray offered eighty-five dollars, right? But his back end stunk."

"Yeah, the blend was sixty-seven dollars tops."

"Okay, Ed will give eighty-five dollars cash front end for fifty-five percent of the company, and you and I will put together a securities package for the back end worth seventy-five dollars. The blend will be eighty dollars. That ought to be enough to get the arbs to pull out of the Martin Marietta offer."

While Gleacher could rattle off the numbers as if they had just occurred to him, Wasserstein knew that a lot of research by Lehman and the financial people at Allied had gone into the calculations. He had run numbers, too. The deal was fair.

"Let's get Ed and Bill together," Wasserstein said. "Ten A.M. at the Palace."

Suite 4509 at the Helmsley Palace had seen double duty during the past few weeks. Not only did Bill and Mary live there, but also, as the time pressure became more extreme and Bill responded by huddling with his advisers, somehow the intimacy of the Palace seemed better suited to Bill's needs than his office at the GM Building.

In preparation for the day-long meetings on Wednesday, the dining-table chairs were pulled back and placed along a wall. The table was moved to be out of the way. Pitchers of grapefruit juice and a large vat of coffee were ordered from room service.

By 7:00 A.M. Wednesday, the suite was bustling with activity. Al McDonald was there, reviewing his discussion from the night before with Donald Trump. Trump himself was expected at the Palace today. Wasserstein was there with the results of his staff's number-crunching during the night. And the lawyers were in and out.

Bill Agee wanted a deal with Tom Pownall. Agee figured that perhaps if he sweetened the price and perhaps minimized the risk for the Martin Marietta directors, the "legal problem" would go away. Steve Fraidin and Tony Grassi were talking in the bedroom on what to offer Martin Marietta. Wasserstein had a plan. He reviewed it with Agee and McDonald. Agee gave the go-ahead.

Wasserstein called Marty Siegel with a new idea to limit the liability of the Martin Marietta directors if they chose not to proceed with their tender offer. Charlie Leithauser had asked during the negotiations in Bethesda if there was a way to "make the Bendix stockholders whole" to allow Marietta to back out of buying. Wasserstein's team at First Boston had stayed up most the night working out the details.

"C'mon Bruce, what have you got for me?" Siegel said during Wasserstein's remarks prefacing his pitch.

"What we're thinking is that instead of you purchasing the stock with cash, what about the idea of Bendix issuing a preferred securities package to the Bendix employees valued at sixty-five dollars? That way, if your guys are sued, they're only liable for the ten bucks—the difference between your seventy-five dollars and our sixty-five dollars—instead of the difference between market and your offer."

"Are you talking the right problem?" Siegel asked.

"Yeah, that would satisfy—or almost satisfy—your liability. We would be giving the Bendix shareholders a good deal. And it would take the cash bite out of your plan for tonight."

The irony was compelling. Bendix was promising to pay off its own stockholders so that Martin Marietta would not saddle the company with an enormous debt of almost $1 billion—due in one year.

"I need an answer soon," Wasserstein said.

Mary answered the door when Ed Hennessy knocked at 10:00 A.M. The chairman of the Allied Corporation led in a group of six men in business suits, some carrying briefcases.

"Hello," Mary said in a cheerful voice. Hennessy introduced his general counsel, Brian Forrow, and his senior VP for planning and finance, Hal Buirkle. With them were Joe Flom and Morris Kramer from Skadden, Arps, and Eric Gleacher and Tom Hill from Lehman Brothers.

The group entered the pastel-colored living room. Bill Agee got up from the L-shaped couch to shake Ed Hennessy's hand. Bruce Wasserstein and Arthur Fleischer exchanged pleasantries with their counterparts. Al McDonald smiled without saying a lot.

Being a large group, it was somewhat awkward, but encouraged by Mary, the men poured themselves coffee and sat down, some balancing a danish on one knee. The setup was not intended so much for negotiations as perhaps reconciliation. Agee had been the disappointed bride before with Ed Hennessy. When the minority-investment deal fell through, Bill was disillusioned. It seemed to him that Hennessy had given his word.

"How should we do this deal?" Hennessy asked matter-of-factly. Having done many deals before, he felt comfortable with establishing the big-picture framework with Agee. The lawyers and bankers would thrash out the details.

"I have a board meeting this afternoon and I'd like to conclude this matter one way or another," Bill said. "Here's where we stand: We're either going to make a deal with Martin Marietta, or we'll do our deal with you. I won't be able to tell you until one P.M. whether we have a deal. But Ed, I will tell you now, I'm not using you as a negotiating ploy with somebody else. It's either Martin Marietta or you."

"How's it going with Pownall?"

"It's still going."

"Okay, so then in terms of our understanding," Hennessy said, "we're looking at offering eighty-five bucks cash a share for thirteen million shares of the Bendix stock."

"Yup."

"Thirteen point one million," Forrow said, "basically fifty-five percent of the outstanding."

"Okay," Hennessy said to the elaboration, "and some kind of package the bankers will put together for the back end at seventy-five dollars."

"Yeah."

"Bill, I frankly don't know what Pownall is gonna do tonight. And I don't know what UTC or somebody else is going to do," Hennessy said. "Once we bid, somebody else may make a play."

Talking in broad strokes, Hennessy and Agee worked out a deal known in the business of mergers and acquisitions as a "crown jewel agreement." By asking Agee to give Allied an option to purchase the lucrative Bendix aerospace-electronics group if any other company made a bid for Bendix at greater than eighty-five per share, Hennessy was in one stroke scaring off potential competitors while guaranteeing Allied a big score no matter what happened.

It was not Agee's idea and he accepted it without great enthusiasm.

"Why don't you guys work out some of these details," Hennessy said to the lawyers and bankers.

"You can use the bedroom," Agee said, pointing to a door off the living room.

Earlier, on the phone, Bruce Wasserstein had spoken with Hennessy about Agee and the presidency of Allied. The position at Allied was open. Hennessy had also instituted a search for a chief operating officer. The right man would hold both jobs. Hennessy knew Bill Agee was ambitious. The vacancies gave him a way to entice Agee into accepting the deal.

"Bill, you will be president of Allied," Hennessy said, "and chairman and CEO of Bendix. I'm gonna need you to make this a smooth transition."*

"Allied, Bendix, and Martin Marietta is going to make one heck of a company," Agee said, smiling. With Bendix already owning 70 percent of Marietta, Hennessy would be buying both companies if the deal went through.

"What about director seats on the Allied board?"

---

*Agee later insisted that Hennessy had also promised to cancel his search for a successor and chief operating officer. "With you on board, Bill, there will be no need for this search to continue," Agee quoted Hennessy as saying.

"Three is the maximum."

"I'd enjoy being on the board," Agee said.

"Of course."

"I'd like you to consider Al McDonald. And maybe Scotty—Jonathan Scott."

"Bill, it's fine that you come on, but not McDonald. I've only got two insiders on my board—Forrow and myself."

"I really want McDonald," Agee said.

"I'll put it in front of my board," Hennessy said.

While Agee and Hennessy talked, Wasserstein and Gleacher were talking in the hall. The lawyers were in the bedroom. With lots of phones but only two phone lines, there was a stackup of people waiting to make calls.

"I'll be over at Skadden," Hennessy said, smiling. The Allied team headed out. "Give me a call when you've made your decision."

THIRTY-TWO

To buy the Bendix stock, Martin Marietta had formed a subsidiary called ML Holding. Charlie Leithauser, Frank Menaker, and Bob Powell were designated as board members. At an organizational meeting on Wednesday morning, Bob Powell was tapped as the man who would actually go to New York and take down the stock.

Tom Mendenhall came into the meeting. He was excited.

"I just got off the phone with Bank of America," Mendenhall said. "Bendix has informed the bank that Martin Marietta is a subsidiary of Bendix and that we are not permitted to borrow the money!"

Bendix had decided to go after the banks in an effort to prevent Martin Marietta from borrowing the money to buy the Bendix stock. The letter was from Hal Barron to Sam Armacost, the president and chief executive officer of Bank of America.

"I think they sent letters to all the banks," Mendenhall said.

"So what did B of A say?" Bob Powell asked impatiently.

"Tegart said we were pretty damn smart to take down the money on Friday," Mendenhall said with a smile. "Now that we got the money in a demand account, there's nothing the banks can do."

"What about the backup three hundred million dollars you were arranging?" Powell asked.

"Sorry," Mendenhall said with a shrug of his shoulders. The new money was intended to be additional operating capital. The Bendix letter stopped that plan cold.

Frank Menaker was thinking hard.

"What happens if somebody stops Powell tonight and gives him an injunction?" Menaker asked, playing devil's advocate. "Something fishy is going on in Delaware. Bendix could go to the court for an order to prevent Martin Marietta from spending the money."

"Let's have Tom go, too," Leithauser said, nodding at Mendenhall. "That way, if Bob gets served with an injunction, Mendenhall will slip through and take down the shares."

It was agreed.

"Tell Tom the codes," Leithauser said.

"Yeah," Mendenhall said with a heavy sigh of anticipation.

The plan was that Bob Powell and Tom Mendenhall would fly to New York separately—Powell taking the company jet, and Mendenhall taking the Eastern shuttle. They would proceed to Dewey, Ballantine for the final briefing. They would then proceed to the Citibank downtown office. Each man would carry a briefcase of official papers authorizing him to spend almost $1 billion. The command would come from Charlie Leithauser or Tom Pownall in a prearranged voice-recognition code.

On Wednesday morning, Martin Marietta vice president Jim Simpson was standing at a telephone at the Bendix headquarters in Southfield, Michigan. The time for the special stockholders' meeting had come. Simpson was talking with Frank Menaker and Tom Pownall in Bethesda.

"So what do you want me to do?" Simpson asked.

Simpson wanted to know if he should challenge the Bendix intention to postpone again the stockholders meeting. The New York lawyers had informed Simpson yesterday that Bendix could not adjourn legally without getting a vote from the stockholders on the motion of adjournment.

"Do you want me to fight?" Simpson asked.

"The lawyers are still talking," Frank Menaker said.

"The way the Bendix guys operate," Simpson said, monitoring his watch, "I've got to have a decision now, or the meeting will be over before I get in there."

There was a long pause. The decision was important. If the meeting was postponed, it would just be a footnote in the long struggle. But if Simpson succeeded in challenging the adjournment, then both sides would have to lay their votes on the table. If Bendix won, the war was over. However, if the amendments were defeated, Martin Marietta could buy the Bendix stock at midnight, and Tom Pownall would be able to deny victory to Bill Agee. Maybe then Agee would agree to a straight stock swap. Each company would go its own way.

At a cost of $2,500,000,000.00!

The men in Bethesda could not decide.

"It's your call, Jim," Menaker said.

With his red badge already pinned to his suit jacket, Simpson walked past the security guards and the assembled Bendix employees at the long table and took his seat among the more than one hundred people assembled in the large conference room for the Bendix special stockholders' meeting.

He had no instructions—only a gut feeling.

"This meeting is called to order. My name is Donald G. Speyer. I am a vice president of Bendix. Yesterday evening, following certain court proceedings, Bendix issued this press release. . . ."

While Speyer read the release about the new postponement, Jim Simpson was looking over at Irv Yoskowitz from United Technologies. The two men sized up the situation. It was now or never.

"In accordance with this announcement, I have been instructed, as chairman of this meeting—"

"Mr. Chairman—" Simpson interrupted.

"—to take the necessary action to adjourn this meeting to Monday, September twenty-seventh, 1982, at ten A.M. This date—"

"Mr. Chairman—"

"—has been chosen in order to avoid the burden on shareholders pending resolution of complex legal matters—"

"Mr. Chairman, I would like to call—" Simpson was on his feet.

"—We are sorry to have inconvenienced you—"

"Mr. Chairman, I would like to call for a quorum count, please."

"—I now declare this meeting adjourned."

With that Don Speyer left the podium. Simpson walked down the aisle and took the podium, adjusting the microphone close to his mouth.

"I am a stockholder of the Bendix Corporation. My name is James Simpson. I'm vice president of Martin Marietta Corporation. It is my belief that there is a quorum present at this meeting, and I believe the proceedings should continue as originally scheduled. At this point since there is no chairman—since the chairman has departed—I would like to call for a vote on electing me chairman of this meeting. All in favor?"

Yoskowitz and the others in the Martin Marietta and United Technologies delegations said "Aye."

"Negative?" Simpson said. There was no response from the Bendix personnel.

"I hereby declare myself chairman of the meeting. The business of the meeting is to consider the two management proposals contained in the notice of meeting. Is there any discussion?"

"Mr. Chairman?" Irv Yoskowitz asked.

"Yes, sir."

"My name is Irving Yoskowitz. I'm vice president and general counsel of United Technologies. We believe the proposals are not in the best interests of the shareholders. We are going to vote against those amendments."

"Thank you," Simpson said.

"Mr. Chairman?"

"Yes, sir," Simpson said to Lewis Black, a Bendix lawyer standing toward the back of the room.

"Mr. Chairman, this meeting has been adjourned," Black said.

"There has not been a proper adjournment," Simpson said.

The two men haggled back and forth with no agreement. Black asked for a recess to discuss the matter further. Simpson agreed.

Andy Samet, Bendix's associate general counsel, was standing in the back with another Bendix lawyer, Dave Young. Samet was a small man, with thinning hair. Young stood head and shoulders above him. A bunch of lawyers from Fried, Frank and Hughes, Hubbard were also milling around. Samet was looking around, thrusting his hands into his jacket pockets, obviously uncomfortable.

"This is a joke," Samet said. "This can't go on. The meeting was adjourned. We can't let them take it over and try to make something out of this!"

When Simpson took the podium again and declared that the

meeting would go on as planned, Andy Samet had had enough. He turned to one of the Bendix audio-video men standing next to a control panel.

"Cut the lights," Samet said. The huge room went black. With more than a hundred people and piles of boxes scattered around the room, it was chaos. There were shouts of surprise.

"I would note for the record that the lights have now been turned out and this meeting is being interfered with! We shall adjourn to the Michigan Inn!" Jim Simpson said.

"Turn off the microphone," Samet told the a/v man.

"This is outrageous!" Simpson yelled when the microphone went dead. "I would like to move for adjournment of the meeting," he said, his hands cupped to his mouth. It was crazy in the darkness.

"So moved!" Yoskowitz called back.

The doors to the room were flung open, and the people filed out.

Simpson told one of the Morrow reps to go ahead to the Michigan Inn and line something up. The man jumped in a cab and went to the hotel. He made a handwritten notice of the special stockholders' meeting and posted it conspicuously.

Simpson and Yoskowitz and their teams filed into the Erie Room off the lobby of the Michigan Inn. There were five round wooden tables—bereft of tableclothes. Boxes of proxies were lugged into the room.

A legion of press people arrived, including local radio and TV crews. There was a lot of jockeying for position among the media. Finally, Simpson had to respond.

"Look, you guys can't participate in this thing. You can sit here. But no pictures and no questions. I'll talk with you afterward."

An hour later, Simpson emerged and was bombarded with questions from the press. The TV crews had turned their lights on, and tape was rolling.

"The amendments have been defeated," Simpson said.

Jim Simpson had removed the last condition.

The Bendix PR department was on full alert.

Dick Cheney from Hill & Knowlton had assembled a team at the GM Building on Fifth Avenue. When word of trouble at the special stockholders' meeting came from the lawyers in Southfield, Cheney immediately issued a story to the wire services saying that the meeting had been adjourned. It crossed the wire at 11:18 A.M.

Then something more disturbing happened.

"Did you hear the latest?" an important Bendix adviser asked Cheney.

"What?"

"Mary went with Agee to Bethesda."

Suddenly the mysterious line about Mary in Bob Cole's story this morning made sense. Cheney found it hard to believe. Almost from the beginning, Cheney had been the one responsible for protecting Agee's soft underbelly. But Cheney had concentrated on preparing for attacks from without. The private investigating company had come up with a list of charges and innuendos capable of being thrown in the face of Harry Gray at United Technologies. To prevent UTC from coming at Mary and Bill, the investigators leaked angles to the press—everything from rumors about Gray's marriage, to a back handed swipe at the authenticity of Harry's World War II decorations.

Armed with that protection, it never occurred to Dick Cheney that Bill Agee would himself red-flag Mary's involvement. With the shock of a sudden realization, Cheney finally knew the danger was from within.

"I want to come over and talk to Bill about Mary," Cheney said to Bob Meyers, the Bendix PR chief who was over at the Palace. Meyers said he would check.

"They don't want you to come over. What Bill said was that you should just go into a private room at the office and call back. Mary and Bill will both get on."

Cheney did as instructed.

"Bill," Cheney said with exasperation in his voice, "to achieve what you want in terms of press reaction and in terms of negotiations with Martin Marietta, Mary has got to take a back seat. Mary, are you on, too?"

"Yes."

"The point is that you are no longer going to be measured in terms of Bendix. You work for Seagram's. Forever, as far as the public is concerned, the game is rigged against you and Bendix. Everybody is waiting to see how you do at Seagram's.

"Bill, now that she appears to be involved with your discussions with Martin Marietta, the world is gonna ask, 'Who's the boss? Who's making the decisions?' You could stir up all kinds of resentments."

"If people want to make of something of Mary's waiting in a back room while I'm in negotiations with Tom Pownall, then that's their problem," Agee said vehemently.

"I didn't mean to insult either of you," Cheney said.

"If my husband tells me that it's helpful to have me nearby at a time as difficult and stressful as this," Mary said, "then I certainly want to be there."

There was little more to say. Bill and Mary hung up.

Minutes before 11:30 A.M., Martin Marietta's lawyer in charge of litigation from Dewey, Ballantine, Robert Myers, was sitting in the ornate boardroom of the old Mattson Chemical Company on the eighteenth floor of the Maryland National Bank in Baltimore. Myers was sitting with George Beall, the senior partner from Miles & Stockbridge. The two men were awaiting word of the decision by Judge Young.

Without his approval, Martin Marietta could not buy tonight.

To pass the time, Myers was reading the transcripts from yesterday's decisive hearing before Judge Young in the federal courthouse down the street.

"Shakespeare, I suspect, had something like this case in mind in Romeo and Juliet when he said 'a pox on both your houses,' " Judge Young had said.

The one line from yesterday's hearing that Bob Myers read and reread was Judge Young's final comment on the Bendix motion for a preliminary injunction to prevent Martin Marietta from buying.

"I am inclined to deny the motion," Judge Young had said.

"We just got a call," a lawyer said, running into the old boardroom. "Judge Young says the opinion is ready! We've sent a messenger."

Myers and George Beall looked to each other, fingers crossed.

When the messenger returned, Myers read quickly.

"Place the call," he said to Beall without any indication.

Twenty some miles away in Bethesda, Tom Pownall, Charlie Leithauser, and a bunch of Martin Marietta staffers were assembled around a speaker phone in Frank Menaker's office waiting to hear the decision.

" 'In conclusion,' " Robert Myers read, starting at the back of the order first, " 'the Court finds that although the balance of hardship is a draw, Bendix has failed to show that it is more likely than not to succeed on the merits of its claims and it is in the public interest for Marietta's offer to go forward. Accordingly, for the reasons stated herein, Bendix's motion for a preliminary injunction BE, and the same IS, hereby DENIED. Signed Judge Young, United States District Judge.' "

The cheer that went up in Bethesda and Baltimore barely needed the speaker phone to be heard. They had done it! The judge had accepted their arguments and decided to stay clear.

With Young's decision, the only hurdles left were the nagging problem out in federal court in Michigan and last-minute action by Bendix in Delaware.

But step by step, if their luck held, in a little more than twelve hours, the Martin Marietta Corporation would be able to buy the Bendix Corporation.

"The Bendix lawyers have already scheduled an appeal tonight," Myers said as a precautionary note.

"Let them," Menaker said. "Read me more of the decision."

The more Bob Myers read of the decision, the better it sounded.

"By refusing to halt its offer, Marietta's board is permitting Bendix' shareholders to freely exercise their own judgment as to whether the Marietta offer is in their own best interests."

The cheer went up again.

"We're gonna do it!" Menaker said.

"What have you decided?" Bill Agee asked Tom Pownall.

The morning was slipping away. Agee wanted to know the status of Pownall's consideration of the indemnification plan. There was an urgency in Agee's voice. In two hours, he had to give an answer to Ed Hennessy.

"We're still looking at it," Pownall said, his voice on an even keel.

"Well, I've got to have your final word by noon—twelve-fifteen P.M. at the latest—and you've got to have your board's authority."

"I can't get them together that fast."

"Tom, I told you I would not allow a collision to occur. If I don't hear from you by twelve-fifteen at the latest, I will pursue another course."

"Pownall wondered what Agee had in mind.

"Tom, I'd like to salvage this if there's any way to do that. I just don't believe your board fully understands the situation. You have got to see what's really going on here."

"Bill, we're not off on a sick moose someplace," Pownall said.

By noon, waiting impatiently at the Helmsley Palace, Agee had heard nothing.

"We'll give them another fifteen minutes," he said sheepishly to Al McDonald and Mary. Bruce and Arthur were standing by.

By 12:30 P.M., still not a word. Bill Agee knew that he had reached a moment of decision that would be with him for the rest of his life.

"What are your thoughts?" Bill asked Bruce and Arthur. They were sitting on the couch. Bill got up to stretch his legs. He wandered over to the window. Outside, a *Newsweek* sign atop a building was staring at him. Through the towering buildings, he could see a glimpse of the Hudson River. Closer, a piece of the rink at Rockefeller Plaza.

"Do we or don't we go give up on Martin Marietta? Do we or don't we go forward with Allied?"

Agee came back and sat down on the couch. Mary came and sat down, too. Outwardly calm, Agee was forcing a smile. He looked at a grim-faced Al McDonald. Both men knew. Bill was glad Mary was there. For a moment, not much was said. Agee was gritting his teeth and staring at nothing in particular.

"Bill, Martin Marietta will not be able to vote the stock. They will not be able to take control of Bendix tonight," Arthur Fleischer said. At that very moment, Bendix lawyers in Delaware were preparing to seek a TRO against Marietta. He was certain in light of the Delaware Supreme Court decision that Martin Marietta would not—at the very least—be able to vote the stock. There was also a chance Bendix could stop them cold. "There are some legal options still open. You don't have to take the Allied deal."

"That's right," Wasserstein said. "It's an option, but there is no necessity. But one thing is for sure: Hennessy's eighty dollars a share is a hell of a lot better than Pownall's sixty-five dollars or Gray's sixty-seven dollars. But it's only one option. There are others."

"Excuse me," Bill said to Art and Bruce. He led Mary into

the bedroom. Agee gestured for McDonald to come also. A few minutes later, they emerged.

"I want to go with Allied," Agee announced. "I don't want to preside over a cripple. If we can still win over Marietta by taking control, what have I really won? The combined company will be so weak, somebody will come after us at a lousy price. I don't want to be in that position."

At minutes to 1:00 P.M., Bill Agee got on the telephone with Ed Hennessy.

"Ed, we'll do the deal."

"Welcome aboard."

"Look, I'm gonna send Fleischer and Wasserstein over to you at Skadden to work out the agreement on paper. We've gotta get word out on this. I figure as soon as my board approves, we'll put out a release. Art will talk to Flom about it."

Not long afterward, the phone rang in the suite. Mary answered. It was Tom Pownall. Bill took the phone. Knowing his deadline had passed, Pownall explained that he had tried to call twice. Once the line was busy. The second time, there was no answer.

"Well, we've been here the whole time," Agee said, hiding his disgust.

"I tried to reach you. But look, I've been thinking. What about a straight stock swap? After I buy, I'll give you yours if you give me mine?"

"It's out of my hands," Agee said. "The thing is done."

"What do you mean?"

"I've made other arrangements," Agee said without inflection.

There was a pause.

"Good-bye," Pownall said.

That was it.

Professor Hugo Uyterhoeven had a busy schedule on Wednesday. He had come down to New York from Boston the afternoon before, following classes at Harvard, and stayed at the Essex House on Central Park. In the morning, he had a board meeting of the Schroeder Corporation. At noon, he had the Bendix board meeting.

After the Schroeder meeting, Uyterhoeven jumped into a taxi to return to the Essex to freshen up. Sitting in the back of the cab was the first chance he had had to check the day's story in *The New York Times*. He read Bob Cole's story and was startled by the mention of Mary Cunningham attending strategy meetings.

"She went to Bethesda?" he questioned aloud.

Agee had not mentioned anything to the board about Mary going to the negotiations with Pownall. If it was true, Uyterhoeven thought, Bill has no idea of the damage he is doing to himself. Mary is Bill's blind spot, he thought, not for the first time.

At the GM Building, Uyterhoeven discovered directors Don Rumsfeld, Paul Hartz, and Jonathan Scott in a small room off the boardroom, grabbing a quick lunch out of the buffet spread. Hugo joined them.

"Are we behind schedule?" Uyterhoeven asked.

"Looks that way," Scott said. "Agee is over at the Palace."

"I understand from reading between the lines in the *Times* that Mary went with Bill yesterday," Uyterhoeven said, fixing a sandwich.

"It's unbelievable," Rumsfeld said knowingly.

"The dumbest thing I've ever heard," Hartz said.

"What the hell is going on with Bill?" Uyterhoeven asked.

"I'll tell you one thing," Scott said. "I've got better things to do than sit around here waiting on Bill Agee."

On occasion, many of the directors had shared off-the-cuff sarcastic remarks about Mary's influence on Bill. Uyterhoeven perhaps a year before had counseled Bill to close that chapter of his life after the Mary story had been dragged up again in *Fortune* magazine. "It's better for you. It's better for Mary. And it's better for Bendix," Uyterhoeven had said. For Bill to take Mary to Bethesda seemed like an unconscious act of sabotage.

With the meeting originally scheduled for 12:00 P.M., and his watch pointing to almost 1:45 P.M., Jonathan Scott was getting mad. He had a close relationship with Bill—they had become even closer in the past year. But this kind of delay was hard to swallow.

Donald Rumsfeld passed the time by trying to teach Hugo Uyterhoeven how to play an intricate card game that utilizes two decks of cards—one large and one small.

"I learned this game from a military officer who played it with Winston Churchill," Rumsfeld said.

THIRTY-THREE

After agreeing to sell the Bendix Corporation to Ed Hennessy, Bill Agee wanted some air.

He and Al McDonald decided to decompress by walking from the Helmsley Palace to the GM Building for the seventh board meeting since Bendix initiated its Martin Marietta takeover attempt. That was twenty-nine days ago. The morning's light rain had all but gone from the streets. The two men walked crosstown one block and then turned north up Fifth Avenue past the display windows of F. A. O. Schwarz.

The GM Building had—appropriately enough—a car display on the ground floor. With the Bendix name built on years in the automobile brake business, it seemed only fitting to pass rows of gleaming station wagons and sports cars, all parked on the carpet, before reaching the elevators and the Bendix offices on the twenty-first floor.

When Bill arrived, the directors were anxious to get down to business. It was almost 2:30 P.M. The meeting was already two and a half hours late in starting. Two directors were missing. Jack Fontaine hoped to arrive in time, but Agee doubted he would attend. That morning, Jack had a scheduled board meeting of another company in Miami. Jewel Lafontant was at a spa in Japan.

"As you know," Bill Agee began, addressing the group of ten men seated in the boardroom, "I went down yesterday to Bethesda to meet with Pownall and his people at Martin Marietta. We were down there from perhaps one P.M. until early this morning. I had hoped to talk with their board of directors, but they decided against it. I delivered to Pownall this letter."

Agee read the letter to the directors, who sat passively. Despite his lack of sleep, Agee projected the image of professionalism. Only the monotone of his voice revealed the strain.

"I received this letter back from Pownall. The important passage states: 'The Martin Marietta board finds it impossible to accept your key proposition that no shares of Bendix stock be purchased under the Martin Marietta offer without Bendix's consent.' We made a sincere effort. They refused our terms. As a result, this morning, I have broken off negotiations with Pownall. I think he will pull the trigger at midnight and take down our shares.

"As I have said all along to the board," Agee said with emphasis returning to his voice, "I am determined to avoid a collision that would be detrimental to the interests of our shareholders. I have held discussions with Ed Hennessy from Allied and they have proposed the following transaction."

Agee detailed the terms of the deal. He was looking around the room for Arthur Fleischer, who had been over at Skadden, Arps hammering out the agreement. Fleischer was not yet back.

"Hennessy is waiting for our answer," Agee said, "before filing with the SEC—thereby automatically granting us a ten-day extension of Martin Marietta's offer. It is my feeling that Hennessy will be able to purchase both companies."

Hearing Agee's plan to sell the Bendix Corporation to Allied, the outside directors were stunned. Perhaps no one was more shocked than a tight-lipped William Tavoularas, the president of Mobil. On Thursday, Tavoularas had left for Alaska after a late discussion with Bill Agee. The select committee decided to buy the Martin Marietta Corporation. Now Bill Agee was standing in front of Tavoularas less than a week later saying he was going to sell Bendix. Tavoularas was completely dumbfounded.

"The last meeting I attended," Tav said, with a withering sarcasm, "we were buying Martin Marietta. Now we're selling Bendix to Allied? What the hell happened since last Friday?"

Agee realized his mistake. He had asked Al McDonald to call Tavoulareas and inform him of the new developments in advance of the meeting. Obviously, McDonald had not succeeded. Agee knew Tavoulareas could be a problem. He had no choice but to confront the man head-on.

"Tav, Tom Pownall will not change his mind. We tried. We cannot reach a negotiated settlement. I cannot accept the possibility of Pownall buying Bendix at midnight."

Agee nodded to Arthur Fleischer, who came into the room discreetly and sat down at the other end of the table. Tavoulareas also noted Fleischer's presence.

"What about the courts?" Tav asked. "Weren't we going to stop their ability to vote the shares?"

"We are trying that now," Fleischer said. "I think they will not be able to vote the stock tonight."

"Bill, look, your own legal advisers say that Martin Marietta cannot win in court," Tavoulareas said, peering over his black bifocals. "You got the judge you need. Will the Martin board be able to unseat us, Arthur?"

"No," Fleischer said, uncomfortable to be between the two men.

"So Bill—see—Bendix should pursue buying the rest of Marietta!"

"They may not be able to vote this year," Agee said defensively, "but if they buy Bendix, the resulting combination would be a financial cripple."

Tavoulareas reacted with a stoic face.

"But I thought our objective was to get Martin Marietta. We're in the winning position, right?" Donald Rumsfeld said, jumping in. "That's where we are supposed to be, isn't it?"

"Yes, Rummy," Agee said. "But I also said that another objective was to make sure that in the course of the acquisition we wouldn't end up in a stalemate position."

Several of the directors ganged up on that one.

"But Bill, you told us that if we did end up in a stalemate position, we could work our way out of it."

"Didn't your own bankers say we could get out of the hole?" Tavoulareas asked incredulously.

"Yes, they did say we could work our way out of it. It would cripple both companies, but we could work our way out of it. But as you may remember, I said that was the least desirable of all the alternatives, and if we found ourselves inadvertently there or in the end that was the only option we had left, we could handle it. But it was at the bottom of the list. Going with Allied represents a much better alternative."

Donald Rumsfeld slumped back into his chair.

"Rummy, look," Agee said, "we have two choices—either let Pownall buy the company at seventy-five dollars or sell out to Hennessy at eighty-five dollars. The Bendix shareholders will be better served by the Allied deal."

"We set out to buy Martin Marietta, not sell Bendix," Tavoulareas said.

"Is it true that Citibank is withdrawing the SESSOP shares from the Martin Marietta offer?" Hugo Uyterhoeven asked. The Citibank board had voted the previous day—with Harry Gray out in the hall—to do just that. Agee had not yet told the board about the situation.

"Yes. Hal, correct me if I'm wrong, some four point three million shares will be withdrawn today." Hal Barron nodded.

"So with those gone, will Martin Marietta be able to purchase a majority of Bendix tonight at midnight?" Tavoulareas asked.

"We're estimating forty-four percent," Agee said matter-of-factly. "But that is not the issue. They'll get fifty percent in a matter of days. The point is, are we going to take the reasonable path to enhance our shareholders' value?"

"Unless I'm missing something, you're asking the board to accept an offer that hasn't even been mentioned before this board meeting," Tavoulareas said angrily. Getting a higher price in a sellout was not Tavoulareas's idea of running a company. He thought Agee was pushing the panic button too soon.

Bill Agee worked hard to control his temper.

"It's especially hard to make a difficult decision with a gun to our heads," Uyterhoeven said, examining Agee's face closely for the friendship the two men had developed over the years. "It puts the board in a bad position. When is the latest we can decide this, Bill?"

"Hennessy was clear: We have until five P.M., or the deal's off. He's been pushing me all day. But it's reasonable. They need to get word out. If we don't tell the market, the arbs won't be able to pull out of the Marietta pool before midnight."

"Why doesn't Allied just file a tender offer and that will delay the Marietta buy?" Uyterhoeven asked. Some of the other directors also thought that was the simple alternative.

"Hennessy is not going to commit to anything until he hears that the Bendix board of directors has approved the deal," Agee said.

"Well, I would like to know if the Allied deal makes sense," General Tom Stafford asked.

"This is pretty broad-brush here. What is this bit about us selling them aerospace, no matter what?" the white-haired Bill Purple, head of Bendix aerospace, asked. He was not enjoying his division being the carrot in Agee's deal with Hennessy. Purple could be a coarse, almost abrasive man. "Aerospace is worth more," Purple added.

The price tag of $720 million for the Bendix aerospace outfit was not impressing any of the board members. Hennessy was driving a hard bargain, and many of the directors resented it.

"How can we decide an issue like this under a clock?" Rumsfeld asked.

"I wish I had time to give you," Agee said, letting a trickle of anger wet his voice. "I don't have it to give."

It was obvious that Tavoulareas, Rumsfeld, and Uyterhoeven were against accepting the Allied deal. Cohen—by saying nothing—was suspect. Scott and Stafford also seemed opposed to the deal, or at least opposed to deciding at that minute. Agee didn't have to count the votes to know he was in trouble.

The discussion back and forth could be heard in the hallways of the Bendix offices. Bill Agee's secretary Marie was almost afraid to make more coffee. She had to pass the angry voices from behind the boardroom door.

"Gentlemen, I'm afraid, looking at the time, I have to ask for a vote on the offer of Allied Corporation," Agee said.

With no fanfare, the directors cast their votes. The "ayes" were polled first—Agee, McDonald, Purple, Hartz, and Searby raised their hands. Then those against the motion—Tavoulareas, Rumsfeld, Stafford, Uyterhoeven, and Scott. Five for, five against.

"Wilbur?" Hal Barron, the board secretary, asked.

"I abstain," Wilbur Cohen said meekly.

The motion was deadlocked.

Hugo Uyterhoeven and William Tavoulareas were sitting next to each other. They huddled for a private discussion.

"I think we ought to have an executive session," Tav whispered, adding, "Why don't you ask for it."

"Why don't *you* ask for it," Uyterhoeven came back nervously. "Look, I've got to go to the can. I'll check with Rumsfeld."

Uyterhoeven pushed back his chair and walked to the door, stopping briefly to whisper something to Don Rumsfeld.

When Uyterhoeven returned from the bathroom, only Bill Agee and some of his executives were left in the boardroom. "Where the hell are they?" Uyterhoeven asked a pale Bill Agee.

"They've adjourned in executive session across the hall."

Waiting outside the boardroom was Arthur Fleischer.

"Get me something," Agee said to Fleischer. He needed Allied to sweeten the deal.

Bruce Wasserstein was sitting in the lobby of the Bendix offices with his partner Tony Grassi, waiting to get the nod to address the board. He was checking his watch and wondering what was taking so long. Art Fleischer was on the telephone with Joe Flom, looking for an improvement in the terms of the Bendix-Allied agreement. It was obvious that Agee was in trouble with the board. He needed some flexibility from Hennessy. Flom and Fleischer kicked it around.

Wasserstein was on the phone with Gleacher, discussing the aerospace lockup or "crown jewel" agreement. Bruce talked to Agee. The two men were getting concerned that maybe Hennessy was going to double cross them and end up just taking the lucrative aerospace division.

Both Agee and Wasserstein were also worried about the stock market.

"The arbs don't like the spread of the front and back end of the Allied deal," Wasserstein said. "They think eighty-five to seventy-five dollars isn't enough. I think the arbs are going to stay with Marietta's deal unless it's a bigger spread—something like ninety to seventy dollars."

If the arbitrageurs did not go for the terms of the Allied deal, then nothing but the courts could stop Martin Marietta from buying the Bendix stock.

Bill Agee heaved a big breath and checked his watch. He was determined to make the deadline. Hennessy would not be given any excuse to back out.

Calls were coming in from Skadden, Arps. The lawyers wanted to know when to call the wire services with the announcement. Agee went into the boardroom to wait for his outside directors to reappear. Hal Barron, Paul Hartz, and Fred Searby were with him.

The men were fidgeting, getting up for coffee, laughingly saying that they wished there was something stronger to drink. Agee was pacing back and forth, trying to control his emotions. Time was slipping away. Agee crossed the hall several times during the next half hour, tapping on the door, only to be told by the outside directors that they were not ready.

"If it's a fight they want, I'll give it to them," Agee said angrily to his executives in the boardroom.

Arthur Fleischer had instructed his Fried, Frank partner Steve Fraidin to draft a press release with Joe Flom over at Skadden, Arps. Periodically, while locked out of the Bendix board meeting, Fleischer checked in with Fraidin.

The strategy conceived by the lawyers and blessed by Hennessy was that Bendix would make the announcement of an agreement in principle after the Bendix board had agreed to the deal. That way the arbitrageurs would be given some warning.

"What's happening?" an anxious Steve Fraidin asked.

"I'm not sure I know," Fleischer responded.

"Art, if we're gonna get this thing out in time to do any good, we gotta do it now."

"I'll get back to you," Fleischer said.

Fraidin and Flom were stewing as the time ticked away. The tender offer by the Allied Corporation promised in the press release was conditioned by the requirement that a minimum of 51 percent of Bendix common stock was tendered to Allied. If word was not put out fast, there would be no chance to convince the investing community to withdraw their Bendix stock from the Martin Marietta pool and tender it for a higher price to Allied.

"What are they doing?" Fraidin asked, checking his watch.

Tavoulareas led the five other outside directors back into the boardroom after their private meeting. It was almost 4:30 P.M. Downtown, the Allied board meeting had begun—only to be put on hold waiting to hear from Agee. Fleischer gave Bill the results of his last-minute negotiations with Flom.

"During the executive session," Agee said, "Art and Bruce have been in communication with Allied. Arthur reports that

Hennessy will agree to up the price for the Bendix aerospace lockup option from seven hundred twenty million to eight hundred million."

"Frankly, I am not persuaded by changes in an agreement I have not really had the opportunity to review in full," Tavoulareas said.

"I'm prepared to answer any questions," Agee said.

"Bill, can't you announce simply that you and Hennessy have agreed in principle and that the two respective boards plan to review the proposals?" Uyterhoeven asked.

"You can't expect a reasoned decision under this pressure," Rumsfeld added.

Agee made one final appeal. He thought his best chance was to swing General Stafford or Jonathan Scott, both of whom were personal friends. Scott was involved with Agee in a private investment. Three weeks earlier, a consulting firm owned in part by Stafford was hired by Bendix for "consulting services" at an annual fee of $100,000 plus expenses. Wilbur Cohen was another matter. He looked obviously uncomfortable and refused to raise his eyes as Agee began to speak.

"Let me repeat again: We have no choice in this situation. I apologize for the rush. I know it's unfortunate. But if we are to prevent Martin Marietta from destroying both companies, we have to do it now. I am asking you—as chairman of the board and chief executive officer—to give me this motion!"

Paul Hartz, an inside director, looked at his watch and said, "If we're going to make the five P.M. deadline, we have to vote now. I present the motion to accept the Allied offer."

"I second," said Fred Searby, another inside director.

The roll was called again, with Cohen voting first.

"Abstain," Cohen said in a nervous voice.

Around the room it went. Tavoulareas, Rumsfeld, and Uyterhoeven again voted "No." The deadlock broke when both General Stafford and Jonathan Scott raised their hands to vote "Aye" along with all of the inside directors.

The motion passed. Seven for, three against, one abstention.

At 4:39 P.M., Arthur Fleischer called Steve Fraidin.

"Okay, we've approved the deal," Fleischer said.

"Tough board meeting, eh?" Fraidin said.

"I'll tell you about it."

Joe Flom's secretary immediately placed the phone call to the Dow Jones wire service. Fraidin was handed the telephone, and he sat in Flom's office and read the press release. By the time he was on the fourth paragraph of the release, the flash headline was printing out on the teletype machine in the office and around the country.*

> BENDIX-ALLIED CORP. AGREE TO MERGE
> 4:45 PM EDT SEPT 22-82
> NY—DJ—William Agee, chairman of Bendix Corp. said that Bendix and Allied Corp. have agreed in principle to a merger in which Bendix shareholders will receive cash and securities of Allied.
>
> The transaction has been approved by the Bendix board of directors.
>
> Edward Hennessy, chairman of Allied Corp. said he intends to recommend approval of the transaction to the Allied board at its meeting this afternoon.
>
> Terms of the transaction provide that Allied will commence a tender offer tomorrow for about 13.1 million shares of Bendix common stock for $85 per share in cash.
>
> Hennessy stated that upon completion of the transaction William Agee will become president of Allied and will remain the chairman and chief executive officer of Bendix. Agee and two additional Bendix directors will join the Allied board.

After the vote, there was an awkward silence in the boardroom.

"Bill, I'd like to make a suggestion," General Stafford said, trying to reconcile the fractured Bendix board. "Perhaps an

---

*When Bendix director Paul Hartz looked at his watch prior to the climactic vote, he noted the time as 4:58 P.M. The "down to the wire" aspect of the situation prompted a vivid remembrance of this otherwise unimportant detail.

Paul Hartz was unaware—until informed by the author—that the merger between Allied and Bendix was announced on the Dow Jones newswire at 4:45 P.M.

Despite the discrepancy, Paul Hartz reaffirmed his story.

If Paul Hartz's recollection is accurate, then the announcement of the merger—and approval of its terms by the Bendix board—was actually made thirteen minutes prior to the showdown vote.

outside director could be represented in your continuing discussions with Hennessy? I'd like to suggest Hugo."

"That's all right with me," Agee said, wondering what was up.

"I think we ought to discuss it among the outside directors," Uyterhoeven said.

Again the outside directors filed out of the boardroom across the hall to the smaller side room.

"I don't want to be part of this," Tavoulareas said emphatically.

"You know," Rumsfeld said, not the worse for wear, "when Joe Blow looks at an annual report and sees your name on the board of directors, he is understandably free to think that A, you basically understand what is going on with the company, and B, that you basically agree. Well, at this point, I don't know what the hell is going on, and I sure as hell don't agree. I'm gonna resign."

There were nods from some of the other men.

The outside directors asked Bill to step into their meeting.

"I'm gonna resign, Bill," Donald Rumsfeld said, combing back a sprig of his black, oiled hair. Tavoulareas and Uyterhoeven announced they also were resigning. Agee looked around the room at the other men.

"I don't think I have an alternative," a reluctant Wilbur Cohen said.

Agee was flabbergasted.

"What about you?" he asked first General Stafford, then Jonathan Scott.

Both men were staying on.

For their loyalty, Scott and Stafford would be presented by Agee to Ed Hennessy for positions on the board of directors of Allied.

"I figure we better prepare something for the press," Tavoulareas said.

The directors drafted a two-sentence press release.

"Our concern is that we came to feel that it was difficult for us to function effectively as directors. We have high regard for the Bendix organization and extend our wishes for success in the period ahead."

Back from his meeting in Miami, director Jack Fontaine arrived at the GM Building in time to be told by a flustered Wilbur

Cohen that he had just resigned. Donald Rumsfeld was standing in the hallway, smiling. He had seen so many crises in government, he knew how to deal with the awkwardness. Tavoulareas was all business. Uyterhoeven seemed to stand back.

After completing the press release, the departing directors shook hands with Bill Agee. Uyterhoeven handed the release to Agee's secretary Marie and then shook her extended hand. People were milling in the offices, trying to look inconspicuous.

"Sorry it turned out this way," an angry Hugo Uyterhoeven said to Bill Agee, who had his hands in his pockets and a blank expression on his face.

Then the directors left.

Director Paul Hartz shared a limousine with Hugo Uyterhoeven. Hugo made it plain that outside directors were disgusted with Agee and his handling of the situation.

"If we had the votes," Hugo said, "we would have removed Agee!"

Ed Hennessy was waiting with his directors in the borrowed boardroom at St. Regis Paper. The meeting was resumed when word came that the Bendix directors had agreed to the merger.

Hennessy did not have to wrestle with any of his directors to convince them that buying Bendix at an $80 blended price was a good deal. The board had been through an earlier, unsuccessful bid in the battle between Marathon Oil and Cities Service. This time victory was for the taking.

The board's strategy of turning down the minority investment in Bendix had paid off. Hennessy was congratulated by his directors.

And because of the $6.4 billion conglomerate's tax situation, a huge portion of the $1.9 billion price tag to buy Bendix would be recouped by tax savings kept in the Allied treasury rather than the U.S. Treasury. With more tax credits than he had domestic income to shelter, it was like the government was giving Hennessy $400 million to buy Bendix.

"At this stage of the game," Ed told the board, "we've announced the deal. The arbs have until midnight to pull out of the Marietta pool and tender their shares to us."

SEC rules dictated that an Allied tender offer filed with the SEC would automatically delay the Martin Marietta offer by ten days. Bill Agee expected Hennessy to direct his lawyers to file

PETER F. HARTZ

the necessary documents. However, Hennessy was not so certain.

After the run-around both Eric Gleacher and Hennessy had experienced with Agee and Bruce Wasserstein, Hennessy's attitude was "I'm not gonna do a damn thing until they sit still and agree to the deal."

By 4:40 P.M.—with only twenty minutes to go before the SEC deadline—Hennessy entertained briefly an outlandish suggestion from his general counsel, Brian Forrow.

"The law says we have to put our materials in the mail, right? Maybe we could gain some time by mailing from Hawaii?"

The idea was dismissed as unworkable.

"Ah, to hell with it," Hennessy said, convinced that if Agee was granted another ten days' reprieve, the deal would evaporate. Hennessy wanted Bendix now.

Joe Flom and Eric Gleacher and his people were on the telephones talking to the arbitrageurs and the big institutional holders of Bendix stock. Flom called a friend, Bob Greenhill, an arb from Morgan, Stanley. Gleacher's people talked with Ivan Boesky and the other prominent names on a prominent list. These were the men who controlled the big blocks of Bendix stock. Whichever way they went, the deal went.

"There's gonna be more cash up front than under the Marietta deal, and overall you've got a higher value of pullout," Gleacher said.

"You're offering eighty-five front end and seventy-five back end, right?" an arb said.

"Right."

"I don't think that's a big enough spread to make me pull out of the Marietta pool. Maybe if it was ninety front and seventy back. But I've already made money on both sides of this transaction. Why should I hassle a few more dollars?"

The more the Allied team polled the arbs, the shakier it seemed that the big money would pull out of the Martin Marietta deal. Looking ahead on how the whole situation would change at midnight, when Tom Pownall bought the Bendix shares, there was really only one place to turn.

"We should go down to Bethesda," Gleacher told Hennessy.

"Ed, Tom Pownall and I are friends. I'd be willing to take you down. I've got my jet parked over at Newark," Allied board member Paul Thayer said. Hennessy knew Pownall, but not well.

"Let's give him a call," Hennessy said.

* * *

In Bethesda, Marty Siegel was on the phone with his office. Kidder, Peabody sources were hearing rumors from friends on the street that Lehman Brothers was polling the arbs to find out what it was going to take to get them to withdraw their shares from the Martin Marietta offer.

It was all beginning to make sense.

Allied Corporation had halted its trading on the NYSE at 2:22 P.M. And there were stories on the wire with sources quoted as saying "It's all over" and "Bendix is very pleased."

Siegel placed a call to Eric Gleacher at Lehman. The two men were friendly, their acquaintance built on the relationship between their wives. The two women had gone to Columbia Business School together. Gleacher was unavailable. Marty left a message.

"Tom, we've got to get word out that we're buying at midnight, or everybody is going to come out of the pool," Marty Siegel said to Pownall.

Given the go-ahead, Siegel called his office in New York and instructed a partner, Dick Wittig, in corporate finance, to get every available body and put them on the phones.

"Tell the institutions and the arbs that a bird in the hand is better than one in the bush," Siegel said. "Tell them they can have messengers at the bank tonight to pick up payments."

Siegel turned to Dick Katcher, Kidder, Peabody's lawyer, and asked him to start drafting a release to that effect. Siegel was pacing, walking in and out of the office where the Dow Jones teletype machine stood. He knew that sometime soon there would be news.

If he got lucky, Allied could save Martin Marietta.

The Martin Marietta board of directors were gathered in the conference room on the third floor of the executive wing. The meeting was scheduled to begin at 5:00 P.M. Tom Pownall came into the room with Charlie Leithauser and the advisers. Siegel came in suddenly and handed a piece of paper to Pownall.

"An announcement has just come over the wire service," Pownall said. "Bill Agee says that Bendix and the Allied Corporation have agreed in principle to a merger. The Bendix board has approved. This says the Allied board is meeting now."

The directors were completely baffled. Pownall passed the press release around the room.

"The Allied offer is supposed to begin tomorrow," Pownall said.

"How does this affect our actions?" a director asked, noting that the wire service report indicated that Allied was going to pay $85 cash for 55 percent of the Bendix stock. In a matter of hours, Martin Marietta intended to pay $75 per share for up to 51 percent of Bendix stock.

Somebody's arithmetic was way off.

"We've been assessing that since we heard Allied trading was stopped," Pownall said. "But from what the lawyers tell me, if Allied files their tender offer right quick tonight, it's a whole new ball game. It would put off our ability to buy for at least ten days."

"We've got a man down at the SEC in Washington," Bob Fullem said. "We ought to get a call from him momentarily."

During the afternoon on Wednesday, as later reported in *The New York Times,* I. Kenneth Bloomberg, a twenty-two-year-old paralegal from Dewey, Ballantine, waited in the file room of the Securities and Exchange Commission in Washington for news about the rumored tender offer by Allied Corporation for Bendix.

At 5:30 P.M., Bloomberg left the SEC Building and went to a telephone.

"Nothing was filed," Bloomberg said.

"Nothing?" Leonard Larrabee asked.

The Allied tender offer to buy the Bendix Corporation— announced on the wire services—had not been filed.

"Oh, jeez, they really screwed up this one," Larrabee told Bob Fullem.

With the deadline for purchasing the Bendix shares only six hours away, Larrabee could not understand why Allied and Bendix had inexplicably missed an opportunity to stop the Martin Marietta offer.

"What the heck is going on?" Fullem asked, completely baffled.

Siegel came into the boardroom again to announce that a story had just run on the tape that the Allied board had approved the purchase of Bendix.

"That press release is just ridiculous now!" a director said. "They're gonna make a tender offer starting tomorrow for fifty-five percent of Bendix, and we're gonna buy up to fifty-one percent tonight? How can that be?"

Tom Pownall's presentation to the board was interrupted by another message.

"Ed Hennessy from Allied is on the phone."

Pownall excused himself from the boardroom to take the phone call. But it wasn't Hennessy on the line; it was Paul Thayer in New York.

"Hey, ol' buddy, I'm here with Ed Hennessy and we've made a little deal up here today with Bendix, and I think it might be advisable if we get together and talk about it."

"I think that's a capital idea," Pownall said, a smile in his voice.

"Well, let me put Ed on here, and you and he can work out the timing."

The two men worked out the schedule. Hennessy would fly down in Thayer's plane and be in Washington by about 8:30 P.M. Pownall would send a car to pick them up at the airport.

"Hennessy is coming down," Pownall told his bewildered board of directors. "Let's recess until 10:30 P.M. At that time, I will apprise the board of my discussions with Ed Hennessy, and we will review the legal situation and then determine where we stand."

THIRTY-FOUR

Wilmington, Delaware, is a small, pleasant train-stop city downriver from Philadelphia. The courthouse commands Caesar Rodney Square in downtown Wilmington. Caesar Rodney Square was named after the man who rode nonstop from Dover to Philadelphia to cast the deciding vote in the Delaware delegation to the Constitutional Convention.

This one was going down to the wire, too.

For several weeks, the Bendix and Martin Marietta lawyers had crossed the square and mounted the steps of the courthouse to argue before Chancellor Grover C. Brown. Martin Marietta's lawyer, Frank Balotti, a good-natured man, five feet, ten inches tall, glasses, and thinning brown hair, had filed suit against the Bendix special stockholders' meeting. He lost. Then appealed to the Delaware Supreme Court. There he lost again.

"A gratuitous tomahawk in my back!" is the way the forty-year-old Delaware attorney described the Delaware Supreme Court ruling against his client, Martin Marietta. The language about a "moral duty" owed Bendix was the sharpest part. It cut to the quick.

The Bendix lawyers in Delaware were instructed to go for broke. Art Fleischer and his head litigator, Marc Cherno, had decided that since Bendix had received the favorable decision from the Delaware Supreme Court, they would go back to the Chancellery Court before Judge Brown and seek what they could not get in Maryland: a temporary restraining order to prevent Martin Marietta from taking down the Bendix shares at midnight.

During the day on Wednesday, while Fleischer was in New York with Bill Agee, Bendix lawyer Dick Sutton, from the prestigious Delaware firm of Morris, Nichols, Arsht & Tunnell, argued forcefully before Chancellor Brown that Martin Marietta should not be allowed to buy the Bendix shares because they could not exercise voting control of the stock.

Sutton pointed to Title VIII, Section 160(c) of Delaware corporate law, which he argued prevented Martin Marietta from voting any shares it may buy of Bendix because Bendix already owned a majority of Martin Marietta.

"If they can't vote, the act of purchasing the shares, Chancellor, becomes at best an unnecessary and, hence, wasteful act or, at worst, a vindictive or damn-the-torpedoes act," Sutton said.

The argument went back and forth between Dick Sutton and Frank Balotti. For his part, Balotti handed up to Chancellor Brown a copy of Section 2509 of the Maryland corporation law. He argued that if Martin Marietta could not vote, then Bendix could not either, because after midnight, Martin Marietta would own a majority of Bendix.

Chancellor Brown held up his hand.

"We ought to quit now. I will go look at it, and as fast as I can, come up with a decision as to what I think has to be done tonight. I will give you a call. We will find a place to assemble. Thank you, gentlemen."

A light drizzle was falling over Caesar Rodney Square.

At shortly before 8:00 P.M., Chancellor Brown called Frank Balotti. The chancellor, a man of considerable comprehension, also had a touch of poetry in him. He had been searching for a figure of speech to cover the enormity of his decision: One way or another, his order would affect how billions of dollars would be spent.

"Frank, why don't we just meet out under the Madonna so this thing will be blessed," the chancellor said, referring to a large statue in Charles Park, just off the square. "Come on over to my office in twenty minutes and I'll have an order."

The two armies met for the decision. Bob Myers was there

from Dewey, Ballantine, along with Balotti. Gerry Goldman from Hughes, Hubbard was there with Dick Sutton. Despite the combat, or perhaps because of it, the lawyers were at ease with each other, glad a decision was in.

Chancellor Brown was also relaxed, wearing a bright yellow pullover sweater and smoking a cigar. The men all sat around a conference table.

"Gentlemen," the chancellor said, holding his cigar low, "I have decided to allow Martin Marietta to proceed with its plan to buy Bendix stock. However, I am restraining and enjoining the same party from voting any Bendix stock that it owns and from otherwise attempting to exercise any rights of a voting Bendix stockholder."

Martin Marietta could buy but not take control.

As the lawyers were leaving Chancellor Brown's chambers on the ground floor of the court building, Dick Sutton and the Bendix lawyers were all smiles. Sutton had validated Arthur Fleischer's reading of the law.

"Well, how can you guys buy now that you can't vote—what's the sense?" Sutton asked.

Frank Balotti shrugged his shoulders.

When Bob Myers returned with Frank Balotti to his office, Myers put in a call to his partner Bob Fullem, who was at Martin Marietta headquarters.

"Bob, how would you feel about being able to buy but not vote?" Myers asked his senior partner.

"I'll take it," Fullem said, getting excited.

"Well, you got it."

Both men knew that the immediate issue was buying. They would deal in court later with the issue of voting.

"The Bendix lawyers down here think that they won. They think we will never buy because we can't vote the damn stuff," Myers said.

"What the hell do they know anyway?" Fullem asked, laughing. "I've got one for you. Ed Hennessy from Allied is on his way down here now to negotiate something with Pownall."

"For what?"

"Probably some kind of swap with us. Maybe we can't vote the Bendix shares, but nobody said Hennessy couldn't."

"What's happening in Maryland?" Myers asked.

"The appeal is scheduled to start before Judge Winter soon," Fullem said. The last-minute Bendix appeal to Judge Winter in Maryland was the final hurdle.

On Paul Thayer's LTV Corporation jet on the way down to Washington, Ed Hennessy was considering his options. Accompanying him were Joe Flom, his lawyer from Skadden, Arps; Eric Gleacher from Lehman Brothers; and Paul Thayer, Allied director and head of LTV.

Both Flom and Gleacher felt that if Hennessy wanted to be really tough, he could acquire both Martin Marietta and Bendix.

"It's a financial nightmare for both of them. They'll look for any way out that will keep them from being locked in a death embrace, waiting for the courts to separate them," Gleacher said.

"Martin Marietta is seventy percent pregnant now," Flom said.

Hennessy knew Agee wanted him to get both companies. But Hennessy was thinking. If Pownall spends the $900 million to take down the Bendix shares, Allied is then looking at assuming the enormous debts of both Tom Pownall and Bill Agee. And Pownall had borrowed the money at expensive short-term rates. The debt load would be almost $3 billion.

"That's one hell of a number to carry," Hennessy said. As an aggressive businessman who had done a slew of acquisitions since coming to Allied from United Technologies, Hennessy was tempted. He would do the whole package if he could convince Pownall not to spend the money. Then it made exquisite sense.

"If Tom will do this on a friendly basis, fine. But I don't think he's gonna do it that way."

Paul Thayer agreed. Pownall was determined. Martin Marietta was not going to sell itself to anyone.

"Then we could do a swap," Joe Flom said. "We'll give them the Martin stock that Bendix owns and get from them the Bendix stock that they'll take down tonight. But if we take that approach, pricing is going to be the whole game."

"We'll do it at cost," Hennessy said. "That way nobody gets cute."

"I'm sure they'll ask for a premium," Flom said.

When they landed at National Airport, the Butler Aviation

terminal was almost empty, except for Alexander Haig, the former Secretary of State and president of United Technologies. As usual, Haig was impeccably dressed, with starched shirt and stickpin collar.

"What are you doing with all those people up in Hartford?" Haig asked, referring to Harry Gray and United Technologies. "You got them in turmoil, Ed."

Haig knew there was no love lost between Hennessy and Gray.

"You've heard what's happening?" Ed asked.

"Yes. Congratulations."

Hennessy felt uncomfortable chitchatting. He wondered if Haig would be on the phone to Harry Gray the moment they parted company.

Pownall had promised a car would meet them. Mistakenly, the Marietta car went to Dulles International Airport. Hennessy and Thayer flew into National Airport. Tired of waiting, they hailed a cab.

Judge Harrison Winter of the U.S. Court of Appeals for the Fourth Circuit had returned from his judicial conference in Washington troubled by what was about to happen in the Bendix vs. Martin Marietta takeover struggle. He had already overruled Federal District Judge Young once in this case, and that was a prospect he did not look forward to again. But having read the briefs of both counsels and having examined in detail Young's decision and a Delaware Supreme Court order in the matter from the day before, Judge Winter found his upcoming decision a heavy mantle to wear.

The meeting was scheduled for 8:30 P.M. Bendix lawyers Marc Cherno, Alex Sussman, and John Henry Lewin met Martin Marietta counsel George Beall and his partner Mark Treanor at the locked glass doors leading into the judge's chambers on the ninth floor of the Federal Courthouse in Baltimore. TV cameras mounted above the doors monitored the lawyers. The judge's clerk buzzed the lawyers in.

It was obvious from the tight-lipped expressions on the attorneys' faces that there was considerable tension. So much was at stake. Marc Cherno shook George Beall's hand.

The men were ushered into Judge Winter's conference

room, where His Honor was already seated at the table. Without formality, the men took available chairs.

"Gentlemen, I know it's late. What say we begin."

"Your Honor," John Henry Lewin said, "I would like to bring to your attention a recent development."

Figuring it was better that he announce it first rather than wait for George Beall to use it to his advantage, Lewin explained to Judge Winter that at close to 5:00 P.M., Bendix had announced an agreement in principle to merge with the Allied Corporation. To Lewin's surprise, George Beall did not react to his announcement in an adversarial way.

"All right, gentlemen, I'm sure we will discuss this development during the course of arguments, but let us proceed to the matters at hand. Bendix is before me on an appeal of a decision by Judge Young dated late this morning in which he denies a Bendix motion for a preliminary injunction preventing Martin Marietta from proceeding with its intent to purchase Bendix shares tonight."

"Less than four hours from now, Your Honor," George Beall said.

"Thank you. Mr. Lewin, who would you have begin?"

"I will, Your Honor," Marc Cherno said. "If I might just state a simple fact to begin with: Bendix is the owner of seventy percent of the available shares of the Martin Marietta Corporation. That underpins all of our discussion. Our point is really quite simple. These two giant corporations are sure to be combined. Both managements have stated that is their desire. All of Martin Marietta's actions have assumed there would be a combination.

"The plain wish of the majority owner of Martin Marietta— the Bendix Corporation—is that this combination be carried out in a way that results in a strong and financially viable commercial entity. Bendix has spent one billion dollars to reach this goal.

"As you have read in our papers, the Delaware Supreme Court has ruled that Martin Marietta owes a moral duty to Bendix, its majority shareholder. We are asking Your Honor to overturn Judge Young's decision and enforce the fiduciary obligations of the Martin Marietta management.

"For Martin Marietta to pursue their tender offer is a violation of the duty they owe to Bendix. And what purpose would it serve? A combination of the companies is a foregone conclusion. They would spend a billion dollars for what? To preserve their management positions? What could possibly be their reasons? The only result will be a financial disaster of unprecedented proportions."

"Your Honor," George Beall said, "last week, when we were before Judge Young trying to stop Bendix from buying our shares, Bendix argued eloquently that the matter must be decided in the marketplace and that the courts should stay out of this. Now that they have succeeded in buying seventy percent of Martin Marietta, they wanted Judge Young to reverse that policy and protect their investment. Judge Young said 'No.' He refused to have the court drawn into the middle. Now, they say, intervene.

"Your Honor, the marketplace should be allowed to work. And seventy-five percent of the Bendix stockholders have tendered their shares to the Martin Marietta offer. Those people believe in what Martin Marietta is doing."

"The board of directors of one corporation owes no fiduciary duty to the shareholders of another corporation," Lewin interjected. "They owe their duty to the shareholders of their own company. The Marietta directors owe their duty to the wishes of the Bendix Corporation, their majority shareholder."

"Your Honor," Bendix attorney Alex Sussman interjected, "I think it is important to understand the consequences of your decision. We have presented a financial analysis of this merger —whatever the outcome, either under the terms of the Bendix offer or under the terms of the Martin Marietta offer. If they are allowed to proceed, this will be a catastrophe for everyone.

"Under the Bendix proposal, stockholder equity would be one point eight billion dollars. Under the Marietta proposal, stockholder equity would be six hundred twenty-two million dollars. Long-term debt will be forty percent greater under their plan. The company would be lucky to survive."

"I do find this most disturbing," Judge Winter said, looking worried. "Why would they do this? Why would rational businessmen do this?"

George Beall had a terrible feeling in the pit of his stomach. His own arguments seemed useless.

"Your Honor, under the Business Judgment Rule, it is not your responsibility to supplant your opinions for those of the management of Martin Marietta."

"They better have a damn good reason to justify killing this company," Cherno said, getting mad and sensing his advantage.

George Beall was getting scared. Sitting across from Judge Winter, he could feel his case slipping away. Just as he was feeling more and more deflated, it was obvious that the judge was becoming more impressed with the Bendix arguments. Beall had one more card to play.

"Now, Your Honor, what about this announcement of the entrance of the Allied Corporation? That changes the entire equation. They intend to commence a tender offer for Bendix tomorrow. Once that happens, that would extend the withdrawal period of the Martin Marietta offer. If you prevent us from buying tonight and Allied makes its offer, the horses would be out of the barn and it would be very, very difficult for Martin Marietta to get them back again."

"I am sympathetic to that problem," Judge Winter said. "Perhaps I could freeze the withdrawal rights."

Beall was now getting desperate. He resorted to a procedural argument.

"Your Honor, as a single federal judge, even if you were thinking of reversing Judge Young and getting into the issue of withdrawal rights, you as a lone judge do not have the authority. You can't do that. . . ."

"I could convene a panel. I could sit on the panel and I could recruit two other judges. We could hold a session within a couple of days."

"Oh, Christ," George Beall thought, "if he delays this thing beyond midnight, all is lost." If Martin Marietta did not buy tonight, then the Allied Corporation when it bought Bendix would automatically become the owner of Martin Marietta.

"Allied is not a party that is before you," Beall said. "All of the Bendix shareholders that have tendered to our offer are standing in line before Allied! You can't do this."

The lawyers argued back and forth. Finally, Judge Winter decided that he needed time alone to deliberate.

"Gentlemen, I would like to take a recess. I think that the arguments presented by Mr. Cherno and Mr. Sussman are interesting arguments. They are significant arguments. As I say, I could grant a stay and convene a panel of judges to consider this further—I'm sure by Friday—but I'm gonna try to figure out whether I can do anything here, whether I have the power to do anything here.

"You can all go off down the hall and use the men's room,

but I don't want anyone making or taking phone calls. Is that understood?"

"Yes, Your Honor," a confident Marc Cherno said.

Ed Hennessy had the cab driver take them to the front door of the Martin Marietta corporate headquarters. Security lights lit up the grounds. The Allied team was met by Tom Pownall, who gave a big smile to Paul Thayer and then shook Ed Hennessy's hand.

They filed into the elevator, trying to make believe this was just a visit among friends. The mix-up at the airport was finally understood.

"Ed, you should congratulate us for having controlled the Bendix stockholders' meeting today," Pownall said. "One of our guys chaired it, and the amendments were defeated."

Both men knew that if the Bendix amendments had passed, the fortune and fate of Martin Marietta would not be subject to negotiations. And Bill Agee would not have had to make a deal with Allied.

"We've got Bendix under control," Hennessy said. Pownall did not even ask Hennessy for a description of the terms of the agreement between Allied and Bendix. It did not matter. The only thing that mattered was that more than likely—when all the paperwork was completed—the way things stood, Allied would own 70 percent of Martin Marietta.

"I understand from the release Agee is to be president of Allied."

"Yeah, but no one at Allied or Martin Marietta will report to him," Hennessy said with a smile. A skillful player, Hennessy had ensured Bill Agee's cooperation by offering him a big job at Allied; but just as skillfully, Hennessy was prepared to isolate Agee in his new position and deprive him of any real power outside of Bendix's operations.

"Agee will help me get a hold on Bendix," Hennessy said.

Don Rauth, the retiring chairman of Martin Marietta, had a conference room attached to his office that was called "the barn." The walls were decorated with barn siding and fake red bricking. It was an inner sanctum. That's where Tom Pownall took Ed Hennessy, Paul Thayer, Joe Flom, and Eric Gleacher. On his side, Pownall had Frank Menaker, Bob Fullem, and Marty Siegel.

"So what are you gonna do about midnight tonight?" Hennessy asked.

"Ed, our board meets in about an hour, and they are going to confirm our purchase of the Bendix stock, and we will buy it sometime between midnight and a minute after."

"Are you sure you wanna do that?"

"Yup. We're gonna own fifty percent of Bendix tonight," Pownall said.

"You're kinda fixed on that, are you?"

"It's not something we started out to do thirty days ago, but that's where we are. That's exactly what we're going to do."

"What do you propose?" Hennessy asked.

"A swap."

"Okay, let's see if we can make that hang together," Hennessy said.

With a growing number of lawyers and advisers in the room and conversations spreading, Joe Flom suggested that Eric Gleacher and Marty Siegel meet separately and discuss the deal. The two bankers went into an adjacent office. Siegel remained standing, leaning against a file cabinet.

"What's this about a tender offer for Bendix?" Siegel asked teasingly, adding with bravado, "We want a premium for the Bendix stock—eighty-five dollars a share, what you say you're gonna pay Agee."

"That's yesterday's deal," Gleacher said with a laugh, remembering Flom's prediction on the plane. "I'll give you cost."

The two men negotiated for less than fifteen minutes. Siegel gave up pretty quickly. The swap would be at cost.

Joe Flom came in followed by Dick Katcher to see how the discussions were going. Gleacher held his calculator in his hands, working out the numbers.

"We will need a stand-still," Siegel said, knowing that at cost, even after the swap, Allied would own almost forty percent of the Martin Marietta stock and Pownall could not afford to buy it all back.

"I'll give you a real stand-still," Flom said. "What do you want?"

"Ten years," Dick Katcher said.

"Fine."

Experienced dealmakers, Joe Flom and Bob Fullem wrapped

all the individual discussions together into the framework of an agreement. Fullem came out of the meeting in the barn to speak with his partner Leonard Larrabee.

"Len, draft a press release that could serve as a memo of intent," Fullem said, detailing the basic points while Larrabee wrote them down. Both Fullem and Flom went back into the meeting between Hennessy and Pownall, and Larrabee set to work. After a series of editorial changes suggested by Flom, the release was shown to both Hennessy and Pownall. Both men agreed.

"Yup, that's our deal," Tom Pownall said.

"We've got to go through the courtesies of presenting this to Agee and packaging it in a way that would be the least embarrassment all the way around," Hennessy said.

While Hennessy and Pownall were talking, their advisers were keeping a close watch on developments. Frank Menaker and the team from Dewey, Ballantine were nervously awaiting word of the appeal in Baltimore. Joe Flom and Eric Gleacher were discreetly staying in touch with New York, monitoring the Martin Marietta stock pool to see if the arbs were indeed staying in. Flom was also waiting to hear about Baltimore. He knew if Judge Young was overturned by Judge Winter—as had happened before—it would be a new ball game.

The thirty minutes that George Beall spent in the corridor outside Judge Winter's offices seemed like an eternity. Beall felt like this was the lowest point of his career. And what made it worse was he could not call Myers or Fullem or Larrabee to talk it over. There was no one he could ask for a miracle solution. Winter seemed to be looking for a way to overrule Judge Young.

Beall talked in a low mumble with his partner Mark Treanor. The Bendix team was loud. Marc Cherno was pacing, glancing at the phone messages a clerk had handed him. New York was calling. Delaware was calling. Under the judge's orders, all Cherno could do was turn the slips of paper in his hands and wait.

"I bet this one is Chancellor Brown preventing them from voting," Cherno said, showing the simple phone-message slip to Sussman.

"Jesus, what's taking so much time?" one of the attorneys asked.

"He's gotta be writing something," Cherno said.

The time ticked by slowly, more slowly than any of the men would have thought possible. Finally the judge's clerk appeared and called them in.

"Gentlemen, this has not been easy. I would like to walk you through my thinking. The first question I have to decide is do I have the power as a single judge to do anything? I have concluded that this is an emergency situation and there is not enough time to convene a panel. The monkey is on my back. The second question is whether Judge Young in denying Bendix any relief was correct or not."

Winter impressed the attorneys with his slow deliberateness and grasp of the issues. He turned his opinion slowly, without betraying what his final decision was. It was as if he had not yet decided.

"Had I been standing in Judge Young's shoes I would no doubt have looked at this situation differently, but as an appellate judge my function is different from a district judge. I can only reverse Judge Young when I find there was no basis for his ruling. I cannot say that Judge Young's findings of fact are clearly erroneous. Therefore, I hereby deny the Bendix appeal."

When George Beall heard those words, it was a huge weight off his shoulders. He emerged with a broad smile on his face from Winter's chambers followed by the other attorneys. When the group rounded the corner, heading for the elevators, they were engulfed by a crowd of perhaps twenty-five people—lawyers representing the arbitrageurs, newspaper reporters from the *Baltimore Sun* and other papers, national papers such as *The Wall Street Journal.* The scene was a madhouse as the onlookers tried to grab the lawyers to find out what had happened.

"What did the judge do? What did he rule?" was the cry from the reporters and arbs' reps. People were shouting and shoving as the elevator doors opened.

"George, how did it go?" Tommy Houston asked. He had known Beall for years. His client, arbitrageur Ivan Boesky, wanted to know badly. "Just a little hint? You look to me like you're smiling, George."

"The judge instructed us to say nothing until he issued his opinion."

"I can see you smiling," Houston said as the elevator doors shut.

When the Martin Marietta board reconvened, the arrangement with Allied was explained to the board primarily by Charlie Leithauser and Marty Siegel. Frank Menaker and Bob Fullem told the directors that the legal issues blocking their decision to buy Bendix had been removed.

Judge Young's decision in Maryland had withstood the Bendix appeal.

Chancellor Brown in Delaware had denied a Bendix request for a temporary restraining order.

And finally, Martin Marietta had found a way around Judge Anna Diggs Taylor in Michigan.

"Our lawyers in Michigan have won on appeal to the Sixth Circuit," a proud Bob Fullem said. "Bendix has been prevented from proceeding in Oakland court to enforce the Michigan takeover act. It's full steam ahead."

It was obvious from the handshakes all the way around the room that the Allied deal was considered an unexpected salvation by the directors. When put to a vote, the deal was adopted with acclaim.

The men were on their feet.

It almost looked as if they intended to put Tom Pownall on their shoulders and march around the room.

"Let's have a drink!" Tom Pownall said.

The barn had a well-stocked bar. Some champagne was uncorked. Pownall introduced Ed Hennessy to the directors. Griffin Bell and Gene Zuckert were overjoyed at the outcome. The men stood around, glasses in hand, congratulating each other.

"I've never seen a group of happier individuals in my life," Fullem said to Larrabee.

Jack Byrne wore a huge smile, but all the same, he did not really feel like celebrating. Tomorrow morning, he realized, the Martin Marietta Corporation was going to wake up with a splitting headache—an 85 percent debt-to-equity ratio. There would have to be a feverish scramble by Tom Pownall and his management team to cover their debts. Large chunks of the business would have to be sold off. Independence would carry an enormous price tag. Holy sakes, Byrne thought, how in the world are we gonna get out of this thing?

Byrne looked at Marty Siegel. Siegel was being congratulated by the board of directors and Martin Marietta management.

"Brilliant! Simply brilliant!" several directors shouted, toasting the investment banker.

Byrne was thinking. Every innovative tactic tried by Siegel had failed. The countertender. The agreement with Harry Gray. The waiving of all but two conditions. All were designed to make Bill Agee back off. Siegel had come within hours of being the goat. Now, thanks to Ed Hennessy, he was the hero.

Byrne knew the vagaries of luck count, too.

"Marty," Byrne said, raising his own glass.

THIRTY-FIVE

On the third floor of the Citibank building on Water Street at the tip of Manhattan, Bob Powell and Tom Mendenhall were nervously reviewing their task with a Citibank official—a brogue-talking Irishman named Farrell. There was a small waiting room facing a cage of tellers' windows, and behind that a large room with a sea of desks separated by waist-high partitions. Men waiting to be paid were milling around in the assigned area.

"What's the time?" Bob Powell asked.

"Eleven fifty-three," a man from Citibank said. His black Casio watch was designated as the official time. The countdown was begun. Tom Mendenhall was on the phone with Charlie Leithauser in Bethesda.

At seconds after midnight, Citibank employee Farrell in his thick accent said to Bob Powell: "You have been tendered eight million, nine hundred eighty-eight thousand, nine hundred twelve shares of Bendix Corporation common stock."

"I accept for payment eight million, nine hundred eighty-eight thousand, nine hundred twelve shares," Powell said. The two men signed off the documents. A notary public affixed his seal.

"We bought the stock," Mendenhall said to Leithauser on

the telephone. In the background, Mendenhall could hear a loud and blowsy cheer go up from the people at Martin Marietta headquarters. Mendenhall suddenly felt as if he had just leaped off a bridge. The water below was coming up fast.

Having done their job, Mendenhall and Powell decided to leave. The two men were quiet. For Mendenhall, the excitement was in raising the almost $1 billion, not in spending it. They worked their way through the crowd of scruffy messengers in the hallway waiting to pick up checks. It was another big payday for the arbitrageurs.

"Now I gotta talk to Bill," Hennessy said. "I don't think he'll like what we've done here." Hennessy smiled. Pownall smiled.

Hennessy left at about 2:30 A.M. with Joe Flom and Eric Gleacher. They went out to Dulles, where an Allied plane was waiting to fly them to Morristown. Flom and Gleacher went back to New York by limo. Hennessy went home and tried to lay down for a while. Unable to sleep, he got up and took a shower. The meeting with Bill Agee was set for 8:00 A.M. at the GM Building on Fifth Avenue.

At 4:00 A.M., Eric Gleacher went to the Skadden, Arps offices where Morris Kramer was still working on details of the deal Gleacher had phoned in. Hennessy wanted some answers before the meeting with Agee.

At 7:00 A.M., Gleacher was at his East Side apartment near Fifth Avenue and Ninety-fifth Street. As usual, his two black Labrador dogs slept at the foot of the bed. When the phone rang, the dogs barked, waking Gleacher and his wife, Annie. It was Ed Hennessy.

"Oh, Ed, God, I must have slept through my alarm," Gleacher said.

"How do the numbers look?" Hennessy asked, his voice bright and crisp.

"The numbers look good," Gleacher said, reviewing the results accumulated a couple of hours before.

"Give one of Agee's guys a call and tell them what's going on," Hennessy said. "See you in an hour."

Gleacher called Bruce Wasserstein at his apartment.

"Hey, here's what happened. We went down to Bethesda last night," Gleacher said.

"You did *what*?" Wasserstein asked incredulously. He realized Hennessy had done an end-around.

"Since they bought Bendix last night," Gleacher said, "Hennessy is going to withdraw the deal we worked out with you yesterday."

"So where are we?" Wasserstein asked. The way it stood, Bendix owned Martin Marietta, and Martin Marietta owned Bendix.

"We still want to make the deal with you, but this is the twist now: If Agee agrees to a merger with Allied, then Pownall will sell Hennessy all the Bendix stock he's got in exchange for a percentage of the Martin Marietta stock owned by Bendix."

"Pownall will take a walk?" Wasserstein asked.

"Yeah. But Hennessy will still have almost forty percent of Marietta stock."

"What about the remaining Bendix stock still in the hands of the Bendix employees?" Wasserstein asked.

"That's what we'll talk about this morning," Gleacher said.

"Well, we're gonna want a lot of money."

"C'mon, Bruce, there's no place for you to go. We've now made a deal to buy half Bendix at seventy-five dollars. If we wanted to play hardball, we could stick to seventy-five for the back end."

The original deal was for $85 cash for a majority of Bendix and a package of Allied securities for the remaining shares. The blended price was $80 per share.

"We're gonna be tough," Wasserstein said.

Just before daybreak on Thursday, September 23, it rained very hard, and in less than ten minutes the clouds broke. The streetlights were still on at the edges of Central Park. Yellow cabs hurtled by the GM Building, enjoying for the last few minutes the open lanes of Fifth Avenue.

Hennessy's lawyer Morris Kramer had not slept. He arrived early at the GM Building for the 8:00 A.M. meeting between Ed Hennessy and Bill Agee. When Al McDonald arrived, Kramer was waiting by the glass and metal front door of the Bendix offices on the twenty-first floor. Within minutes, the full complement of Allied advisers—Joe Flom; Eric Gleacher; and Tom Hill, from Lehman Brothers—arrived. In came Bill Agee, followed by Bruce Wasserstein and Arthur Fleischer.

When Ed Hennessy arrived, looking tired, accompanied by

the towering Hal Buirkle and Allied's general counsel, Brian
Forrow, the coffee was already up. The group of lawyers, bankers, and businessmen followed each other into the Bendix conference room. The Bendix board of directors was scheduled to
meet at 10:00 A.M. Bill Agee and Ed Hennessy had alot of
negotiations to complete before then.

Hennessy gave Bill Agee the memo of intent he had agreed
to with Tom Pownall ten hours earlier in Bethesda. Agee read
the sheet, sitting quietly in his chair. Hennessy watched his
reaction carefully.

Agee knew he had been outmaneuvered.

When he agreed to sell Bendix yesterday to Hennessy, Agee
found consolation in the fact that Martin Marietta would also be
owned by Allied. In his promised position as president of Allied,
Agee thought he would be able to exert control over Martin
Marietta.

But now Martin Marietta would remain an independent company.

"Bill, before the market opens today, we're gonna announce
that our tender for Bendix shares is off," Hennessy said. "Pownall was not interested in any arrangement that stopped him
from taking down your shares. I understand from my people
that he has some forty-two percent of your shares. And they're
still buying. We're going to have to talk about another way to
do this deal."

"Our deal couldn't be done?" Agee asked.

"Not that deal," Hennessy said.

Both Agee and Hennessy knew that Allied would succeed in
acquiring a majority of Bendix from Martin Marietta without
using any Allied cash. Ed Hennessy had skillfully played both
sides.

"Ed, once you take possession of the Bendix stock Marietta
bought, that still leaves over eleven million shares outstanding,
and four point five million of those are owned by Bendix employees, the SESSOP people.

"I want to see that those people who were loyal to the end
get the deal they deserve. The arbs and the street dealers got
seventy-five dollars. I want a better deal for my people," Bill
Agee said.

"We could work out a nice package," Hennessy said.

"How nice?"

"Something about seventy-five, maybe eighty dollars."

"I'm gonna need ninety dollars a share, Ed," Agee said.

"There's no way," Hennessy said with a smile, adding, "Let's get our people talking about this."

As was always the case, the group broke into smaller groups, with the bankers talking to the bankers and the lawyers talking to the lawyers. Art Fleischer and Joe Flom were already looking beyond price to the complicated process of drafting the agreements. There would be a document to cover the Bendix and Allied merger. And another document to cover the stock swap understanding that would also include Martin Marietta's lawyers. Another document would cover a stand-still agreement between Allied and Martin Marietta. Flom hoped to wrap up the drafting by late in the afternoon. But price was still a sticking point. Eric Gleacher buttonholed Bruce Wasserstein in the hall.

"God, Bruce, we're right where we were on the phone," Gleacher said.

Back in the room, Ed Hennessy was looking very tired.

"Let's take a walk on Fifth Avenue," Agee said.

"Bill, we're going to just sit here and work this out. Then I'll take a walk."

"The price yesterday was eighty-five for control with a seventy-five back end," Agee said. "So the blended was eighty. You're getting control from Pownall at seventy-five, so give my people eighty-five on the back end."

Hennessy thought about the package. The deal had essentially been turned on its head. The blended price came out the same. The number-crunching his staff had done would be essentially the same. And at $85—set up to be tax-free for the sixteen thousand SESSOP holders—Hennessy would gain valuable "goodwill" with his new employees.

"It's a deal," Hennessy said, knowing that his board would rubber-stamp the final agreements when they were drafted.

While Bill Agee moved into his office to conduct the Bendix board meeting—which had already been delayed an hour and a half—Hennessy and Buirkle, Forrow, and the Allied bankers and lawyers stayed in the conference room. At one point, Hennessy emerged to ask one of the secretaries if she had any "Bendix Unity Day" balloons left. She went into a desk drawer and produced some, wondering what was going on. Sitting at her desk, she could hear laughter coming from the conference room.

The eighth Bendix board meeting since the attempted take-over of Martin Marietta was almost a family affair. With Jewel Lafontant still in Japan, Jack Fontaine unavailable, and the resignations of the four directors—Tavoulareas, Rumsfeld, Uyterhoeven and Cohen—the entire board could comfortably fit in Agee's corner office. General Tom Stafford and Jonathan Scott were the only two outside directors. The rest of the board besides Agee and McDonald was comprised of three men: Bill Purple, Fred Searby, and Paul Hartz.

Waiting for Agee to begin, Scott talked in a lowered voice with the director seated next to him. Scott was talking about the resignations. "It ticks me off," he said, "they come off looking lily white in the *Times,* and we look like whores."

"At a couple of minutes before ten A.M.," Agee said, "Allied announced to the wire services that it does not intend to commence today the tender offer the board approved yesterday. I am in negotiations now on a new agreement."

Bill Agee outlined the latest developments—Marietta's purchase of 42 percent of Bendix stock, Hennessy's visit with Pownall and the new revised merger agreement in principle between .Allied and Bendix, with terms subject to approval by both boards.

"I am requesting that the board give its approval to the Allied merger in principle subject to a follow-up meeting when all of the necessary documents are before us. This represents an opportunity for our remaining stockholders to receive eighty-five dollars for their shares."

"Since I made the big motion yesterday, I might as well make this one today," director Paul Hartz said.

The board gave its unanimous approval.

Bill Agee went into the conference room to talk .with Hennessy.

"Did your board approve?" Hal Buirkle asked, sitting with Forrow and Hennessy.

"Well, it's okay," Agee said, making a joke, "the rest of the board resigned. I am the board!"

After the directors and Hennessy and his team departed, Agee had some last-minute words with Arthur Fleischer, who was on his way over to Skadden, Arps to begin work on the agreements. A group of almost forty lawyers were planning on a large session to resolve the outstanding legal points of the contracts among Bendix, Martin Marietta, and Allied.

*   *   *

When Fleischer left, Bill Agee was alone in his office. He was thinking about the directors who resigned. He sat with his hand resting on the telephone receiver, looking out his window at the expanse of Central Park. He placed a call to Jewel Lafontant in Japan.

It was 2:00 A.M. the following morning in Japan. Jewel Lafontant was asleep in her lavish suite at the Okura Hotel in Toyko. Startled by the phone, she woke up to hear a voice say "This is Bill Agee in New York."

She turned on the light, trying to wake herself up as Agee began the story of the resignation of the four directors. Lafontant scribbled notes on a pad on the nightstand. Agee sounded depressed. He thanked a bewildered Jewel for her support in the past and explained that he had agreed to a merger with the Allied Corporation.

"I'm sorry I missed all of the events," Lafontant said. Hours later, when she was fully awake, she reviewed her notes with her son, who had accompanied her on the trip. "He couldn't have said that," she said. "Allied?"

Throughout the day, spokespersons for the Allied Corporation fielded questions from the press corps gathered at the company offices, eager to know if the most complex and celebrated merger war in the history of Wall Street had ended. The only two approved statements issued were "Discussions are still continuing between Bendix and Allied" and "Negotiations are proceeding satisfactorily."

While the suspense would continue throughout the night and into the early morning, the deal was essentially done as Bill Agee and Mary Cunningham took the Bendix navy blue limousine from the Helmsley Palace to fly back to Michigan in a Bendix jet. Agee told his secretary Marie, "Mary and I are going home. You know how to get me."

On the plane, Bill comforted Mary. Her name had been splashed in the day's newspapers. *The Wall Street Journal* ran a headline "CUNNINGHAM ATTENDS BENDIX-MARIETTA TALKS." And the papers had a preliminary catalogue of the "mistakes" committed by Bill.

Agee was outraged at the newspaper accounts.

The Bendix employees and remaining shareholders would receive $85 per share of Bendix common stock—a 70 percent increase in value from the day Bendix announced its intention to take over the Martin Marietta Corporation.

His own 47,055 Bendix shares were worth almost $4 million on paper.

Agee was excited about being named president of Allied, the No. 2 man in an $11 billion a year corporation. Allied was ranked No. 55 on the list of largest U.S. industrial concerns. Having acquired Bendix, it would shoot up in the rankings.

On Friday, September 24, in a press release with a dateline from Morristown, New Jersey; Southfield, Michigan; and Bethesda, Maryland, the three companies would jointly announce the signing of a peace treaty that would result after government clearance in the merger of Allied and Bendix and a resolution of the dueling tender offers between Bendix and Martin Marietta.

Edward L. Hennessy, Jr., chairman of Allied, would be quoted as saying, "We'll be delighted to welcome Bendix into Allied."

Agee would be quoted as saying, "I am pleased and enthusiastic about this agreement, which will achieve many of our objectives."

Thomas G. Pownall, president and chief executive officer of Martin Marietta, adamant to the end about being left alone, would not be quoted in the press release.

But that would all happen the following day. That night, Bill and Mary would just enjoy the peace, high above it all in the Bendix jet. At 8:00 P.M., at Al McDonald's home in Bloomfield Hills, they would have dinner with former President Jimmy Carter and talk for hours about the serialization of his memoirs in *Time* magazine.

EPILOGUE

On Friday, September 24, 1982, Roy Calvin, the VP of corporate communications for Martin Marietta, wrote the editors of *The Washington Post* in response to speculation that the presence of Mary Cunningham at the meeting in Bethesda had distracted the negotiations. "Miss Cunningham's presence was not an irritant," Calvin wrote, adding with a subtle jab, "it was apparent that Mr. Agee took some comfort from his wife's presence."

Two days later, Tom Pownall was sitting in Roy Calvin's office at Martin Marietta headquarters, reviewing for the press conference he planned to hold on Monday. Ed Hennessy had already held a press conference on Saturday at the Pierre Hotel in New York. Hennessy was quoted as saying he thought Bill Agee had "received some bad advice" and that it would more than likely take Pownall "a several-year period" to straighten out the finances of Martin Marietta.

Calvin was leaning back in his chair amid a haze of cigarette smoke. Suddenly, the graying, bespectacled executive began to cough violently. Calvin was surprised to find blood in his mouth. Tom Pownall gathered the man up and drove him to the emergency room of a local hospital. The diagnosis was a hemorrhaging lung. The tension of the past month and the five packs a day of Tareytons finally slowed the ex-newspaperman down. After several months at slow speed, Calvin took his retirement—and began smoking again.

Tom Pownall—named the chairman of Martin Marietta following the retirement in January 1983 of J. Donald Rauth—was consumed with salvaging the balance sheet of the company. The peak 1982 debt was $1.341 billion. The debt-to-capitalization ratio topped 80 percent. Tom Pownall assembled a team under Charlie Leithauser to tackle the problem. The company issued more stock in December. Between March and July 1983, the company sold six cement plants in Maine, Oklahoma, Iowa, Alabama, Georgia, and West Virginia.

By May 1983, the one-year bank loan of $930 million, set up by Tom Mendenhall in the first hectic days of the battle, was refinanced. The company sold more businesses in May and five office buildings in June. In September, ten industrial sand plants were sold.

By the end of 1983, a year after the battle with Bendix, Martin Marietta was on the road to recovery. The proceeds of the sale of a public offering were used to buy back Martin Marietta stock from Allied and to continue to fund the company's ambitious development plans.

Having completed his assignment, Charlie Leithauser retired in February 1984 and went scuba diving in Florida.

In October 1984, Tom Pownall announced that he intended to sell the company's aluminum business, which in 1983 had lost $45.9 million. The total value of the deal was $500 million.

For his contribution to the corporation, Tom Mendenhall was awarded a silver Jefferson Cup at an annual ceremony held to honor excellence. He also received a year's scholarship to the Sloan School in Boston.

Doris Rush did not receive a silver cup. Instead, in a small informal ceremony on the second floor, Rush was surprised by colleagues in the legal and treasury departments who approached her and proclaimed, "We hereby tender unto you this Styrofoam cup." She keeps it on her desk as a remembrance.

Harry Gray at United Technologies has been seen sporadically in the news. In May 1983, Robert J. Carlson was elected president of UTC. Apparently, he was being groomed for the chairmanship when Gray retired—something Gray has been averse to do. But like Ed Hennessy who was forced out of UTC in a power struggle with Gray, Carlson "resigned" in September 1984.

Several directors were furious and were anonymously quoted as saying so in *The Wall Street Journal*. Printed reports said that Harry Gray's days were numbered. A week later, stories anounced that the board had "full confidence" in Harry Gray.

In October 1984, Robert F. Daniels was named president of United Technologies. Insiders said the appointment was part of the firm's place to find a successor to Harry Gray whose current contract expires December 31, 1985.

On October 14, 1984 (as later disclosed in the *WSJ*), members of the United Technologies board of directors met in Manhattan to investigate sensational accusations against Harry Gray that he had allegedly ordered the wiretapping or bugging of Robert Carlson and possibly other employees.

In the same article, Ed Hennessy was referred to as saying that when he was at United Technologies, he was tipped off by an employee that the company's own security department had placed listening devices in his office.

Speculation centered on the possibility that Gray was "looking to get something" on his chosen successors.

Harry Gray for his part denied the accusations and said the charge "amounts to dragging a dead cat across the boardroom table."

Several days later, there were printed reports that United Technologies had prepared a study for the possible acquisition of the Allied Corporation.

The title of the Allied Corporation's 1983 annual report was "Making a Merger Work." From all signs, Ed Hennessy has done just that. Even before the merger cleared the government regulatory agencies and became official on January 31, 1983, a merger management task force was established drawing key executives from Bendix and Allied. The team members went directly to the employees in an effort to sustain morale. A daily shuttle-flight service was established between Bendix's Southfield, Michigan, headquarters and Allied headquarters in Morristown, New Jersey.

Eventually, the Southfield headquarters building was sold by Allied and leased back to Bendix. About 175 employees out of 875 in the facility lost their jobs. In all, according to Allied, 300 people were laid off as a result of the merger. ·

And Hennessy sold off the money-losing Bendix machine tool business.

At his first news conference, Ed Hennessy skirted the issue of Bill Agee. He said in response to a question that Bill Agee "has no employment contract with Allied. At the present moment, the only agreement we have is that he will be chairman and chief executive officer of Bendix."

Upon further probing, Hennessy made an amendment to his statement.

"He's also president of Allied. All right?"

Late in the fall of 1982, Hennessy visited an elaborate international Bendix seminar in Boca Raton, Florida. In private, Hennessy jokingly referred to the meeting as "the last supper."

Bill Agee was in charge of the meeting. Mary Cunningham was with him. Promised the presidency of Allied, Agee coveted the more important job of chief operating officer. According to Agee, Hennessy had promised him the position during the final tense moments of negotiations in September. Behind the scenes in Boca Raton, Bill buttonholed key executives in an attempt to surround Hennessy with glowing assessments of his abilities. By design, Mary was seated next to Ed Hennessy.

Bill and Mary were named 1982's Most Intriguing Couple by *People* magazine. The couple was pictured in their bedroom with Mary wearing a cable knit sweater sitting on the edge of the bed. Bill was on his knees before her, holding her hands. The publication of the photo provoked howls of derision in the business community. Ed Hennessy—when shown the photo by a reporter—grumbled, "I sure as hell wouldn't have done it!"

Shortly after the merger became official, Bill Agee was startled.

"I found out," Agee said later, "that Hennessy had, without telling me, reactivated his search for a chief operating officer. It was in this context . . . that it became clear that I would not be able to work with him successfully."

Bill Agee left the company.

Al McDonald also "resigned" after being summoned by Ed Hennessy.

Ironically, the two loyal Bendix directors who were responsible for breaking the deadlock over the Allied deal—J. L. Scott and Thomas P. Stafford—went on to become members in good standing of the Allied board.

Two years after the events of the Bendix versus Martin Marietta war thrust Bendix into the arms of the Allied Corporation, Bill Agee was still bitter toward Hennessy.

"I admit to being trusting but not stupid. I was not used to dealing with many people like Ed Hennessy," Agee wrote in a letter to the author.

Eager for his contributions to Bendix to be acknowledged, Agee noted that before the merger attempt with Martin Marietta, Bendix stock was worth around $50 per share; the Allied deal made the stock worth $85 per share. Agee added, "I have many letters from secretaries, clerks, and general managers thanking me for making their retirement years more secure."

Mary resigned her executive VP, strategic planning post at Joseph E. Seagram & Sons in October 1983 and went on to form an investment company with her husband.

Bill Agee unfurled his golden parachute contract that guaranteed him a salary of $805,000 per year for five years. Bill and Mary bought a $1 million home on Cape Cod.

Mary wrote a book about her experiences at Bendix and spent several weeks on the talk show circuit.

INDEX

411

INDEX

INDEX

413

INDEX

Forrow, Brian, 355, 356, 380, 401, 402, 403
Fortune, 14, 141, 154, 368
Fraidin, Stephen, 324–325, 326, 327, 329, 333, 334, 340, 341, 342–343, 375, 376–377
Frankel, David, 250
Fried, Frank, Harris, Shriver & Jacobson, 11, 12, 24, 87, 189, 361
Friedman, Milton, 16
Fullem, L. Robert, 63–65, 68–69, 118, 155, 157, 270–271, 328, 339, 347
  Agee-Pownall meetings and, 308–309
  Allied-Martin Marietta deal and, 392, 393, 395
  Bendix charter amendments and, 161
  Bendix SESSOP and, 172–174
  indemnification of Martin Marietta directors and, 336–337, 340–341
  Martin Marietta countertender offer and, 73–74, 75, 340
  Martin Marietta "Doomsday Machine" maneuver and, 228, 229
  Martin Marietta litigation and, 281–282, 286, 287, 386–387, 396
  UTC-Martin Marietta agreement and, 125, 126, 217–218

Gamson, Bernie, 44
Garrett, Dave, 193
Geico Corporation, 47, 225, 297
Gibson, Duncan, 70
Gleacher, Eric, 303, 304, 310, 319, 323, 326, 341, 348, 355, 374, 380, 381
  Allied-Martin Marietta deal and, 387, 392, 393, 399–400, 402
  Allied minority investment in Bendix and, 351–352
  Wasserstein and, 348, 351–352, 357
"Golden parachute" contracts, 62–63, 113, 133–134, 148, 149–150, 197–198, 410
Goldman, Gerald, 243, 277, 386
Grassi, Tony, 169, 221, 222, 287–288, 289, 326, 327, 352, 374
Grasso, Dick, 159–160
Gray, Harry, 107, 108–110, 114, 117–118, 131, 183, 193–194, 198, 363, 372, 407–408
  Agee and, 118, 153, 154, 193, 194–195, 218–219, 262–265
  Hennessy and, 132, 133, 274, 388
  Martin Marietta "Doomsday Machine" maneuver and, 230, 231–232, 234, 235
  Pownall and, 110, 114, 119–120, 194, 209

UTC-Martin Marietta agreement, 120, 127–128, 129, 140, 142, 143–144, 146–147, 210, 211, 216–217
Greenhill, Bob, 380
Grumman v. *LTV*, 88
Gutfreund, John, 25, 82, 133, 139, 170, 171

Hagerty, Bill, 62, 80
Haines, Gordon, 277, 280
Hamilton Standard, 109, 133
Hanigan, John, 62, 63, 80, 156, 227
Harkins, Peter, 188–189, 215
Harris, Ira, 18, 104, 136–139, 170, 171
Hartz, Paul F., 22, 102, 149, 261–262, 266, 267, 317, 368, 375, 376, 377n, 379, 403
Harwood, Bill, 106, 321, 350, 351
Haselton, William R., 318
Hennessy, Edward L., Jr., 131–133, 264, 316
  Agee and
    Allied minority investment in Bendix, 293, 302, 303, 304, 309–311, 318–319, 323–324, 353
    Allied takeover of Bendix, 367, 369, 370, 372, 373, 379–380, 392, 399–402
    bitterness between, 409, 410
    chief operating officer position, 356n, 409
    "crown jewel" agreement, 356–357, 373, 374, 376
    Allied takeover of Bendix and, 348, 353, 367, 377, 379–380, 405
    Gray and, 132, 133, 274, 388
    Pownall and, 383, 386, 387, 388
    Allied-Martin Marietta deal, 392–395, 396, 397, 399, 405
Herlihy, Ed, 215
Higgins, Jay, 10, 18, 35–36, 55–56, 59, 95, 96, 100, 104, 133, 137, 138, 139, 151–152, 154, 170, 171, 199, 220, 224, 263, 265, 272
Hill, Tom, 355, 400
Hill & Knowlton, 18, 188, 213, 320, 362
"How Companies Should Use Their Cash: Lessons from Bendix" (Agee), 47
Hugel, Charlie, 46, 47, 62, 80
Hughes, Hubbard & Reed, 11, 12, 16, 17, 24, 86, 87, 95, 361, 386
Huplits, Earl, 181
Hurtt, Caleb, 62, 176, 238, 239

Iacocca, Lee, 14
Inman, Virginia, 92
Inmont, 108
Ivan F. Boesky Corporation, 106

414